# Rethinking Rape Law

*Rethinking Rape Law: International and Comparative Perspectives* provides a comprehensive and critical analysis of contemporary rape laws, across a range of jurisdictions. In a context in which there has been considerable legal reform of sexual offences, *Rethinking Rape Law* engages with developments spanning national, regional and international frameworks. It is only when we fully understand the differences between the law of rape in times of war and in times of peace, between common-law and continental jurisdictions, between societies in transition and societies long inured to feminist activism, that we are able to understand and evaluate current practices, with a view to change and a better future for victims of sexual crimes. Written by leading authors from across the world, this is the first authoritative text on rape law that crosses jurisdictions, examines its conceptual and theoretical foundations, and sets the law in its policy context. It is destined to become the primary source for scholarly work and debate on sexual offence laws.

**Clare McGlynn** is Professor of Law at Durham University in the UK. She is the author of *The Woman Lawyer: Making the Difference* and *Families and the European Union: Law, Politics and Pluralism*, and editor of *Legal Feminisms: Theory and Practice*.

**Vanessa E. Munro** is Professor of Socio-Legal Studies at the University of Nottingham in the UK. She is author of *Law and Politics at the Perimeter: Re-Evaluating Key Debates in Feminist Theory* and co-editor of *Sexuality and the Law: Feminist Engagements* and *Demanding Sex: Critical Reflections on the Regulation of Prostitution*.

# Rethinking Rape Law

## International and Comparative Perspectives

Edited by Clare McGlynn and
Vanessa E. Munro

a GlassHouse book

First published 2010
by Routledge
2 Park Square, Milton Park, Abingdon, Oxfordshire OX14 4RN
Simultaneously published in the USA and Canada
by Routledge
711 Third Avenue, New York, NY 10017
A GlassHouse book
*Routledge is an imprint of the Taylor & Francis Group,
an informa business*

First issued in paperback 2011

© 2010 editorial matter and selection Clare McGlynn and Vanessa E. Munro, individual chapters the contributors

Typeset in Times and Gill Sans by
RefineCatch Limited, Bungay, Suffolk

All rights reserved. No part of this book may be reprinted or reproduced or utilized in any form or by any electronic, mechanical, or other means, now known or hereafter invented, including photocopying and recording, or in any information storage or retrieval system, without permission in writing from the publishers.

*British Library Cataloguing in Publication Data*
A catalogue record for this book is available
from the British Library

*Library of Congress Cataloging-in-Publication Data*
Rethinking rape law : international and comparative perspectives /
edited by Clare McGlynn and Vanessa Munro.
      p. cm.
   Includes bibliographical references.
1. Rape. I. Munro, Vanessa, II. McGlynn, Clare.
K5197.R48 2010
345′.02532–dc22                                     2009044979

ISBN13: 978–0–415–55027–7 (hbk)
ISBN13: 978–0–203–85219–4 (ebk)
ISBN 13: 978-0-415-61066-7 (pbk)

# Contents

*List of contributors* — viii

**Foreword** — xiv
BY NAVANETHEM PILLAY, UN HIGH COMMISSIONER FOR HUMAN RIGHTS

*Acknowledgements* — xvi

**Rethinking rape law: an introduction** — 1
CLARE McGLYNN AND VANESSA E. MUNRO

**PART I**
**Conceptual and theoretical engagements** — 15

1. **From consent to coercion: evaluating international and domestic frameworks for the criminalization of rape** — 17
VANESSA E. MUNRO

2. **Rethinking the criminal law's response to sexual penetration: on theory and context** — 30
JONATHAN HERRING AND MICHELLE MADDEN DEMPSEY

**PART II**
**International and regional perspectives** — 45

3. **International criminal law and sexual violence: an overview** — 47
ALISON COLE

4. **Learning our lessons? The Rwanda Tribunal record on prosecuting rape** — 61
DORIS BUSS

5  The force of shame 76
   KAREN ENGLE AND ANNELIES LOTTMANN

6  Everyday rape: international human rights law and
   violence against women in peacetime 92
   ALICE EDWARDS

7  Defining rape under the European Convention on
   Human Rights: torture, consent and equality 109
   PATRICIA LONDONO

8  Rape law reform in Africa: 'more of the same' or
   new opportunities? 122
   HELÉNE COMBRINCK

## PART III
## National perspectives 137

9  Feminist activism and rape law reform in England
   and Wales: a Sisyphean struggle? 139
   CLARE McGLYNN

10 All change or business as usual? Reforming the law
   of rape in Scotland 154
   SHARON COWAN

11 Rethinking Croatian rape laws: force, consent and
   the 'contribution of the victim' 169
   IVANA RADAČIĆ AND KSENIJA TURKOVIĆ

12 Rape in Italian law: towards the recognition of
   sexual autonomy 183
   RACHEL ANNE FENTON

13 Rethinking rape law in Sweden: coercion, consent
   or non-voluntariness? 196
   MONICA BURMAN

14 Canadian sexual assault law: neoliberalism and the
   erosion of feminist-inspired law reforms 209
   LISE GOTELL

15 Rape, law and American society 224
   DONALD DRIPPS

| | | |
|---|---|---|
| 16 | Criminal law and the reformation of rape in Australia<br>PETER D. RUSH | 237 |
| 17 | Reforming the law of rape in South Africa<br>SHEREEN W. MILLS | 251 |

**PART IV**
## New agendas and directions 265

| | | |
|---|---|---|
| 18 | Independent legal representation for complainants in rape trials<br>FIONA E. RAITT | 267 |
| 19 | Jury deliberation and complainant credibility in rape trials<br>LOUISE ELLISON AND VANESSA E. MUNRO | 281 |
| 20 | The mythology of male rape: social attitudes and law enforcement<br>PHILIP N.S. RUMNEY AND NATALIA HANLEY | 294 |
| 21 | Violence against women in South Asian communities in the UK: a culture of silence<br>AISHA GILL | 308 |
| 22 | Sexual assault of women with mental disabilities: a Canadian perspective<br>JANINE BENEDET AND ISABEL GRANT | 322 |
| | *Index* | 335 |

# Contributors

**Janine Benedet** is an Associate Professor at the Faculty of Law, University of British Columbia in Vancouver, Canada, where she teaches criminal law, labour law and sexual offences law. Her research focuses on sexual violence against women, including prostitution and pornography. She is currently writing about the criminal law's treatment of external conditions that might vitiate consent, as well as offering a feminist critique of harm reduction approaches to prostitution.

**Monica Burman** is a Senior Lecturer and a Research Fellow at the Department of Law and Umea Centre for Gender Studies, Umea University, Sweden. Formerly, she worked for seven years as an associate judge. Her main publications are in the field of violence against women and the criminal law and include, amongst others, 'The Ability of Criminal Law to Produce Gender Equality – Judicial Discourses in the Swedish Criminal Legal System' (*Violence against Women* (2010)). She is currently working on a project on legal protection and legal processes for immigrant women exposed to male partner violence.

**Doris Buss** is Associate Professor of Law at Carleton University, Ottawa, Canada. She teaches and researches in the areas of international human rights, women's rights and social movements. She is the author (with Didi Herman) of *Globalizing Family Values: The International Politics of the Christian Right* and editor (with Ambreena Manji) of *International Law: Modern Feminist Perspectives*. She is currently working on a project examining identity, war crimes and international criminal prosecutions. Her chapter in this volume is based on research for the first stage of this project.

**Alison Cole** has worked at the International Criminal Tribunal for Rwanda and the Former Yugoslavia and the International Criminal Court, and has recently taken up a post at the Extraordinary Chambers of the Courts of Cambodia. She previously worked on various human rights projects, such as refugee issues in central Africa, death row appeals in the Caribbean and rights-based development in India. She is the author of several law review articles and book chapters examining international law.

Heléne Combrinck is a Senior Researcher at the Centre for Disability Law and Policy at the Faculty of Law, University of the Western Cape, South Africa. She previously worked as a senior researcher at the Community Law Centre at the University of the Western Cape, where she co-ordinated the Centre's Gender Project. She has published extensively on women's equality and women's rights, and has been involved in various submissions on law reform to parliamentary committees and the South African Law Reform Commission.

Sharon Cowan is a Lecturer in Law at the School of Law, Edinburgh University, UK, where she is the co-director of the Centre for Law and Society. Her research interests include feminist legal theory; sexuality, gender and the law; criminal law; and criminal justice. Her current projects include a book on feminist perspectives on consent in the criminal law; and a national empirical project (with Helen Baillot and Vanessa Munro) exploring the Asylum and Immigration Appeal Tribunal's treatment of women asylum applicants who claim to have been raped.

Donald A. Dripps is Professor of Law at the University of San Diego, US. He has written widely about criminal justice in the US, including *About Guilt and Innocence* (Greenwood Press 2003) and dozens of articles. His writings on rape law include 'Beyond rape' (*Columbia Law Review*, 1992); 'For a negative, normative model of consent, with a comment on preference-skepticism' (*Legal Theory*, 1996); and 'After rape law: will the turn to consent normalize the prosecution of sexual assault?' (*Akron Law Review*, 2008).

Alice Edwards is Lecturer in International Refugee and Human Rights Law in the Refugee Studies Centre, Oxford University, UK. Her research focuses on issues of gender/feminist theory, human rights, and refugees and displacement. She has published widely on these issues, including as co-editor of *Human Security and Non-Citizens: Law, Policy and International Affairs* (Cambridge University Press, 2008). She is a past recipient of an Arthur C. Helton Fellowship of the American Society of International Law and, in 2008, she was awarded the Audre Rapoport Prize for Scholarship in the Human Rights of Women for her work on violence against women and the UN human rights treaty bodies.

Louise Ellison is a Senior Lecturer in Law in the School of Law at the University of Leeds, UK. She is author of *The Adversarial Process and the Vulnerable Witness* (Oxford University Press, 2001) and co-editor of *Feminist Perspectives on Evidence* (Cavendish, 2000). In addition, she has published a number of articles and book chapters on the topic of rape – focusing in particular on the credibility barriers that rape survivors confront within the criminal process – and has conducted research (with Vanessa Munro) on the impact of educational guidance on (mock) juror decision-making in rape cases (funded by the ESRC).

**Karen Engle** is Cecil D. Redford Professor in Law and founding Director of the Bernard and Audre Rapoport Center for Human Rights and Justice at the School of Law, University of Texas, US. She is author of *Indigenous Roads to Development: social movements and international law* (Duke University Press, 2009) and co-editor (with Dan Danielsen) of *After Identity: a reader in law and culture* (Routledge, 1995). She has published extensively on gender and international law and has critically chronicled the development of the women's human rights movement over the past 20 years.

**Rachel Anne Fenton** is a Senior Lecturer at Bristol Law School, University of the West of England, UK. She has published a number of articles on Italian law, rape and sexual assault and assisted reproduction. She is currently co-editing a book on gender, sexualities and law to be published by GlassHouse.

**Aisha Gill** is a Senior Lecturer in Criminology at Roehampton University, UK. She has been involved in addressing the problem of violence against women (VAW) at the grassroots and activist levels for the past 10 years. She is Chair of Newham Asian Women's Project, management committee member of Imkaan (a national VAW charity) and a member of Liberty's Project Advisory Group and the End Violence Against Women coalition. Her current research interests include the following: rights, law and forced marriage; crimes related to patriarchy; so-called 'honour'-based violence and femicide in Iraqi Kurdistan and the Kurdish/South Asian Diaspora; post-separation violence and child contact; trafficking; missing women; and sexual violence.

**Lise Gotell** is Professor of Women's Studies at the University of Alberta in Canada. She has published on such topics as feminist litigation, constitutional equality, pornography and sexual violence. She is a co-author of *Bad Attitude/s on Trial: feminism, pornography and the Butler decision* (1997) and a co-editor of *Open Boundaries: a Canadian women's studies reader* (2009). Her recent work focuses on the implications of 1990s' Canadian sexual assault reforms, including interrogating the legal standard for consent and evaluating the effectiveness of legislative restrictions on sexual history evidence and confidential records.

**Isabel Grant** is a Professor at the Faculty of Law at the University of British Columbia, Canada, who specializes in criminal law. She has written a number of papers exploring male violence against women and most recently has published two papers on the sexual assault of women with mental disabilities (with Janine Benedet). She is currently completing a study on sentencing of men who kill their intimate partners. She is also a member of the Law Program Committee for the Women's Legal Education and Action Fund.

**Natalia Hanley** is a Lecturer in Criminology at the University of Melbourne,

Australia. She has recently completed an ESRC CASE-funded PhD at the University of Manchester on the impact of gangs on the work of the Probation Service.

**Jonathan Herring** is a Fellow in Law at Exeter College, University of Oxford, UK. He has written on family law, medical law and criminal law. His most recent books include *Criminal Law* (6th edn, Palgrave, 2009); *Family Law* (4th edn, Pearson, 2009); *Older People in Law and Society* (Oxford University Press, 2009); and *Criminal Law* (3rd edn, Oxford University Press, 2008).

**Patricia Londono** is the John Collier Fellow in Law at Trinity Hall, Cambridge and a member of the Faculty of Law, University of Cambridge, UK. Her doctoral thesis 'Women, human rights and criminal justice' (2006) won the Bapsybanoo Marchioness of Winchester Thesis Prize at Oxford University (2007). She has published on sexual violence and the ECHR, as well as on the human rights of women prisoners. She is currently working on a monograph, entitled *Human Rights and Violence Against Women*, which is due to be published by Oxford University Press.

**Annelies Lottmann** has worked on human rights issues around the world, including a brief time at the Office of the Prosecutor at the International Criminal Tribunal for Rwanda. She is the author of 'No direction home: nationalism and statelessness in the Baltics' (*Texas International Law Journal*, 2008). She has a JD from the University of Texas, School of Law, and is currently an associate at Weil, Gotshal and Manges in New York, US.

**Clare McGlynn** is a Professor of Law at Durham University, UK. She has written widely in the field of feminism and law, including *The Woman Lawyer: making the difference* (Oxford University Press, 1998), *Families and the European Union: law, politics and pluralism* (Cambridge University Press, 2006) and, as editor, *Legal Feminisms: theory and practice* (Ashgate, 1999). She is a co-organizer of the ESRC-funded Feminist Judgments Project (www.feministjudgments.org.uk) for which she has written a dissenting judgment in the rape trials case *R v A* (2001). In the field of rape law, she has published on 'Rape, Torture and the ECHR' (*International and Comparative Law Quarterly*, 2009) and her current work focuses on the legal regulation of extreme pornography.

**Michelle Madden Dempsey** is an Associate Professor at Villanova University School of Law in Pennsylvania, US, and formerly a CUF Lecturer in Law at the University of Oxford, UK. She is the author of *Prosecuting Domestic Violence: a philosophical analysis* (Oxford University Press, 2009) and several articles regarding the criminal justice system's response to violence against women. She is a former criminal prosecutor and is presently working on projects regarding prostitution and trafficking. With Jonathan Herring, she is writing a book for Oxford University Press regarding sexual offences, which develops the line of argument outlined in their contribution to this volume.

**Shereen Mills** is an attorney and senior researcher based at the Centre for Applied Legal Studies at the University of the Witwatersrand, in Johannesburg, South Africa. She has worked in the areas of race and gender equality, participating in the drafting of key legislation as well as advocacy. She currently engages in research, advocacy and strategic litigation on gender-based violence, poverty and women's access to justice. She has been involved as amicus curiae in a number of groundbreaking cases involving gender-based violence. She also teaches gender and the law. She currently sits on the Board of the Gender Education and Training Network in Cape Town, as well as the Women's Legal Centre Trust.

**Vanessa E. Munro** is Professor of Socio-Legal Studies at the University of Nottingham, UK. She has published widely on feminist legal and political theory, and combines this with empirical projects exploring popular and penal responses to sexual violence. Recent works include *Demanding Sex: critical reflections on the regulation of prostitution* (Ashgate, 2008), *Law and Politics at the Perimeter: re-evaluating key debates in feminist theory* (Hart, 2007), and *Sexuality and the Law: feminist engagements* (Routledge, 2007). She has advised the UK Government on both human trafficking and rape law reform, and presented research on these issues to – amongst others – the Metropolitan Police, Judicial Studies Board, Rape Crisis, the Mayor of London's Office, Royal College of Psychiatrists, and the New Zealand Ministry of Justice.

**Ivana Radačić** is a Researcher at the Ivo Pilar Institute of Social Sciences in Zagreb, Croatia. Her research and teaching interests are in international human rights law, and feminism and law; and her PhD thesis was on the women's rights jurisprudence of the European Court of Human Rights. She has published in international law and human rights journals, and worked at different academic institutions. She has also worked as a lawyer at the European Court of Human Rights, acted as an Expert for the Council of Europe on the European Convention on Human Rights, and collaborated with a number of NGOs.

**Fiona Raitt** is Professor of Law at the University of Dundee, UK. She researches in the areas of evidence law, family law, domestic abuse and sexual violence, often from an interdisciplinary perspective, for example the book co-authored with Suzanne Zeedyk, *The Implicit Relation of Psychology and Law – women and syndrome evidence*. Current research projects include the completion of a book co-authored with Jane Mair, *Scots Family Law – a critical analysis*, and further publications linked to the Rape Crisis Scotland-funded research on independent legal representation for complainers of sexual offences.

**Phil Rumney** is a Reader at Bristol Law School, University of West of

England, UK, where he teaches courses on criminal justice. His research interests include legal responses to male rape, false allegations of rape and the problems of rape law enforcement. He is currently writing a book for Willan Publishing examining the debate over the use of torture as an interrogation tool in cases of terrorism.

**Peter Rush** is an Associate Professor in Law at the University of Melbourne, Australia. He is the author of several books on the jurisprudence of criminal law, journal articles in legal theory and criminology, and a film on colonial legal relations and the art of the city. His areas of research include law and literature, aboriginal justice, and sexual politics. He has participated in law reform projects in the area of rape law and in policy advocacy on the criminalization of HIV transmission. His current work concerns trauma and the jurisprudence of witnessing in national and international criminal justice.

**Ksenija Turković** is Professor of Criminal Law and Head of the Department of Criminal Law at the Faculty of Law, University of Zagreb, Croatia. She is Head of the Commission of the Ministry of Justice responsible for drafting the new Croatian Criminal Code. She is also a member of the Commission of the Ministry of Family, Veterans and Intergenerational Solidarity, responsible for preparing the national strategy of protection against domestic violence. She is Vice President of a Council of Europe group of specialists on child-friendly justice and a member of the committee on preventing and combating violence against women and domestic violence. She was Vice President of the Council of Europe committee of experts that drafted the Convention against sexual exploitation and sexual abuse of children.

# Foreword

## *Akayesu* 10 years on

It is the inequality and systematic de-humanization against certain groups which makes them susceptible to violence. When those who perpetrate sexual violence can do so with impunity, without justice being done, the violence and gender inequalities which give rise to such violence are perpetuated, with no solace for victims. As a Judge in the International Criminal Court, and former President of the International Criminal Tribunal for Rwanda, I heard many harrowing accounts of human rights violations and sorrow from individuals who refused to remain silent, seeking justice rather than revenge. To redress the suffering, individual accountability and responsibility for crimes of sexual violence must be pursued. The aim must be not only to punish perpetrators, but to deter violations of human rights and advance gender equality; and in times of war, also to promote justice and peace.

Rape and sexual violence are sustained by the patterns of gender inequality which cut across geo-political, economical and social boundaries. Justice is needed on the individual and national level to redress rape and other expressions of sex inequality that women experience as a part of their everyday lives, as well as on the international level for sexual violence and other crimes perpetrated in times of conflict and war that are not effectively addressed at the national level. I was appointed UN High Commissioner for Human Rights in 2008. On behalf of the United Nations, my Office seeks national and international co-operation to assist and support governments in their efforts to promote human rights. This is not just a matter of overseeing the equality of laws which protect fundamental human rights, but also of focusing on the implementation and enforcement of those laws to make changes which will affect and improve individuals' lives in the struggle for social justice.

Accordingly, I was pleased to be invited to speak at the Durham University conference *Rethinking Rape Law: Akayesu 10 Years On* in July 2008. This conference marked the tenth anniversary of the judgment of the ICTR in the case of *Akayesu* in which the mayor of Taba commune in Rwanda was convicted for genocide, explicitly including rape as a form of genocide, and in which rape was defined with a focus on the coercive circumstances in which the violence took place rather than the absence of consent. In this case, the Trial Chamber, of which I was a member, greatly expanded the international community's ability to prosecute gender-based war crimes. Equally significantly, the jurisprudence it provided has been taken as a starting point to review laws of rape elsewhere, to debate reform strategies in other arenas, and to consider the role of women and feminists in bringing about change at national and international levels.

It is from this successful forum of discussion and debate that this collection of essays has emerged. Contributions are made from internationally renowned scholars across the world, providing fascinating insights into the laws across different cultures, continents and contexts. To this end, the book encourages different ways of thinking about rape law and reform – from substantive legal changes, to implementation and enforcement – in order to rethink rape in different contexts – from sexual violence in the home as a method of dominance, to rape as a weapon of war in armed conflict.

In reading the chapters of this book, I am reminded of the obstacles which block the path to gender equality and women's freedom from sexual violence. However, we must not only look forward to the difficulties and challenges we face, but also reflect on how far we have come and the fundamental changes that we have witnessed, such as *Akayesu*. Our past and our progress can inform our thinking, providing the insight and encouragement to consider the ways forward towards gender equality and social justice, welfare and peace.

Navanethem Pillay, UN High Commissioner for Human Rights
Geneva, September 2009

# Acknowledgements

The original inspiration for this collection came from the 2008 conference, *Rethinking Rape Law: Akayesu 10 Years On*, held at Durham University, UK, and organized by Clare McGlynn. The conference brought together an impressive range of scholars, activists, lawyers and policymakers from all over the world. The plenary presentations, from Navanethem Pillay (UN High Commissioner for Human Rights), Catharine MacKinnon (Michigan University), Liz Kelly (London Metropolitan University), Karen Engle (Texas University) and Jessica Neuwirth (Equality Now), amongst others, generated challenging debates about all aspects of feminist thinking and strategy around rape law.

The conference was only possible due to the sponsorship of the British Academy, the Society of Legal Scholars and the Government Office for the North East. Durham University also helped with the administration of the conference, as well as providing financial support via its Institute of Advanced Study, the Centre from Criminal Law and Criminal Justice and the research group 'Gender & Law at Durham' (GLAD). Particular acknowledgment is due to Erika Rackley at Durham University who provided organizational help and assistance which was well beyond the call of duty or friendship.

A collection of this sort does not come into existence without the involvement of a great number of people. We are indebted to Colin Perrin for his enthusiasm towards the project and to the copy-editors and production team at Routledge for their assistance. We are also grateful to both Nikki Godden and Laura Graham for their help in formatting the manuscript prior to submission and Nikki also helped with the index. We extend our thanks also to the contributors, whose diligence in meeting deadlines and constructive approach to engaging with our editorial comments has been hugely appreciated throughout.

Finally, we would like to express our gratitude to the many colleagues and friends who have supported our work on this project, most especially Fiona Raitt, Ian Ward, Celia Wells and Nicole Westmarland.

# Rethinking Rape Law: an introduction

*Clare McGlynn and Vanessa E. Munro*

Rape, and rape law, have been key sites of feminist struggle – whether nationally, regionally or internationally – for decades. The need to lift the veil of privacy in order to protect the vulnerable has been increasingly acknowledged and respect for a person's right to sexual and bodily integrity has become a prevalent theme in contemporary legal and policy discourse. At the same time – and despite the fact that, in several countries, there has been a marked increase in the number of sexual assaults reported to police – conviction rates for rape typically remain disconcertingly low. There is convincing evidence which suggests that spurious and highly gendered 'rape myths' continue to inform both the popular and penal imagination; and rape complainants who make it into the courtroom often still endure invasive and hostile questioning from defence counsel without any form of representation, and often with inadequate witness preparation or post-trial support.

Progressive reform of rape law has been an ongoing process: and often a painfully slow one. While in some jurisdictions any change to existing doctrinal frameworks for conceptualizing and criminalizing rape has been stubbornly resisted, in others there has been an almost incessant process of consultation and legislative 'tinkering' as new initiatives are developed to address old problems, often with disappointing, limited- or unintended counter-productive results. Common-law legacies have bestowed a level of doctrinal and/or operational scepticism in relation to rape. Sir Matthew Hale's seventeenth-century insistence that rape allegations are easy to make and hard to dispute, especially given the frequent absence of corroborating evidence, though less explicitly endorsed in modern times, continues to inform investigative and prosecutorial perspectives in most jurisdictions. The historical conceptualization of women as property – first of their fathers and then of their husbands – as well as the more contemporary correlation between women and 'honour', accentuated in certain minority communities – has generated obstacles to the recognition of all forms of non-consensual sexual activity as violence, and has embedded into the law – if not substantively, then evidentially – a requirement that women resist their assailant's advances to the utmost (both verbally and physically). In this context, difficult questions have been asked about the ability of legal doctrine – however reformulated – to produce real improvements at the level of practice.

These challenges have been particularly evident at the international level over the past decade or more. While the link between sexual violence against women and militarism is by no means new, the highly visible and instrumental use of rape as a weapon of war in recent conflicts, together with the blossoming of an international criminal jurisprudence, has provided impetus for increased condemnation. The applicability of conventional consent-based analyses of rape in these contexts of displacement, violence and intimidation has been the subject of much critical concern, generating alternative conceptualizations that some have argued also provide a more appropriate response to sexual violence in times of 'peace'. While debate on this issue continues, it is clear that the multiple axes of oppression – racial, ethnic, gender, and so on – that stratify the use, and meaning, of sexual violence in wartime has promoted a more intersectional and complex approach, and that this too can generate fruitful insights in non-conflict contexts.

This collection of essays arose out of a conference, held at Durham University (UK) in 2008, to mark the tenth anniversary of the *Akayesu* judgment of the International Criminal Tribunal for Rwanda (ICTR), which saw the first conviction for genocide and war crimes based on rape (ICTR-96-4-T, Judgment 2 September 1998). The *Akayesu* decision has been heralded by many as a victory for feminist activism – experiences of sexual violence initially marginalized in the indictment were repositioned as central and were met by the Chamber (and in particular – perhaps not coincidentally – by its sole female member, Judge Pillay) with staunch condemnation (see Buss, Cole, and Engle and Lottmann in this collection). Reflecting on the significance of *Akayesu* provides an occasion for engaging with broader debates about the role and relevance of law as a mechanism for securing change in the context of rape – and indeed other entrenched socio-cultural phenomena. More substantively, the judgment also affords an opportunity for reappraising foundational assumptions about the nature of the wrong of rape and the appropriate legal response thereto. The Chamber in *Akayesu* expressly eschewed attempts to prescribe a list of sexual acts that would constitute rape and purported to abandon the consent threshold, replacing it with a focus on the coercive circumstances in which the act took place (paras 598 and 688). This, some have argued, rightly privileges surrounding context and structural inequality, and moves away from the inappropriately individualistic focus on sexual autonomy reflected in the consent threshold (MacKinnon 2006; but see also Munro in this collection). In these ways, then, the concerns that the *Akayesu* judgment gave, and continues to give, rise to render it a symbol of the myriad broader debates about feminism and rape law which are currently taking place both across and within national jurisdictions. And while the contributions in this collection create a profile that is far wider in its remit than a narrow focus on *Akayesu* would permit, they all speak – explicitly or implicitly – to the debates that engaged the ICTR in that case.

The aim of this book is to provide a critical appraisal of recent developments in rape laws, across a range of diverse jurisdictions. Spanning national and international responses, the book explores the parallels and dissonances between rape in times of war and in times of peace. It is innovative in a number of ways, not least in bringing together perspectives on international criminal law, human rights law and domestic criminal justice law and policy, alongside a theoretical interrogation of some of the foundational concepts in rape law and pioneering new research which seeks to move the reform agenda forward in progressive, evidence-based ways. Across the chapters that follow, there is an unfolding interrogation of the relationship between power hierarchies and sexual violence, and a challenge – echoed in different registers and from different locations – is lodged against the normalization of male (hetero)sexual aggression. Leading authors from across the world have contributed critical 'stocktakes' of the current responses to rape in their respective national jurisdictions and have evaluated the successes and failures of international and regional initiatives to improve domestic policy, protect victims and punish perpetrators. The collection reflects on the differences between common law and continental jurisdictions, as well as between societies in transition and societies that have been long inured to feminist activism. And yet, at the same time, it identifies a number of consistent challenges that plague rape laws, regardless of state borders and boundaries.

In this introduction, we highlight four overarching themes which emerge across the following chapters: first, the theoretical complexities of responding to the 'wrong' of rape; secondly, the relationship between feminist activism and legal reform; thirdly, the limits of law reform in bringing about social change; and finally, the 'secondary victimization' of rape complainants during the criminal investigation and trial process.

## RESPONDING TO THE WRONG OF RAPE

While there has been a greater feminist consensus regarding rape than in relation to other areas of concern to feminists, such as prostitution or pornography, there have always been distinctive feminist approaches to conceptualizing the wrong of rape, and therefore to strategies and proposals for reform. The debates of second-wave feminism revolved around the dichotomy of conceptualizing rape as either 'violence' or 'sex'. Thus, while Susan Brownmiller argued that rape is not about sex but about violence and the exertion of male power (Brownmiller 1975), Catharine MacKinnon challenged this approach, suggesting that 'to say rape is violence not sex preserves the "sex is good" norm by simply distinguishing forced sex as "not sex" ' (MacKinnon 1989: 173). Violence against women, MacKinnon argued, is always sexual. Notwithstanding the often polarized nature of these debates, both approaches were seeking to challenge cultural assumptions about rape and to reimagine the wrong of rape as a precursor to reform and change.

The conflicts in the former Yugoslavia and Rwanda, particularly the revelation of mass rape and sexual violence, gave fresh impetus to these debates. While feminist discord over how to conceptualize rape in times of war in the former Yugoslavia was initially downplayed in order to pursue legal reforms and challenges, they have resurfaced as the legacies of early international activism and tribunal judgments are being reviewed. Debate has flourished between those demanding a central focus on the coercive circumstances surrounding rape (MacKinnon 2006), an approach operationalized in *Akayesu*, and those who seek to retain a more consent-based, individualized approach to women's experiences and victimization (Engle 2005; Halley 2008).

Vanessa Munro's chapter begins by establishing the central features of these debates and goes on to interrogate the suitability of coercion- and consent-based legal responses, at both national and international levels. She suggests that while there are clear merits to a focus upon coercive circumstances, this should supplement rather than supplant reliance upon the consent threshold, particularly in the context of domestic rape laws. Defending a 'consent-plus' model that centres on the 'wantedness' of sexual interaction, she integrates the contextual potential of coercion-based accounts into a framework that continues to conceptualize the wrong of the rape through the lens of personal violation and disregard of bodily autonomy. Meanwhile, in their chapter, Michelle Madden Dempsey and Jonathan Herring extend the critical focus further by troubling the normative distinction between (hetero)-sex and rape which underpins conventional analyses. In so doing, they defend the position that the former is prima facie wrongful – at least under current social conditions – and insist that it is in need of further scrutiny and justification in order to be tolerated, let alone valorized as fulfilling and valuable. This innovative and challenging approach advances a new way to put radical feminist thinking about rape and rape law into practice. It demonstrates the possibilities of shifting the burden from women victims having to demonstrate non-consent, towards a justification for any sexual intercourse.

These engagements with feminist conceptualizations of the harm of rape are also raised in later chapters. Karen Engle and Annelise Lottmann, for example, challenge feminists to think afresh about how we characterize the harm of rape. They suggest that shame may not be an inevitable result of wartime rape and warn against humanitarians and feminists exacerbating the very harm which they hope to relieve by emphasizing shame and stigma. Their ambition is to imagine alternative responses to wartime rape which do not assume the inevitability of shame; at the same time recognizing that such a turn would be likely to reduce the possibilities of prosecutions for war crimes such as genocide. The scope for recasting the harm of rape within legal discourse is also considered in the chapters by Alice Edwards and Patricia Londono, which explore the wrong of rape through the paradigm of gender discrimination – in both European and international contexts.

These contributions do not speak with one voice when conceptualizing the wrong of rape. The extent to which violations of sexual integrity are to be privileged as a uniquely serious form of abuse varies across the different accounts, as well as – in the case of some authors – across the contexts of war and peace in which rape occurs. The commonalities that unite sexual assault with consensual heterosexual encounters are afforded greater emphasis by some authors than by others, and some chapters prioritize harm or injury at the systemic and structural level, while others focus more on the individual and experiential. Critical interaction between feminists regarding rape, and the legal and theoretical responses thereto, should be neither 'taboo' (Mardorossian 2002: 743), nor the status quo 'sacrosanct' (Halley 2008: 122). The complexities of rape – both as a social phenomenon and as a personal abuse – require diversity, and feminist analysis is, we believe, enriched by the kinds of critical engagement to be found in this collection.

## THE RELATIONSHIP BETWEEN FEMINIST ACTIVISM AND LEGAL REFORM

The establishment of rape and other forms of violence against women as legitimate concerns for state and civil institutions is widely accredited to the pioneering efforts of feminist campaigners. Although causal correlations are difficult to establish, and usually involve a complex interlocking of a number of conditional factors, the abolition of the marital rape exemption in many national jurisdictions and the steady evolution of rape laws away from a narrow focus upon force, towards what was at least anticipated to be a more progressive emphasis on consent, have certainly been secured following spirited episodes of lobbying and activism by women's groups. It is also true that the official consultations which often precede sexual offences law reform have increasingly – in some jurisdictions at least – sought out and engaged with feminist organizations.

In each of the chapters examining the experiences of different national jurisdictions in responding to rape, the role played by feminists and women's groups in demanding and often securing legal reform (albeit to varying degrees) is demonstrated. At the same time, however, as Monica Burman's discussion of recent developments in Sweden illustrates, the mere presence of a vocal feminist community and, indeed, of a government which purports to pride itself on its gender-sensitive and progressive equality politics does not necessarily ensure the uptake of feminist-inspired rape laws. In addition, the analyses offered by Lise Gotell of Canada and Clare McGlynn of England and Wales demonstrate the extent to which, while feminists may make 'gains' in terms of specific legal reforms, such changes are often met with great resistance and undermined when put into practice.

Moreover, as the chapters by both Peter Rush and Lise Gotell highlight, securing greater political currency with state law-makers and law-enforcers comes with its own costs for feminist organizations. While infiltration of governmental institutions and bureaucratic machinery is necessary in order to bring about legal reform, co-option by the state remains a perpetually present danger. Experiences in Australia and Canada, as well as in other jurisdictions, illustrate that engaging the state on its own terms risks distorting feminism's theoretical paradigms, requiring a 'repackaging' of women's concerns to fit governmental mandates of cost-efficiency and measurability. That this is confounded when funding for NGOs is contingent upon state favour is no surprise – but its consequences in terms of the provision of victim support, for example, may be profound.

The emergence of increasingly powerful international human rights and criminal justice regimes provides a new avenue for activism, and there has been a visible feminist presence in key negotiations and consultations at the international level. Indeed, Janet Halley and others have charted the rise of what is referred to as 'governance feminism' within these contexts, insisting that a particular perspective on violence against women – one closely associated with more radical feminist analyses – has secured unprecedented currency in international responses to rape, prostitution and people trafficking (Halley et al. 2006; Halley 2008). At the same time, however, others have starkly disputed Halley's claim, insisting that feminism remains in a 'scholarly ghetto' in both international law and its institutions (Charlesworth forthcoming). It is against the background of these debates that several of the chapters in this collection emerge. Karen Engle and Annelise Lottmann, for example, lend some support to Halley's perspective, tracing the ways in which shame has been deployed by (some) feminists to amplify the harm associated with rape and the urgency of responding thereto. Doris Buss offers a nuanced analysis of the legacy of *Akayesu* and the ICTR, recognizing both its merits and demerits. In particular, she urges feminists to look beyond conviction rates when considering the 'success' or otherwise of investigations, prosecutions and judgments (on this latter point see also Gotell). Meanwhile, Alice Edwards exposes how feminist activism, despite its increased presence in international dialogue, has failed to secure the recognition of its insistence that rape and sexual violence represent quintessential forms of gender discrimination.

## THE LIMITS OF LAW REFORM IN BRINGING ABOUT CHANGE

In contrast to formalist conventions that see the law as a coherent and complete system, it is widely acknowledged in contemporary socio-legal analysis that, since the 'law is not a brooding omnipresence in the sky' (*Southern Pacific Company v Jensen* 244 US 205 per Holmes J at 222), caution is needed in extrapolating assumptions about law's operation from 'mere paper rules' (see, further, Llewellyn 1931). Carol Smart, highlighting – alongside Michel Foucault – the increasingly disciplinary operation of modern power, has urged feminists to resist the siren call of law, to de-centre it from reform agendas and reappraise our faith in its ability to provide 'solutions' (Smart 1989; Foucault 1980). To the extent that this highlights the limits of law reform as a strategy for change, reminding us of the multiple sites beyond law in which norms are constructed and enforced, as well as of the myriad ways in which human agency (and discrimination) interact with formal conventions to produce alternate outcomes, these interventions are clearly important.

At the same time, there are perils associated with the expulsion of law which must not be underestimated. For one thing, as Catharine MacKinnon has argued, this leaves the terrain of law undefended and enables men to reinscribe patriarchal norms therein without any prospect of challenge (MacKinnon 1993). In addition, it risks trivializing the symbolic function of law as an index of social norms – even where its operation does not currently follow policy, the existence of a formal condemnation provides potential for progressive development. Moreover, it ignores the extent to which legal power – particularly in its emerging quasi-regulatory and governmental guises – is profoundly disciplinary in its operation, creating perpetual sites of resistance and challenge beyond the narrow confines of state regulation and juridical structures (Munro 2001).

In the context of rape, this uneasy combination of optimism about the potential of legal reform, together with a critical awareness of the limits of law's power, marks the terrain in which activism is undertaken. Several of the chapters in this collection expose, in some detail, the dilemmas which this gives rise to. At the international level, for example, both Alison Cole and Doris Buss reveal the ways in which, despite the promising jurisprudence developed by the International Criminal Tribunal for the former Yugoslavia (ICTY) and the ICTR in particular, the legacy left by these tribunals is one replete with failures in the charging and prosecution of sexual violence claims.

Similar patterns are evidenced, and parallel conclusions are reached, in the chapters on national responses to rape. Several authors here highlight factors which have given rise to the failure of legal regimes to fully implement the protections formally provided under domestic criminal laws. For example, Sharon Cowan's analysis of the recent reforms to Scottish sexual offence laws concludes that, despite the changes, many of which are positive in terms of their symbolism and technical improvements, the practice of the law will likely continue, with 'business as usual'. The Italian experience, examined by Rachel Fenton, also suggests that while recent transformations in Italian rape law are welcome, the impact has been more at the level of the expressive, symbolic function of the law, rather than in terms of changing social or cultural mores which impact significantly on prosecutorial practice. Similarly, Clare McGlynn's analysis of recent substantive and evidential law reform in England and Wales provides a number of examples where welcome legislative initiatives have been undermined by judicial attitudes or inaction.

Despite significant variety in the legislative history and socio-economic conditions of the jurisdictions in question, the chapters examining national contexts illustrate common concerns about the adequacy of police training and investigative techniques, and parallel patterns of increased reporting to authorities being met with decreased rates of trial conviction. The tenacity of 'rape myths' and misconceptions in relation to the prevalence of false rape reporting – endorsed by the judiciary, criminal justice officials and members of the public – also represent a shared focus of critical attention. The chapters by Louise Ellison and Vanessa Munro, and Phil Rumney and Natalia

Hanley, draw out the nature and extent of such myths through experimental techniques, while other authors rely on judicial commentary, attrition patterns or social attitude surveys to support their concerns.

While these 'real world' obstacles lead some contributors – such as Sharon Cowan, Clare McGlynn, Rachel Fenton, and Janine Benedet and Isabel Grant – to emphasize the need for social change as a precursor to legal change, others – such as Ivana Radačić and Ksenija Turković, and Heléne Combrinck – remain more optimistic about the power of legal doctrine; and Peter Rush even calls for a renewed focus upon this aspect.

## THE SECONDARY VICTIMIZATION OF RAPE COMPLAINANTS

It has often been argued that rape complainants endure a 'secondary victimization' at the hands of the criminal justice system. In many jurisdictions, recent decades have seen a number of improvements in policy and practice (for example, specialist training of rape investigators, increased availability of in camera testimony, and formal restrictions on the types of questioning permitted at trial), designed to ameliorate the difficulties associated with bringing a rape complaint. It is hoped that such domestic reforms will both increase rates of reporting and improve the prospects for conviction by promoting more effective case-building by police and prosecutors and reducing scope for juror/judicial prejudice, for example in relation to complainants' previous sexual history. These initiatives are certainly to be commended, and should not be thought to have been without positive consequences, at least for some complainants. At the same time, concerns have been expressed – at national and international level – about the extent to which best practice has been incorporated into criminal justice responses, as well as about the ways in which reforms have been circumvented through the ingenuity of determined defence barristers.

Across the 'national perspective' chapters in this collection, a consistent frustration emerges with procedural reforms which – though well-intentioned – have failed to live up to their promise in terms of respecting the rights and dignity of rape complainants. This encompasses common and civil-law jurisdictions, as well as adversarial and inquisitorial systems (see Donald Dripps, Clare McGlynn, Lise Gotell, Rachel Fenton, Monica Burman, Ivana Radačić and Ksenija Turković, and Janine Benedet and Isabel Grant).

In turn, this frustration has provoked other contributors to explore alternative and additional mechanisms by which the armoury of protection afforded to rape complainants might be strengthened. Fiona Raitt recommends the introduction of independent lawyers to provide advocacy and representation for rape complainants – a move that would both empower victims and reclaim their disputes from the 'stolen' grip of the state (Christie 1977). Meanwhile, Louise Ellison and Vanessa Munro consider the positive impact which educating jurors in a rape trial might have in terms of promoting less prejudiced assessments of complainant credibility and more nuanced analyses of the questions of consent and belief therein, which are central to criminal liability. In addition, several authors highlight the need for more effective – and better, as well as independently, funded – support services for victims, with Aisha Gill making a compelling case for this in the particular context of women from black and minority ethnic communities.

## THE STRUCTURE OF THE BOOK

The chapters of this book are organized into four parts. While the themes outlined above can be traced across the entire collection, there are also certain issues of concern that are unique to each of these parts. The chapters contained in the 'Conceptual and Theoretical Engagements' section – by Vanessa Munro, and Michelle Madden Dempsey and Jonathan Herring – revisit and reappraise key debates around the 'wrong' of rape, the relationship between rape and 'normal' sexual relationships and the role of sexual violence as a technique of patriarchal oppression. In addition to theorizing the phenomenon of rape, these chapters also evaluate competing legal frameworks for responding thereto. More specifically, the chapters explore the merits and demerits of consent-based approaches, and engage with crucial questions about the role that consent plays in legitimating intercourse, about the levels of freedom that must be enjoyed before normatively meaningful consent can be given, and about the extent to which a focus on coercive circumstances can – or should – by-pass consideration of personal autonomy.

The second part of the book focuses upon 'International and Regional Perspectives'. Several of the chapters here continue the engagement with, for example, debates over consent and coercion or the 'wrong' of rape initiated in the previous section, with the emphasis here placed upon exploring these issues in the context of international or regional level regimes. The chapters by Alison Cole, Doris Buss, and Karen Engle and Annelise Lottmann focus upon the relatively recent international criminal law response to sexual violence perpetrated during military conflicts. Cole sets the scene by tracing the origins of this jurisprudence from Nuremberg through subsequent international tribunals for Yugoslavia, Rwanda, Sierra Leone, and on to the creation of the International Criminal Court. Buss focuses specifically upon the lessons – positive and negative – to be learned from the Rwanda tribunal's prosecution of rape. Meanwhile, Engle and Lottman explore the role of shame in simultaneously amplifying the harm of rape in international legal doctrine while imposing a barrier to its prosecution in the tribunal context. The chapters by Alice Edwards, Patricia Londono and Heléne Combrinck turn from criminal law to explore human rights frameworks – at the international, European and African levels. Each author examines the emergence of sexual violence as an issue of concern within these respective regimes. In addition, critical consideration is given to the extent to which human rights principles, and the political currency that they have enjoyed, have imposed more demanding thresholds upon state parties in terms of criminalizing sexual violence, responding appropriately to victims and punishing perpetrators.

In the third part, attention shifts to the domestic level and to a range of divergent 'National Perspectives'. As a collective, these chapters provide valuable insights into the ways in which, across often diverse legal and socio-political territories, comparable dilemmas, debates and difficulties are encountered in responding to sexual violence. The authors here provide a critical overview of key provisions in their own jurisdiction, highlighting the shifts which have occurred over time, hypothesizing about the causes of these developments, engaging with ongoing controversies and indicating avenues for future reform. Mindful of the complexities of comparative analysis, which requires detailed knowledge and understanding of different cultures and practices, the authors in this section have immersed their analyses of rape laws in their social and institutional context as much as possible, in many cases providing data about the overall political environment (for example, Sharon Cowan, Rachel Fenton, Clare McGlynn, Lise Gotell, and Ivana Radačić and Ksenija Turković) and the status of feminist/civil society campaign groups (for example, Lise Gotell, Clare McGlynn and Peter Rush), as well as more general information on socio-sexual attitudes research, the statistical incidence of rape reporting and the national trends in relation to attrition and conviction.

The various national jurisdictions covered by contributors to this section were selected in a broad attempt to embrace a diversity of approaches and traditions. England and Wales has often been seen as responsible for 'exporting' a reactionary approach to rape law across the common-law world and it continues to have one of the lowest rape conviction rates in Europe. Clare McGlynn analyses the recent attempts to break free from this historical legacy and evaluates the reforms that have been introduced in recent years to tackle the high rate of attrition and improve the experiences of victims. While sharing a similar cultural and social context, Scotland's legal system is separate from that of England and Wales, and has long been resistant to the claims of feminist reformers. Nonetheless, in 2009, it adopted a new Sexual Offences Act which draws on the lessons learnt from other jurisdictions. Sharon Cowan's chapter is one of the first examinations of this new law and, particularly, challenges the instantiation of rape as a gender-specific crime, exposing the lack of protection therefore afforded to lesbian women.

These common-law traditions are contrasted with the civil-law approaches in Italy, Croatia and Sweden. As a democracy recently emerging from both totalitarian rule and internal conflict, analysis of the Croatian experience presents an insight into the political negotiations, compromises and opportunities of a state in transition. We learn from this analysis that the voices of feminists and women's activism are essential to place the issue of sexual violence on the political agenda; but also that compromise is necessary. These lessons are also demonstrated in Rachel Fenton's analysis of Italy's reform of sexual offence laws which shows the often painstakingly slow process of change, as well as the complex interaction between progressive reforms in the jurisprudence and the tenacity of conservative social attitudes. Sweden then provides a contrasting example. With a long history of women's rights, and regularly heralded as an exemplar of women's equality, one could be forgiven for assuming that an analysis of the Swedish law on rape would provide the answers to the questions that other jurisdictions are asking. Unfortunately, this is not so, as Monica Burman lays bare. Indeed, it is often the assumptions about there already being equality between women and men which hinders progress within Sweden.

In a similar vein, and moving beyond Europe, Canada is often lauded as a jurisdiction promoting a positive, and progressive, conception of consent and women's rights. While Canada has indeed moved closer towards the kind of affirmative model of consent that many feminists have advocated, Lise Gotell's analysis suggests that this has come at the price of consolidating the individualizing approach of the criminal law. This, in turn, produces new forms of victim-blaming as women are required to demonstrate their individual responsibility, and sexual violence is decontextualized from the social power relations which define it. This also raises particular concerns for women with mental disabilities, as developed in the later chapter by Janine Benedet and Isabel Grant.

Although their vast array of different state jurisdictions entails caution in relation to any general conclusions, both Australia and the US are often offered as exemplars of countries within which sustained feminist activism has achieved changes to the formal laws and policies on rape. Indeed, the 'culture wars' in the US have mainstreamed debates about rape, rape law and women's rights. However, promising changes in US law, towards greater recognition of sexual autonomy and female equality, have often been met with a tenacious backlash against feminist gains (Roiphe 1994; Paglia 1992; Hoff Summers 1995). Indeed, in his chapter, Donald Dripps concludes that popular opinion in the US, which could be said to harbour resentment against female sexual freedom, has a decisive influence on the law-in-action, often at the expense of the more progressive law-in-the-books. Peter Rush's analysis of Australian developments critically examines the effects of an increasing reference to social science literature and research findings to justify law reform; a practice which has become more and more evident in many other jurisdictions. While this turn to social science research has many benefits, particularly the highlighting of the failures of the processing of rape complaints, in his chapter, Rush warns against a preoccupation with the procedures of the criminal justice system, and urges a reconsideration of the substantive laws of the offence of rape.

Finally, Shereen Mills examines the South African experience. This chapter provides an intriguing and valuable analysis of a country which, at the same time as exhibiting unprecedented levels of sexual violence, has also introduced much-lauded constitutional protections of human rights. In recent years, while law reform agencies in South Africa contemplated eschewing a consent-based approach to rape law, focusing instead on the coercive circumstances of the acts, this was not borne out in practice. Mills shows how the realities of poverty, high incidence of HIV and the persistence of customary laws and practices regarding women's subordinate role and lack of rights together restrict the opportunities for progressive reform of the law and particularly its practice.

Though offering a range of diverse national perspectives, this section is not intended to be, and nor could it ever have been, exhaustive. Asian and Latin American experiences are not represented, for example. In addition, the significance of the Germanic tradition within Europe is worthy of further examination. Nonetheless, the analyses offered here provide an important cross-section of developments and perspectives, some of which, though well known, are brought together in valuable comparison; others, such as Croatia and Italy, are little known or explored beyond those particular nation states, and their inclusion here enriches our understanding of rape law and policy in varied societies.

In the final part of the book, 'New Agendas and Directions', the chapters draw upon several of the criticisms and calls for reform that have been voiced by other contributors in relation to international, regional or national jurisdictions. The various authors here identify ongoing challenges in responding to rape – for example, in relation to the representation of victim witnesses during criminal proceedings (Fiona Raitt) or the tenacious assumptions that inform juror assessments of complainant credibility (Louise Ellison and Vanessa Munro, and Phil Rumney and Natalia Hanley). In addition, they marshal evidence-based arguments that can be deployed in support of reform agendas. Also drawn into the frame here are the perspectives of, and problems encountered by, constituencies who seek redress for sexual violence but who are often marginalized from 'mainstream' analyses – namely, men (Phil Rumney and Natalia Hanley), women from black and minority ethnic communities (Aisha Gill) and persons with mental disabilities (Janine Benedet and Isabel Grant). While many of the concerns raised in the preceding chapters also have a direct relevance for these groups, a dedicated focus on them in this final section is intended to underline the need for their greater inclusion in debates and reform activities, as well as to foster a more intersectional analysis of the ways in which rape can be afforded different meanings and engender different experiences depending upon a person's location within a network of identity categories and contexts.

The primary focus of this book, then, is upon rethinking rape *laws*, but the boundaries between the legal and the non-legal are by no means as sharp or impenetrable as is often implied. While law may be something more than bare politics, there is little doubt that its content and operation is closely bound up with political agendas, as well as social and cultural norms, economic and pragmatic imperatives, and moral/ethical aspirations. In engaging the legal, the contributors to this collection have implicated these other phenomena, highlighting their mutually supportive and constitutive operation. In the area of rape law, there remain a number of 'known unknowns'; for example, in relation to rates of prevalence (as opposed to reporting) and even, in some countries, in relation to rates of attrition. Attitudinal surveys, though instructive, may not translate predictably into jury deliberations, and – despite their central role as the ultimate arbiters of guilt or innocence in many jurisdictions – prohibitions on research with juries often leave us to fill the gap between judicial direction and verdict with conjecture. In addition, as noted above, there are several groups whose perspectives have been inadequately represented or understood in the creation and implementation of rape laws – in many cases despite the fact that such groups are amongst the most vulnerable to sexual assault. These, and many other, issues provide a programme for future research that is gargantuan both in its scale and its importance. Though this will take us well beyond the immediate confines of state legislatures, courtrooms and international protocols, it remains intimately bound up with the framing and operation of future rape laws. By bringing a range of perspectives together, and traversing the local and global, abstract and concrete, structural and individual, and theory and practice, the chapters which follow – and the collection as a whole – seek to contribute to and inform this enterprise of rethinking rape law.

## Bibliography

Brownmiller, S. (1975) *Against Our Will: men, women and rape*, London: Penguin.

Charlesworth, H. (forthcoming) 'Talking to ourselves: feminist scholarship in international law', in Z. Pearson and S. Kouvo (eds) *Between Resistance and Compliance? Feminist Perspectives on International Law in an Era of Anxiety and Terror* (manuscript in progress).

Christie, N. (1977) 'Conflicts as property', *British Journal of Criminology*, 17: 1–15.

Engle, K. (2005) 'Feminism and its (dis)contents: criminalizing war time rape in Bosnia and Herzegovina', *American Journal of International Law*, 99: 778–816.

Foucault, M. (1980) *Power/Knowledge – Selected Interviews and Other Writings 1972–77* (C. Gordon, ed.), New York: Harvester Press.

Halley, J. (2008) 'Rape at Rome: feminist interventions in the criminalization of sex-related violence in positive international criminal law', *Michigan Journal of International Law*, 30: 1–123.

Halley, J., Kotiswaran, P., Shamir, H. and Thomas, C. (2006) 'From the international to the local in feminist legal responses to rape, prostitution/sex work and sex trafficking: four studies in contemporary governance feminism', *Harvard Journal of Law and Gender*, 29: 335–425.

Hoff Summers, C. (1995) *Who Stole Feminism? How women have betrayed women*, London: Simon and Schuster.

Llewellyn, K. (1931) 'Some realism about realism', *Harvard Law Review*, 44: 1222–64.

MacKinnon, C. (1989) *Toward a Feminist Theory of State*, Cambridge, MA: Harvard University Press.

—— (1993) 'Reflections on law in the everyday life of women', in A. Sarat and T. Kearns (eds) *Law in Everyday Life*, Ann Arbor: University of Michigan Press.

—— (2006) 'Defining rape internationally: A comment on *Akayesu*', in C. MacKinnon (ed.) *Are Women Human? And Other International Dialogues*, Cambridge, MA: Harvard University Press, 237–46.

Mardorossian, C. (2002) 'Toward a new feminist theory of rape', *Signs: Journal of Women in Culture and Society*, 27: 743–75.

Munro, V. (2001) 'Legal feminism and Foucault: A critique of the expulsion of law', *Journal of Law and Society*, 28(4): 546–67.

Paglia, C. (1992) *Sex, Art and American Culture*, London: Viking.

Roiphe, K. (1994) *The Morning After: fear, sex and feminism*, London: Hamish Hamilton.

Smart, C. (1989) *Feminism and the Power of Law*, London: Routledge.

# Part I
# Conceptual and theoretical engagements

Chapter 1

# From consent to coercion
Evaluating international and domestic frameworks for the criminalization of rape

*Vanessa E. Munro*

The decision of the International Criminal Tribunal for Rwanda (ICTR) in the case of *Prosecutor v Akayesu* (ICTR-96-4-T, Judgment 2 September 1998) has been heralded by many as signalling a new, and improved, approach to defining the offence of rape (at least, although not necessarily solely, for the purposes of international criminal law). The background to the *Akayesu* judgment is discussed in detail in subsequent chapters (see, in particular, the discussion by Cole and Buss in this collection). For current purposes suffice it to say that, in its judgment, the ICTR sought to ensure that the fundamentally aggressive nature of the act of rape should not be eclipsed by a mechanical obsession with what needs to be done (e.g. penetration) with which body parts. Thus, a 'conceptual' rather than 'cataloguing' approach was adopted, emphasizing that rape represents a violation of personal dignity, which can be used to intimidate, degrade, humiliate, discriminate, punish, control or destroy a person. Rape was defined as a 'physical invasion of a sexual nature, committed under circumstances which are coercive' (paras 597–8), although it was noted that, for it to constitute a crime against humanity, the rape(s) must have been committed as part of a systematic/widespread attack on a civilian population and grounded in national, ethnic, political, racial or religious discrimination.

This conceptualization of rape as paradigmatically involving sexual invasion under coercive circumstances has received an uneven reception in subsequent international criminal cases. In *Prosecutor v Kunarac, Kovac and Vukovic* (case no. IT-96-23-T & IT-96-23/1-T, Judgment 22 February 2001), the International Criminal Tribunal for the former Yugoslavia (ICTY) reinserted the reliance upon a consent threshold that had been deliberately omitted in *Akayesu*. Here, rape was defined as requiring proof of a lack of consent, albeit that it was emphasized that the issue of voluntariness would need to be assessed in the context of the surrounding circumstances, with due attention being paid to the fact that coercion need not be limited to a narrow focus upon force or the threat of force. Acknowledging that in most cases charged as war crimes or crimes against humanity, the prevailing circumstances will indeed give rise to coercion (and thus to a lack of 'true' consent), the ICTY nonetheless sought to preserve the definitional significance of consent, or more specifically non-consent, to the offence of rape.

While any suggestion that this created a competing and contradictory authority has been formally disputed by the ICTR (*Prosecutor v Muhimana* (case no. ICTR-95-1B-T, Judgment 28 April 2005) and *Prosecutor v Gacumbitsi* (case no. ICTR-2001-64-A, Judgment 7 July 2006)), the ideological compatibility of the coercive circumstances approach in *Akayesu* and the consent-based approach in *Kunarac* have been questioned by several commentators, many of whom have insisted that the former represents the more progressive, and more accurate, framework for responding to (wartime) rape.

With Ines Peterson, Wolfgang Schomburg – an Appeals Chamber judge at both the ICTR and ICTY – has insisted that 'the peculiar characteristics of crimes of sexual violence under international law militate in favour of shifting the focus away from consent as an element of the crime' (2007: 139). Acknowledging that the familiarity of domestic criminal law responses to rape, the vast majority of which retain a consent threshold, may make transposing the same model into the international context seem prima facie appropriate, Alison Cole makes a similar argument, emphasizing that 'in this national context, there is no attack against an entire population' and 'the issue is typically the interactions between two individual people who are treated in law as equally autonomous individuals' (2008: 75). While this may make a definitional focus upon (non-)consent more appropriate in the national context, Schomburg and Peterson suggest that 'the general assumption of equal autonomy . . . cannot indiscriminately be transferred to the level of international criminal law' (2007: 126), and Cole insists that the 'need to reflect the imbalance in interpersonal relations that exist in wartime' and the fact that in 'a context of armed conflict, the victims . . . by definition are under a non-consensual attack' renders this domestic approach problematic in the international criminal arena (2008: 75).

Meanwhile, Catharine MacKinnon has gone further, insisting that the approach initiated in *Akayesu* is not only to be preferred at the international level, in responding to wartime rape, but should also provide a template to be adopted at the domestic level. MacKinnon traces the origins of a conflict strategy of instrumentalizing sexual violence as a tactic of genocide to patriarchal peacetime structures within which women are marked as inferior, conspicuous and vulnerable. In this context, she seeks – without conflating the two phenomena – to emphasize the continuum which unites genocidal rape and sexual violations that occur on the domestic scale, outwith conflict zones, and between individual acquaintances or intimates (2006a: 225). Having done so, MacKinnon laments the retreat from the coercive circumstances approach of *Akayesu* in subsequent ICTY jurisprudence, highlighting the extent to which the return to non-consent in *Kunarac* ignores the contextual and collective dimensions of rape, focusing, she argues, upon an atomistic, one-at-a-time model of sexual negotiation that is ill-fitting in circumstances of both war and peace, since it ignores the foundational patterns of gender inequality that frame the parameters within which (hetero)sexual agency is exercised.

The *Akayesu* approach has, as MacKinnon advocates, now been incorporated in several national jurisdictions, including both California and Illinois, where gender violence for civil purposes is defined to include 'a physical instruction or physical invasion of a sexual nature under coercive conditions' (MacKinnon 2006b: 956). This chapter seeks to evaluate the merits and demerits of this turn from consent to coercion. Exploring the transferability of this model from international contexts marked by war and genocide to national contexts in which the profoundly mundane nature of sexual violence against women has been emphasized, it argues that abandoning consent risks practical obstacles to prosecution, as well as doctrinal contortions (and, indeed, distortions). It suggests that while there are clear merits to a focus upon coercion, this should be seen to supplement rather than supplant our reliance upon consent in domestic rape laws. Indeed, it illustrates that many of the apparent advantages of coercion over consent-based frameworks are attributable to a tendency amongst commentators to contrast a minimalist conception of consent against a rich conception of coercion, which underestimates the potential for a more contextual understanding of agency and autonomy within the confines of existing consent regimes.

## FROM COERCION TO CONSENT, AND BACK AGAIN?

Historically, the tendency to conceive of female chastity/fidelity in terms of financial or (male) status value, together with a palpable unease at the prospect of women's false rape allegations (e.g. Hale 1736 (reprinted 1971); for recent commentary, see Rumney 2006), led to the creation of laws in many national jurisdictions which defined the offence of rape to require the use of physical force to overpower the victim's resistance. While, over time, these force-based accounts were often expanded to accommodate, for example, the coercive effect of threats of physical force upon the victim, they continued to expect that a female victim would resist unwanted sexual contact with utmost vigour, and retained a trigger for criminalization which lay in the forceful actions of the assailant, rather than in the 'wantedness' or otherwise of the encounter from the victim's perspective.

While in some jurisdictions, such as Scotland and certain US states, the retreat from such narrow forced-based accounts has been a relatively recent phenomenon (see, further, Cowan and Dripps in this collection), in many other jurisdictions – including, for example, England and Wales (see McGlynn in this collection) – the law has long since converted (at least at the level of formal doctrine) to a response to rape that is grounded in the existence of a lack of victim consent. Within this genre of approach, and particularly with the passage of time and consecutive efforts at substantive and evidential law reform, there have been significant points of divergence – for example, in relation to the conceptualization of consent as a state of mind or a performative act, to the need for positive dissent to be communicated, and to the level of knowledge/concern about the victim's lack of consent that the defendant must exhibit in order to be criminally liable.

Campaigns to reform force-based rape laws have often held out such consent-based frameworks as providing a more progressive and responsive alternative. But these too have generated significant difficulties and concerns. Although non-consent is a required element in many crimes, critics have pointed out that, in rape law, this threshold is operationalized in a context of profound suspicion of female sexuality (Naffine 1994). It is argued that using consent to distinguish instances of (socially prized and personally endorsed) intimacy from instances of sexual violation has encouraged a disproportionate focus upon the will and behaviour of the complainant rather than upon the conduct and intentions of the perpetrator. While force and resistance are no longer definitional requirements of the offence, they continue to be seen as evidentially highly significant, and their absence in many experiences of rape ensures that a large share of the sexual violence perpetrated upon women is never brought to the attention of, or is summarily dismissed by, domestic criminal justice systems (for England and Wales, see Kelly et al. 2005; Munro and Kelly 2009). In addition, there is substantial evidence that a woman who exhibits other non-conforming behaviour, for example, by drinking alcohol, dressing provocatively, or initiating intimacy, will often be deemed – by defendants, criminal justice officials and jurors – to have sent out signals of sexual interest which cannot easily be revoked when subsequently relied upon by a male perpetrator (for England and Wales, see Home Office 2009; Temkin and Krahé 2008; Brown et al. 2007; Finch and Munro 2007).

In addition, it has been emphasized that while they assert a foundation that is grounded in freedom, capacity and choice, consent-based models often fail to adequately interrogate these concepts, and in so doing fail to acknowledge their profound malleability (e.g. Temkin and Ashworth 2004; Finch and Munro 2006). The deference afforded to the conventional (and highly abstract) conception of consent in rape laws disguises the extent to which men and women do not operate in, choose from, or communicate on the basis of an equal and mutually respectful terrain. On the contrary, it is argued, social stereotypes about 'appropriate' gendered behaviour, as well as material considerations and inter personal/structural power differentials, inform women's subjectivities, activities, choices and assessments of the scope for refusal. In a patriarchal world in which women experience systematic disempowerment and inequality, critics have cautioned that women's tokens of heterosexual interest, acquiescence or even initiative may be as much a mechanism for survival as an expression of legitimate choice (see MacKinnon 1987, 1989). And yet, as MacKinnon emphasizes, consent-based criminal thresholds have tended to pay scant regard to this complexity: 'when the law of rape finds consent to sex, it does not look to see if the parties were social equals in any sense, nor does it require mutuality or positive choice in sex, far less simultaneity of desire' (2005: 243).

These, and other, concerns have led some commentators to argue for a reformulation of rape laws, proposing either to relegate non-consent from being a constitutive element to being solely of defensive relevance or to establish a differentiated 'familial' system within which a substantive definitional content will describe the harm in its absence (e.g. rape by coercion, rape by force, drug-assisted rape, etc.) (e.g. Tadros 2006). The shift in *Akayesu* away from reliance upon consent, and towards a definition of rape grounded in the existence of a physical invasion of a sexual nature in coercive circumstances, in many ways represents a concrete attempt at such a reformulation in the international context.

Yet, there are reasons to be sceptical of these so-called alternative models. For one thing, it has been argued that, in the context of rape, some concept of consent is necessary to allow people to act, and be respected as, moral agents who police the boundaries of their own personal intimacy by inviting as well as denying sexual access (Gardner and Shute 2000: 207–8). One may respond to this assertion, as Victor Tadros has done, by insisting that 'even if the concept of consent is central to the most appropriate theoretical investigation into the scope of the law of rape', its excessive and inherent ambiguity mean that it is simply not useful in the delineation of the law itself (2006: 518). But this begs crucial questions, in particular about the wisdom of generating conceptual frameworks for law reform that are consciously detached from – and arguably at odds with – the wrong that occasions their development. At a more practical level, moreover, it is far from clear that reforms which purport to abandon the consent threshold at the level of doctrine can succeed in avoiding its reinsertion in trial proceedings. Research by Regina Graycar and Jenny Morgan (2002) has illustrated the extent to which legal reforms that formally relegate consent to the status of a defence in rape have failed to prevent disputes about its presence from arising in the courtroom, and have done little to prevent dubious claims about 'proper' female socio-sexual behaviour from informing both judicial and jury reasoning. Similar findings in Jennifer Temkin's exploration of alternative legal regimes in New South Wales, Michigan and Canada led her to conclude that 'the problem of consent is unlikely to vanish whatever means are adopted to deal with it' (2002: 176).

Yet, there are some who maintain that the coercion-based approach pioneered in *Akayesu* offers a far more robust alternative than those models that simply relegate consent to the status of a defence; and that, as such, it offers a genuine prospect of moving beyond the limitations of the consent threshold in both theory and practice. MacKinnon, in particular, has argued that the definition provided by the ICTR offers a third model that bridges the divide between consent and force-based accounts by seeing the wrong of rape as grounded in inequality rather than in a lack of autonomy or in physical violation per se. This account, she insists, cannot be subsumed within a consent-based model, since its conceptual orientation is quite distinct – as she puts it, 'where coercion definitions of rape see power – domination and violence – nonconsent definitions envision love or passion gone wrong' and, as such, where consent definitions focus on the individual psychic space inhabited by victim and perpetrator, coercion definitions focus on the material plane and 'turn on proof of physical acts, surrounding context, or exploitation of relative position: who did what to whom and, often, in some sense, why' (2006a: 237–8).

To the extent that consent-based models have too often adopted a thin understanding that privileges the existence (express or implied) of an affirmative token over a more concrete and contextualized exploration of the various pressures that operate to construct and constrain sexual agency, it is true that they have been disappointing, and are ripe for feminist reconstruction. At the same time, however, it should be recalled that models of rape law grounded in coercion can also be interpreted in narrow and restrictive terms, giving rise to a return to an essentially force-based framework. To contrast a very thin understanding of consent with an expansive understanding of coercion is, thus, to amplify the appearance of improvement at the cost of giving consent a fair hearing and at the risk of being too optimistic about the (progressive and expansive) ways in which coercion-based accounts will be interpreted and applied in legal practice. For all the legitimate concerns that have been expressed about the consent threshold, its potential for more productive deployment in a way that both better secures justice for rape victims and tackles hetero-normative power dynamics should not be discounted. As Sharon Cowan has emphasized, 'consent is a concept which we can fill with either narrow liberal values, based on the idea of the subject as an individual atomistic rational choice maker, or with feminist values encompassing attention to mutuality, embodiment, relational choice and communication' (2007: 53). The challenge, then, should not be to abandon consent as the transformative channel between the permissible and impermissible, but to reformulate it in a way that enables it to take greater account of the peculiarities of context, constraint and construction, and to operate with renewed vigour in the pursuit of social justice.

### 'Consent-plus': toward a more adequate conception of consent

In support of this ambition to formulate a richer, and more responsive, conception of consent, I have previously argued (contra Wertheimer 2003) for a 'consent-plus' account, according to which something more than 'consensual minimalism' – that is, a mere token of acquiescence or affirmation in the absence of force or deception – is required to render sexual contact permissible (Munro 2005). A token of consent must be accompanied, under this approach, by a critical endorsement of a reciprocal benefit (be it emotional, relational, physical, or even material), which accrues as a result of engaging in sexual intercourse. Genuine, and transformative, agency is expressed not simply when individuals are in a position to articulate and implement their desires, but when they have hitherto 'taken charge' of those desires in a particular way. Without underestimating the impact of disciplinary norms and disparities of power/resources, this 'consent-plus' approach refuses to surrender agency to these forces, imposing instead a procedural insistence on reflection about the reasons that underpin, constrain, construct and motivate our choices. It goes beyond the minimalist baseline by requiring not only that there be an absence of immediate obstacles (e.g. force or fraud), but that education be provided to enable people to manage their long-term self-determination, that a range of genuine and realistic alternatives be made available to choose from, and that a culture be promoted in which introspection about one's desires is actively encouraged.

This 'consent-plus' model creates a forum in which agency can be encouraged, fostered and exercised without resort to a utopian vision of self-determination in which constraint and construction are transcended, avoided or eliminated. It does not demand – or rely on the misguided hypothesis – that people be elevated from the practical and theoretical limitations that impinge upon their decision-making. Instead, it is enough that the parties, exercising agency within the social constraints incumbent upon them, have critically evaluated and endorsed the values reflected in the choices that they make. Crucially, this in no way entails that we should divert attention away from interrogating the broader socio-economic constraints that impact upon a woman in her reflective process, challenging them where necessary in pursuit of a more just distribution of resources and expectations. But it does ensure that the focus is on those instances in which the parties experience the pain of self-alienation and a lack of 'wantedness' through their sexual participation. Thus, it fosters our critical engagement with the discursive and relational circumstances that frame the parameters of a person's sexual decision-making, without thereby submerging that person's ability to speak within the structural dictates of these circumstances – and it makes it clear that, as Brenda Baker has argued, 'it is not reasonable to expect consent to do all the work needed for sexual equality' (1999: 64).

Coercion-based analyses are crucial to the operation of this 'consent-plus' model. They provide a vital supplement to conventional 'consensual minimalism', ensuring that structural and systemic pressures, as well as material, interpersonal and communal imperatives, are acknowledged as impacting upon both the ability to exercise, and the nature of, a choice. But they do not, and cannot, supplant the consent threshold. The approach set out in *Akayesu* is clear that coercion need not be limited to physical force, but can include circumstances of duress and intimidation. Under a 'consent-plus' approach, such duress or intimidation also emerge as pertinent considerations, which – together or separately – contra-indicate a valid expression of agency. Their relevance, however, lies precisely in the fact that they have operated to prevent the critical reflection and endorsement that must accompany a valid token of affirmation. Thus, the need for their recognition and eradication is central to, rather than distinct from, the ethos of a consent-based model; and it is only by assuming a thin, one-dimensional and abstract conception thereof that matters could appear otherwise. Granted, such a thin notion has often animated historical and contemporary liberal legal responses, but as the 'consent-plus' model indicates, this is far from inevitable. Richer conceptualizations of consent (and its core concepts of freedom, capacity and agency) are capable of being deployed.

The 'consent-plus' model sketched here does, to some extent, retain its core focus upon the individual psyche of the rape complainant, but it does not do so at the exclusion of societal and contextual considerations of inequality and power, as MacKinnon suggests. To the contrary, it incorporates these factors, and the critical conditions that are required in order to make sense of them, into its exploration of psychic spaces, taking seriously the voices of women themselves without rubber-stamping averred expressions of autonomy as representative of genuine, critically endorsed and reflected upon self-determination.

## CONSENT AND COERCION IN TIMES OF 'PEACE'

The suggestion that coercion-based frameworks can replace, and obliterate the need for, non-consent in rape emerges as particularly problematic, it will be argued here, in the domestic context. Even accepting MacKinnon's compelling assertions of a continuum which unites the scripts and practices of gender inequality, and sexual violence as an expression and enforcer thereof, there are clearly some distinguishing characteristics which mark out (many) rapes in times of conflict from (many) rapes in times of peace.

The cases that engage international criminal law on rape often involve the co-existence of myriad other forms of wrongdoing, including physical violence, homicide and sexual slavery. The perpetrators and victims are often strangers to one another – both literally in terms of their lack of previous acquaintance and also metaphorically in terms of the significance attached to their divergent ethnic identities. The rapes take place in a context in which the antagonism between the groups to which the victim and perpetrator belong is not only deeply felt and fiercely actualized, but overt, public and publicized. By contrast, in domestic contexts, the majority of rapes are perpetrated by acquaintances, partners or former partners. The rapes may be accompanied by acts or threats of physical violence, but a significant proportion are not. And while social relations between men and women may be structurally problematic, and the parties' personal relationships may be abusive or unequal, the manifestations of this are often more complex and elusive.

In these latter contexts, the ability of the law to identify and respond to coercive conditions becomes increasingly problematic. As feminist commentators, including MacKinnon, have established, while patriarchy may be alive and well, its modes of operation and exclusion are often subtle, pervasive and cloaked in claims to authority, legitimacy and inevitability. This not only makes patriarchy a resilient adversary, it sets its modus operandi apart, in some significant ways, from the more overtly oppressive and coercive mechanisms that are deployed in support of military conflicts. MacKinnon argues that, in contrast to the focus in consent-based accounts on the parties' subjective psyche, the focus within a coercion-based account on the external world yields factors that 'are more susceptible to standard forms of legal proof' (2006a: 246). While this may be true to an extent, it would be misleading to suggest that all evidential difficulties will be eliminated, particularly, it is submitted here, within the domestic context.

It might be objected, of course, that these evidential difficulties would also continue to apply in relation to the 'consent-plus' model defended above. After all, this model purports to incorporate some of the valuable insights of the coercion framework, and in so doing it too demands attention to the complex, and subtle, operations of patriarchal power. At the same time, however, the 'consent-plus' approach has the advantage of flexibility in that it includes within its remit of consideration all factors that construct and/or constrain the realization of 'genuine' (that is, non-self-alienating) agency. As a result, it avoids the additional, and significant, obstacle posed in coercion frameworks, which require not only the identification of influencing factors, but the determination of such factors as operating in a coercive manner. In this context, it is also worth noting that while these probative difficulties would be amplified by the courts'/legislatures' adoption of a restrictive interpretation of coercion, this is a prospect which the history of rape law reform, together with MacKinnon's own general hypothesis of a structural privileging of male interests in legal institutions, suggests cannot be ruled out.

There are, moreover, other reasons to be wary of jettisoning consent in preference for a focus on coercive circumstances in the domestic criminal arena. There are, after all, certain scenarios of rape, populating the domestic landscape with alarming regularity, which would be conceptually ill-suited to a coercion-based analysis. Take, for example, situations in which a complainant, who is voluntarily intoxicated, is raped by an opportunistic male assailant. No doubt, there are some coercive factors operating in the background – including, for example, contemporary associations between alcohol consumption and (wanted and unwanted) sexual activity, as well as the existence of social norms that disapprove of sober sexual initiation from women while condoning, and rationalizing as 'natural' and 'uncontrollable', men's attempts to push the boundaries of any limited permissions granted in pursuit of sexual gratification (e.g. Ellison and Munro 2009). At the same time, this is far from a paradigmatic case of coercion, and the harm experienced by the victim is far more straightforwardly conceptualized as a violation of her sexual autonomy, in line with the consent-based account. Where the victim lacks capacity to make or express a choice owing to her intoxication, the defendant's conduct in having sex with her is clearly blameworthy, but the nature of his wrongdoing lies most centrally in his disregard of her entitlement (as a moral and legal agent) to make a choice; and it is in the denial of this opportunity that the victim would most likely locate the feelings of violation and disempowerment that she experiences. This is not to say that, despite the fact that the defendant did not compel the victim to become intoxicated, coercion *could* not be constructed from the broader, contextual backdrop. Nor is it to say that such contextual factors ought not to play a central role in evaluating the wrongdoing and blameworthiness of the defendant's conduct. But it is to say that focusing on this coercive paradigm at the expense of the violation of autonomy that prima facie encircles the scenario would significantly misrepresent the nature of the wrongdoing, and the nature of the harm. Removing consent from the frame in this context would, in other words, alter and impoverish the expressive contours of the picture.

It is true that consent is a threshold that can only be invoked with considerable caution. Amongst other things, it requires the addition of a coercion-based analysis to ensure that the background conditions constructing and constraining women's (sexual) choices are acknowledged, and their impact evaluated. However, it provides a triggering condition for criminalization that cannot, and should not, be abandoned, particularly in a liberal society that purports to hold dear the values of freedom of, and respect for, choice. In contrast to MacKinnon, who insists that a coercion-based framework provides a complete alternative to, and significant improvement upon, its consent-based predecessor, in both international and domestic contexts, it has been argued here that a 'consent-plus' account, which incorporates a focus on coercive circumstances without abandoning a concern with sexual autonomy, provides a more desirable model. A thin analysis of consent yields a soft target for critique, but it ignores the extent to which the concept is capable of being infused with richer, more demanding and profoundly contextualized standards. At the same time, relying on an expansive analysis of coercion ignores the difficulties involved in dismissing women's averred expressions of agency where they appear to reflect or support existing patterns of power. It also trivializes the risk that the concept of coercion will be interpreted minimally in practice, reinstituting a narrow and problematic focus on physical force. Aside from these concerns of over- and under-inclusivity, a coercion-based account may encounter additional problems in being relied upon as the exclusive model for responding to rape in the domestic context, where patriarchal power relations are often fluid, complex and subtle in their operation, and where many rapes, such as those involving a voluntarily intoxicated complainant, are more straightforwardly understood as violations of autonomy rather than as expressions of systemic coercion.

Finally, it should be noted that an exclusive focus on coercion fails to avoid the risks of 'secondary victimization' that critics have associated with the consent threshold (e.g. Regan and Kelly 2003; Bacik et al. 1998; Campbell and Raja 1999). Indeed, while a coercion-based model may remove some of the critical glare from the behaviour of the complainant (at least in theory), it also has the effect of interpreting and framing her personal violation in a way that prioritizes its reflection of macro-level struggles for power. This risks further alienating her experiences from the legal process. By contrast, retaining a focus on the consent threshold, infused with a greater sensitivity to context and coercion, permits recognition that rape is both a personal and a systemic attack.

## CONCLUSION

George Fletcher has argued that 'no idea testifies more powerfully to individuals as a source of value than the principle of consent' (1996: 109). This chapter supports this approach and argues that, particularly in the context of sexual self-determination, where our identities as incarnated beings are crucially implicated (Archard 1998), the symbolic and practical value of consent should not be dismissed lightly. At the same time, the defence made here of consent, or more accurately of 'consent-plus', models for rape laws does not seek to trivialize the difficulties involved in their realization. Law is a notoriously blunt instrument. Legislative protocols and courtroom procedures limit the law's ability to recognize, let alone problematize, the complex and multiple ways in which entrenched power disparities, material inequalities, relational dynamics, and socio-sexual norms construct and constrain women's agency. The requirement in 'consent-plus' accounts to trace the integration of values and choices within a person's life-plan will undoubtedly pose challenges in its implementation by conventionally detached legal decision-makers. It may also prove too demanding to insist that a defendant who has taken reasonable steps to secure the woman's token of consent also ensures that this is not tainted with self-alienation (generated, perhaps, by social or psychic dynamics that are both outwith his immediate control and beyond his appreciation).

As has often been the case in the context of rape law, these concessions may mean that feminist victories won at the *actus reus* stage will continue to be undone when it comes to assessments of the defendant's *mens rea*. This, in turn, will be disappointing for those who measure the success of reform initiatives exclusively by the index of increased conviction rates. At the same time, however, it should not be forgotten that the societal role and significance of law extends beyond the confines of the criminal courtroom. Re-engaging with, and demanding more of, the consent threshold affords an opportunity for the law to lead by example, holding out a model of sexual relations that takes mutuality and reciprocity seriously, and generating attitudinal changes that may, in time, permit holding defendants to a higher level of accountability in regard to their sexual strategies. In addition, the ability of this approach to reflect the experiential perspective of the complainant is important, since this has too often been neglected, distorted or rejected in the rape context. As Louise du Toit puts it, the law has typically not asked 'whether the woman unambiguously intended, wanted or desired the sexual actions under consideration, but rather whether she *allowed* them to take place' (2007: 62). Emphasizing the importance of 'wantedness' by requiring that a token of consent should be issued in conditions in which the benefits associated with a sexual act have been critically endorsed (with a range of alternatives being available and adequate resources to assist the development of 'autonomy competence' (Raz 1986; Meyers 1989) does not offer a panacea to the difficulties associated with the prosecution of rape, but it does provide an important starting point from which further vital questions can be asked.

## Bibliography

Archard, D. (1998) *Sexual Consent*, Oxford: Westview Press.
Bacik, I., Maunsell, C. and Gogan, S. (1998) *The Legal Process and Victims of Rape*, Dublin: Dublin Rape Crisis Centre.
Baker, B. (1999) 'Understanding consent in sexual assault', in K. Burgess-Jackson (ed.) *A Most Detestable Crime: new philosophical essays on rape*, Oxford: Oxford University Press, 49–70.
Brown, J., Hamilton, C. and O'Neill, D. (2007) 'Characteristics associated with rape attrition and the role played by scepticism or legal rationality by investigators and prosecutors', *Psychology, Crime & Law*, 13(4): 355–70.
Campbell, R. and Raja, S. (1999) *Secondary Victimisation of Rape Victims: insights from mental health professionals who treat survivors of violence*, Chicago: University of Illinois Press.
Cole, A. (2008) '*Prosecutor v Gacumbitis*: the new definition for prosecuting rape under international law', *International Criminal Law Review*, 8: 55–85.
Cowan, S. (2007) 'Freedom and capacity to make a choice: a feminist analysis of consent in the criminal law of rape', in V. Munro and C. Stychin (eds) *Sexuality and the Law: feminist engagements*, London: Routledge-Cavendish Publishing, 51–71.
Du Toit, L. (2007) 'The conditions of consent', in R. Hunter and S. Cowan (eds) *Choice and Consent: feminist engagements with law and subjectivity*, London: Routledge-Cavendish, 58–73.
Ellison, L. and Munro, V. (2009) 'Of normal sex and real rape: exploring the use of socio-sexual scripts in (mock) jury deliberation', *Social and Legal Studies*, 18(3): 1–22.
Finch, E. and Munro, V. (2006) 'Breaking boundaries?: Sexual consent in the jury room', *Legal Studies*, 26(3): 303–20.
—— (2007) 'The demon drink and the demonised woman: socio-sexual stereotypes and responsibility attribution in rape trials involving intoxicants', *Social and Legal Studies*, 16(4): 591–614.
Fletcher, G. (1996) *Basic Concepts of Legal Thought*, Oxford: Oxford University Press.
Gardner, J. and Shute, S. (2000) 'The wrongness of rape', in J. Horder (ed.) *Oxford Essays in Jurisprudence (Fourth Series)*, Oxford: Clarendon Press, 193–217.
Graycar, R. and Morgan, J. (2002) *The Hidden Gender of Law*, 2nd edn, Sydney: Federation Press.
Hale, M. (1736) *Historia Placitorum Coronea: The History of the Pleas of the Crown* (S. Emlyn ed.) (Reprinted in 1971), London: Professional Books Limited.
Home Office (2009) 'Violence Against Women Opinion Poll', London. Online. Available at: <http://www.homeoffice.gov.uk/documents/violence-against-women-poll?view=Binary>.
Kelly, L., Lovett, J. and Regan, L. (2005) *A Gap or a Chasm? Attrition in reported rape cases*, London: Home Office Research Study 293.
MacKinnon, C. (1987) *Feminism Unmodified: discourses on life and law*, Cambridge, MA: Harvard University Press.
—— (1989) *Toward a Feminist Theory of State*, Cambridge, MA: Harvard University Press.
—— (2005) *Women's Lives, Men's Laws*, Cambridge, MA: Harvard University Press.
—— (2006a) *Are Women Human? And other international dialogues*, Cambridge, MA: Harvard University Press.

—— (2006b) 'Defining rape internationally: a comment on *Akayesu*', *Columbia Journal of Transnational Law*, 44(3): 940–58.

Meyers, D. (1989) *Self, Society and Personal Choice*, New York: Columbia University Press.

Munro, V. (2005) 'Concerning consent: standards of permissibility in sexual relations', *Oxford Journal of Legal Studies*, 25: 335–52.

Munro, V. and Kelly, L. (2009) 'A vicious cycle? Attrition and conviction patterns in contemporary rape cases in England and Wales', in J. Brown and M. Horvath (eds) *Rape: challenging contemporary thinking*, Cullompton: Willan Publishing, 281–300.

Naffine, N. (1994) 'Possession: erotic love in the law of rape', *Modern Law Review*, 57: 10–37.

Raz, J. (1986) *The Morality of Freedom*, Oxford: Clarendon Press.

Regan, L. and Kelly, L. (2003) *Rape: still a forgotten issue*, London: London Metropolitan University, Child and Woman Abuse Studies Unit.

Rumney, P. (2006) 'False allegations of rape', *Cambridge Law Journal*, 65(1): 128–58.

Schomburg, W. and Peterson, I. (2007) 'Genuine consent to sexual violence under international criminal law', *American Journal of International Law*, 101: 121–40.

Tadros, V. (2006) 'Rape without consent', *Oxford Journal of Legal Studies*, 26: 515–43.

Temkin, J. (2002) *Rape and the Legal Process*, 2nd edn, Oxford: Oxford University Press.

Temkin, J. and Ashworth, A. (2004) 'The Sexual Offences Act 2003: rape, sexual assaults and the problems of consent', *Criminal Law Review*, 328–46.

Temkin, J. and Krahé, B. (2008) *Sexual Assault and the Justice Gap: a question of attitude*, Oxford: Hart Publishing.

Wertheimer, A. (2003) *Consent to Sexual Relations*, Cambridge: Cambridge University Press.

Chapter 2

# Rethinking the criminal law's response to sexual penetration

## On theory and context

*Jonathan Herring and Michelle Madden Dempsey*

In this chapter, we will explain and defend our approach to thinking about the criminal law's response to sexual penetration. This will involve us making the following four claims:

1   Engaging in sexual penetration calls for justification.
2   The penetrated person's consent does not fully justify sexual penetration.
3   The penetrated person's consent plus other reasons (i.e. reasons in favour of engaging in sexual penetration) *can* justify sexual penetration.
4   In any given social context, if sexual penetrators are typically justified in engaging in sexual penetration, then sexual penetration per se should not be prohibited in that society; however, if sexual penetration typically is *not* justified in a given social context, then the penetration itself becomes a proper target for prohibition.

This chapter will elaborate upon these four principles, which we see as central to developing a sound approach to the law's response to sexual offences. In adopting these principles, we reject what we have previously coined the 'orthodox approach', which starts with the assumption that a sexual penetration is not in itself wrongful and that only penetrations which are not consented to require a justification (Madden Dempsey and Herring 2007). We will clarify how and why we depart from this orthodoxy in the following discussion.

### ENGAGING IN SEXUAL PENETRATION CALLS FOR JUSTIFICATION

We claim that when a man penetrates a woman's anus or vagina he commits a prima facie moral wrong (Madden Dempsey and Herring 2007). Sexual penetration requires justification and, in the absence of any justification, it will be wrongful, all things considered.

To clarify our claim, it may help to distinguish it from the orthodox view, which is that sexual penetration does not require justification. According to this account, it is only if there is some additional element (such as an absence of consent) that the act is in need of justification. Victor Tadros captures the orthodox view well in his claim that 'there is no prima facie reason against having intercourse' (2005: 106). Similarly, Stephen Shute, supporting the orthodox view, claims that '[w]e simply do not think that there is always a reason against sexual intercourse' (1996: 690); and John Gardner insists that sexual intercourse is not per se prima facie wrongful, but rather becomes so 'in virtue of being non-consensual' (2004: 820).

Our view differs from these accounts because we believe there *is* a general reason not to engage in sexual penetration, and that its prima facie wrongfulness is not limited to cases where the penetration is non-consensual. We base our argument on three claims.

## Argument 1: physiology and force

When force is used by one person against the body of another that is a prima facie wrong. Sexual penetration of the vagina or anus requires the use of force. A penis does not simply fall into a vagina, nor is it enveloped by an anus. Rather, if a penis is to achieve penetration, it must push through muscled walls into the vagina or anus. A vagina or anus is not a penis-shaped hole. Of course, often when a person uses force on another, its use is justified. For example, grabbing your absent-minded friend's arm as she is about to walk out into the road in front of a car would be justified. Thus, insofar as sexual penetration requires the use of force, it requires justification.

## Argument 2: harm and risks of harm

Harming someone requires justification, and so does posing a non-trivial risk of harm. These are not controversial claims. There is a substantial body of academic material recognizing the wrongfulness of acts based on their endangering qualities, and, of course, there are many examples of such offences in the criminal law (e.g. Finkelstein 2003; von Hirsch 1996). Antony Duff writes:

> [T]he fact that a contemplated action might well injure others' interests is, normally, a good reason against undertaking that action, or for taking precautions against the prospective harm; and it often provides conclusive reasons against the action. If we act, without justification, in a way that we realise might harm others, when the prospective harm provides a conclusive reason against acting thus, we do wrong; we do wrong to those whom we thus endanger.
>
> (Duff 2005: 53)

Even where the risk does not materialize, it is still a setback to an individual to be exposed to the risk. By exposing a person to a risk, they are put into a class of people who are more likely to develop that harm than others; and they have a legitimate interest in not being in such a class (Finkelstein 2003: 973).

Sexual penetration typically presents a non-trivial risk of harm and, for this reason, often requires justification. The risks that are attached to sexual penetration include sexually transmitted diseases, pregnancy, injuries ranging from tearing or chafing to the delicate tissues of the vagina or anus to vaginal lacerations or anal fissures, and psychological harm (e.g. reliving memories of rape or dehumanizing sexual experiences) (see Madden Dempsey and Herring 2007 for detailed discussion). We accept that in some acts of sexual penetration none of these risks arises and, thus, these concerns would not ground the prima facie wrongfulness of sexual penetration in those particular instances. However, we suspect such instances are atypical.

## Argument 3: social meaning

Acts can have social meanings. Where an act has a negative social meaning, this can lead it to being a prima facie wrong. By saying that an act has a social meaning, we suggest simply that an act takes on significance beyond that attaching to the mere act itself. So, for example, raising a middle finger at a person conveys (in Anglo-American societies at least) a certain offensive social meaning, while displaying the Confederate flag (say, in the southern United States) carries a racist social meaning (Blackburn 2001; Anderson and Pildes 2000).

We claim that one of the social meanings which attaches to the sexual penetration of a woman's vagina or anus is negative – so negative as to render the act prima facie wrongful. Specifically, as we explain below, the social meaning we have in mind is the devaluing of women qua women and disrespecting women's humanity. Importantly, we do not claim that this is the only social meaning which attaches to sexual penetration, nor that every social meaning attached to sexual penetration is negative. Indeed, both positive and negative meanings can attach to a sexual penetration. Moreover, our claim that sexual penetration has a negative social meaning does not imply that men *intend* to express something negative through sexual penetration, nor that women *perceive* sexual penetration as expressing something negative about themselves (Madden Dempsey and Herring 2007: 483–4). Rather, we mean to endorse a version of Blackburn's credibility principle in identifying the social meaning of actions. According to this principle, an action may be properly recognized as having a particular social meaning if 'there is no way – no credible way – that the group could rationally sustain their open affirmations were they not also prepared to stand by the belief' entailed by the social meaning of the action (2001: 483). The proof that an act bears a particular social meaning is that 'there is no way to make sense of the explicit statements of the body, unless they were also committed to the implicit principle or premise teased out this way' (2001: 484).

On what basis do we conclude that sexual penetration has a negative social meaning of devaluing women qua women and disrespecting women's humanity? One strong reason in favour of this conclusion is that our society could not use, depict and describe penile sexual penetration of women's vaginas and anuses the way it does if the social meaning of such conduct were not, at least in part, a way of devaluing women qua women and disrespecting their humanity. There is no credible explanation for the terminology and depictions used to represent sexual penetration, which does not attach a negative social meaning to the act of sexual penetration per se.

This social meaning is betrayed by the language we use to describe the act of sexual penetration: fuck, bang, screw, nail, drill, smash, hit it, hump, let her have it, poke, shaft, slay, etc. The grammatical structure of our language is such that these verbs feature in sentences which take the form: 'subject-verb-object'. Notably, it is typically the person who plays the male role who is assigned as subject and the person who plays the female role who is assigned as object (MacKinnon 1989: 128). Not only this but also the words used to describe sexual penetration indicate that the woman is being harmed. Notice that phrases such as 'Bobbie fucked Marion' or 'Bobbie screwed Marion' are, in fact, ambiguous (Baker 1984: 263). They could mean that Bobbie sexually penetrated Marion or that Bobbie deceived or took advantage of Marion. The most credible explanation for these terminologies and depictions is that sexual penetration is an act through which the woman is rendered less powerful, less human, while the male is rendered more powerful and more human.

We hope that there will be a time in the future when the social meaning of sexual penetration will have transformed to such a degree that our interpretation will no longer hold. Perhaps in a post-patriarchal world, where the social meaning of sexual penetration has changed so radically, it will strain credibility to interpret the uses, depictions and descriptions of sexual penetration as conveying the devaluation or disrespect of women. When that day arrives, sexual penetration will no longer be a prima facie wrong by virtue of its social meaning, and the generality of our thesis will be defeated. That day, however, has not yet arrived. Thus, the negative social meaning discussed above remains very much part of the current meaning of sexual penetration in our culture and continues, we argue, to ground its prima facie wrongfulness.

## CONSENT DOES NOT FULLY JUSTIFY SEX

In the previous section we explained why we believe that sexual penetration is a prima facie wrong, while emphasizing the action could, all things considered, be justified. Here, we will consider how much work consent can do in justifying this prima facie wrong.

### Requesting v consenting

As a preliminary matter, it is important to distinguish the normative effect of *requests* (either to be penetrated or not to be penetrated) from the normative effect of *consent/non-consent* to penetration. Requests typically generate new, additional reasons for action: thus, a woman's request *not* to be penetrated (e.g. saying 'no') generates a new, additional reason for the man not to penetrate her. This reason further strengthens the prima facie wrongfulness of his penetration and makes justification of his act all the more difficult (indeed, perhaps, impossible). However, the woman's non-consent (e.g. when unconscious) has no normative force whatsoever: it is an absence, a void. Normatively speaking, it is a non-starter. It does not add to or alter any of the reasons which already exist against sexual penetration.

There are two important consequences which flow from the distinction between 'requests not to be penetrated' and 'non-consent to penetration'. First, the distinction counsels against the widespread orthodox assumption that sexual penetration is only prima facie wrongful when it is non-consensual: i.e. that non-consent is the normative ground of the wrongfulness of the act. However, if we are correct in arguing that non-consent is normatively inert, this insight opens a new way to considering the moral quality of sexual penetration – one which investigates whether sexual penetration itself is prima facie wrongful. Second, the distinction counsels against (albeit more obliquely) rules which require evidence of a victim's *request* that the defendant not sexually penetrate in order to establish her *non-consent* to being penetrated. Since *non*-consent is precisely that, a *lack* of consent, this point would suggest that rules of evidence should not require proof of the victim's *request* not to be penetrated (e.g. saying 'no') when seeking to establish her mere non-consent. Of course, while a victim's request that the defendant not penetrate her certainly entails her non-consent to being penetrated (i.e. 'no means no'), it does much more than that by generating a new, additional reason against sexual penetration. By confusing the two, evidence laws do a disservice both to the rationality of the law and to particular victims, who are required to prove that they *requested* not to be penetrated, despite a legal framework which purports to require their mere *non-consent*.

## What consent does do and how it does it

We argue against those who claim that if sexual penetration has been consented to then no wrong has taken place. As discussed above, this claim has been defended by those who hold the orthodox view, which claims that consensual sexual penetration is not prima facie wrongful (Gardner 2004; Tadros 2005: 106). The claim has also been defended by those who believe that consent contains a 'moral magic' which does all the justificatory work necessary to render sexual penetration not-wrong-all-things-considered (Hurd 1996; Wertheimer 2003: 119–43). In this section, we argue against this 'moral magic' view regarding the normative effect of consent.

One way of seeking to present our case against the moral magic view would be to examine how consent is understood in our society, and in the law; and to demonstrate the inadequacies that would flow from using consent as a justification for sexual penetration. Such arguments have been richly developed in existing feminist literature regarding consent, and we will not seek to add to this literature here (see e.g., MacKinnon 1989, 171–83; Munro 2005;

Cowan 2007, Herring 2009). Instead, we will approach the issue of the normative effect of consent by assuming a quality of consent in the richest sense possible – consent that is granted by one who is socially empowered, and is given under conditions in which the consent is fully informed, voluntary, competent, etc. By approaching the issue in this way, we shall attempt to put to one side the difficulties which arise in cases where these qualities are lacking. Later, we will briefly consider the normative effect of consent in cases where consent is somewhat inadequate and thus fails to bear its full normative force.

We will summarize our conclusion regarding what consent does before seeking to justify and expand on it. We reject two extreme views: (1) that where a woman consents to being sexually penetrated, her consent alone renders the penetration justifiable; and (2) that her consent is irrelevant to the issue of whether or not the penetration is justified. Rather we seek to establish a middle path whereby consent gives what Joseph Raz has coined an 'exclusionary permission':

> The simplest case of giving an exclusionary permission is a case of [woman] who consents that another shall perform an act harmful to [her] interests. The permission does not alter the reasons against the action ... [rather] it allow[s] the man who contemplates the action to disregard the interests of the [woman] who granted the permission.
> (Raz 1975, reprinted 1999: 96–7)

While we borrow the language of exclusionary permissions from Raz, we think he puts the point too strongly in the quote above when he says that consent allows such reasons to be *disregarded*. In contrast, we think the normative effect of consent is better captured by saying that the woman's consent to sexual penetration allows the man to *opt not to conform* to some set of reasons he otherwise has not to sexually penetrate her (Madden Dempsey and Herring forthcoming b). We agree with Raz, however, in identifying the scope of reasons affected by consent as those which are grounded in the woman's self-interest; and we follow Raz's characterization of these reasons as grounded in an array of needs and desires which are related to, yet distinct from, the woman's well-being (see further Raz 1986: 294–300).

If our claims regarding sexual penetration are correct, then (at least some of) the reasons against sexual penetration are grounded in the interests of the woman who is being penetrated (specifically, reasons regarding the use of force on her body and the harm/risks of harm she may suffer from penetration). We argue that the woman's consent affects these reasons by allowing the man an option not to conform to what these reasons would have him do. It is a logical truth that if the man conformed to what these reasons would have him do, he would not engage in sexual penetration. The woman's consent, however, changes the man's normative situation, by providing him with the option not to conform to those reasons. This effect of consent – the granting of an exclusionary permission – is the extent of its normative force.

Consent does not (unlike a request) generate any additional reason to engage in sexual penetration. Moreover, consent does not generate any reason in favour of disregarding the interests of the person who gave it. It merely allows the recipient of consent not to conform to those reasons (Raz 1975, reprinted 1999: 97).

Of course, one who is granted an exclusionary permission might nonetheless opt to conform to what the affected reasons would have him do in any event and thus, in the case of consent to sexual penetration, refrain from engaging in penetration out of concern for the woman's interests. Our point is simply that her consent gives him the legitimate option to do otherwise. (Of course, it bears noting that obligations of friendship or other special relationships between the parties may require him to make his own assessment of her self-interest and, in some cases, even challenge her assessment (Jeske 1998)).

The account of the normative force of consent set out above reflects the full extent of the work consent can possibly do in justifying sexual penetration. In its richest, most perfect instances, consent will affect the full scope of reasons against penetration that are grounded in the woman's interests, by granting the recipient of consent an exclusionary permission not to conform to those reasons. However, in instances where the quality of consent is lacking (due, for example, to inadequate information, voluntariness, capacity or other considerations) consent will not bear its full normative force. By this, we mean that the scope of reasons affected by the woman's consent will be limited: it will not extend to *all* the reasons grounded in her self-interest (Madden Dempsey and Herring forthcoming b). So, while perfectly genuine consent may potentially affect the entire range of reasons against sexual penetration, which are grounded in the women's interests, imperfect consent will affect a narrower scope of reasons. The scope of reasons affected depends on a number of considerations, including imperfections in the quality of consent. It follows that consent which borders on mere submission will bear very little normative force indeed. Given the quality of consent to sexual penetration typically granted under conditions of sex inequality (MacKinnon 1989: 171–83), we suspect that the normative force of consent is typically limited in scope.

Moreover, even when consent does bear its full normative force, recall that it *only* affects reasons grounded in the woman's self-interest. If our arguments above regarding the relevance of social meaning to the prima facie wrongfulness of sexual penetration are plausible, then at least some of the reasons against sexual penetration are not grounded solely in the woman's self-interest, and as such these reasons are not subject to being affected by even the most perfectly genuine consent. Thus, even at its most forceful, consent does not have the normative force to affect the full range of reasons that render sexual penetration prima facie wrongful. If these reasons remain undefeated, then sexual penetration in that instance will not be justifiable, and thus the full justification for it must lie in considerations other than consent.

## WHAT DOES JUSTIFY SEXUAL PENETRATION?

In the above discussion, we have established three reasons why sexual penetration is prima facie wrong. We have argued that, even putting the claim at its strongest, consent does not provide a justification to a sexual penetration; and at its very best, it provides reasons which allow the penetrator to accept the other party's assessment of their self-interest. Consent will not, therefore, provide a justification for the negative social meanings that attach to a sexual penetration.

So, what might provide a justification for these? These would require that the act is conducted in circumstances which challenge the negative social meaning attached to the act and contain no elements which reinforce that message. Rather, the act should emphasize some of the positive social meanings that can be attached to it. The act of sexual penetration, if it is to be justified, must be in circumstances that give humanity to the woman rather than dehumanize her; recognize her value rather than devalue her; recognize the respect due to her, rather than disrespect her.

The value of sexual penetration (i.e. the positive aspects of sexual penetration) can be found in a wide variety of things. Since the range of reasons for engaging in sexual penetration vary widely, as do the circumstances in which it takes place, it is difficult to generalize about the benefits of sexual penetration. For this reason, we doubt the plausibility of Hyman Gross's sweeping generalization that '[h]aving sex is one of nature's blessings, a commonplace of life that is meant to be enjoyed no less than eating or sleeping' (2007: 220). While sexual penetration involves 'harmless pleasures' for some, for others 'it is the stuff of abuse, oppression and a tool of war' (Herring 2007: 229). Our view, however, is certainly not 'anti-sex'. Indeed, we fully acknowledge and appreciate the wide array of important values that can be realized through the act of sexual penetration. Indeed, by starting our analysis where we do (in the claim that sexual penetration is prima facie wrongful), our attention is focused more upon these values than it would be under an approach which simply assumed that sexual penetration was entirely unproblematic.

The values of sexual penetration can be found in the circumstances surrounding the act, the meaning the parties attach to it, and the consequences of it. Amongst its most commonly realized values is the extent to which it contributes to the formation and maintenance of valuable relationships between the parties: contributing to commitment to, or stability of, a relationship, openness in the relationship and overall satisfaction with the relationship (Brezsnyak and Whisman 2004). Closely related to this point is the sense in which sexual penetration can realize values in terms of expressing and/or communicating a range of valuable feelings or emotions to the other (e.g. 'I'm sorry'; 'I am glad you are back'). It can also mark a defined stage in a relationship that the couple undertake a degree of commitment to each other, and operate as a confirmation that the relationship is still ongoing and is still strong. For some people, as well as the advantages already mentioned, sexual penetration may have religious or spiritual value. And, of course, a potential value realized by sexual penetration in some cases is the production of children. No doubt this is a partial list and many others could be found, too. To the extent that these values can be realized through sexual penetration, they generate reasons in favour of the act; reasons which potentially serve to justify the prima facie wrongdoing at issue.

## PRINCIPLES OF CRIMINALIZATION

We have, so far in this chapter, been discussing when a sexual penetration is justified in moral terms. We now turn to when the criminal law would be justified in intervening to prohibit sexual penetration. First, we need to develop an approach to criminalization. It is not possible here to defend the approach we wish to take, except in the briefest of ways (see Madden Dempsey and Herring forthcoming a).

Our approach to criminalization starts from the assumption that the claim to authority entailed by criminalization must be justified. We then question whether a particular criminal prohibition is justified as an authoritative directive. We do not, therefore, follow the more standard approaches of considering whether punishment of an offence is justified, whether the harm principle is satisfied, or whether the conduct at issue is a matter of 'public' concern, because we believe each of these approaches fail to appreciate that many laws would not be justified as authoritative directives in the first place, let alone as criminal laws with criminal sanctions.

By criminalization, we are referring to the enactment of a criminal law (such as when a legislature votes to pass a criminal statute into law). Criminalization involves the state claiming authority over its subjects by offering them a directive which it intends the subjects to treat as a binding, content-independent reason for action. Common examples include directives not to commit murder, battery, theft, rape, etc. In criminalizing these actions, the state is not merely offering advice to its subjects to refrain from committing such conduct: it is not merely suggesting to its subjects that their lives would go better if they refrained from committing these acts, or that it might be nicer if everyone would just agree not to murder, batter, thieve or rape one another (Green 2008: 26–9). Rather, by enacting these directives as law, the legislature is claiming authority over its subjects (Raz 1975, reprinted 1999). It is, in effect, telling its subjects not to act on the balance of reasons that apply to them as they understand those reasons to be, but instead to act in accordance with content-independent reasons not to commit murder, battery, theft, rape, etc. and not to act on (at least some) reasons in favour of committing these acts.

We believe that criminalization is prima facie wrongful, which is to say, inter alia, that it calls for justification. One important aspect of its prima facie wrongfulness is that it often establishes an authority relationship between the state and its subjects, whereby the subjects repeatedly obey the authority's directives. The moral problem created by repeated obedience to authority is that it tends to weaken one's rational capacities and threaten one's autonomy. These considerations are what we might call the downside of obedience to authority. Joseph Raz has famously argued that authority will (normally) be justified when the subject is more likely to comply with right reason 'if he accepts the directive ... as authoritatively binding, and tries to follow [it], than if he tries to follow the reasons which apply to him directly' (1994: 214). Where these conditions obtain, obedience to authority can have its upside as well. As Raz puts it, obedience to authority can provide a service by helping subjects better to comply with right reason (Raz 1994).

Since the capacity to engage in first-order practical reasoning is central to our humanity, it should not be squandered through disuse unless the pay-off is worth it. Raz's test above, which he coins the 'normal justification thesis', provides a means of testing whether the pay-off is indeed worth it. The following three principles can be derived from the service conception of authority as a test for determining whether the pay-off of obedience to authority is worth it:

1   One should always act for an undefeated reason.
2   Other things being equal, one should act for reasons which one has discerned for oneself on the merits of the case, rather than obey authority.
3   It is permissible (justifiable) to violate principle (2) if doing so makes one more likely to comply with principle (1).

One implication from the above argument is that, in drafting criminal offences, legislators should define the elements of offences to include only that conduct which, when committed in that particular society, is typically not justified. In other words, if people typically fail to act for an undefeated reason when they engage in that conduct, it would be justifiable for the legislature to authoritatively prohibit that conduct. Thus, the fact that a given type of action is prima facie wrongful never establishes a prima facie case in favour of criminalization. Those who have assumed as much are mistaken insofar as they concede far too quickly and easily the basic question of the authority of criminal law. Rather, in defining criminal offences, a responsible legislator must inquire as to whether the prima facie wrongdoing in question is typically justified in their society.

These considerations point to the fact that the project of creating justifiable criminal law is a highly context-sensitive one. The legislature must remain alive to the possibility (indeed, the likelihood) that a criminal law which is justifiable in one society at one time may not be justifiable in another society or at another time. Below, we argue that this context-sensitive approach leads to the conclusion that sexual penetration per se can be justifiably prohibited in particular contexts.

## FROM THEORY TO CONTEXT: PROSTITUTE-USE

In this section, we move from the rather abstract theoretical concerns set out above to what we believe to be some of the practical implications of our argument. One key point is that prohibitions against sexual penetration per se may be justifiable depending on the social context in which the penetration takes place. In other words, although sexual penetration is typically only criminalized when it occurs without consent (e.g. in England and Wales, under the Sexual Offences Act 2003, section 1), it may also be justifiable to prohibit sexual penetration per se, if the act of penetration is typically unjustified in that particular social context. Below, we consider the social context of prostitute-use and consider the implications of our argument for determining whether sexual penetration in this social context is typically justified in moral terms and whether it should be criminalized.

Sexual penetration in the context of prostitute-use, like sexual penetration in any context, is typically prima facie wrongful by virtue of the considerations outlined above regarding force and harm/risks of harm. Typically, risks of harm – both physical and psychological – will be heightened in the context of prostitute-use (Farley et al. 2003). Moreover, our arguments regarding social meaning and the extent to which it grounds the prima facie wrongfulness of sexual penetration strike us as having at least as much, if not more, relevance in the context of prostitute-use. As such, like all acts of sexual penetration, prostitute-use calls for justification.

Whether justification is available in any given instance of prostitute-use will depend on a variety of considerations. The consent of the prostituted-woman, for one, forms an important starting point in any inquiry into the justification of the penetration. Prostitute-use in the absence of consent is, of course, seriously wrongful conduct which falls under the general heading of rape (Madden Dempsey 2005). While not all prostitute-use may best be understood as rape (cf. Giobbe 1991), our analysis helps illuminate the myriad of reasons why even consensual prostitute-use is typically not justified.

First, even where the prostituted-woman can be said to have consented, the conditions under which such consent is formed are typically detrimental to the quality of her consent. Economic desperation and prior abuse are but two of the many conditions which affect the normative force of many prostitute-women's consent (Farley et al. 2003). Given these and other considerations which negatively impact upon the quality of consent, the scope of reasons affected by the consent will be considerably narrowed. At its best quality, her consent would have the normative force to grant an exclusionary permission to the prostitute-user to opt not to conform to the reasons against sexual penetration which are grounded in her self-interest: e.g. reasons grounded in the use of force and harm or risks of harm she may suffer from penetration. At its less-than-best, her consent will leave some, or indeed many, of these reasons unaffected. Thus, the prostitute-user will not have the legitimate option of failing to conform to what these reasons would have him do. These reasons against engaging in sexual penetration will continue to feature on his rational horizons and, barring exceptional circumstances, will render his conduct (in moral terms) unjustifiable-all-things-considered.

Of course, even at its best, consent does not affect the entire range of reasons against sexual penetration, but merely those reasons grounded in the self-interest of the penetrated person. Thus, to the extent that prostitute-use contributes to generalized conditions of sex inequality in a given society, the consent of the prostituted-woman has no normative bearing on these reasons to refrain from such conduct. Moreover, insofar as sexual penetration in the context of prostitute-use bears the negative social meaning discussed above, there are reasons against such conduct which the prostituted-woman's consent does not affect. Where such reasons continue to bear rational force, it will typically be the case that sexual penetration in the context of prostitute-use is unjustified. As such, we argue that such conduct may be a candidate for criminalization. It can be justifiably prohibited through an authoritative directive, such as the criminal prohibitions adopted in Sweden, which target prostitute-use without criminalizing the conduct of the prostituted-woman. Similar, albeit more narrow, reform have recently been enacted in England and Wales (see Policing and Crime Act 2009, section 14, which creates the offence of 'paying for sexual services of a prostitute subjected to force etc.').

Our argument, as applied to sexual penetration in the social context of prostitute-use, differs from arguments against prostitution which are grounded in concerns regarding the commodification of sexual activity (Radin 1996). According to the commodification argument, prostitute-use is problematic principally because something has been commodified which should not be. The wrongness, in other words, is grounded in the fact that there was an exchange of money for sex. On our account, in contrast, prostitute-use is problematic principally because sexual penetration in that social context is typically unjustified. The fact that money was provided to someone who needs it is, other things being equal, a good thing: it does not, however, generate the kind of reason capable of defeating the prima facie wrongness of the conduct.

## CONCLUSION

As will be clear from our approach, the scope of criminal laws prohibiting sexual penetrations can vary justifiably across different societies and contexts, reflecting the likelihood that the penetration will be justified when performed in dissimilar social context. Furthermore, although we have not explored the matter here, it is clear that the justification of criminalization itself will depend in part on the varying levels of success achieved by complementary forms of social control. This is simply to say that the mere fact that a criminal prohibition would be justifiable does not entail that it should be used in circumstances where less severe alternatives for social control exist.

Turning to the case of whether it would be permissible to prohibit sexual penetration per se, while leaving matters such as consent to play the role of an affirmative defence, the key question which arises from our investigation should now be clear. To resolve this matter, we must begin by asking, 'is sexual penetration as it is typically performed in our society justified?' If the answer to that is 'no', then a prohibition on sexual penetration per se would be permissible. If the answer is 'yes', then the *actus reus* of any offence targeting such conduct would need to be defined in a way as to build in additional wrong-making considerations.

Although we have identified the key issues to address, we find it difficult to opine on whether, in our society, sexual penetration is typically unjustified or not. No doubt we can all agree there are instances of where it is and where it is not, but what evidence could be gathered to further our inquiry is hard to identify, particularly given the relevance of social meaning to our inquiry and the difficulty of capturing data regarding such an illusive and malleable consideration. If we take it for now that sexual penetration is not typically justifiable in the sense outlined in this chapter, either due to the restricted normative scope of consent or considerations regarding social meaning which consent is incompetent to affect, then an offence could properly be created that has as its *actus reus* the sexual penetration by a man of a woman's vagina or anus. The man would be permitted to offer an affirmative defence grounded in a claim that his partner's consent was especially rich, and thus bore greater normative force than is typical for the society or social context, and that his act was not one that devalued, degraded or dehumanized his partner.

## Bibliography

Anderson, E. and Pildes, R. (2000) 'Expressive theories of law: a general restatement', *University of Pennsylvania Law Review*, 148: 1503–75.

Baker, R. (1984) 'Pricks and chicks: a plea for persons', in R. Baker and F. Elliston (eds) *Philosophy and Sex*, Buffalo, NY: Prometheus Books, 281–305.

Blackburn, S. (2001) 'Group minds and expressive harms', *Maryland Law Review*, 60: 467–91.

Brezsnyak, M. and Whisman, M.A. (2004) 'Sexual desire and relationship functioning: the effects of marital satisfaction and power', *Journal of Sex and Marital Therapy*, 30: 199–218.

Cowan, S. (2007) 'Freedom and capacity to make a choice: a feminist analysis of consent in the criminal law of rape', in V. Munro and C. Stychin (eds) *Sexuality and the Law: feminist engagements*, London: Routledge-Cavendish Publishing, 51–71.

Duff, R.A. (2005) 'Criminalizing endangerment', in R.A. Duff and S. Green (eds) *Defining Crimes*, Oxford: Oxford University Press, 43–64.

Farley M., Cotton A., Lynne J., et al. (2003) 'Prostitution and trafficking in nine countries: an update on violence and Posttraumatic Stress Disorder', in M. Farley (ed.) *Prostitution, Trafficking and Traumatic Stress*, Binghamton, New York: Haworth Press, 33–74.

Finkelstein, C. (2003) 'Is risk a harm?', *University of Pennsylvania Law Review*, 151: 963–1001.

Gardner, J. (2004) 'Fletcher on offences and defences', *Tulsa Law Review*, 39: 817–27.
Giobbe, E. (1991) 'Prostitution buying the right to rape', in A.W. Burgess (ed.) *Rape and Sexual Assault III: A Research Handbook*, New York: Garland Press, 143–60.
Green, L. (2008) *The Authority of the State*, Oxford: Oxford University Press.
Gross, H. (2007) 'Rape, moralism and human rights', *Criminal Law Review*, 220–29.
Herring, J. (2007) 'Human rights and rape: a reply to Gross', *Criminal Law Review*, 228–31.
—— (2009) 'Relational autonomy and rape', in S. Day-Sclater, F. Ebtehaj, E. Jackson and M. Richards (eds) *Regulating Autonomy: sex, reproduction and family*, Oxford: Hart, 53–71.
Hurd, H. (1996) 'The moral magic of consent', *Legal Theory*, 2: 121–46.
Jeske, D. (1998) 'Families, friends, and special obligations', *Canadian Journal of Philosophy*, 28: 527–56.
MacKinnon, C. (1989) *Toward a Feminist Theory of the State*, Cambridge, MA: Harvard University Press.
Madden Dempsey, M. (2005) 'Rethinking Wolfenden: criminal law, remote harms and prostitute-use', *Criminal Law Review*, 444–55.
Madden Dempsey, M. and Herring, J. (2007) 'Why sexual penetration requires justification', *Oxford Journal of Legal Studies*, 27: 467–91.
—— 'The typical justification of criminalisation', forthcoming a.
—— 'How consent works', forthcoming b.
Munro, V. (2005) 'Concerning consent: standards of permissibility in sexual relations', *Oxford Journal of Legal Studies*, 25(2): 335–52.
Radin, M.J. (1996) *Contested Commodities*, Cambridge, MA: Harvard University Press.
Raz, J. (1975) *Practical Reason and Norms*, London: Hutchinson (2nd edn, reprint 1999).
—— (1986) *The Morality of Freedom*, Oxford: Oxford University Press.
—— (1994) *Ethics in the Public Domain*, Oxford: Clarendon Press.
Shute, S. (1996) 'Second Law Commission Consultation Paper on Consent: (1) something old, something new, something borrowed: three aspects of the project', *Criminal Law Review*, 684–98.
Tadros, V. (2005) *Criminal Responsibility*, Oxford: Oxford University Press.
von Hirsch, V. (1996) 'Extending the harm principle: "remote" harms and fair imputation', in A. Simester and A. Smith (eds) *Harm and Culpability*, Oxford: Oxford University Press, 259–76.
Wertheimer, A. (2003) *Consent to Sexual Relations*, Cambridge: Cambridge University Press.

Part II

# International and regional perspectives

# Chapter 3

# International criminal law and sexual violence

## An overview

*Alison Cole*

The international crime of rape is part of two overlapping systems of law, namely international law and criminal law. Any analysis, therefore, has to be alert to potential biases or difficulties in each of these systems. The first international criminal prosecutions at Nuremberg after the Second World War demonstrated how these biases can result in a failure to address rape. After a nearly 50-year hiatus following Nuremberg, the international community again instituted prosecutions through the establishment of the International Criminal Tribunal for the Former Yugoslavia (ICTY) in 1993. This chapter provides an overview of the landmark prosecutions by the ICTY and then considers, in turn, the other tribunals which followed, namely the International Criminal Tribunal for Rwanda (ICTR), the Special Court for Sierra Leone (SCSL) and the International Criminal Court (ICC). The different ways in which these institutions have treated the prosecution of rape and sexual violence will be examined, providing some insight into future possibilities.

## INTERNATIONAL LAW AND INTERNATIONAL CRIMINAL LAW

International law is distinct from national laws in that there are various sources of law, a range of courts applying only limited jurisdiction, and no overarching global executive charged with ensuring enforcement. This unique character of international law is a result of its origin as a means to regulate relations between nations. Under this approach, questions relating to the treatment of individuals remained within the purview of the nation state, on the basis of a general principle that no country should interfere in the treatment of another country's citizens. This has had a predictably negative impact in terms of advancing and protecting the rights of women. Certain aspects of national law, which were established without reference to women's concerns, have been transferred into the foundations of international law. As an example, the divide between the 'public' and 'private' spheres, which historically left family relations and abuse in the home outside the protection of national law, is also present in the foundations of international law where the treatment of citizens is a private matter for each state. Indeed, it has been argued that international law is inherently gendered because its rules have developed as a response to the experiences of a male elite (Charlesworth and Chinkin 2000: 50, 52, 56).

The initial position that only states could be subjects of international law leads also to the conclusion that only states could breach international law. In this regard, however, a seismic shift occurred with the establishment of the military tribunals after the Second World War. While this created the theoretical possibility for sexual violence to become a topic of international law, and for individual perpetrators of rape to be subjected to international criminal prosecution, this did not occur in practice until almost half a century later.

An examination of the three key aspects to prosecuting international crimes – jurisdiction, law and evidence – demonstrates the particular challenges facing the prosecution of rape as an international crime. As a matter of jurisdiction, international settings generally require that only the most responsible persons can be indicted, which means those who mastermind the atrocities far from the subordinates on the ground who directly perpetrate the violence. As a matter of law, it is necessary to satisfy three conditions to establish responsibility: (i) the crime on the ground must be proved (the 'crime base'), (ii) the crime must fall within the context of a civilian attack or an armed conflict (the 'threshold' or 'chapeau' elements), and (iii) there must be a link between the crime base and the accused (the 'linkage' or 'mode of liability' issue). As a matter of evidence, there are further difficulties in rape cases. Rape is distinct from other crimes in that, in many cases, more conventional forms of evidence – such as documents or eye-witness accounts – may not be readily available. These challenges are particularly acute, moreover, where the charge is against an accused who may not be the direct perpetrator of the assault.

While thoughtful investigators, creative prosecutors and sensitive judges can ensure that justice is done, each actor in international justice must also guard against any prejudices inherited from their national systems to ensure that these are not transferred into the international courtroom. As the following discussion illustrates, though there have been some significant improvements in the use of international criminal law as a mechanism of redress against sexual violence, there have been – and remain – a number of obstacles.

## NUREMBERG

It is undeniable that sexual violence was a weapon of war during the Second World War (Pietila and Vickers 1994: 146); for example, there were reportedly over 100,000 rapes in Berlin during the final two weeks of the war (Conot 1983: 278; Brownmiller 1975: 48–78). Rape was invoked in propaganda campaigns to stir hatred towards the enemy (Brownmiller 1975: 41, 44–8, 70). Mass gang rape and sexual mutilation (for example, the severing of breasts) were weapons of war spreading terror throughout the affected communities (IMT Official Documents 1945–46 vol. VII: 455, 456 and 494).

At the end of the war, the Allied victors decided to stay the hand of vengeance and commit to trial those considered responsible for the atrocities perpetrated by the defeated armies. There are three main sources of law from this time. First, the International Military Tribunal (IMT), established in Nuremberg, held one main trial against 24 key actors in the Nazi regime (Charter of the International Military Tribunal, Annexed to the London Agreement, 8 August 1945). Secondly, there were several subsequent trials governed by the Control Council Law No. 10 (Allied Control Council Law No. 10, Punishment of Persons Guilty of War Crimes, Crimes against Peace and against Humanity, 20 December 1945). And thirdly, the Tokyo Trials prosecuted Japanese defendants (Charter of the International Military Tribunal for the Far East, 19 January 1946, Annexed to the Special Proclamation by the Supreme Commander for the Allied Powers at Tokyo). Despite the available evidence, none of these courts charged anyone with rape.

The Nuremberg IMT Charter did not refer to rape or sexual violence. However, the war crimes provision in Article 6(b) referred to ill-treatment or slave labour and the crimes against humanity provision under Article 6(c) referred to enslavement and to other inhumane acts. These could have provided a basis for prosecuting sexual slavery and other forms of sexual violence (Askin 1997: 131). Witnesses during the trial gave details of the crimes of sexual violence that they had witnessed, but this was not pursued by prosecutors (Askin 1997: 98 and footnote 322).

Control Council Law No. 10, on the other hand, defined crimes against humanity with reference to rape under Article 2(d). Across the 12 US trials at Nuremberg based on Control Council Law No. 10, however, no gender-specific crimes were charged (Askin 1997: 125 and footnote 434).

The International Military Tribunal for the Far East (IMTFE) was established to prosecute 28 war criminals from Japan, although only accused persons listed as 'Class A' criminals were in fact tried at the Tokyo Tribunal. Like the Nuremberg IMT Charter, the IMTFE Charter did not enumerate rape as a prosecutable violation. Despite the lack of a specific separate charge of sexual violence, the indictment did charge the accused of war crimes, including inhuman treatment committed by the rape of female prisoners, mistreatment of female nurses by acts of rape, and failure to respect family honour and rights through committing rape (IMTFE Indictment: para. 1, 5(c), 12). At trial, the prosecution asserted that during the first six weeks of the Japanese occupation of Nanking in China, over 20,000 women and girls were raped (IMTFE vol. 2, transcript p. 4592; Roeling and Ruters 1977: 385). However, the overwhelming majority of gender crimes were ignored, in particular for the sexual slavery of so-called 'comfort women', for which limited civil litigation took place nearly 50 years later (the Comfort Women Case: Judgment of April 27, 1998, Shimonoseki Branch, Yamaguchi Prefectural Court, Japan).

This first step into international criminal law, taken after the atrocities of the Second World War, is thus a damning indictment of the gender gap existing under the law at that time. Crimes of rape and sexual violence were not only slipping through the cracks of international law, but were blocked and ignored to the point of almost denying they even happened. It may be seen, however, that with each of the three initiatives after the war, the situation slightly improved. While there was no reference to rape at all at the Nuremberg trial, in Control Council No. 10, the word 'rape' was at least referred to in the legislation, and in the Tokyo Indictment, rape was included in the descriptive list of crimes charged.

It took the thaw of the Cold War to revive the development of international criminal law started at Nuremberg. By this time, a second wave of feminism had brought forward a greater level of awareness of sexual violence, such that there were greater expectations that rape should be addressed internationally.

## THE INTERNATIONAL CRIMINAL TRIBUNAL FOR THE FORMER YUGOSLAVIA (ICTY)

Ethnic tensions played a key role in the conflict in the former Yugoslavia and, as a result, women were targeted on the basis of both their gender and ethnicity. In 1989, Slobodan Milosevic became President of Serbia and proceeded to impose greater Serb authority on the republics which constituted the federal Yugoslavian state. The republics resisted and in 1991 Slovenia, Croatia, Macedonia and Bosnia-Herzegovina declared independence. Intense warfare targeting civilians followed, within which sexual violence was deliberately utilized as a weapon of war. The UN Special Rapporteur on Human Rights estimated that approximately 20,000 women were victims of sexual violence in the former Yugoslavia between 1992 and 1994 (1996). Women were detained, interrogated, gang raped, mutilated and subjected to enforced pregnancies in deliberate efforts to affect the region's ethnic composition.

In response to these atrocities, the UN Security Council Resolution 827 (under Chapter VII of the UN Charter) established the ICTY in 1993. In a remarkable leap forward from prior precedent at Nuremberg, the UN Security Council explicitly stated that it was 'appalled by reports of massive, organised and systematic detention and rape of women' (UN SC Res. 789, 18 December 1992). The ICTY Statute explicitly established rape as a crime against humanity under Article 5. The Rules of Procedure and Evidence governing ICTY proceedings also specifically provided for sexual crimes. Rule 96 established that corroboration of the testimony of a sexual assault victim is not required and that evidence relating to consent is to be first presented to the judges in camera (in private) to determine whether it is relevant and credible. It was also stated that consent could not be raised as a defence if the victim had been threatened or had otherwise submitted to the assault through fear. Rule 34 required the Victims and Witnesses Unit to 'provide counselling and support . . . in particular in cases of rape and sexual assault' and it emphasized that 'due consideration shall be given, in the appointment of staff, to the employment of qualified women' to do so.

Despite this impressive advancement from the Nuremberg precedent, the ICTY faltered in its first step. In the *Tadic* case (ICTY-94-1-T, Trial Chamber, 7 May 1997), rape was presented merely as a 'background' issue (Copelon 2000). An amicus brief was filed by civil society groups and the *Tadic* indictment was amended at the ICTY to include rape charges (Copelon 2000). However, the charges were later dropped because the witness was unwilling to testify without the guarantee of full protective measures, albeit that charges did remain regarding sexual violence involving male victims. This case showed that formal provisions to support the prosecution of rape are insufficient: strategies for investigating gender crimes need to be implemented from the outset and maintained through to trial, inparticular, to provide adequate protection and security to witnesses.

Convictions for rape as a crime against humanity were established in several cases at the ICTY but, importantly, the ICTY case law also pioneered the approach of using rape to satisfy the elements of other crimes such as torture, enslavement or persecution (Sellers and Okuizumi 1997: 59). For example, in *Furundijza* (ICTY-95-17/1, Trial Chamber, 10 December 1998) acts of rape were found to constitute torture and outrages against personal dignity as a violation of the laws of war. In this case, Witness A was detained in a house and interrogated while she was repeatedly raped orally, anally and vaginally. The Trial Chamber found that the relevant harm threshold for torture can be established through acts of rape or other forms of sexual violence. The accused, who was present during the assaults though not a direct perpetrator, was found guilty by the Trial Chamber. Other cases have since also found acts of sexual violence to constitute torture (such as *Celebici*, ICTY-96-21-T, Trial Chamber, 16 November 1998: paras 172–8).

As another example of this approach, *Kunarac et al.* (ICTY-96-23&23/1, Trial Chamber, 22 February 2001) addressed rape and sexual violence in the context of enslavement. Here, women were detained in a house, raped repeatedly, and forced to render household services. It was held that the key element of enslavement, namely ownership, could be established even though the women were physically able to leave their accommodation, since they were psychologically detained in that they had nowhere else to go even if they managed to escape. Although the ICTY Statute did not specifically provide for sexual slavery, the prosecution in the *Kunarac* case continued the precedent of showing that gender crimes can be incorporated into other, broader crimes, which previously had not been litigated in the context of gender violence. Significantly, the *Kunarac* decision may also be thought of as paving the way for the Special Court for Sierra Leone to later bring successful charges under its Statute for sexual slavery.

Several ICTY judgments have also found that acts of sexual violence constitute persecution as a crime against humanity under Article 5 of the ICTY Statute. Persecution involves the denial of rights on discriminatory grounds, including through the discriminatory commission of crimes against humanity such as rape and sexual violence (see, for example, *Kvocka et al.*, IT-98-30/1, Trial Chamber, 2 November 2001: para. 186). Although the case law did not go so far as to find that gender could constitute a discriminatory basis, since the Statute only refers to persecution on political, racial or religious grounds (although the ICC Statute later recognized discrimination on a gender basis), sexual violence was recognized as effecting a denial of rights.

Finally, the ICTY took steps to address the more basic omissions of Nuremberg in failing to construe sexual violence crimes as a grave breach of the Geneva Conventions through wilfully causing great suffering or serious injury to body or health under Article 2(c) and also inhuman treatment under Article 2(b) (see *Celebici*, IT-96-21-A, judgment of 20 February 2001: para. 511). Additionally, the ICTY has emphasized the non-exhaustive nature of the list of offences under the war crimes provision in Article 3 of the ICTY Statute, thereby finding that it covers acts prohibited by Common Article 3 of the Geneva Conventions, including rape as an outrage upon personal dignity (see, for example, *Kunarac et al.*, IT-96-23, Appeals Chamber, 12 June 2002: para. 161). This demonstrates the extent to which the ICTY not only addressed the omissions of Nuremberg, but went on to interpret their Statute to permit further characterizations of sexual violence crimes.

The ICTY also clarified the standard with respect to the so-called 'threshold' requirement in proving crimes against humanity, namely that the crime must be committed within a widespread or systematic attack against a civilian population. In the *Kunarac* trial judgment, the ICTY established that it is not necessary to prove that the crime-base acts, such as rape, were themselves widespread or systematic (para. 417). A crime against humanity can therefore be established by proof of one rape within the context of a widespread or systematic attack.

Furthermore, at an evidential level, the ICTY made an important finding on the role of post-traumatic stress disorder (PTSD) in assessing apparently contradictory evidence of rape victims. The Trial Chamber in *Furundijza* found that 'survivors of such traumatic experiences cannot reasonably be expected to recall the precise minutiae of events, such as exact dates or times. Neither can they reasonably be expected to recall every single element of a complicated and traumatic sequence of events. In fact, inconsistencies may, in certain circumstances, indicate truthfulness and the absence of interference with witnesses' (para. 113). This is an important breakthrough, not yet fully replicated in many national systems, which recognizes the realities of trauma and memory recall for rape victims. This also provides the prosecution with a useful tool for protecting witnesses from cross-examination which seeks to suggest that inconsistency undermines credibility.

Despite these advancements, however, there have also been occasions when sexual offences have not been charged or when they have been dropped during plea bargaining (for example *Todorovic*, IT-95-9/1, Trial Judgment, 31 July 2001: paras 37–40). In some cases, even though sexual assaults are described in the judgment, there has been no formal charge of rape (for example, *Kordic and Cerkez*, IT-95-14/2, Trial Judgment, 26 February 2001: para. 29; *Kupreskic et al.* IT-95-16, Trial Judgment, 14 January 2000: para. 199). However, there have been a few cases where the accused pleaded guilty to charges of rape (for example, *Nikolic*, IT-94-2, Trial Judgment, 18 December 2003; *Cesic*, IT-95-10/1-S, Trial Chamber, 11 March 2004: paras 3–4). To date, the ICTY has completed cases against over 80 individuals, of which – including indictments eventually withdrawn – 21 were charged with sexual offences.

In the final assessment, it can be seen that the ICTY has set several important precedents. The ICTY demonstrated how rape and other forms of sexual violence are prevalent in armed conflict and, as a consequence, sexual crimes can now form elements of other international crimes, such as torture. This offers a valuable counter to any structural bias in international criminal law inherited from the origins of international law and national criminal law. While, as will be discussed below, the International Criminal Tribunal for Rwanda did not follow the lead set by the ICTY in terms of prosecuting sexual violence as a range of international crimes, prosecuting rape in this manner is crucial in order to reflect the range of circumstances in which sexual violence can be perpetrated. This approach, pioneered by the ICTY, has made a lasting impact on how gender crimes are conceptualized in international criminal law, paving the way for the recognition of the crime of forced marriage by the Special Court for Sierra Leone and the establishment of comprehensive sexual violence provisions under the Rome Statute of the International Criminal Court.

## THE INTERNATIONAL CRIMINAL TRIBUNAL FOR RWANDA (ICTR)

The Rwandan genocide started in April 1994 following ethnic tensions within Rwanda stretching back several decades, principally between the communities identified as Hutu and Tutsi. The targeting of women in the media began years before the genocide and sexual violence was a key method by which the genocidaires inflicted harm and spread terror. Up to 500,000 women were raped during the approximately 100 days of the genocide, predominantly by a Hutu militia group known as the Interahamwe (Brouwer 2005: 11). Women were raped in open view, in public buildings and in private homes. Many were held in collective or individual sexual slavery. Sexual mutilation was common, with public displaying of women's severed breasts and sexual organs. Little was done by the international community to halt the atrocities. However, in November 1994, the Security Council followed the precedent it set with the ICTY by creating the ICTR under Chapter XII of the UN Charter.

As with the ICTY, the Rules of Procedure and Evidence established for the ICTR included provisions to support sexual violence testimony, and sex crimes were specifically included in the ICTR Statute. Rape was included under the provisions addressing crimes against humanity in Article 3(g) and outrages to personal dignity including rape as violations of common Article 3 of the Geneva Conventions under Article 4(e).

The first case of the ICTR, *Akayesu* (ICTR-96-4-T, Trial Chamber, 2 September 1998), made the groundbreaking finding that genocide can be committed by acts of rape and sexual violence, since these crimes constitute the 'serious bodily or mental harm' referred to under the Genocide Convention, if coupled with specific intent to destroy the targeted group. However, like the first case of *Tadic* at the ICTY, rape was not initially charged – the prosecutor even went so far as to say that it was impossible to document rape because the women would not talk about it (Copelon 2000: 225). The error of this assertion was established during the oral testimony of Witness J who, of her own volition and without direct questioning from counsel, described the gang rape of her six-year-old daughter by three Interahamwe. She also asserted that she had heard about other gang rapes. Witness H later testified that she was raped and described other rapes that she had witnessed. This trial was presided over by Judge Pillay, the only woman judge out of the nine at the ICTR at the time. She adjourned proceedings to permit the prosecution to investigate the crimes raised by Witnesses J and H with a view to amending the charges to include rape. An amicus brief was also filed urging the bringing of rape charges. Akayesu was then additionally charged with rape and inhumane acts as crimes against humanity and outrages upon personal dignity as a war crime under violations of Common Article 3 of the Geneva Conventions. These acts were also encompassed under the genocide count.

One of the greatest contributions of the ICTR to the jurisprudence on gender and sexual violence crimes is the definition of rape and sexual violence. The *Akayesu* judgment is an impressive demonstration of how actors involved in the development of international criminal law have the capacity to step outside any innate structural biases embedded in both international law and criminal law. Rape is traditionally defined as a crime against personal autonomy, which plays out in the courtroom as a battle over whether or not the victim consented. This can be problematic since the factual circumstances of rape usually do not permit the discovery of corroborating evidence such as additional witnesses. Forensic evidence can assist in identifying the perpetrator, but if there is no evidence of a physical struggle, determination of guilt can often depend on an evaluation of the credibility of the victim and accused. For this reason, the witness can be exposed, during her/his testimony, to intrusive questioning on her/his private life, designed to raise questions about consent and belief in consent, as well as to present her/him as unreliable or disreputable.

*Akayesu* stepped out of this framework entirely. According to the *Akayesu* judgment, the key focus is on the context of the acts, in particular focusing on factors which establish the existence of coercive circumstances. This approach is especially warranted in relation to international crimes, which typically occur during armed conflict. The judgment made an analogy with torture, which follows a conceptual approach (harm committed to attain a prohibited purpose) rather than setting out a precise list of which particular acts constitute torture. In *Akayesu*, the broader category of sexual violence was held to include rape, and rape was defined as 'a physical invasion of a sexual nature, committed on a person under circumstances which are coercive' (paras 597–8; see further Munro in this collection).

However, the *Akayesu* definition has not been consistently applied in subsequent cases. The ICTY reverted to a consent-based definition of rape in the Appeals Chamber judgment in *Kunarac* (ICTY-96-23&23/1, Appeals Chamber, 12 June 2002), which defined rape as the sexual penetration of the vagina or anus by the penis or any other object, or the penetration of the mouth of the victim by the penis of the perpetrator without consent of the victim. More recently, in *Gacumbitsi*, the Appeals Chamber affirmed the *Kunarac* approach, but incorporated aspects of *Akayesu* by finding that lack of consent could be proved by coercive circumstances (ICTR-2001-64, Appeals Chamber, 7 July 2006). The *Akayesu* definition is, thus, significant since it provides a standard that can be referred to as precedent in legal argument or used to lobby national legislatures for reform.

The main jurisprudential shortcoming of the ICTR has been the failure to follow the ICTY approach of charging sexual violence under a range of international crimes, in particular since there is evidence to suggest that such charges could be made. For example, NGOs have documented testimonials demonstrating that sexual enslavement was widespread during the genocide (Nowrojee: 1996). The ICTR Statute includes provisions which the ICTY has shown could be used in prosecuting sexual violence, namely enslavement, inhuman treatment and persecution under crimes against humanity and violations of common Article 3 of the Geneva Conventions. However, the ICTR has failed to prosecute such crimes (for further discussion, see Buss in this collection). There are a mere handful of ICTR sexual violence cases, despite the fact that it is accepted and documented that rape was widely used in implementing the genocide.

One case where rape was successfully prosecuted at the ICTR was that of *Semanza* (ICTR-97-20, Trial Chamber, 15 May 2003), in which a conviction for torture against the perpetrator was secured. The accused, having made statements suggesting that Tutsi women should be raped before being killed, was found to have engaged in an ethnic targeting that constituted the discriminatory purpose necessary to establish torture. There are three other cases at the ICTR which have resulted in convictions for sexual violence. First, *Muhimana* (ICTR-95-1-I, Trial Chamber, 28 April 2005) involved a notorious rapist who was convicted for crimes against humanity and for committing genocide through rape. Second, *Gacumbitsi* involved a government official who incited others to commit rape. Here, however, the appellate judges were not able to find that the rapist had been influenced by Gacumbitsi, despite the fact that during the rape he made statements to the victim that were similar to those statements previously made by Gacumbitsi. This demonstrates the high threshold involved in finding accused persons *individually* responsible for crimes. However, with respect to *command* responsibility, the third case concerning *Bagosora* (ICTR-96-7, Trial Chamber, 18 December 2008 – currently on appeal) found a military leader responsible for rapes committed by his subordinates: the rapes were so widespread that he was deemed to have known about them and was held accountable since he did nothing to prevent the crimes, or to punish the perpetrators under his control. For the remainder of the ICTR proceedings, however, rape charges have – for one reason or another – ultimately failed. This is clearly a disappointing legacy and one out of which it can but be hoped that lessons will be learned (see, further, Buss in this collection).

## THE SPECIAL COURT FOR SIERRA LEONE (SCSL)

The conflict in Sierra Leone was extreme in its brutality. It targeted the civilian population through crimes such as amputations, enlisting child soldiers and horrendous forms of sexual violence, including the practice of taking 'forced wives'. The key warring factions were the Revolutionary United Front (RUF) and the Armed Forces Revolutionary Council (AFRC), although allies of the government, namely the Civil Defence Forces (CDF), also committed serious crimes. Sexual and gender-based violence was a deliberate tool of warfare designed to inflict extreme harm on women, keeping the population in fear, while destroying traditional community norms and systems of order.

The establishment of the SCSL marked the creation of a 'hybrid' or 'mixed' international court, so named because it was established based on an agreement between the national government and the UN. It thus lacked the UN Chapter VII powers of the ICTR and the ICTY. Unlike the ICTR and the ICTY, the SCSL incorporates national as well as international crimes and is located inside the country itself. Although other hybrid models existed in East Timor and Kosovo, they constituted part of a domestic justice system as opposed to an independent institution. The SCSL was also unique since, at the time of its establishment, a national Truth and Reconciliation Commission (TRC) was taking place in the country. In order to ensure that people were as forthcoming as possible at the TRC, the SCSL Prosecutor did make it clear, however, that he would not make use of that process to obtain evidence for criminal purposes. Following the concern that the ICTY and ICTR were proving costly, in terms of time and resources, the SCSL was mandated to charge only those bearing the greatest responsibility. Trials were initially expected to take no more than three years, and costs were to be met on the basis of voluntary donations.

The first SCSL case against the CDF forces (SCSL-04-14-T, Trial Chamber, 2 August 2007) represented a failure in the prosecution of sexual and gender-based violence. The initial indictment did not contain any sexual violence charges and the Chamber denied a subsequent request by the prosecution to include such charges on the basis that late notice would prejudice the accused. This demonstrates a consistent theme: once again, sexual violence was not factored into the initial stages of the investigative strategy and it proved impossible for prosecutors to remedy this omission at the trial stage.

However, the next SCSL case made a stunning contribution to the jurisprudence. As noted above, the ICTY had previously demonstrated that acts of rape and sexual violence could be characterized as elements satisfying the requirements of other crimes such as torture, persecution or enslavement. The ICTR did the same for rape as genocide. In its turn, the SCSL in the case against the AFRC (SCSL-04-16OT, Trial Chamber, 20 June 2007) used the provisions of the crime against humanity of other inhumane acts to articulate a form of sexual violence, namely, the crime of forced marriage. Inhumane acts are considered as a residual category under crimes against humanity and require proof that the criminal acts are of similar seriousness, that is, resulting in levels of harm on a par with other acts considered to be crimes against humanity, such as rape or torture (see *Vasiljevic*, IT-98-32-A, Appeals Chamber, 25 February 2004: para. 165). The Appeals Chamber of the SCSL emphasized that these elements could be satisfied when a person is placed under forced conjugal association, resulting in harm to the victim. The Chamber was careful to distinguish forced marriage from arranged marriages, which it held typically involved community consensus. This unique legal interpretation of inhumane acts to include forced manage marriage allows emerging forms of sexual violence to be punished through a more general criminal provision, on the proviso that international customary law supports a finding that it was a crime at the time of the offence.

Most recently, the Trial Chamber in the case against the RUF forces (SCSL-04-15-T, Trial Chamber, 20 June 2007) found all three accused responsible for sexual and gender-based violence crimes. They were convicted of rape as a crime against humanity, of forced marriage as the crime against humanity of inhumane acts, and of outrages against personal dignity as a violation of common Article 3 to the Geneva Conventions. In addition, for the first time, the judges also entered convictions for the crime of sexual slavery, building upon the enslavement case of *Kunarac* at the ICTY. This will be an important precedent for the International Criminal Court, which also criminalizes sexual slavery in its Statute.

The final case for the SCSL is against Charles Taylor, who is currently on trial accused of committing rape, sexual slavery and outrages upon personal dignity according to a joint criminal enterprise with members of the RUF and AFRC (case no. SCSL-03-01-PT).

Overall, the SCSL has made a marked effort to include sexual violence crimes in its cases, despite the initial setback in the *CDF* case. That convictions have been entered for all such charges demonstrates that it is possible both to investigate sex crimes and to bring successful prosecutions under international criminal law, including against high-level accused who may not have been the direct perpetrators. The experience of the SCSL has also demonstrated that there is still scope for examining each specific conflict scenario and pressing charges that reflect the experience of its victims, such as through utilizing inhuman acts under crimes against humanity to criminalize forced marriage.

## THE INTERNATIONAL CRIMINAL COURT (ICC)

The concept of a permanent international court addressing the gravest crimes of international concern has been under consideration since Nuremberg. Starting in 1951, the International Law Commission has been developing drafts of an international criminal code. These culminated in the 1998 Rome Statute, which entered into force in 2002, establishing the ICC.

The Rome Statute crystallized the advancements in prosecuting sexual and gender-based violence which had arisen out of the ICTY, ICTR and SLSC. Indeed, it went further than the previous tribunals, for example by referring to enforced prostitution and female trafficking as a form of sexual slavery and finding that persecution can be committed on the basis of gender discrimination. The ICC also has several provisions relating to protective measures for victims of sexual violence, such as Article 68(1) of the Rome Statute, which requires the court to take appropriate steps to protect victims and witnesses. The Rules of Procedure and Evidence and the Regulations provide additional details on the methods by which this can be done, such as permitting a support person to be present during the testimony of a sexual violence witness (Rule 88). In addition to these various statutory provisions, it is hoped that the ICC will inherit the precedents of the ICTR and ICTY in finding that rape and sexual violence can constitute other general crimes such as torture and genocide, as well as following the jurisprudence of the SCSL in establishing forced marriage as an other inhumane act under crimes against humanity.

To date, the ICC has commenced one trial, the *Lubanga* case (ICC-01/04-01/06). Again, this first case did not include sexual violence charges, although during the prosecutor's opening statement, he referred to the sexual violence which took place under Lubanga's watch and members of the Bench have been questioning witnesses on sexual violence during the trial. The second ICC case, against *Katanga* and *Ndjulu-chou* (ICC-01/04-01/07), did charge the accused with rape and sexual slavery as both crimes against humanity and war crimes. This case went to trial at the end of 2009. The third ICC case, *Bemba* (ICC-01/05-01/08), is expected to proceed to trial in 2010 and relates to crimes in the Central African Republic. The Accused is charged with rape and it is considered likely to be a key ICC case concerning sexual crimes. The ICC also has two situations at the pre-trial stage, namely Darfur and Uganda, both of which include sexual violence charges in the various arrest warrants. It is hoped that – through these and other indictments – the ICC will further the ongoing global efforts to end impunity for sexual and gender-based violence by continuing a progressive and responsive approach to addressing victims' concerns and developing international criminal law jurisprudence.

## CONCLUSION

The track record in relation to the international criminal prosecution of rape and sexual violence has been mixed. Nuremberg and the Tokyo proceedings essentially ignored the vast majority of sexual violence crimes which took place during the Second World War. The early indictments of the ICTY, ICTR, SCSL and ICC all initially failed to include charges relating to sexual violence. At the same time, lessons have been learned with experience, and each institution has made its own unique and valuable contribution to the jurisprudence. This demonstrates the necessity for groups which provide accountability frameworks for these institutions to persist in ensuring that crimes of sexual violence remain on the agenda. At the same time, it is crucial to bear in mind that each conflict is factually distinct and that the prosecution of sexual violence crimes needs to be sensitive to the local dynamic. This is well exemplified by the SCSL initiative to address the phenomenon of forced marriage. As the work of the ICTY, ICTR and SCSL comes to an end, the responsibility for improving investigation and prosecution standards, developing jurisprudence and securing justice will fall on the ICC and new ad hoc institutions, such as the hybrid Extraordinary Chambers in the Courts of Cambodia prosecuting the Khmer Rouge. Although the ICC has a fairly detailed and progressive Statute, vigilance is still essential. Perhaps the most pressing challenge relates to mode of liability issues which have been a consistent basis upon which rape charges have resulted in acquittals. It is essential not only that charges for rape are brought in the international arena, but that convictions are secured. There have been remarkable improvements, but the work of ensuring that international criminal cases adequately address sexual violence will continue as long as tribunals and courts exist.

## Bibliography

Allied Control Council Law No. 10 (1945) *Punishment of Persons Guilty of War Crimes, Crimes against Peace and against Humanity*, 20 December.
Askin, K. (1997) *War Crimes Against Women*, The Hague: Martinus Nijhoff Publishers.
Brouwer, A-M.L.M. de (2005) *Supranational Criminal Prosecution of Sexual Violence: the ICC and the practice of the ICTY and the ICTR*, Antwerp: Intersentia.
Brownmiller, S. (1975) *Against Our Will: men, women and rape*, London: Penguin.
Charlesworth, H. and Chinkin, C. (2000) *The Boundaries of International Law: a feminist analysis*, Manchester: Manchester University Press.
Charter of the International Military Tribunal, Annexed to the London Agreement, 8 August 1945.
Charter of the International Military Tribunal for the Far East, 19 January 1946, Annexed to the Special Proclamation by the Supreme Commander for the Allied Powers at Tokyo.
Conot, R.E. (1983) *Justice at Nuremberg*, New York: Harper & Row.
Copelon, R. (2000) 'Gender crimes as war crimes: integrating crimes against women into international criminal law', *McGill Law Journal*, 46: 217–40.
IMT Official Documents of Nuremberg Trial, 14 November 1945–1 October 1946.
Nowrojee, B. (1996) *Shattered Lives: sexual violence during the Rwandan genocide and its aftermath*, New York: Human Rights Watch.

Pietila, H. and Vickers, J. (1994) *Making Women Matter: the role of the United Nations*, London: Zed Books.

Roeling, B.V.A. and Ruter, C.F. (eds) (1977) *The Tokyo Judgement: The International Military Tribunal for the Far East*, vol. 1, Amsterdam.

Sellers, P.V. and Kaoru, O. (1997) 'Prosecuting international crimes: an inside view: international prosecution of sexual assaults', *Transnational Law and Contemporary Problems*, 7: 45–80.

The Comfort Women Case: Judgment of April 27 1998, Shimonoseki Branch, Yamaguchi Prefectural Court, Japan.

UN SC Res. 789, 18 December 1992.

UN Special Rapporteur on Human Rights (1996) 'Preliminary Report of the Special Rapporteur on the Situation of Systematic Rape, Sexual Slavery and Slavery-Like Practices during Periods of Armed Conflict', UN ESCOR, Hum. Rts. Comm. 48th Session, Provisional Agenda Item 15, UN Doc E/CN.4/Sub.2/1996/26.

Chapter 4

# Learning our lessons?
## The Rwanda Tribunal record on prosecuting rape

*Doris Buss*[1]

The Rwanda Tribunal was scheduled to complete its trial work by the end of 2008 and appeals by 2010. While it is now clear these deadlines will not be met,[2] the Tribunal is beginning to wind down its operations and to plan for when it is no longer in existence. As part of that process, the Office of the Prosecutor (OtP) is starting to write the story of the Tribunal's legacy. One aspect of that legacy is to determine the 'lessons learned' from its experiences of prosecuting sexual violence cases.

The Rwanda Tribunal's record on sexual violence prosecutions is mixed. Though often treated as the poor second cousin to the Yugoslav Tribunal, the Rwanda Tribunal was the leader of the two in establishing that wartime rape was committed as part of, and was instrumental to, genocide (see Cole in this collection). The period following that promising start, however, has been disappointing. Tribunal scholars and activists (Nowrojee 2005; Haffajee 2006; de Londras 2009;Van Schaak 2009) have identified a number of institutional failings that negatively impacted on the number and success rate of rape prosecutions. The result is that, as the Tribunal begins the process of defining its legacy, its record on sexual violence is uneven and, for many, disappointing.

Producing an authoritative record of atrocities is often listed as one of the important accomplishments of war crimes prosecutions (Lattimer and Sands 2003; Minow 1998; Orentlicher 1991; for a discussion, see Leebaw 2008). The criminal courtroom, with its teams of lawyers, phalanx of investigators, and panel of international judges, provides a space for vetting information and evidence. The final judgments, it is hoped, will be a thorough and careful accounting of who did what to whom, when and how. For transitional justice, the body of judgments should produce a historical record that will operate as a 'form of truth' (Louise Arbour, quoted in Todorov 2004), making it possible to 'counter the denial about the extent and impact of systematic violence' (Leebaw 2008: 107).

The question of exactly what the record will achieve in post-genocide Rwanda is subject to debate (Maogoto 2004; Koskenniemi 2002; Alvarez 1998). Both the Rwanda and Yugoslav tribunals, while leading the way in post-conflict prosecutions, highlight some of the fault-lines in the initial enthusiasm for international war crimes courts. Both Tribunals are located outside the regions where the conflicts took place, and it is not clear to what extent individuals from these regions will accept the judgments of *international* courts, located elsewhere, as truthful records of what happened. Further, the criminal trial model itself has come under justifiable critique for limiting the range of 'truths' that can be testified to, and recorded, in legal judgments focused on the narrower task of assessing criminal culpability (Campbell 2007; Dembour and Haslem 2004; Mertus 2004). Nonetheless, the prevailing view of the Rwanda Tribunal is that it has been instrumental in establishing evidence about the 1994 genocide that otherwise would not be part of the historical record (author interview with Linda Bianchi, Appeals Counsel, Office of the Prosecutor, Rwanda Tribunal 2008; see also Nowrojee 2005).

Prosecuting rape and sexual violence poses its own challenges to the Tribunal record. As Cynthia Enloe notes, making rape visible as a matter of political and legal concern can be 'dangerously easy' (2000: 108–9). The public portrayal of rape, including in legal decisions, is invariably enmeshed in competing discourses of nationalism, belonging, insecurity, violence and responsibility. The difficult task, Enloe suggests, is to 'make visible the mass rapes of women by men as a systematic weapon of war in a way that does not turn those raped women into new commodities: commodities for our angst; commodities for human rights activism; commodities, especially, for galvanizing the next generations of nationalists to seek revenge' (2004: 177–8).

One means to disrupt the commodification of sexual violence against women is to continually 'roll back the canopy that discourages observers from taking a close look at women's varied experiences of nationalist conflict and thereby to specify the conditions and decisions that have turned some women into victims' (Enloe 2004: 104). In previous work (Buss 2009), I considered how the formulation of rape as an instrument of the Rwanda genocide operates to distract scrutiny of the conditions that create conflict and position some individuals more at risk than others. In this chapter, I want to consider how 'learning our lessons' about prosecuting rape may also discourage scrutiny, this time of the multiple objectives of feminist engagement in international criminal law and the place of rape prosecutions within that project.

The first section of this chapter outlines the Tribunal's record on sexual violence, including the number of rape prosecutions, convictions and acquittals. In the next section, I examine some of the institutional failings identified by Tribunal watchers, drawing on the facts of individual cases to illustrate how these failings impact upon the Trial Chambers' decision-making. The level of description of individual cases found in this section is intentional. My aim, in part, is to demonstrate the complex factual circumstances within which the Trial Chamber makes its decisions, and which are recounted in detail in the written judgments. I then consider, in the final section, how the level of detail found in Tribunal decisions yields different readings of the Tribunal record.

My analysis in this chapter is based on a close reading of the Rwanda Tribunal decisions up to December 2008, as well as interviews that I conducted with Tribunal staff and some defence counsel in April and May 2008. The Chief Prosecutor's 'legacy project' was mentioned by some interview subjects, but I was not able to directly access this project. All interviews referred to were conducted in Arusha, Tanzania.

## DEFINING THE RECORD

In setting out to look at the record of the Rwanda Tribunal, the starting – and finishing – place for many observers is the Tribunal's first decision in *Akayesu* (ICTR-96-4-T, Trial Chamber, 2 September 1998). The story of *Akayesu* is now well known (see also Cole in this collection); part way through the trial, and in response to questioning by one of the three Trial Chamber judges, Navanethem Pillay, evidence emerged of acts of rape conducted by individuals under the accused's authority. The trial was suspended while an application was made to include rape charges in the indictment against the accused (Copelon 2000; Van Schaak 2009). The Chamber's eventual judgment on the merits of the case concluded that rapes were widespread, the accused knew of and aided and abetted the rapes, and rapes 'were committed with the specific intent to destroy, in whole or in part, a particular group' (*Akayesu*: para. 731), namely the Tutsi. The Tribunal went further to rule that the rapes in fact 'resulted in physical and psychological destruction of Tutsi women, their families and their communities. Sexual violence was an integral part of the process of destruction, specifically targeting Tutsi women and specifically contributing to their destruction and to the destruction of the Tutsi group as a whole' (para. 731). Rape was used, the Tribunal held, to commit the crime of genocide.

*Akayesu* represents a high-water mark in the Tribunal's work which, post-*Akayesu*, has been much more uneven in its attention to, and treatment of, sexual violence. The Tribunal has largely failed to charge individual accused with sexual violence crimes, or where these charges are included in the indictment, the OtP has either not pursued them at trial, or pursued them unsuccessfully.

The numbers tell the story. As of December 2008, the Tribunal has overseen the completed trials and guilty pleas of 48 men, only 15 of whom went to trial on charges including rape or sexual violence.[3] Only five men[4] in total have been found guilty of rape-related charges. Further, eight men have pleaded guilty before the Tribunal, five of whom were charged with sexual violence crimes. All five were able to have their sexual violence charges dropped in exchange for guilty pleas on other counts. No one has pleaded guilty to any sexual violence offences.

## AND THEN THERE WERE NONE: WHAT WENT WRONG IN RAPE PROSECUTIONS?

The dismal statistics on rape prosecutions have given rise to a number of different investigations into what went wrong. The OtP, as part of its 'legacy project' to establish a best practices manual for other war crimes institutions, has been looking at what worked, and what did not, in the prosecutions of rape at the Rwanda Tribunal. Feminist scholars and activists have also been conducting studies of the Rwanda record (see, for example, de Londras 2009; Van Shaak 2009). While the Rwanda Tribunal has not yet finished its work, and the 'legacy' of the OtP has yet to be publicly released, there appears to be an emerging consensus, at least among Tribunal watchers, about the specific institutional failings of the Tribunal, together with some difficulties inherent in connecting individual acts of rape to the leaders of the genocide and senior military and government members. For the purposes of this discussion, I highlight some of the larger institutional problems that impacted upon Tribunal decisions: namely, the lack of political will in the OtP, inadequate or flawed investigations, and defective and incomplete indictments.

Binaifer Nowrojee, together with the Coalition for Women's Human Rights in Conflict Situations (Brunet 2003; Nowrojeee 2005; see also de Londras 2009), have been particularly critical of Carla del Ponte, chief prosecutor from 1999 to 2003.[5] Del Ponte's decision to discharge the Sexual Assault Team in 2000 was seen as part of a larger failing to pursue or adequately resource sexual violence prosecutions. The Coalition and Nowrojee also point to instances where the OtP, under del Ponte, chose not to pursue or advance sexual violence charges, even when it had the evidence to do so. They point, in particular, to the *Cyangugu* case (*Prosecutor v Bagambiki et al.*, ICTR-99-46-T, Trial Chamber, 25 February 2004), in which three men were tried together for crimes committed in south-western Rwanda. The prosecutor in that case had evidence of sexual violence crimes but delayed, apparently due to 'personnel problems' in the OtP, filing an application to add sexual violence charges to the indictment. Without explanation, the OtP then withdrew its application. No charges for sexual violence crimes were advanced, despite pressure from women's groups within and outside Rwanda. Two of the three men were eventually acquitted.

This lack of political commitment to prosecute rape was compounded by problems in investigations, particularly those conducted in the early years of the Tribunal. These problems included lack of diversity and specialized training for investigators. Until very recently, no Rwandans were included in investigation staff and training on pursuing sexual violence inquiries was not conducted until several years into the Tribunal's work. When Binaifer Nowrojee conducted her research in early 2000, most of the investigators were men, many of whom came from backgrounds that made them unfamiliar with and/or unconvinced about the importance of investigating sexual violence, and they lacked the 'training and direction on how to elicit information about sexual violence' (2005: 12–13). Nowrojee also found investigation results were skewed by internal OtP policies that paid a higher stipend to investigators depending on the region where the interviews were conducted. The result was that some areas of Rwanda, such as the capital Kigali, 'have been neglected [by investigators] despite their high levels of sexual violence' (2005: 12). Nowrojee's conclusions, confirmed in part by OtP investigators

I interviewed, were that investigation reports were of poor quality, emphasizing quantity over quality (2005: 12).

The combined impact of lack of political will and faulty investigations can be seen throughout the Rwanda Tribunal's body of judgments. In some cases, like *Cyangugu* referred to above and *Muvunyi* (ICTR-2000-55A-T, Trial Chamber, 12 September 2006), discussed below, the OtP either did not bring charges or tried to drop them before trial. Part of the reason for the OtP's dithering on sexual violence charges can be attributed to an uncertain political commitment, but there were also parallel problems with securing witness testimony, as well as enduring problems in drafting indictments.

The Rwanda record, read as a whole, reveals numerous incidents where charges listed in the indictments were struck out by Trial Chambers on the basis that they were too vague or incomplete about the time frame, specific facts or identities of individuals involved in alleged incidents. The rationale behind striking charges in an indictment is that the lack of specificity impairs the defendants' ability to mount an adequate defence.

Defects in the indictments affect the prosecution of a range of offences, but their impact on sexual violence charges has been described as 'a plague' (author interview with Tim Gallimore, Spokesperson, OtP, Rwanda Tribunal 2008). Indeed, there are repeated instances where evidence of rape exists on the trial record, but does not result in a conviction because the charge was not pleaded correctly or fully in the indictment. In several cases, the Trial Chamber heard from women who gave what the Tribunal characterizes as 'spontaneous' evidence of their own rapes. This evidence, often compelling, is generally dismissed because those particular rapes were not included in the indictment against the accused. For example, Witness AQ gave evidence against Mikaeli Muhimana (ICTR-95-1B-T, Trial Chamber, 28 April 2005) that she and her sister were held captive in Muhimana's house. She testified about the multiple rapes of her sister by the defendant, which she witnessed, but she also testified that she too was raped on at least three occasions by Muhimana (paras 90–4). The indictment, however, was not specific enough about the rapes committed against Witness AQ and the OtP failed to properly amend the indictment to include these charges. The Chamber ruled that the evidence about AQ's rapes could not be used against Muhimana.

The case of Tharcisse Muvunyi might be one of the more extreme and recent examples of the impact defective indictments can have on sexual violence charges. Muvunyi was convicted by the Trial Chamber for genocide and crimes against humanity, but in August 2008, the Appeal Chamber (ICTR-2000-55A-A, Appeals Chamber, 29 August 2008) overturned these convictions and made the unusual order for a retrial on one charge of incitement to genocide, of which Muvunyi was subsequently convicted (ICTR-2000-55A-T, Trial Chamber, 11 February 2010). The convoluted legal issues in *Muvunyi* provide something of a road map of the various problems experienced by the OtP with poorly drafted indictments and inadequate attempts to amend indictments.

A Lieutenant Colonel in the Rwanda Army, Muvunyi was the commanding officer for Butare *préfecture*. Throughout the genocide, he had control over École des Sous-Officers (ESO) soldiers and responsibility for the security of the local civilian population (Trial Chamber 2006: para. 90). Muvunyi was charged with incitement to genocide, superior responsibility for genocide and crimes against humanity, including rape. Both Trial and Appeal Chambers found the indictment against Muvunyi to be flawed in various ways: failing to plead crucial elements of the crimes, omitting essential information about the details of the crime, or adducing evidence at trial of crimes not listed in the indictment. The Appeal Chamber went further in its determinations on the indictment than the Trial Chamber and ruled that all convictions of Muvunyi were suspect as a result, sending one remaining charge back for a retrial.

The initial indictment against Muvunyi contained allegations of rapes and sexual assaults. The OtP applied to strike the rape and sexual violence charges in January 2005, six weeks before the start of the trial, on the basis that it was having problems locating and convincing witnesses to testify to rape. That application was unsuccessful, as was the OtP's attempt at the same time to amend the indictment to provide more details of other charges. The Chamber refused the amendments on the grounds that the OtP was introducing new charges which, coming so close to the trial, would prejudice the accused.[6] In any event, the Chamber reasoned, the OtP had already amended the indictment in 2003 and could (and should) have made all necessary changes at that time.

The rape charges went to trial and the Chamber heard, and found to be true, evidence of widespread incidents of sexual violence by soldiers in Butare. It heard victim-witness testimony about rapes of Tutsi women at road blocks manned by soldiers of the Rwanda Army (2006: paras 451–3). It heard evidence, again directly from victim-witnesses, that some Tutsi women were held captive at bars where they were repeatedly raped by soldiers of the Rwanda Army (para. 386). And it heard evidence about the rape of virgins, and rape in front of family members, usually accompanied by killing (para. 378).

The Tribunal believed Witnesses AFV, QY and TM's testimony that they were raped, humiliated and abused. But while the Tribunal 'sympathised' (para. 409) with these rape victims, and it concluded that the rapes were committed by soldiers under Muvunyi's command, it refused to convict Muvunyi. The indictment alleged that the rapes were committed by a particular camp of soldiers – Ngoma camp – yet all the trial evidence related to rapes committed by ESO soldiers. Even though the evidence also showed that the ESO soldiers were under Muvunyi's command, the indictment did not refer to rapes by ESO soldiers and so the Tribunal treated the evidence relating to ESO soldiers as a new allegation that was not properly pleaded in the indictment. Muvunyi's acquittal on all sexual violence charges was upheld on Appeal.

*Muvunyi* crystallizes many of the problems outlined by Tribunal watchers: the indictment was poorly drafted, there appear to have been flaws in gathering and reporting on evidence, the OtP prevaricated on whether to pursue rape evidence, and both Trial and Appeal Chambers seemed unsatisfied with the performance of the OtP in preparing the case for trial in a timely and effective way. These problems are also found in cases where rape charges make it to trial and survive challenges to the indictment. Once at trial, rape allegations suffer from lack of evidence and/or inadequately prepared witnesses.

The combined effect of these various institutional problems – lack of political will, flawed investigations, poor indictments, inadequate evidence – is to gradually, step by step, erode the charges and evidence of sexual violence until few convictions can result. The overall process of reading the decisions is like a counting song that starts at 100 but loses one item each round until there is only one remaining. The Trial Chamber decisions similarly begin with a large number of charges but with each section of the decision, individual charges are dropped: this one is dropped because the indictment was faulty, that one because the witness was confused, and another was never fully proved in any event. By the end of the judgment, just like in a counting song, there are only a few charges left. Or there are none.

The case against Alfred Musema follows just this pattern (ICTR-96-13-A, Trial Chamber, 27 January 2000). Musema was a Director of the Gisovu tea factory and a leading community figure in Butare. The range of indictments against him was lengthy, including a number of rape and sexual violence charges. While he was eventually convicted of genocide and crimes against humanity, all sexual violence charges were dismissed either at trial or on appeal. The Prosecutor led evidence on five separate counts of rape/sexual assault at trial. The first was an allegation that Musema had incited rape by giving a speech at a Karongi Hill meeting in which he said 'those who wanted to have fun could rape their [Tutsi] women and their [Tutsi] children' (para. 800). The next day, five men raped Witness M's cousin and niece (para. 801). The charge was dismissed (Judge Pillay dissenting) because the Prosecutor had not proved beyond a reasonable doubt, in light of Musema's alibi evidence, that he had in fact attended the meeting.

Second, Musema was alleged to have been responsible for the rape and murder of Annunciata Mujawayezu, a woman who worked in the Gisovu tea factory. Witness I was hiding, she testified, when the accused and two assistants discovered Annunciata. Witness I said she heard Musema order his two assistants to rape and cut off Annunciata's breast. Witness I, who could not see into the room, heard sounds of what she took to be a rape, including sounds of physical violence (para. 809). The Tribunal ruled that the Prosecution had proved beyond a reasonable doubt that Musema ordered the rape of Annunciata, but refused to deduce from the sounds Witness I heard that Annunciata was raped (paras 828–9, 889). As a result, this charge too was dismissed.

Third, Musema was charged with the rape and killing of Immaculée Mukankuzi, and with encouraging men under his supervision to rape. Witness J testified that on 13 May, Musema arrived with a group of men to attack Tutsi refugees on Muyira Hill. Witness J and other women were caught by the men and Witness J testified that Musema told the men 'What I do, you will imitate after me' (para. 832). Musema raped and killed Immaculée and this emboldened the men to rape Witness J, her daughter and five other women (paras 833–4).

This charge too was dismissed because Witness J gave confusing testimony about how many children she had, how many children were with her at the time of her daughter's rape, and which of her children was subject to rape (see, for example, paras 840–5). The Tribunal ruled that there was insufficient evidence of the rapes of Immaculée and the other women.

Finally, Musema was convicted of the remaining rape charge: the rape and killing of Nyiramusgi. At appeal (ICTR-96-13-A, Appeals Chamber, 16 November 2001), however, the defence led new evidence from two witnesses which raised doubt about whether Nyiramusgi was raped by Musema or someone else, and the conviction was overturned (paras 193–4).

And then there were none; all rape and sexual violence charges against Musema were dismissed.

The Rwanda record on rape prosecutions, read in its entirety, follows a pattern similar to *Musema*. A large number of charges relating to various incidents are brought at the outset. But, as each allegation is weighed and assessed, the charges and some of the evidence are whittled away until few convictions for rape result. The record of rape prosecutions, as a consequence, is remarkably low compared with the available evidence of rape enacted during the Rwanda genocide (see below).

But while the number of formal convictions is low, the Tribunal record may be more promising than it initially appears. I began this chapter noting that the production of a record of events is often seen as one of the important contributions of post-conflict justice mechanisms, and particularly so for the Rwanda Tribunal. The telling of the Rwanda genocide, like so many other conflicts, is the subject of complex political manoeuvrings (Pottier 2002), and the capacity of the Rwanda court system to deliver authoritative judgments on the wrongs of the genocide has been seriously questioned by international observers and the Tribunal itself (see, for example, Human Rights Watch 2008 and *Prosecutor v Munyakazi*, ICTR-97-36-R11bis, Appeals Chamber, 8 October 2008). The work of the Rwanda Tribunal is thus likely to be the most fulsome process for hearing and weighing evidence on, and making determinations about, what happened during the 1994 genocide. In the following section, I consider the different ways in which the Tribunal record can be read. My interest here is to explore the relationship between reading the record and identifying what lessons should be learned from the Rwanda Tribunal.

## (RE)READING THE RECORD

While it has failed to consistently convict individual defendants of rape as a crime, the Rwanda Tribunal has, paradoxically, repeatedly acknowledged the existence of widespread sexual violence against Tutsi women. Rape, as an instrument of the genocide, is present on the Tribunal record even while few individual accused are held legally responsible.

A number of Tribunal judgments, including those where rape was not prosecuted, make passing note of the existence of widespread rape and sexual violence as part of the genocidal violence. For example, in *Prosecutor v Jean-Bosco Barayagwiza, Hassan Ngeze and Ferdinand Nahimana* (ICTR-99-52-T, Trial Chamber, 3 December 2003: paras 114 and 1079), known as the Media case, the Tribunal ruled that the sexualization of Tutsi women was part of the genocidal campaign against all Tutsi, and, as a result of the media propaganda orchestrated by the three defendants, 'Tutsi women were often raped, tortured and mutilated'. Similarly, in *Prosecutor v Clement Kayishema and Obed Ruzindana* (ICTR-95-1-T, 21 May 1999: paras 294 and 547), the Chamber referred to acts of rape, among other crimes, committed at roadblocks and on a widespread basis, as part of the larger genocide committed against the Tutsi. And in 'Military 1' (*Prosecutor v Théoneste Bagasora, Gratien Kabiligi, Aloys Ntabakuze, Anatorle Nsengiyumva*, ICTR-98-41-T, Trial Chamber, 18 December 2008: para. 1728), the Tribunal noted that 'it is well known that rape and other forms of sexual violence were widespread' in the genocide. Thus, the overall image presented in the body of the Tribunal decisions is that rape of women was widespread and part of the genocide.

More importantly, the judgments in cases where rape charges are heard, even if unsuccessful, provide substantial discussion of witness evidence about sexual violence. Witness I's testimony of hiding from Musema and his assistants and overhearing the killing (and likely rape) of Annunciata makes for hard but vivid reading. By the end of the judgment, whatever the outcome, the reader is left with powerful stories about what happened to some individuals during the genocide. The actual outcome of the trial – conviction, acquittal and sentence – feels, in some respects, like an add-on chapter to a much larger story.

The Tribunal decisions are a rich source of information from which one can glimpse larger patterns and stories about the genocide. The format of the Trial Chamber decision, with its methodical recounting and weighing of witness evidence, results in a lengthy, factually driven document. The focus of the decision tends to be on marshalling the pool of factual evidence to make an assessment of the existence of crimes, first, and individual responsibility for those crimes, second. But even where the second step is not completed – the individual accused is not found responsible, for example – the Chamber's decision still provides an accounting of the evidence of crimes committed, and it reproduces, albeit in a constrained way, narratives of individuals' experiences. As such, the judgments are themselves a resource for information about what happened to some groups and individuals during the genocide.

For example, neither prostitution nor 'forced marriage' have been prosecuted by the Tribunal and yet some of the decisions contain information pointing to these practices. For example, *Muvunyi* includes evidence of witnesses being held captive and used as prostitutes (para. 386 and discussion above), and in *Muhimana* (ICTR-95-1B-T, Trial Chamber, 28 April 2005:

paras 308–17), the Tribunal heard evidence that Muhimana authorized, in his leadership capacity, the abduction of Witness BG, who was held by another man as a de facto sex slave for a short duration (when she escaped). Muhimana's defence to this charge was that Witness BG was going to be married to her captor and, hence, no crime had resulted. The Tribunal rejected this evidence stating that it was not persuaded that BG had consented to marriage given the 'coercive circumstances prevailing' (para. 322).

While this result seems appropriate, Witness BG's experience points to another dimension of sexual violence in the genocide: forced marriage. Human rights reports of the genocide (see, for example, Human Rights Watch 1996) provide further information that many women were in fact 'married' to Hutu men during the genocide. Some women were able to leave their 'marriages' at the end of the genocide, but others chose to stay (Human Rights Watch 1996; African Rights 1995: Ch. 10). While the Rwanda Tribunal record would be stronger had it pursued prosecutions for forced marriage, the decisions themselves can function as an additional source of information about some women's experience of violence during the genocide.

I want to be careful here not to overstate my case. The Tribunal record is limited by the very structure of a criminal trial setting, which curtails the range of stories that can be told (Buss 2009; Campbell 2007; Mertus 2004; Dembour and Haslem 2004). For example, the record contains few, if any, references to sexual violence against men (Buss 2009; Sivakumaran 2007), Hutu women are rarely seen as victims of sexual violence unless their rapes are defined as an attack against their Tutsi husbands (Buss 2009; Buss 2007), and the Tribunal has failed to charge the Rwanda Patriotic Front for any crimes at all, including rape (Human Rights Watch 2009). Further, feminist scholars have traced the ways in which both war crimes trials and truth commissions reproduce distorted accounts of women's experiences in conflict settings (Kelsall and Stepakoff 2007; Franke 2006; Mertus 2004; Ross 2003), a charge that no doubt can also be levelled at the Rwanda Tribunal.

But, the examples of prostitution and forced marriage demonstrate the different ways in which the Tribunal record can be read. If it is read in terms of numbers of convictions, the record does not look so promising. If it is read as an accounting of what happened to some individuals during the genocide, it is an important, if incomplete, resource. There is a disjuncture between what is visible at the level of convictions (and legal determinations of fact and law) and what can be found in the factual backdrop to individual stories.

The significance attributed to these different readings of the record immediately calls to mind long-standing debates about the promises and perils of post-conflict truth processes versus war crimes tribunals, and the possible therapeutic promises of testimony. These are larger debates that I do not pursue here (see, for example Mendeloff 2009; Nikolic-Ristanovic 2005; Fletcher and Weinstein 2002; Minow 1998; Alvarez 1998). Rather, I want to consider the relationship between how the record is read and the 'lessons' identified as needing to be learned.

For Tribunal-watchers and staff, the lessons to be learned focus, with good reason, on how to do rape investigations and prosecutions better. While this is a laudable goal, I want to consider two other lessons that might be learned from the experience of rape prosecutions at the ICTR. The first of these lessons is that law operates unevenly and that feminist engagement with law is – and should be – focused on a range of political goals and not simply the numbers of rape convictions. The second lesson, following on from this, is that *how* rape is prosecuted is as important as *whether or not* rape is prosecuted.

The mixed record of rape prosecutions at the Rwanda Tribunal can be seen as an example of what Carol Smart refers to as the 'uneven operation' of law, where developments in one legal area to enhance women's legal remedies are undermined by regressive developments in another ([1986] 1995: 154–5). For example, the Tribunal's groundbreaking work in defining rape as an international crime (of genocide and against humanity) came at the same time that other legal actors – investigators, staff in the OtP – were failing to pursue investigations and charges on sexual violence crimes. Similarly, developments in the Witness and Victim Support Section designed to strengthen support for rape victims were undermined by lack of political resolve to effectively prosecute sexual violence crimes. The Tribunal, viewed as a whole, was thus simultaneously advancing and undermining the legal recognition of sexual violence crimes.

What implications does this 'uneven operation' of international criminal law have for feminist engagement with the tribunals and courts that are increasingly active in prosecuting wartime sexual violence? At one level, institutional changes to strengthen rape prosecutions are important, but, on their own, they are insufficient. As Fionnuala Ni Aolain and Ellish Rooney (2007) remind us, 'underenforcement' of post-conflict and transitional agreements is itself a product of gendered and other forms of social power. Institutional failing, like under-enforcement, is not an innocent act, and post-conflict transition processes, whether peace agreements or war crimes prosecutions, are sites at which gender and other relations of power are re/constituted (see also Buss 2009; Campbell 2007; Ross 2003). Recognizing that law operates in multiple sites, and at varying levels, underscores the importance of feminist engagement with a range of legal sites associated with post-conflict reconciliation – not just courts, but also peacekeeping and peacemaking operations, economic reparations (see Engle and Lottmann in this collection), reconstruction, and so on.

But just as there are multiple challenges facing feminist-inspired reforms of international criminal law, there are also multiple potential political gains from such a project. Feminist efforts in the 1990s to strengthen international legal recognition of sexual violence may have started with the (simple) demand that rape be recognized as a war crime and not (merely) a side-effect of war (for a discussion, see Buss 2009). But the impact of that recognition always held the possibility for more extensive social change. For example, the recognition of rape as an international crime also might have led to increased resources for women fleeing sexual violence, a more substantive understanding of the relationship between violence against women in war *and* peace, an appreciation of the significance of gender to the conditions of, and recovery from conflict, a zero-tolerance approach to violence against women whenever it occurs – and the list could go on. Convictions for sexual violence crimes are only one part of what presumably is a much larger and richer array of political goals that, one hopes, would be strengthened by the recognition of rape as an international crime. But if 'lessons learned' focus exclusively or primarily on the conviction rate for rape prosecutions, we may fail to track how, and to what extent, related feminist goals are pursued or implemented.

A second, and related, lesson that might be learned from the Rwanda experience is the importance of tracking *how* rape is prosecuted. At the outset of this chapter, I referred to Cynthia Enloe's injunction to 'roll back the canopy' that prevents a closer scrutiny of the complexity of wartime sexual violence. The Tribunal decisions, with their focus on individual responsibility, may provide an important record of what happened to some individuals at different times and places in the genocide. But the Tribunal does little to explain what made individuals engage in rape, and what factors positioned some women more at risk than others. As discussed above, the record of Tribunal decisions can be mined for rich evidence of types of sexual violence during the 1994 genocide. A focus on whether or not rape is prosecuted avoids asking other questions, such as: Why is it that some women are visible as victims and other women (and men) are not? What type of sexual violence is subject to prosecution and which types (that is, forced marriage and/or prostitution) are not?

## CONCLUSION

This chapter has aimed to do three things. First, it provides an overview of the work of the Rwanda Tribunal after its first, and much-lauded, decision in *Akayesu*. Activists and feminists committed to ending sexual violence against women see *Akayesu* as a success story about international prosecutions. But, as I show in this analysis, *Akayesu* is only the first chapter in a much longer story about the merits and limits of international war crimes prosecutions on sexual violence.

My second objective was to mediate, in some respects, the opposite tendency: to see the Rwanda Tribunal as consistently failing to realize the promise of *Akayesu*. This chapter has mapped the various ways in which the Tribunal, while manifesting a series of problems in prosecuting sexual violence crimes, has produced an important, if incomplete, record on rape committed as part of the 1994 genocide.

The resulting picture that emerges of the Rwanda Tribunal is a mixed one. The third objective of this chapter has been to use this mixed result to think more critically about how to read the Tribunal record and the resulting recommendations for institutional reform. While there is no doubt that rape prosecutions should be done better, the task of 'learning our lessons' should not stop there.

## Notes

1 My thanks to the editors, Vanessa Munro and Clare McGlynn, for their helpful comments on earlier drafts of this chapter, and to Brittany Sheridan for her editing assistance. An earlier version of this chapter was presented at *Reforming the Law on Sexual Violence*, workshop, Centre for Criminal Justice and Human Rights, University College Cork, Ireland, 27 June 2008 and my thanks to the organizers and audience for their comments. Research for this paper was funded by the Social Sciences and Humanities Research Council of Canada.
2 See 'Statement of the President of the Security Council', S/PRST/2008/47, 10 December 2009. Online. Available at: <http://www.un.org/Depts/dhl/resguide/scact2008.htm> (accessed 28 February 2009).
3 There are many different ways to count cases at the ICTR and I have focused only on contested decisions on the merits of the case, and excluded, for example, convictions for perjury.
4 The five men found guilty of rapes, as of December 2008, are Akayesu, Bagasora, Gacumbitsi, Muhimana and Semanza.
5 She was removed as Chief Prosecutor of the Rwanda Tribunal in 2003, but remained as Chief Prosecutor of the Yugoslav Tribunal until 2007.
6 On Appeal, the Chamber disagreed that the OtP's amendments introduced new charges but agreed the accused would be prejudiced in any event. The amendments were not allowed.

## Bibliography

African Rights (1995) *Rwanda: death, despair and defiance*, London: African Rights.
Alvarez, J. (1998) 'Rush to closure: lessons of the Tadic judgment', *Michigan Law Review*, 96: 2031–112.
—— (1999) 'Crimes of state/crimes of hate: lessons from Rwanda', *Yale Journal of International Law*, 24: 365–483.
Brunet, A. (2003) 'Letter to Kofi Annan, Secretary General of the United Nations, concerning the reappointment of Carla Del Ponte as Prosecutor to the International Criminal Tribunal for Rwanda', on behalf of the Coalition on Women's Human Rights in Conflict Situations. Online. Available at: <http://www.ichrdd.ca/english/commdoc/prelease/letterICTR.html> (accessed 15 July 2009).
Buss, D. (2007) 'The curious visibility of wartime rape: gender and ethnicity in international criminal law', *Windsor Journal of Access to Justice*, 25: 3–22.
—— (2009) 'Rethinking rape as a weapon of war', *Feminist Legal Studies*, 17: 145–63.
Campbell, K. (2007) 'The gender of transitional justice: law, sexual violence and the International Criminal Tribunal for the Former Yugoslavia', *The International Journal of Transitional Justice*, 1: 411–32.
Copelon, R. (2000) 'Integrating crimes against women into international criminal law', *McGill Law Journal*, 46: 217–40.
De Londras, F. (2009) 'Prosecuting sexual violence in the *Ad Hoc* International Criminal Tribunals for Rwanda and the Former Yugoslavia', *University College Dublin Working Papers in Law, Criminology & Socio-Legal Studies*: 06/2009.
Dembour, M.B. and Haslem E. (2004) 'Silencing hearings? Victim-witnesses at war crimes trials', *European Journal of International Law*, 15: 151–77.
Enloe, C. (2000) *Maneuvres: the international politics of militarizing women's lives*, Berkeley, CA: University of California Press.

—— (2004) *The Curious Feminist: searching for women in a new age of empire*, Berkeley, CA: University of California Press.
Fletcher, L. and Weinstein, H. (2002) 'Violence and social repair: rethinking the contribution of justice to reconciliation', *Human Rights Quarterly*, 24: 573–639.
Franke, K. (2006) 'Gendered subjects of transitional justice', *Columbia Journal of Gender and the Law*, 15: 813–28.
Haffajee, R.L. (2006) 'Prosecuting crimes of rape and sexual violence at the ICTR: the application of joint criminal enterprise theory', *Harvard Journal of Law and Gender*, 29: 201–21.
Human Rights Watch (1996) *Shattered Lives: sexual violence during the Rwandan genocide and its aftermath*, New York: Human Rights Watch.
—— (2008) 'Law and reality', report, 24 July 2008. Online. Available at: <http://www.hrw.org/en/node/62097/section/1> (accessed 20 July 2009).
—— (2009) 'Letter to the Prosecutor of the International Criminal Tribunal for Rwanda regarding the Prosecution of RPF Crimes', Letter: 1 June 2009. Online. Available at: <http://www.hrw.org/node/83536> (accessed 20 July 2009).
Kelsall, M.S. and Stepakoff, S. (2007) ' "When we wanted to talk about rape": silencing sexual violence at the Special Court for Sierra Leone', *International Journal of Transitional Justice*, 1: 355–74.
Koskenniemi, M. (2002) 'Between impunity and show trials', *Max Planck Yearbook of United Nations Law*, 6: 1–35.
Lattimer, M. and Sands, P. (2003) 'Introduction', in M. Lattimer and P. Sands (eds) *Justice for Crimes against Humanity*, Oxford: Hart Publishing.
Leebaw, B.A. (2008) 'The irreconcilable goals of transitional justice', *Human Rights Quarterly*, 30: 95–118.
Maogoto, J.N. (2004) 'The International Criminal Tribunal for Rwanda: a paper umbrella in the rain? Initial pitfalls and brighter prospects', *Nordic Journal of International Law*, 73: 187–221.
Mendeloff, D. (2009) 'Trauma and vengeance: assessing the psychological and emotional effects of post-conflict justice', *Human Rights Quarterly*, 31: 592–623.
Mertus, J. (2004) 'The impact of international trials for wartime rape on women's agency', *International Feminist Journal of Politics*, 6: 110–28.
Minow, M. (1998) *Between Vengeance and Forgiveness*, Boston: Beacon Press.
Ni Aolain, F. and Rooney, E. (2007) 'Underenforcement and intersectionality: gendered aspects of transition for women', *International Journal of Transitional Justice*, 1: 338–54.
Nikolic-Ristanovic, V. (2005) 'Sexual violence, international law and restorative justice', in D. Buss and A. Manji (eds) *International Law: modern feminist approaches*, Oxford: Hart Publishing.
Nowrojee, B. (2005) 'Your justice is too slow: will the ICTR fail Rwanda's rape victims?', Occasional Paper 10, United Nations Research Institute for Social Development, New York: United Nations.
Orentlicher, D. (1991) 'Settling accounts: the duty to prosecute human rights violations of a prior regime', *Yale Law Journal*, 100: 2537–615.
Pottier, J. (2002) *Re-Imagining Rwanda: conflict, survival and disinformation in the late twentieth century*, Cambridge: Cambridge University Press.
Ross, F.C. (2003) *Bearing Witness: women and the Truth and Reconciliation Commission in South Africa*, London: Pluto Press.

Sivakumaran, S. (2007) 'Sexual violence against men in armed conflict', *European Journal of International Law*, 18: 253–76.
Smart, C. (1986) 'Feminism and law: some problems of analysis and strategy', *International Journal of the Sociology of Law*, 14(2): 109–23 [Reprinted in Smart, C. (1995) *Law, Crime and Sexuality: essays in feminism*, London: Sage Publications].
Todorov, T. (2004) 'The limitations of justice', *Journal of International Criminal Justice*, 2: 711–15.
Van Schaack, B. (2009) 'Obstacles on the road to gender justice: The International Criminal Tribunal for Rwanda as object lesson', *American University Journal of Gender, Social Policy and the Law*, forthcoming.

Chapter 5

# The force of shame

*Karen Engle and Annelies Lottmann*[1]

In 1998, the International Criminal Tribunal for Rwanda (ICTR) convicted Jean-Paul Akayesu of genocide and crimes against humanity (*Prosecutor v Akayesu* (ICTR-96-4-T, Judgment 2 September 1998)). The decision was considered landmark for many reasons, including that it connected acts of rape to genocide, even without finding that Akayesu himself committed the rapes. Patricia Viseur-Sellers, former prosecutor and Legal Advisor for Gender at the International Criminal Tribunal for the Former Yugoslavia (ICTY) and a legal advisor to the ICTR trial team for *Akayesu*, calls *Akayesu*'s jurisprudence, particularly with regard to sex-based crimes, 'stunning' (2008: 42).

Nevertheless, many contend, including Viseur-Sellers, that the ICTR has not lived up to the promise suggested by *Akayesu*. Indeed, it might be fair to say that *Akayesu* has had more impact outside of the ICTR – at least in terms of the drafting of statutes, rules of evidence and doctrinal linking of rape to genocide – than it has had within the Tribunal itself. Among other things, the ICTR has been criticized for its relatively few successful convictions for rape, given that rape and sexual violence were endemic during the Rwandan genocide (Bianchi 2008; Buss 2009; Nowrojee 2005a; see, further, Buss in this collection).

Although the low number of convictions has been attributed to a number of different factors, we focus this chapter on the internal analyses of rape prosecutions at the Tribunal, which have frequently suggested that the reluctance of victims to testify about their own rapes has been a serious hindrance to effective investigation, trial testimony, and, ultimately, conviction (Bianchi 2008; ICTR Newsletter 2005). Shame and the stigma that sometimes accompanies it are often seen as the culprit of that reluctance.

The terms 'shame' and 'stigma' have both been widely theorized, and there is much disagreement about their meaning. In this chapter, rather than propose our own definition, we consider the terms in the ways that they are used by many feminists, humanitarians, prosecutors and the ICTR itself in discussing the harm of rape. In general, though, we believe that the Oxford English Dictionary (OED) definition of shame covers many of the ways in which we find it used. The first definition it offers describes shame as '[t]he painful emotion arising from the consciousness of something dishonouring, ridiculous, or indecorous in one's own conduct or circumstances (or in those of others whose honour or disgrace one regards as one's own), or of being in a situation which offends one's sense of modesty or decency' (OED 1989). Thus, individuals and groups can experience shame on behalf of themselves as well as of others. We agree with Silvan Tomkins, the founder of affect theory in psychology in the early 1960s, that shame is 'a theoretical construct, rather than an entity unambiguously defined by the word "shame" ' (1987: 134). The OED definition suggests that the same situation – rape, for example – might cause shame for different people for different reasons.

The shame of rape is often seen as accompanied by stigma. Raped women in war are considered stigmatized, or marked, by the known fact of the rape. In this sense, the term 'stigma' does not generally refer to the bodily signs for which the term was originally coined, but, as sociologist Erving Goffman uses it, 'to an attribute that is deeply discrediting' (at least, if known, and vis-à-vis those who do not possess it) (1963: 3–4). The literature we examine here assumes that women who are known to have been raped would likely be ostracized by their families and their communities, and that the families would also be discredited by the communities. Moreover, for rape to be considered to be an effective weapon in war, the communities – even entire ethnic groups – must be thought to be both stigmatized and shamed by the rapes.

Shame thus functions as both a noun and a verb here. Raped women and their families, and sometimes their communities, are seen to be shamed. Not only the perpetrators, but the groups to which both the perpetrator and victim belong, participate in the shaming, albeit at different levels and in different ways.

While, or perhaps because, shame and stigma are seen as inevitable, they are often treated as technocratic problems. Prosecutors and investigators, as well as policymakers and feminists who continually put pressure on them to increase the Tribunal's number of convictions for rape, have expressed concern that shame inhibits individual victims' ability or willingness to testify about the rape and that making the rape public marks the victims in stigmatizing ways. They have thus devised a number of responses to *manage* shame, most of which aim to coax witnesses to tell their stories of sexual violence to investigators and to testify at trial.

At the same time that shame constitutes a technical problem for prosecutors, it also functions as a doctrinal link between rape and genocide. At least in the ICTR's legal analysis that rape constitutes genocide, both individual and communal shame resulting from rape constitute a significant part of the link to genocide (*Akayesu* 1998: para. 731). Paradoxically, then, a feminist victory in diminishing the force of shame might also reduce rape's efficacy as a tool of war, as well as its value as evidence of genocide.

In this chapter, we suggest that shame might not be an inevitable result of wartime rape, and encourage feminists and humanitarians not to assume that women who have been raped in wartime are necessarily stigmatized by their families and communities or that they are emotionally destroyed. By seeing rape as a 'fate worse than death', in part because of the shame they assume it brings, feminists and humanitarians risk exacerbating the very harm that they hope to relieve.

We begin the chapter by demonstrating the significant roles that assumptions about shame play both doctrinally and procedurally in the context of the ICTR. While not denying that many rape victims experience shame and are stigmatized on a variety of levels, we hope to imagine alternative responses to wartime rape that do not assume the inevitability of shame. We do so by considering three alternative strategies for combating the necessary association of stigma and shame with rape, which we borrow largely from areas outside of criminal law.

## THE FUNCTIONS OF SHAME

As noted above, shame serves two different, and often competing, functions with regard to rape prosecutions in the ICTR. On one hand, shame is essential to the doctrine tying rape to genocide. On the other, it is viewed as an obstacle to prosecutions. In this section, we will explore each in turn.

### Doctrinal function

In the context of war, shame is often seen as the goal of rape and other forms of sexual violence. Its incidence is attributed to a desire on the part of the perpetrators to bring shame to individual victims and their communities. When considering rape as an instrument of genocide, individual harm is not necessarily the focus, given that the rape must be found to be part of a systematic or widespread attack on an ethnic group (*Akayesu* 1998: para. 731). Thus, intent to cause physical or even emotional harm to an individual woman would not, in and of itself, qualify as genocide. Rather, a finding of rape as genocide is dependent upon group harm, which is often located in communal shame and stigmatization.

Binaifer Nowrojee has described this understanding of intended communal shame in a report on Rwanda:

> The humiliation, pain and terror inflicted by the rapist is meant to degrade not just the individual woman but also to strip the humanity from the larger group of which she is a part. The rape of one person is translated into an assault upon the community through the emphasis placed in every culture on women's sexual virtue: the shame of the rape humiliates the family and all those associated with the survivor . . .
> 
> (Nowrojee 1996: 2)

Nowrojee's assessment, not limited to Rwanda here, is echoed in the *Akayesu* decision; it assumes a collective motivation against a woman because of the 'larger group' to which she belongs.[2]

Doris Buss has identified 'three aspects of rapes [in the *Akayesu* judgment] that made them distinctive acts committed with the intent to destroy the Tutsi community' (Buss 2007: 8). One of the three is physical in nature – the intent to inflict acute suffering on Tutsi women before they were killed. But the other two are emotional harms related to shame: public humiliation and an effort to destroy the 'will to live' of the Tutsi community. The Trial Chamber concluded that sexual violence was 'a step in the process of destruction of the Tutsi group – destruction of the spirit, the will to live, and of life itself' (*Akayesu* 1998: paras. 731–2).

The Trial Chamber cited specific instances of acts by the Interahamwe, the semi-professional militias who carried out much of the genocide, against Tutsi women, which were intended to humiliate them, asserting that 'these rapes resulted in physical and psychological destruction of Tutsi women, their families, and their communities . . . and to the destruction of the Tutsi group as a whole' (para. 731). Part of the psychological harm the Chamber attributes to some women who were raped comes from their subjection to the 'worst public humiliation' (para. 731). Humiliation, of course, is often used as a synonym for shame. Thus, rape's nexus to communal shame was an essential bridge connecting rape and genocide.

The *Akayesu* decision has been considered progressive by many feminists, but there is an irony here. Feminists have long criticized justifications for criminalizing rape based on protecting men's or women's honour. The recent wave of feminist treatment of rape as a serious violation of international humanitarian law has thereby, as Janet Halley has shown in detail, deliberately avoided reference to its effect on a woman's 'honour' (2008: 57). Yet, this doctrinal understanding of rape as destructive because of its power to destroy communities, largely through shame, perpetuates many of the same social constructs that supported the concept of honour. Indeed, the understanding resonates with the OED's third definition of shame, which includes 'disgrace, ignominy, loss of esteem or reputation' and offers as a specific example of disgrace the '[v]iolation of a woman's honour, loss of chastity' (OED 1989).

Moreover, this view of the harm of rape implicates the gender prejudices of the affected group and even its agency in its own persecution. In this case, Tutsi biases against women are presumed to lead them to shame and stigmatize individual women who have been raped. In doing so, they participate in raising the harm to a genocidal level.

## Procedural function

At the same time that communal shame is crucial to the equation of rape and genocide for prosecutors, individual shame (whether or not resulting directly from communal shame) is seen as a significant obstacle to prosecution and justice. Because shame is seen to impede the gathering and demonstration of evidence necessary to tie the accused to acts of sexual violence, the shame of rape victims, along with their fear of stigmatization, is often called upon by prosecutors, as well as outside observers, to explain the low rate of indictment and conviction for sexual crimes at the ICTR. In particular, stigma and shame are considered responsible for the reluctance of female victims to report rape and/or to testify about it.

ICTR prosecutor Alex Obote-Odora, for example, has described the difficulty of investigation, or even gaining an accurate count of the number of rape survivors: 'Sex-based crimes are not easily identified ... because these crimes inflict physical and psychological wounds, which women can conceal, avoiding further emotional anguish, ostracization, and retaliation from perpetrators who may live nearby' (2005: 139). This description invokes the stigma associated with rape, suggesting the incentive for women who have been raped either to 'pass' or 'cover', in Goffman's terms (1963: 91–104). It is invoked in part to limit the accountability of ICTR investigators for the failures to prosecute rape; if the women will not talk to them, investigators cannot do their job.

The *Akayesu* Trial Chamber judgment accepts that shame affects the willingness of those who have been raped to talk about the incident, thereby impeding investigation. It describes its reasons for amending the indictment halfway through trial to include a charge for rape by explaining that: '[t]he Prosecution stated that evidence previously available was not sufficient to link the Accused to acts of sexual violence and acknowledged that factors to explain this lack of evidence might include the shame that accompanies acts of sexual violence as well as insensitivity in the investigation of sexual violence' (*Akayesu* 1998: para. 417).

Even while she is wary of excusing investigators and prosecutors for failing to get women to talk to them about sexual violence, Binaifer Nowrojee echoes this part of the *Akayesu* decision, as well as Obote-Odora's identification of the problem of stigma. In doing so, she specifically discusses Rwanda, but generalizes from it as well: '[I]in Rwanda, as throughout the world, there is profound shame and stigma associated with rape. In Rwanda, this shame is compounded by a sense of guilt for having survived' (Nowrojee 1996: 19).

Many of the proposals for increasing the number of convictions for sexual violence in the ICTR respond to the concerns about shame and stigma through technical suggestions largely aimed at soliciting witness statements about sexual violence. Suggestions include training of investigators and witnesses, the addition of more female investigators and better translation work (Bianchi 2008: 5; Nowrojee 1996: 16). The idea is that women *can* be encouraged to talk under the right circumstances.

Many commentators assume, however, that once solicited, testimony about rape and the adversarial system in which the testimony takes place causes even more trauma and harm. Linda Bianchi of the ICTR's Sexual Violence Committee has noted, for example, that '[d]ue to the extreme sensitivity of eliciting and obtaining this type of evidence, and the detrimental impact and re-traumatization providing such evidence often has on a victim, thought should be had as to alternative methods by which to bring evidence of sexual violence into the courtroom' (2008: 6). Elsie Effange-Mbella, the former gender adviser at the ICTR, has further contended that judicial proceedings regarding rape and sexual assault 'often have a devastating and long lasting impact on the victim and witness'. She suggests that '[t]he elements of stigmatization by the family and community, including fear of reprisals upon testifying, are almost permanently present' (2006: 10).

Some argue that ensuring that victims have access to psychological counsellors after testifying will help manage the harm. For others, the testimony itself is mitigating. Nowrojee, for example, sees the testimony as therapeutic: 'For rape victims, breaking the silence that surrounds sexual violence is all the more important because of the particular stigma and shame that attaches to rape' (2005b: 104). Of course, both assessments might be correct. For *some* victims, testifying is traumatic, while for others it is healing; for some, it is likely both. But if shame is an internal, psychological affect resulting, at least in part, from structurally biased external judgment, individual healing – either through testimony or after the fact – does little to respond to the structural harm.

## ATTACKING SHAME AND STIGMA

### International criminal justice and the redistribution of shame

Why put women through the ordeal of testifying if there is a significant risk that at least some of them will be more harmed by the process and that, with or without psychological healing, their lives will be endangered when they return home? The response is almost certainly embedded in a theory of criminal justice by which criminal liability for rape and sexual violence reinforces societal acknowledgment of the harm by punishing the perpetrator. We are willing to risk the harm to individuals for the sake of justice.

For some, criminal justice is a means for attacking the shame itself. Nowrojee, for example, insists that criminal liability (not just testimony) is ultimately therapeutic for victims: '[T]he importance of holding perpetrators responsible for their actions cannot be underestimated as an aspect of healing the victims of, and witnesses to, major atrocity' (2005b: 104). Obote-Odora takes the argument further, seeing the ICTR as providing a way to put the shame and stigma on the perpetrator:

> The victims of these atrocious crimes feel ignored and invisible. If these crimes are not severely punished the message the international legal community sends is that impunity and grave injustice will be tolerated . . . The perpetrator should bear the shame and stigma that society now attributes to the victim.
>
> (2005: 157)

The ICTR thus offers to rape victims the possibility that the burden of shame and stigma that they now carry may, upon conviction, shift to the masterminds of the genocide. The criminal justice system engages in its own sort of shaming, displacing it from the victim onto those who caused the harm.

In this way, international criminal law functions similarly to the 'naming and shaming' process that human rights NGOs have been involved with for several decades. As Kenneth Roth, director of Human Rights Watch, writes of his own organization: '[T]he core of our methodology is our ability to investigate, expose, and shame. We are at our most effective when we can hold governmental (or, in some cases, nongovernmental) conduct up to a disapproving public' (2004: 67). Obote-Odora's perspective also seems aligned with a recent report by the United Nations, entitled 'The Shame of War'. The report calls for the waging of 'a different war, one against violence against women and girls and against the culture of impunity that protects the perpetuators and their accomplices' (UNOCHA 2007: introduction). Again, at least part of this war is to be waged in the criminal justice system, with the understanding that attribution of legal guilt and its attendant shame might mitigate, if not erase, the harm of shame to the victims.

While Obote-Odora and the UN Report suggest the possibility of redistributing shame – from individual victims and their communities to the perpetrators themselves – they do so by reinforcing the inevitability of shame as a response of individual rape victims and of the communities to which they belong. They also, of course, assume that those convicted of rape will experience shame and that the shame will be productive. Such an acceptance of the positive process of shaming, particularly through courtroom (as opposed to certain types of restorative) justice, fails to attend to arguments that 'shame can be a destructive emotion because it can lead one to attack others, attack self, avoid, or withdraw' and even 'promote crime' (Braithwaite 2002: 79).

In the remainder of this chapter, we would like to return to the idea of reimaging rape, and the harm of rape, by turning to mechanisms outside of international criminal law. In particular, we will look to other legal and non-legal mechanisms that, explicitly or not, attack shame and stigma: economic reparations in the context of Sierra Leone; various grassroots efforts to respond to stigma and shame associated with HIV/AIDS and its treatment; and the consideration of raped women as political actors or even combatants.

## Justice and economic (re)distribution

A number of scholars have begun to criticize transitional justice today for its focus on individual accountability, which neglects and obscures systemic responsibility and economic justice (Mamdani 2001; Keenan and Nesiah 2004; Miller 2008). One way in which issues of economic justice have been addressed is through the consideration of economic reparations, generally for individual victims, including families of those victims who have been killed. We would like, for the moment, to use the idea of reparations to think about a remedy that might replace or augment a criminal justice focus. How might a consideration of reparations for victims of sexual violence affect the substantive and procedural harms of shame noted above? To work through these questions, we turn to Sierra Leone and the responses provided by the Truth and Reconciliation Commission (TRC) and the Special Court to the rape and sexual violence that took place during the more than decade-long civil war in that country.

Amnesty International reports that, even though nearly one-third of the female population in Sierra Leone is thought to have been subjected to crimes of sexual violence, women still experienced stigma and shame from that violence. As a result, some victims were reticent to participate in the TRC and in the Disarmament, Demobilization and Reintegration process, and to access the social and health services made available to them (Amnesty International 2007). Nevertheless, women turned out in large numbers to testify, particularly before the Truth and Reconciliation Commission. Some testified anonymously and behind the protection of a screen, while others chose to testify openly (Hayner 2004).

One reads little about any difficulties in encouraging women in Sierra Leone to testify; in fact, indications are that, at least in one case before the Special Court, women wanted to have the opportunity to give more detail and testimony about sexual violence than the court would permit. In an article detailing that case, Kelsall and Stepakoff, the latter of whom was a psychologist for the Special Court, conclude that six of seven women who took the stand 'expressed considerable psychological distress regarding the silencing' (Kelsall and Stepakoff 2007: 372). They were obviously not alone in their desire to tell their stories. One female aid worker in Sierra Leone explained: 'We want to break the silence. We want to say what happened to us. We want to understand why it happened. We need somebody to acknowledge that these things happened to us, to reclaim our dignity, so that this doesn't happen again' (Ben-Ari and Harsch 2005: 1).

This account seems quite different from that given about the ICTR. What might explain the difference? Although there has been, to our knowledge, no study examining this question, the TRC was praised, at least early on, for holding special hearings solely for women to testify about rape and sexual violence (Nowrojee 2005b). Moreover, some have noted that the statute of the Special Court (a joint effort by the UN and the state) explicitly permitted the prosecution of 'rape, sexual slavery, enforced prostitution, forced pregnancy and any other form of sexual violence', thereby deliberately extending the statute's explicit reach in this area beyond that of the ICTR or ICTY (Kelsall and Stepakoff 2007; see also Cole in this collection). Finally, the Special Court has two full-time investigators working solely on gender crimes (Jefferson 2004: 342), and all investigators have received sensitivity training on gender issues.

Of course, each conflict and context in which wartime rape occurs is different. In Sierra Leone, women might have wanted to testify to ensure their victim, as opposed to perpetrator, status. Rape had occurred on all sides of the conflict, and lack of consent was not always easy to infer. Indeed, there were many women who had become 'bush wives' during the war – forcibly taken, but then in some cases apparently choosing to remain and even support the war efforts of the groups they were with. Dyan Mazurana and Khristopher Carlson summed up this paradoxical experience in their 2004 paper on women's participation in the Sierra Leone disarmament process, stating that 'the experience of women and girls in the fighting forces was complex. They were captives and dependents, but they were also involved in the planning and execution of the war' (2004: 2). Given this context, it is not hard to imagine that, for at least some women, testifying might have been a way to avoid a presumption of consensual sexual (and military) activity that could have constituted something akin to treachery.[3]

We want to suggest that something else might also have been at play. Vasuki Nesiah, former director of the gender project at the International Center for Transitional Justice, points out that the victims in Sierra Leone saw the possibility for reparations for the harm to which they testified. Women in this war-torn country with little means of survival were told that they might receive monetary compensation if they were found to be a victim. Amnesty International has since reported that those reparations have not been realized,[4] but it appears that the possibility of reparations might have nevertheless influenced women's decision to testify. Discussing the TRC, the Report quotes a woman from Makeni:

> Well they did tell us that we would not benefit directly from participating but some help would come later. It has been such a [sic] long time since, almost three years, and we haven't seen anything. We are truly discouraged now because the hope that was created then is now gone.
> (Amnesty International 2007: 22)

The final report of the TRC outlines the close connection it sees between reparations and truth. The Report acknowledges that victims of all types of violence must bear the brunt of the responsibility for the reconciliation process and describes the way to do this through telling the story, and thus making a public, communal documentation of the events that transpired, and by providing reparations to assist survivors on their road to recovery. According to the report, '[i]f the Commission had not intended to pursue a reparations policy for victims, truth-telling without reparation could conceivably be perceived by the victims to be an incomplete process in which they have revealed their pain and suffering without any mechanism being put in place to deal with the consequences of that pain' (Sierra Leone TRC 2004: para. 33).[5]

Without choosing one causal explanation for women's decisions to testify about rape in Sierra Leone, we hope the above possibilities demonstrate that the silencing force of shame and stigma is not absolute or universal. We also hope to elicit greater attention to the role that economic distribution at both the local and global levels play in internal conflict and in post-conflict attempts at resolution. If the economic reparations explanation fits for even some of those who testified, it suggests that shame and stigma that might accompany testimony could at least be partially mitigated by the promise of economic compensation.

We do not want to suggest that reparations, particularly the way that we normally conceive of them, are the proper response either to the harm of rape or the shame and stigma that may accompany it. Indeed, as Zinaida Miller contends, '[b]y definition ... reparations do not redistribute either wealth or power on a scale that would dramatically alter the balance of power in the country during or after transition' (2008: 284).

We believe that the examples above call for putting sexual violence in a larger context that, both inside and outside the courtroom, attends to issues of economic distribution. A recent study by Physicians for Human Rights (PHR) on the situation of women in Darfuri refugee camps illustrates both the need for and some positive consequences of placing sexual violence in such a broader context (PHR 2009).

Though the focus of the PHR's study was meant to be sexual violence, researchers believed that very few women would come to speak with them about this topic because of 'social stigma and humiliation and the risk of re-traumatization' (PHR 2009: 13). To provide women with a more ambiguous and thus secure situation to reveal information about sexual violence, interviewers placed a broad invitation for women in the camps to speak with them about their 'health and lives in the camps'. While the interviewers included questions about sexual violence, they were not made to appear the central concern of the interviews (2009: 12–13).

Of the 88 women interviewed (anonymously, in private areas and by female investigators accompanied by female translators), 32 reported at least one incidence of sexual violence. But the researchers learned crucial, additional information about women's concerns. A majority of the women interviewed reported health and safety concerns other than sexual violence, particularly their need for more and better quality food and their profound desire to return home to their farms in Darfur (2009: 21). The women held these other issues at least equal to the importance of sexual violence. The variety of primary concerns expressed by the women led the PHR to recommend a combination of tactics to be used in the camps (providing safer access to firewood, better food security and rations, more access to and encouragement to use psychological and social services within the camps) and suggestions for the future (returning home in peace, economic reparations, judicial recourse for prosecution of perpetrators) (2009: 47).

## Anti-stigmatization efforts of HIV/AIDS activists

HIV/AIDS health workers note that the stigma associated with the condition often stems from a fear, not of actual contraction of the virus, but 'a fear of "symbolic contagion", a threat to both the health and well-being of individuals and to the well-being and legitimacy of the status quo' (Campbell et al. 2005: 1). Similar to the communal shame of rape, HIV-positive people, particularly in small communities, report widespread stigmatization and attendant feelings of shame. And, like those who work with women who have suffered sexual violence, aid workers and researchers working with HIV and

AIDS acknowledge up front that shame and stigma both accompany and fuel the spread of HIV/AIDS, albeit in different ways from rape (International Center for Research on Women 2002).

Rather than simply attempting to manage the stigma and shame at an individual level, advocacy and activism around HIV/AIDS have often sought to change community attitudes in order to address both the causes and effects of shame and stigma. We offer two examples. First, since 2003, HIV-positive women in Botswana have competed in a very public 'Miss HIV Stigma Free' competition (Philips 2005). Run like a traditional beauty pageant, the competition's mission is to combat the prejudices and stereotypes against individuals, particularly women, with HIV. The winner of the competition receives a scholarship and a monthly stipend, and spends a year travelling across the country and the continent working on projects to break down fear and prejudice.

In Thailand, monks and nuns have undertaken a multi-point initiative to minister to HIV/AIDS-positive individuals (New Tactics in Human Rights 2003, UNICEF 2002). They interact with HIV-positive people as normal members of the community – eating food offerings prepared by them and spending time with them in close quarters. The monks view the community stigma of HIV/AIDS sufferers as an opportunity to teach tolerance and community support. As one monk said about the project, 'the problem was on both sides – people who had HIV/AIDS were secretive, while the community would not accept them . . . [s]o we set out to teach people about the importance of solidarity, helping others – not only in relation to HIV/AIDS but as a whole' (Williams 2001: 1). In this way, the monks provide an example to the entire community, demystifying HIV and including HIV-positive individuals in daily life and ritual.

Although both of these examples offer the possibility of responding to individual feelings of shame, their focus is on combating negative community perceptions and reactions. Could we imagine similar responses to rape? What if religious or community leaders engaged in everyday life with women who had suffered sexual violence? Could we/would we want to imagine a Miss Rape Stigma Free beauty pageant? Would there be resonance for rape victims of the aims of the 2003 winner of Miss HIV Stigma Free who said she hoped the publicity gained from winning the competition would encourage people to respect victims: 'I'm going around the country to talk to people to say that (being) an HIV positive person does not mean you have done something wrong. You are still who you are' (BBC News 2003).

## Rape victims as political actors and combatants

In David Kennedy's 1985 account of a human rights delegation to Uruguay in which he participated, he self-critically and consciously revisits the role that the 'manipulat[ion] of gender distinction' played in the delegation's 'feeling of simultaneous engagement and distance' (1985: 1405). After visiting female political prisoners who described some of the torture they had experienced,

Kennedy discusses how gender differentiation allowed the three-member, all-male delegation to exploit the spatial and temporal distance between the female prisoners and the government and military members they met with in the capital:

> In prison we had been with the women, the victims, and we were returning to the men, the victimizers, in Montevideo. This spatial difference was partly sustained by contrasting the sacred woman with the profane man and partly by contrasting the female victim with the male avenger.
>
> (1985: 1404)

Although, as Kennedy notes, the delegation had made 'elaborate efforts to connect with [Ana, one of the female prisoners] as a person, a politico sympatico [sic]', those efforts were lost or forgotten not just when meeting with the 'avengers', but with male political prisoners as well. Rather, the delegation began to 'reimagine Ana's torture as an abomination', making it 'possible to relate more objectively to [a male political prisoner] Ramon's tales. Ramon seemed subjugated, not violated. His pain was instrumental, his body political. Ana had been trespassed upon, Ramon punished' (1985: 1404).

Neither the female nor male victims Kennedy interviewed expressed that they had been subjected to sexual violence.[6] Nevertheless, the gender distinctions marked both short- and long-term perceptions of the harm. Ramon was a political activist, a fighter. He had been tortured, but he had 'used his body, deployed it, spent it'. In contrast, Ana's pain seemed 'extra, gratuitous, imposed' (1985: 1401). She would not, it seems, be able to don her battle marks in the same way as Ramon who, not coincidentally, was her boyfriend.

In cases of sexual violence against women, we would argue, the distinction is even more pronounced. Those feminists, humanitarians and prosecutors who blame communities and cultures (and sometimes each other) for the shame and stigmatization of rape victims sometimes make it so. By maintaining that sexual violence is uniquely, especially and universally harmful to women and to their communities, they reinforce the gender biases within the communities. They also exploit those biases through the doctrinal connection of rape to genocide. Meanwhile, whether in their communities or in front of tribunals, women are given little room to manoeuvre in terms of claiming their political identity. Both women who are raped and those who are not continue to bear the costs.

What would it mean for women to be recognized for having 'used', 'deployed', 'spent' their bodies in war? Might recognizing women as political and even perhaps military actors in this way constitute another means for attacking shame?

## CONCLUSION

This chapter has meant to show the animating power of shame for many of those who have sought to prosecute rape as genocide. We have attempted both to question the inevitability of shame and stigmatization in the context of rape, and to consider ways of diminishing the harm of shame to the extent it exists. Without the harm of shame, of course, rape would lose a degree of its legal force as rape; sexual violence might not constitute genocide or even a crime against humanity. Given that the diminishment of shame and stigma associated with rape would presumably weaken it as a tool of war, that is a risk we are willing to take. We also hope that a decrease in shame and stigma – and in the assumption of it – would facilitate a broader understanding of women's (and men's) role in war and consider the economic, social and political contexts in which both war and attempts at post-conflict justice occur.

## Notes

1 We are extremely grateful to Clare McGlynn for organizing the Rethinking Rape Law conference and to her and Vanessa Munro for their insightful editing of this piece. We have also benefitted from Annelies Lottmann's internship at the ICTR, feedback at a variety of conferences and comments from a number of individuals. Special thanks to Doris Buss, Neville Hoad, Vasuki Nesiah and Patricia Viseur-Sellers for their useful conversations about this work.
2 Nowrojee contends and complains that communal shame often takes precedence over individual shame after the rape. She argues, for example, that '[i]n the aftermath of such abuse, the harm done to the individual woman is often obscured or even compounded by the perceived harm to the community' (Nowrojee 1996: 2).
3 After the Second World War, for example, French women accused of engaging in sexual activity with German soldiers during the war were publicly shamed by having their heads shaved and being forced to walk naked through the streets. Engle uses this incident to offer a possible explanation for the ICTY's jurisprudence that essentially defines as nonconsensual all sexual relations between Bosnian Muslim women and Serbian men in conflict regions during the war in Bosnia (Engle 2005: 811 and n. 194).
4 At the time of writing, some of the promised reparations are being provided by a $3 million dollar grant from the UN Peacebuilding Fund plus about $250,000 from the government of Sierra Leone, to be distributed through Sierra Leone's NACSA (National Commission for Social Action) and some are on the verge of finally being meted out. On the list of reparations to be provided are housing (at $6,500 per unit), skills training, health care, education and agricultural assistance, as well as symbolic activities such as reburials, memorials and remembrance ceremonies (IRIN 2009).
5 The report continues: 'Similarly, reparations without truth-telling could be perceived by the beneficiaries as an attempt to buy their silence. Restorative justice requires not only truth telling but reparations which will strengthen the reconciliation process' (Sierra Leone Truth and Reconciliation Commission, 2004, para. 33).
6 While the men described having had electrodes attached to their genitalia, they did not appear to consider that torture to be 'sexual' (Kennedy 1985).

## Bibliography

Amnesty International (2007) *Sierra Leone: Getting Reparations Right for Survivors of Sexual Violence*, Amnesty International Report.

BBC News (2003) 'Beauty pageant battles AIDS stigma', *BBC News Health Report*. Online. Available at: <http://news.bbc.co.uk/2/hi/health/3087366.stm> (accessed 8 June 2009).

Ben-Ari, N. and Harsch, E. (2005) 'Sexual violence: an "invisible" war crime', *Africa Renewal*, 18. Online. Available at: <http://www.un.org/ecosocdev/geninfo/afrec/vol18no4/184sierraleone.htm> (accessed 7 June 2009).

Bianchi, L. (2008) 'The investigation and presentation of evidence relating to sexual violence', *Roundtable on Cooperation Between the International Criminal Tribunals and Prosecuting Authorities*. Online. Available at: <http://www.ictr.org/ENGLISH/international_cooperation/papers_presented/> (Link to this paper under 'Panel 5') (accessed 7 June 2009).

Braithwaite, J. (2002) *Restorative Justice & Responsive Regulation*, New York: Oxford University Press.

Buss, D. (2007) 'The Rwanda Tribunal and the making of ethnic rape', presented at *Sexual abuse and the exploitation of women in violent conflict*, Amsterdam.

—— (2009) 'Rethinking rape as a weapon of war', *Feminist Legal Studies*, 17(2): 145–63.

Campbell, C., Foulis, C., Maimane, S., and Sibiya, Z. (2005) ' "I have an evil child at my house": stigma and HIV/AIDS management in a South African community', *American Journal of Public Health*, 95: 808–15. Online. Available at: <http://www.ajph.org/cgi/reprint/95/5/808> (accessed 8 June 2009).

Carlson, K. and Mazurana, D. (2004) *From Combat to Community: women and girls of Sierra Leone*, Hunt Alternatives Fund series on Women Waging Peace, 2–4. Online. Available at: <http://www.smallarmssurvey.org/files/portal/spotlight/disarmament/disarm_pdf/2004_Mazurana_Carlson.pdf > (accessed 8 June 2009).

Effange-Mbella, E. (2006) 'On support measures to victims and witnesses summoned to appear before the tribunal', *ICTR Conference on Challenging Impunity*, November 7–9 2006. Online. Available at: <http://www.ictr.org/ENGLISH/challenging_impunity/support_measures.pdf> (accessed 8 June 2009).

Engle, K. (2005) 'Feminism and its (dis)contents: criminalizing wartime rape in Bosnia and Herzegovina', *American Journal of International Law*, 99: 778–816.

Goffman, E. (1963) *Stigma: notes on the management of spoiled identity*, Englewood Cliffs: Prentice-Hall.

Halley, J. (2008) 'Rape at Rome: feminist interventions in the criminalization of sex-related violence in positive international criminal law', *Michigan Journal of International Law*, 30: 1–123.

Hayner, P. (2004) 'The Sierra Leone Truth and Reconciliation Commission: reviewing the first year', *Case Studies Series*, International Center for Transitional Justice. Online. Available at: <http://www.ictj.org/images/content/1/0/100.pdf> (accessed 8 June 2009).

ICTR Newsletter (April 2005) *ICTR Attendance at Boston Conference: The ICTR Ten Years After*, 7. Online. Available at: <http://www.ictr.org/ENGLISH/newsletter/april05/april05.pdf> (accessed 8 June 2009).

Integrated Regional Information Networks (IRIN) (2009) 'Sierra Leone: lack of aid funds for amputees, rape survivors, war widows', *UNHCR Refworld*. Online.

Available at: <http://www.unhcr.org/refworld/publisher,IRIN,SLE,49a660d01a, 0.html> (accessed 8 June 2009).

International Center for Research on Women (2002) *Addressing HIV-Related Stigma and Resulting Discrimination in Africa*, ICRW Information Bulletin, Washington DC. Online. Available at: <http://www.icrw.org/docs/Stigma_Africa_InfoBulletin_302.pdf> (accessed 8 June 2009).

Jefferson, L.S.R. (2004) 'In war as in peace: sexual violence and women's status', *World Report: human rights and armed conflict*, Human Rights Watch, 325–48.

Keenan, A. and Nesiah, V. (2004) 'Human rights and sacred cows: framing violence, disappearing struggles', in N. Gordon (ed.) *From the Margins of Globalization: critical perspectives on human rights*, Lanham, MD: Lexington Books, 261–96.

Kelsall, M. and Stepakoff, S. (2007) ' "When we wanted to talk about rape": silencing sexual violence at the Special Court for Sierra Leone', *International Journal of Transitional Justice*, 1: 355–74.

Kennedy, D. (1985) 'Spring break', *Texas Law Review*, 63: 1378–424.

Mamdani, M. (2001) 'Amnesty or impunity? A preliminary critique of the report of the Truth and Reconciliation Commission of South Africa (TRC)', *diacritics*, 32: 33–59.

Miller, Z. (2008) 'Effects of invisibility: in search of the "economic" in transitional justice', *International Journal of Transitional Justice*, 2: 266–91.

New Tactics in Human Rights (2003) 'Using traditional leaders to combat ignorance and bring communities together', *New Tactics Report*. Online. Available at: <http://www.newtactics.org/en/tactics/using-traditional-leaders-combat-ignorance-and-bring-communities-together> (accessed 9 July 2009).

Nowrojee, B. (1996) *Shattered Lives: Sexual violence during the Rwandan genocide and its aftermath*, Human Rights Watch Africa.

—— (2005a) *'Your Justice Is Too Slow': will the ICTR fail Rwanda's rape victims?* United Nations Research Institute for Social Development: Geneva.

—— (2005b) 'Making the invisible war crime visible: post-conflict justice for Sierra Leone's rape victims', *Harvard Human Rights Journal*, 18: 85–104.

Obote-Odora, A. (2005) 'Rape and sexual violence in international law: ICTR contribution', *New England Journal of International and Comparative Law*, 12: 135–59.

Oxford English Dictionary (OED) (1989) 'shame', Oxford: Oxford University Press. Online. Available at: <http://dictionary.oed.com/cgi/entry/00181778> (accessed 12 July 2009).

Philips, B. (2005) ' "I am beautiful and HIV Positive" ', *BBC News, Africa*, 3 March 2005. Online. Available at: <http://news.bbc.co.uk/2/hi/africa/4311807.stm> (accessed 9 June 2009).

Physicians for Human Rights (PHR) (2009) *Nowhere to Turn: failure to protect, support and assure justice for Darfuri Women Physicians for Human Rights*. Online. Available at: <http://physiciansforhumanrights.org/sudan/news/nowhere-to-turn.pdf> (accessed 14 June 2009).

*Prosecutor v Akayesu* (ICTR-96-4-T, Judgment 2 September 1998).

Roth, K. (2004) 'Defending economic, social and cultural rights: practical issues faced by an international human rights organization', *Human Rights Quarterly*, 26: 63–73.

Sierra Leone Truth and Reconciliation Commission (2004) *Witness to Truth*, Report of the Sierra Leone Truth and Reconciliation Commission, Vol. 1 Ch. 3, GPL Press: Ghana.

Tomkins, S. (1987) 'Shame', in D. Nathanson (ed.) *Many Faces of Shame*, New York: The Guilford Press, 133–61.
UNICEF (2002) 'The Sangha Metta monks demonstrate compassion in action in assisting orphans', *UNICEF Children and HIV and AIDS*.
United Nations Office for the Coordination of Humanitarian Affairs (UNOCHA) (2007) *The Shame of War: sexual violence against women and girls in conflict*, United Nations OCHA/IRIN.
Viseur-Sellers, P. (2008) ' "Tokyoisation" of the ICTR's Gender Jurisprudence', *Africa Legal Aid Quarterly*, June 2008: 41–6.
Williams, J. (2001) 'Thai Temples and AIDS'. Online. Available at: <http://www.buddhanet.net/sangha-metta/articles.html> (website of the Sangha Metta project).

Chapter 6

# Everyday rape
## International human rights law and violence against women in peacetime

*Alice Edwards*[1]

Much has now been written and theorized about rape in the context of war (Copelon 1995; Buss 2002; Askin 2003; Engle 2005; MacKinnon 2006). The violent conflicts in the former Yugoslavia and Rwanda in the 1990s, in which women were routinely raped, sexually assaulted, incarcerated and forcibly impregnated as part of deliberate military and political strategies to debase and humiliate them and others (read: men) from the same ethnic group, turned the tide on impunity for international war crimes against women. These forms of sexual violence have been responded to by international condemnation and outrage, albeit belatedly (for example, *Akayesu* ICTR-96-4, ITCR, 1998; *Kunarac, Kovac and Vukovic* IT-96-23 and 23/1, ICTY, 2002; *Furundzija* IT-95-17/1, ICTY, 2000; SC res. 1325 (2000) and 1820 (2008); Statute of the International Criminal Court 1998, Articles 7(1)(g), (c) and (h), and 8(1)(b)(xxii)).

Much less, by comparison, has been written in the context of international human rights law about rape of women in peacetime, or outside the so-called 'exceptional' circumstances of armed conflict. According to MacKinnon:

> When no war has been declared, and life goes on in a state of everyday hostilities, women are beaten and raped by men to whom we are close. Wives disappear from supermarket parking lots. Prostitutes float up rivers or turn up under piles of rags in abandoned buildings ... In the record of human rights violations [these acts] are overlooked entirely because the victims are women and what was done to them smells of sex.
>
> (2006: 180–81)

These 'everyday' forms of rape and other violence against women (VAW) are the focus of this chapter. According to the United Nations, women are subjected to violence on a widespread scale and on a daily basis regardless of culture, religion, class or nationality (UN The World's Women 2005). The UN Secretary-General stated in his 2006 report that '[t]he scope and extent of violence against women are a reflection of the degree and persistence of discrimination that women continue to face' (S-G Report 2006: 1). Despite this, the international legal system has struggled to conceive of various forms of VAW as human rights violations, primarily because of the theory of state responsibility for human rights abuses.

This chapter interrogates how international human rights law (IHRL) has responded to rape and other forms of VAW outside the context of armed conflict. I summarize the main feminist critiques of IHRL, before tracing the major developments that have taken place at the level of human rights law and policy. I then examine the workability of the available definitions of 'violence against women' and the 'due diligence' standard of state responsibility, the latter having been developed in order to incorporate non-state abuse under the rubric of IHRL.

## FEMINIST NARRATIVES

According to feminist theories of international law, the UN human rights system privileges the realities of men's lives and ignores or marginalizes the experiences of women (Charlesworth et al. 1991). This is particularly so in relation to VAW, which is not, for example, explicitly prohibited in any of the eight 'core' human rights treaties,[2] except specific types (for example, the Convention on the Elimination of All Forms of Discrimination Against Women 1979 (CEDAW), Article 6 on trafficking in women and enforced prostitution). According to many feminist scholars, this is because IHRL prioritizes and reflects the masculine experience; in particular by defining rights in terms of what men fear will happen to them. Men, for example, are more likely than women to be subjected to torture at the hands of public officials within state custody, which is recognized as an explicit prohibition (International Convention on Civil and Political Rights, ICCPR Article 7), including having its own treaty (UN Convention Against Torture, UNCAT). This is to be compared with the fears of women, such as being beaten and raped in the home, which have until the late 1990s been considered entirely outside the scope of international law.

Claims to gender-neutrality and objectivity in the articulation and application of these human rights norms institutionalize male power (MacKinnon 1983) and they raise questions about whether women's voices and experiences have a place in the existing system (Scales 1986: 1382). The omission of women's interests from mainstream human rights is attributed to 'male hegemony over public life and institutions' (Mahoney 1996), which in practical terms has ensured the exclusion of women from any meaningful participation in negotiating, drafting, monitoring, implementing and enforcing human rights norms (Fraser 1999).

It was not the intention, however, to exclude women from general human rights instruments. The principles of non-discrimination on the basis of sex and equality between men and women are found in all the major human rights instruments (Benninger-Budel 2008a). Nonetheless, VAW in the home has been considered to fall outside the state-based system of international law because that system is primarily concerned with inter-state relations, rather than interpersonal relations (Copelon 1994). This so-called public/private dichotomy is manifest in the theory of state responsibility for human rights abuses (Romany 1994). It is argued that this construction of two separate spheres of life – one in the public, one in the private – creates a 'hierarchy of oppressions' in which men fear oppression from the state, whereas women fear oppression by men in the private world (Olsen 1983). Many violent acts committed against women at the hands of men occur prior to or without direct state involvement (MacKinnon 1993) and legal concepts such as privacy preserve male supremacy by 'shield[ing] the place of battery, marital rape, and women's exploited labour' (MacKinnon 1987: 101).

This construction of the public/private fails, however, to acknowledge the complicity of the state and its power-brokers in reinforcing (and often benefiting from) a system that excludes and marginalizes women (Binion 1995). In fact, the state is not absent from the crimes committed against women. It has been argued that rape and other sexual violence are 'neither random nor individual' but 'defined by the distribution of power in society' (MacKinnon 1993: 25). That is, they are structural representations of patriarchal inequality. VAW is 'systematic and known, the disregard is official and organized, and the effective governmental tolerance is a matter of law and policy' (MacKinnon 1993: 25). More recently, jurisprudential imagination has brought some non-state violence within the scope of IHRL where the state has been complicit in that violence, or where it has failed in its duties of due diligence (explained below) (Benninger-Budel 2008b). Questions remain, however, as to the effectiveness of these jurisprudential strategies and what they mean for female victims.

## MAJOR DEVELOPMENTS RELATING TO VIOLENCE AGAINST WOMEN AND HUMAN RIGHTS

As noted above, VAW was not considered of concern to the international community until the mid-1990s. Despite women's entitlement to equality before the law and equal protection of the law being recognized as rights in all the major human rights treaties, VAW was not a major issue in the 1975 and 1980 global women's conferences (Merry 2006: 21). Rape was nonetheless identified specifically as a human rights violation in 1975, alongside prostitution, physical assault, mental cruelty, child marriage, forced marriage and marriage as a commercial transaction (Mexico 1975: para. 28). A decision at the 1980 global conference on 'battered women and violence in the family' recognized domestic violence as 'an intolerable offence to the dignity of human beings' (Copenhagen 1980: 67). An explicit provision outlawing VAW was not, however, included in CEDAW, the key women's rights treaty adopted in 1979. This glaring omission has required the committee supervising the treaty's implementation to issue two general recommendations in 1989 and 1992 respectively characterizing VAW as a form of sex discrimination in order to bring the issue within its mandate.

The 1985 Nairobi Forward-looking Strategies identified VAW as interconnected with the achievement of peace, but did not deal with the same in relation to equality or development, the other themes of the 1985 global women's conference (Nairobi 1985). Interestingly, a draft resolution on 'sexual violence against women and children', sponsored by Austria, Liberia, Spain, Tunisia and the US, urged governments to take steps to ensure that women are not re-victimized under penal law by providing, inter alia, for confidential proceedings at the request of the victim and measures to protect the privacy of the victim (Nairobi 1985: 216–17).

It has been asserted that VAW was central to deliberations at the 1993 World Conference on Human Rights (Friedman 1995: 27–31) in which women's rights were recognized as human rights (Vienna 1993, Pt 1: para. 18). Both public and private forms of violence were included, as well as gender bias in the administration of justice. The Vienna Declaration specifically called for the drafting of a declaration prohibiting VAW and the appointment of a special rapporteur on the same subject (Pt II: para. 38).

In 1994, the UN Declaration on the Elimination of Violence against Women (DEVAW) was adopted and the first Special Rapporteur on Violence against Women appointed. Positively, unlike the human rights treaty bodies, the mandate of the Special Rapporteur is not circumscribed by ratifications to international treaties or periodic reporting cycles and therefore has a wider mandate (Spec. Rapp. 2009: 8). On the other hand, there is no obligation on the part of a state to co-operate with the Special Rapporteur as an extra-treaty measure.

Still in 1994, the International Conference on Population and Development in Cairo acknowledged the interlinkages between women's empowerment and autonomy and protection from gender-based violence (Cairo 1994: Ch. IV).

The following year, the Beijing World Conference placed VAW squarely on the women's rights agenda, identifying it as one of 12 priority areas of concern (Beijing 1995: D). Beijing highlighted particular harms not specifically mentioned in the DEVAW, including systematic rape and forced pregnancy during armed conflict (not, however, during peacetime), sexual slavery, forced sterilization and forced abortion, female infanticide and pre-natal sex selection (Beijing 1995: paras 114–15; Spec. Rapp. 2009: 5). As a follow-up to DEVAW and Beijing, the UN General Assembly called upon the UN Development Fund for Women to strengthen its role in eliminating VAW (para. 2). The Beijing +5 review further called for the criminalization of all forms of VAW (Beijing +5: para. 69(c)) and recognized links between gender-related violence and prejudice, racism and racial discrimination, xenophobia, pornography, ethnic cleansing, armed conflict, foreign occupation, religious and anti-religious extremism, and terrorism (Spec. Rapp. 2009: 5).

By the late 1990s, and following developments in international criminal law, rape perpetrated by state officials for the purposes of interrogation or to force a confession from women within state custody had been recognized as a form of torture under international and regional human rights instruments (*Mejìa v Peru* I-A Comm. HR 5/96 case 10.970 1996; *Aydin v Turkey* ECtHR

App. 25660/94 1997; *Miguel Castro-Castro Prison v Peru* I-ACtHR 2006; *CT and KM v Sweden* CAT Comm. 279/2005; Edwards 2006).

In 2000, two further human rights treaty bodies issued general comments on the gender-related dimensions of human rights violations, recognizing in particular that rape is a form of torture (HRC 2000: para. 11; CERD 2000). In 2005, the Committee on Economic, Social and Cultural Rights followed suit by specifically mentioning that obligations upon states to protect the family included taking measures against domestic and other gender-related violence in the family (CESCR 2005: para. 27).

In 2006, the UN Secretary-General issued his first comprehensive report on VAW and the UN General Assembly adopted a resolution calling for the intensification of efforts to eliminate all forms of VAW, thus reaffirming the international focus on VAW. Building on this momentum, the current Special Rapporteur issued her second report in 2008 in which she acknowledges that there are no agreed benchmarks or indicators to assess progress at the international level and she sets out to develop these (Spec. Rapp. 2008: para. 21).

At the regional level, the Inter-American Convention on the Prevention, Punishment and Eradication of Violence against Women (IA-VAW) was agreed in 1994 and entered into force in 1995; meanwhile a Protocol to the African Charter on Human and Peoples' Rights on the Rights of Women in Africa was agreed in 2003 and entered into force in 2005 (APWR).

The above catalogue of developments is testament to an international human rights legal system in transition. There has been a significant shift from a system that excluded entirely the issues of everyday rape and other forms of VAW from the international human rights agenda to one that now recognizes its elimination as a necessary precondition to the enjoyment of all human rights for women, acknowledges the structural causes of women's inequality and the associated risk of violence, and the role of the state in fostering directly and indirectly women's subordinate position in society.

## DEFINING RAPE AND VIOLENCE AGAINST WOMEN

Nowhere is rape defined under IHRL. However, human rights jurisprudence demonstrates endorsement of the consent school of thought. Rape has been identified as a violation of sexual autonomy, regardless of the use of physical force (see, for example, *MC v Bulgaria* ECtHR App. 39272/98 2003; Gormley 2008: 179). The Committee on the Elimination of Discrimination against Women (the Women's Committee) has given specific focus to the entitlement of women who have been trafficked or who are in prostitution to equal protection of laws relating to rape (CEDAW 1992: para. 15), to the repeal of laws that permit marital rape and rape within the family (para. 23), and to the risk of HIV/AIDS infection through harmful traditional practices including marital rape (CEDAW 1999: para. 18). Although rape is explicitly listed in the DEVAW and in the regional women-specific instruments (DEVAW

Article 2(a) and (b); IA-VAW Article 2; APWR Articles 11 (in armed conflict) and 14), international human rights institutions have focused less on rape specifically than on the range of forms of VAW broadly defined.

Ultimately, two strategies have been employed by international decision-making bodies to include VAW under international law in the absence of an explicit provision at the level of international law: the first, to conceptualize VAW as a form of sex discrimination, and the second, to creatively interpret existing human rights so that the experiences of women are included. Legal norms analysed in the latter context include the rights to life and to liberty and security of the person, provisions relating to freedom of movement, privacy and health, rights pertaining to marriage, and the prohibition against torture and other ill-treatment. Of these, the torture provision has been the most extensively considered to date so it will be the focus of this chapter as illustrative of the second strategy.

The CEDAW General Recommendation 1992 provides that '[g]ender-based violence is a form of discrimination that seriously inhibits women's ability to enjoy rights and freedoms on the basis of equality with men' (paras 1 and 7). 'Gender-based violence' is defined as: 'violence that is directed against a woman because she is a woman or that affects women disproportionately. It includes acts that inflict physical, mental or sexual harm or suffering, threats of such acts, coercion and other deprivations of liberty' (para. 6). In particular, the Committee states that '[g]ender-based violence may breach specific provisions of the Convention, regardless of whether those provisions expressly mention violence' (para. 6).

This strategy of categorizing and conceptualizing VAW as discrimination has been both commended and criticized. It has been praised as a 'conceptual breakthrough' since VAW is no longer perceived as an individual criminal act but part of a systemic and political problem, requiring a systemic, political solution (Goldfarb 2002–2003: 254). VAW is viewed as a social justice issue rather than an individual anomaly. Positively, such a focus permits deeper excavations of its causes and consequences (Edwards 2009). However, it has also been criticized on a number of grounds.

First, characterizing VAW as sex discrimination or a form of inequality is reliant on understandings of these terms, which are complex and contested concepts. These terms are regularly interpreted as permitting excuses for unequal treatment based on 'reasonable and objective' criteria, which are in turn treated and applied by decision-makers as neutral terms and thereby failing to take account of particular social-cultural and gendered perspectives (Kaufman and Lindquist 1995). Secondly, the rhetoric of sex discrimination is weaker than the language of violence and conjures up lower levels of societal disapproval and punishment systems (Edwards 2009). Thirdly, and most importantly, equating VAW with sex discrimination results in the unequal treatment of women under the law. This approach does not make VAW prohibited conduct per se. Instead, female victims of violence are only protected to the extent that they can substantiate that the harm they have suffered is discriminatory or otherwise fits within another provision of international law. This can be problematic because gender may not be the main or sole determinant of the act in question. Moreover, violence that disproportionately affects men, such as physical assault in police custody, in contrast, is not burdened with additional legal criteria, as such conduct is already the accepted subject-matter of a specific prohibition (that is, torture) (Edwards 2009).

Likewise, the DEVAW adopts the language of 'violence against women', which it defines in turn by reference to 'gender-based violence', as:

> any act of gender-based violence that results in, or is likely to result in, physical, sexual or psychological harm or suffering to women, including threats of such acts, coercion or arbitrary deprivation of liberty, whether occurring in public or in private life.
>
> (DEVAW Article 1)

[VAW] shall be understood to encompass, but not be limited to, the following:

> (a) physical, sexual and psychological violence occurring in the family, including battering, sexual abuse of female children in the household, dowry-related violence, marital rape, female genital mutilation and other traditional practices harmful to women, non-spousal violence and violence related to exploitation;
> (b) physical, sexual and psychological violence occurring within the general community, including rape, sexual abuse, sexual harassment and intimidation at work, in educational institutions and elsewhere, trafficking in women and forced prostitution;
> (c) physical, sexual and psychological violence perpetrated or condoned by the State, wherever it occurs.
>
> (DEVAW Article 2)

Appearing also in the Beijing Platform for Action (para. 113) and most recently reconfirmed by the UN General Assembly in their 2006 resolution on VAW, this is the leading definition relied upon in international discourse. Broadly construed and non-exhaustive, it nonetheless has a number of limitations. First, it conflates VAW with gender-related violence. That is, it is concerned only with VAW that contains an element of sex discrimination and this arguably narrows the experiences of women worldwide by ignoring the many violations women suffer in public, and for which gender may not be the main or even a contributing factor (Edwards 2006 and 2009). Secondly, the definition refers to physical, sexual or psychological harm or suffering, or acts likely to cause such harm or suffering. It does not mention structural or economic violence, although such issues have been taken up where an equality rubric has been applied (Edwards 2009). This is to be compared with the APWR, in which 'economic violence' is expressly identified (Article 1(j)). A third concern is that the definition appears to create a hierarchy of harms, with the primary focus on family violence, followed by violence within the general community, and finally violence perpetrated or condoned by the state. The ordering of this provision is intended to reverse the general presumption of international law that it applies exclusively to state-sponsored violence. However, such attempts to dismantle the public/private dichotomy may have the effect of simultaneously reaffirming stereotypes about women by downplaying the violence they suffer and the roles they play in the public realm (Edwards 2009).

The IA-VAW adopts a similar approach. Article 1 provides that VAW 'shall be understood as any act or conduct, based on gender, which causes death or physical, sexual or psychological harm or suffering to women, whether in the public or the private sphere'. Like the DEVAW, Article 2 identifies the site, rather than the nature, of the violence; and it is likewise concerned with violence perpetrated against women attributed to their gender. Many of the criticisms outlined above can also be levelled against this treaty. However, the IA-VAW has also been criticized because it does not include acts that are 'likely to cause harm' and so only applies to any act that has actually caused harm (Ewing 1995).

The APWR, although a women's rights treaty rather than a VAW treaty, nonetheless contains a definitional clause which defines 'violence against women' as:

> all acts perpetrated against women which cause or could cause them physical, sexual, psychological, and economic harm, including the threat to take such acts; or to undertake the imposition of arbitrary restrictions on or deprivation of fundamental freedoms in private or public life in peace time and during situations of armed conflicts or of war.
>
> (Article 1(j))

This definition is distinct from those contained in the DEVAW or the IA-VAW in four key ways. First, it makes clear that it covers both actual violence and acts that could lead to violence. That is, unlike the IA-VAW, it specifically covers threats of violence. Secondly, it encompasses acts that are not usually viewed as violence per se, but which could lead to physical, sexual, psychological or economic harm, such as restrictions on freedom of movement, unequal rights in marriage, media campaigns that portray women in negative images, polygamy or customary, traditional or religious practices that view women as inferior or second-class citizens (Odinkalu 2002). Thirdly, the definition is not limited to gender-related violence but applies to VAW in a global sense. That is, the definition is broader in scope than its predecessors. Fourthly, it is the only definition to include explicitly economic harm as a form of VAW. While it does not use the language of systemic or structural violence, the inclusion here of economic harm complements that approach. This is an important breakthrough in international discourse on this subject and revisits earlier global women's conferences that linked VAW with the issues of equality, peace and development.

The above definitions have tended to treat VAW as an issue of inequality and discrimination on the basis of sex, or at least to couple VAW with these issues. An alternative approach, as already noted, has been the characterization of various forms of VAW as torture or cruel, inhuman or degrading treatment or punishment (ICCPR Article 7; UNCAT Articles 1 and 16; European Convention of Human Rights, ECHR Article 3; American Convention on Human Rights, ACHR Article 5(2); African Charter on Human and People's Rights, ACHPR Article 5). The Grand Chamber of the European Court of Human Rights, for example, has recognized rape as a particular form of torture, because it results in 'deep psychological scars' as well as 'acute physical pain of forced penetration, [which was considered to] have left [the victim] feeling debased and violated both physically and emotionally' (*Aydin v Turkey* ECtHR 1997: para. 83; see also *MC v Bulgaria* ECtHR 2003; *Mejia v Peru* I-A Comm. HR 1996; *Miguel Castro-Castro Prison v Peru* IACtHR 2006).

Torture has also been used to apply to VAW outside the context of state custody, such as applying to domestic violence, female genital mutilation, forced abortion or sterilization (see Edwards 2006). The feminist argument is that 'when stripped of privatization, sexism and sentimentality, private gender-based violence is no less grave than other forms of inhumane and subordinating official violence' (Copelon 1994: 295–96). Identifying control, intimidation or elimination as the 'generally recognized' purposes of torture, MacKinnon argues that there is little difference between torture and rape or other forms of sexual violence (1993: 22).

Why torture? Feminist activists and scholars have harnessed torture as the site to argue against VAW owing to the status attached to the norm under IHRL. Viewing rape as a form of torture equates the severity of the assault with one of the most serious human rights violations. That is, '[the torture label] give[s] the crime specific symbolic significance that recognizes it as an affront to personal integrity, rather than as a crime against honour or custom' (Pearce 2003: 540). Similar arguments have been framed in the context of rape and sexual violence as genocide. Franke, for example, has praised the Prosecutor and the International Criminal Tribunal for Rwanda (ICTR) for finding that rape in the Rwandan conflict constituted a form of genocide. She states:

> Rather than rely upon special laws that isolate rape and/or sexual assault as a privileged kind of injury . . . [the Tribunal] has chosen to tailor the construction of these crimes to the way in which sex-related violence figures in the physical or mental destruction of a people or person.
> (Franke 1998: 1177)

In other words, some feminist scholars acknowledge the benefit of the rhetorical connection of rape to genocide or torture because it captures worldwide attention and condemnation on a scale that would not be achieved by provisions on rape or VAW alone.

On the other hand, the rape as genocide strategy has been criticized because it serves to 'reify ethnic difference, diminish women's capacity to engage in sexual activity with the "enemy" during the war, and downplay the extent to which any but extraordinary women could be perpetrators in war' (Engle 2005: 784). It might also be argued that focusing so heavily on rape and sexual violence results in debate that ignores the fact that women are subject to torture and genocide under their traditional constructions. This strategy therefore plays into the masculine international system by seeking to raise the profile of VAW through equating the seriousness of the harm with male conceptions of torture rather than as grave human rights violations in their own right (Edwards 2006 and 2008).

McGlynn (2008) has questioned the merit of pursuing the feminist strategy of 'rape as torture' on two fronts. First, she argues that state complicity cannot extend to every rape. The difficulty of linking the state to the rape in question appears more punctuated in peacetime than in wartime, where in the latter, deliberate strategies targeting particular women for sexual violence may be identified. In peacetime, governments may pursue a range of policies and programmes to combat VAW that may be entirely ineffective. While acknowledging that 'rape does happen because of gender inequalities', McGlynn additionally asserts that viewing rape as torture will have no effect on reducing the prevalence of the crime or on ensuring that more perpetrators are brought to justice (2008: 84).

Secondly, McGlynn considers that the rhetoric of 'rape' is perhaps as powerful, if not more powerful, than that of 'torture' (2008: 78). It is not, however, clear that 'rape' as a crime has gained the status of abhorrence at a domestic level in any society that is attributed to torture at an international level. The symbolism of labelling an act as 'rape' is socially and culturally contingent. Precisely because it is a crime generally considered to be perpetrated against women, it has not attained the same status under domestic or international laws. Perversely, the same could be said of the language and practice of torture. Not every society objects to torture or comprehends its boundaries in the same way. Nonetheless, at the level of international law, torture has attained a particular peremptory status. Rape, on the other hand, is not an identifiable international crime or human rights violation in its own right, although – as discussed in other chapters in this collection – this is slowly changing and should be furthered. Other scholars have argued that strategies that include the language of both rape and torture ought to be pursued, in order 'to recognize the general – rape as torture – as well as the particular – rape as rape' (Sivakumaran 2007: 257). An accurate classification of abuse is considered important to give victims a voice, to breakdown stereotypes and to accurately record the events in question.

While recognizing that both the strategies of incorporating VAW under IHRL outlined in this chapter have been necessary in the absence of an explicit prohibition, they nonetheless reinforce an international legal system that disadvantages women by subjecting them to additional, different or unequal criteria. By requiring women to characterize the violence they suffer as sex discrimination or as torture, rather than as violence (or rape) per se, women are treated unequally under the law. This is my primary objection to these strategies, at the same time as acknowledging the conceptual and political breakthroughs that they represent.

## STATE RESPONSIBILITY AND DUE DILIGENCE

However rape and VAW are defined or conceptualized, the state-based international legal system requires that the state is the responsible actor. The International Law Commission's (ILC) Articles on State Responsibility for Internationally Wrongful Acts (2001) provide that a state is responsible for actions and omissions that are attributable to the state and breach an international obligation (Article 2). Attributable actions or omissions include those which are committed by legislative, executive, administrative, judicial or other organs of the state (Article 4), persons and entities not organs of the state but exercising governmental authority (Article 5), including where either the organ or the empowered person or entity acts, exceeds its authority or contravenes instructions (Article 7), and persons or entities acting under instructions from the state (Article 9).

Under IHRL, it is generally accepted that a state has an obligation to respect, protect and fulfil human rights. As early as 1988 a 'due diligence' standard of state responsibility for human rights abuses committed by non-state actors was developed by the Inter-American Court of Human Rights (I-ACtHR), albeit having its antecedents in the area of state responsibility for injuries to aliens abroad (ILC *Yearbook* 1957, vol. II: 121–28). The I-ACtHR held that:

> An illegal act which violates human rights and which is initially not directly imputable to a State (for example, because it is the act of a private person or because the person responsible has not been identified) can lead to international responsibility of the State, not because of the act itself, but because of the lack of due diligence to prevent the violation or to respond to it as required by the Convention.
> (*Velásquez Rodriguez v Honduras* I-ACtHR Ser. C no. 4 judgment 29 July 1988: para. 172)

This articulation of state responsibility has been accepted by most human rights judicial or quasi-judicial mechanisms (for example, HRC 2004: para. 8) and it has been praised for its particular relevance to women's human rights (Ertürk 2008; Gormley 2008), although the initial decision itself involved no analysis of gender. The emergence of the due diligence standard in a typically 'male' scenario of a disappeared male political dissident in *Velásquez Rodriguez* reminds us that women are not the only beneficiaries of the collapsing of the public/private dichotomy (Edwards 2006). At the same time, it makes us reflect, too, on the fact that, even though 'private' abuse disproportionately affects women, the issue was not pursued at the level of international law until it was also seen as being of relevance to men.

Building on the work of regional human rights instruments (for example *Maria Da Penha Maia Fernandes v Brazil* I-ACtHR case no. 12-051 2001; *MC v Bulgaria* ECtHR 2003), in 2005, the Women's Committee (under the Optional Protocol to the CEDAW) found Hungary to have failed to provide effective protection from domestic violence (*AT v Hungary* Comm. 2/2003: para. 9.3). In breach of its CEDAW obligations, Hungary had failed to enact specific legislation to combat domestic violence and sexual harassment. In addition, no shelters existed for the immediate protection of a woman in the victim's circumstances with a disabled child and there was no injunctive relief, such as a restraining order, available to her. Two further domestic violence cases have been decided under the new individual communications mechanism (*Goekce (deceased) v Austria* Comm. 5/2005; *Yildirim (deceased) v Austria* Comm. no. 6/2005), confirming domestic violence as an actionable breach where the state fails in its duties of due diligence.

These cases now represent a statement of the general position at international law. In the context of VAW, duties on states include the obligation to ratify relevant international instruments; to establish national legislative and administrative frameworks outlawing VAW, which provide for gender-sensitivity in the criminal justice system; and to introduce protective measures consisting mainly of the provision of services such as telephone hotlines, healthcare, counselling centres, legal assistance, shelters, restraining orders, and financial aid to victims of violence (Spec. Rapp. 1999, Report: para. 25; S-G 2006, Report: para. 261). Ertürk notes that implementation of such measures is inconsistent and in many cases ineffective and that protection measures are also frequently based on short-term emergency assistance rather than on sustainable solutions to avoid re-victimization (2008: 37). These mechanisms are not well geared towards complaints arising from two or more states, such as trafficking of women and children across national boundaries or sex tourism (Byrnes 1994: 204). They also do not address systematic patterns or trends of human rights violations.

Despite these developments, women are still treated unequally under international human rights law by virtue of the state-based system. The due diligence standard does not change this fact. Women must mount two hurdles before gaining redress under international law for so-called 'private' violations. They need to establish, first, that they have been subjected to or threatened with violent conduct by a non-state actor (in some cases, this may require them to prove that they have been raped or sexually assaulted first), and secondly, that the harm can be attributed to the state by reason of its failure to act with due diligence to prevent or prosecute it. At no time has IHRL recognized the right of individuals to bring actions directly against their perpetrators, whether government officials or private individuals, before an international court (Nowak 2007). International law does not have direct horizontal effect. This is arguably the real barrier to dismantling the public/private dichotomy, because although private acts can now be brought within the purview of IHRL, these cases are still on the periphery, considered an exception to the rule, and a close linkage with the state is still required.

A further concern is that the standard of due diligence does not prohibit VAW per se, but demands only that a state takes 'reasonable steps' to prevent or respond to the harm. Reliance on standards such as reasonableness has proven problematic in other areas of law as such terms risk a biased interpretation. Feminist scholars, such as Cornell, have argued that '[r]easonableness is not natural and objective but rather socially and politically constructed through the identification of this supposedly neutral concept with masculinity' (2003: 206). It is also problematic because what is required to eradicate or prevent VAW is not easily defined. Although the due diligence standard is a broadly framed concept that has substantially extended the reach of IHRL and the obligations of states thereunder, it also has limitations (Byrnes and Bath 2008).

## CONCLUSION

Significant progress has been achieved since the mid-1990s in securing recognition by the international community that VAW is a human rights issue. Starting with VAW in armed conflict, it can now be argued that VAW in peacetime and by non-state actors is on the UN's human rights agenda, if not one of its priority areas. Although the strategies outlined in this chapter are worthy of praise on many grounds, their effect is that women are treated unequally under the international legal system. Female victims of non-state violence are subject to additional or supplementary legal criteria, which in turn operate to deter women from fully utilizing and benefiting from the UN human rights redress mechanisms.

### Notes

1  I would like to thank Lydia Gény for her help with the research for this piece.
2  International Covenant on Civil and Political Rights 1966, G.A. res. 2200A (XXI), 16 Dec. 1966, 999 UNTS 171; entered into force 23 Mar. 1976 (ICCPR); International Covenant on Economic, Social and Cultural Rights 1966, G.A. res. 2200A (XXI), 16 Dec. 1966, 993 UNTS 3; entered into force 3 Jan. 1976 (ICESCR); International Convention on the Elimination of All Forms of Racial Discrimination 1965, G.A. res. 2106 (XX), 21 Dec. 1965, 660 UNTS 195; entered into force 4 Jan. 1969 (ICERD); Convention against Torture and Other Cruel, Inhumane or Degrading Treatment or Punishment 1984, G.A. res. 39/46, 10 Dec. 1984, 1465 UNTS 85; entered into force 26 June 1987 (UNCAT); Convention on the Rights of the Child 1989, G.A. res. 44/25, 20 Nov. 1989, 1577 UNTS 3; entered into force 2 Sept. 1990 (CRC); Convention on the Elimination of All Forms of Discrimination against Women 1979, GA res. 34/180, 18 Dec. 1979, 1249 UNTS 13; entered into force 3 Sept. 1981 (CEDAW); International Convention on the Protection of the Rights of All Migrant Workers and Members of Their Families 1990, GA res. 45/48, 2220 UNTS 93; entered into force 1 July 2003 (IMWC); and Convention on the Rights of Persons with Disabilities 2006, GA res. 61/106, 13 Dec. 2006; entered into force 3 May 2008 (ICRPD).

## Bibliography

Askin, K.D. (2003) 'Prosecuting wartime rape and other gender-related crimes under international law: extraordinary advances, enduring obstacles', *Berkeley Journal of International Law*, 21: 288–349.

Benninger-Budel, C. (2008a) 'Introduction', in C. Benninger-Budel (ed.) *Due Diligence and Its Application to Protect Women from Violence*, Leiden and Boston: Martinus Nijhoff Publishers.

—— (ed.) (2008b) *Due Diligence and Its Application to Protect Women from Violence*, Leiden and Boston: Martinus Nijhoff Publishers.

Binion, G. (1995) 'Human Rights: a feminist perspective', *Human Rights Quarterly*, 17: 509–26.

Buss, D. (2002) 'Prosecuting mass rape: *Prosecutor v Dragoljub Kunarac, Radomor Kovac and Zoran Vukovic*', *Feminist Legal Studies*, 10(1): 91–9.

Byrnes, A. (1994) 'Toward more effective enforcement of women's human rights through the use of international human rights law and procedures', in R.J. Cook (ed.) *Human Rights of Women: national and international perspectives*, Philadelphia: University Pennsylvania Press, 189–227.

Byrnes, A. and Bath, E. (2008) 'Violence against women, the obligation of due diligence, and the Optional Protocol to the Convention on the Elimination of All Forms of Discrimination against Women – recent developments', *Human Rights Law Review*, 8: 517–33.

Charlesworth, H., Chinkin, C. and Wright, S. (1991) 'Feminist approaches to international law', *American Journal of International Law*, 85: 613–45.

Copelon, R. (1994) 'Recognizing the egregious in the everyday: domestic violence as torture', *Columbia Human Rights Law Review*, 25: 291–367.

—— (1995) 'Gendered war crimes: reconceptualizing rape in time of war', in J. Peters and A. Wolper (eds) *Women's Rights, Human Rights: international feminist perspectives*, New York and London: Routledge, 197–214.

Cornell, D. (2003) 'Living Together: Psychic Spaces and the Demand for Sexual Equality', in A.J. Cahill and J. Hansen (eds) *Continental Feminism Reader*, London: Rowman & Littlefield, 196–220.

Edwards, A. (2006) 'The "feminizing" of torture under international human rights law', *Leiden Journal of International Law*, 19: 349–91.

—— (2008), *Women, Feminist Theory, and the United Nations Human Rights Treaty Bodies*, unpublished PhD thesis, The Australian National University.

—— (2009) 'Violence against women as sex discrimination: judging the jurisprudence of the United Nations Human Rights Treaty Bodies', *Texas Journal of Women and the Law*, 18: 101–65.

Engle, K. (2005) 'Feminism and its (dis)contents: criminalizing wartime rape in Bosnia and Herzegovina', *American Journal of International Law*, 99: 778–816.

Ertürk, Y. (2008) 'The due diligence standard: what does it entail for women's rights', in C. Benninger-Budel (ed.) *Due Diligence and Its Application to Protect Women from Violence*, Leiden and Boston: Martinus Nijhoff Publishers, 27–46.

Ewing, A.P. (1995) 'Establishing state responsibility for private acts of violence against women under the American Convention on Human Rights', *Columbia Human Rights Law Review*, 26: 751–800.

Franke, K.M. (1998) 'Putting sex to work', *Denver University Law Review*, 75: 1139–80.

Fraser, F. (1999) 'Becoming human: the origins and development of women's human rights', *Human Rights Quarterly*, 21: 853–906.

Friedman, E. (1995) 'Women's human rights: the emergence of a movement', in J. Peters and A. Wolper (eds) *Women's Rights, Human Rights: international feminist perspectives*, New York: Routledge, 18–35.

Goldfarb, S.F. (2002–2003) 'Applying the discrimination model to violence against women: some reflections on theory and practice', *American University Journal on Gender Social Policy and Law*, 11: 251–70.

Gormley, L. (2008) 'Violence against women by non-state actors, a responsibility for the state under human rights law: Amnesty International's work on domestic violence', in C. Benninger-Budel, (ed.) *Due Diligence and Its Application to Protect Women from Violence*, Leiden and Boston: Martinus Nijhoff Publishers, 173–84.

Kaufman, N.H. and Lindquist, S.A. (1995) 'Critiquing gender-neutral treaty language: the Convention on the Elimination of All Forms of Discrimination Against Women', in J. Peters and A. Wolper (eds) *Women's Rights, Human Rights: international feminist perspectives*, New York: Routledge, 114–25.

McGlynn, C. (2008) 'Rape as "torture"? Catharine MacKinnon and questions of feminist strategy', *Feminist Legal Studies*, 16: 71–85.

MacKinnon, C. (1983) 'Feminism, Marxism, method, and the state: toward feminist jurisprudence', *Signs*, 8: 635–58.

—— (1987) *Feminist Unmodified: discourses on life and law*, Cambridge, MA: Harvard University Press.

—— (1993) 'On Torture: a feminist perspective on human rights', in K. Mahoney and P. Mahoney (eds) *Human Rights in the Twenty-First Century: a global perspective*, Dordrecht: Martinus Njihoff Publishers, 21–32.

—— (2006) 'Rape, genocide, and women's human rights', in *Are Women Human? And other international dialogues*, Cambridge, MA: Belknap Press of Harvard University Press, 180–91.

Mahoney, K. (1996) 'Theoretical perspectives on women's human rights and strategies for their implementation', *Brooklyn Journal of International Law*, 12: 799–856.

Merry, S.E. (2006) *Human Rights and Gender Violence: translating international law into local justice*, Chicago and London: The University of Chicago Press.

Nowak, M. (2007) 'The need for a World Court of Human Rights', *Human Rights Law Review*, 7: 251–9.

Odinkalu, C.A. (2002) 'Africa's regional human rights system: recent developments and jurisprudence', *Human Rights Law Review*, 2: 99–116.

Olsen, F.E. (1983) 'The family and the market: a study of ideology and legal reform', *Harvard Law Review*, 96: 1497–578.

Pearce, H. (2003) 'An examination of the international understanding of political rape and the significance of labeling it torture', *International Journal of Refugee Law*, 14: 534–60.

Romany, C. (1994) 'State responsibility goes private: a feminist critique of the public/private distinction in international human rights law', in R.J. Cook (ed.) *Human Rights of Women: national and international perspectives*, Philadelphia: University of Pennsylvania Press, 85–115.

Scales, A.C. (1986) 'The emergence of feminist jurisprudence: an essay', *Yale Law Journal*, 95: 1373–403.

Sivakumaran, S. (2007) 'Sexual violence against men in armed conflict', *European Journal of International Law*, 18: 253–76.

## UN documents (in date order)

*Yearbook of the International Law Commission*, 1957, vol. II.

World Conference on Women, Declaration of Mexico on the Equality of Women and their Contribution to Development and Peace, Mexico, 1975, UN Doc. E/CONF.66.34, 2 July 1975 [Mexico 1975].

World Conference on Women, Equality, Development and Peace, Copenhagen, 1980 UN Doc. A/CONF.94/35, 19 Sept. 1980 [Copenhagen 1980].

World Conference on Women, Report and Nairobi Forward-looking Strategies for the Advancement of Women, 1985, UN Doc. A/CONF.116/28/Rev.1 [Nairobi 1985].

Committee on Elimination of All Forms of Discrimination against Women (CEDAW), General Recommendation No. 19: Violence against Women (1992), UN Doc. HRI/GEN/1/Rev.7 [CEDAW 1992].

World Conference on Human Rights, Vienna Declaration and Programme of Action, UN Doc. A/CONF.157/23, 12 July 1993 [Vienna 1993].

UN Declaration on the Elimination of Violence against Women, GA res. A/RES/48/104, 23 Feb. 1994 [DEVAW].

International Conference on Population and Development, Cairo Programme of Action, 5–13 Sept. 1994 (no UN Doc.) [Cairo 1994].

World Conference on Women, Beijing Declaration and Platform for Action, UN Doc. A/CONF.177/20 (1995) and A/CONF.177/20/Add.1 (1995) [Beijing 1995].

UN General Assembly res. A/RES/50/166, 16 Feb. 1999, UN Development Fund for Women to strengthen its role in eliminating violence against women.

Report of the Special Rapporteur on Violence against Women, Its Causes and Consequences, UN Doc. CN/4/1999/68, 10 Mar. 1999 [Spec. Rapp. 1999].

CEDAW, General Recommendation No. 24: Women and Health, 1999 [CEDAW 1999].

Committee on the Elimination of Racial Discrimination (CERD) General Comment No. 25: Gender-Related Dimensions of Racial Discrimination, UN Doc. A/55/18, 20 Mar. 2000 [CERD 2000].

Human Rights Committee General Comment No. 28: Equality of Rights between Men and Women, UN Doc. A/55/40, 29 Mar. 2000 [HRC 2000].

Beijing +5, Further Actions and Initiatives to Implement the Beijing Declaration and Programme for Action, UN Doc. A/RES/S-23/3 (2000) [Beijing +5].

Human Rights Committee General Comment No. 31: The Nature of General Legal Obligations Imposed on States Parties to the Covenant, UN Doc. CCPR/C/74/CRP/4/Rev.6, 29 Mar. 2004 [HRC 2004].

Committee on Economic, Social and Cultural Rights (CESCR), General Comment No. 16: Equal Rights of Men and Women to the Enjoyment of All Economic, Social and Cultural Rights, UN Doc. E/C.12/2005.4, 11 Aug. 2005 [CESCR 2005].

United Nations Department of Economic and Social Affairs, *The World's Women 2005: Progress in Statistics*, UN Doc. ST/ESA/STAT/SER.K/17, UN Sales No. E/05/XVII.7 (2006) [UN The World's Women 2005].

Report of the UN Secretary-General, *In-Depth Study on All Forms of Violence against Women*, UN Doc. A/61/122/Add.1, 6 July 2006 [S-G Report 2006].

UN General Assembly res. A/RES/61/143 30 Jan. 2007 (resolution dated 19 Dec. 2006), on *Intensification of Efforts to Eliminate All Forms of Violence against Women*, Report of the Special Rapporteur on Violence against Women, Its Causes and Consequence, *Indicators on Violence against Women and State Response*, UN Doc. A/HRC/7/6, 29 Jan. 2008 [Spec. Rapp. 2008].

Report of the Special Rapporteur on Violence against Women, Its Causes and Consequences, 15 Years of the United Nations Special Rapporteur on Violence against Women, Its Causes and Consequences: A Critical Appraisal 1994–2009, no UN Doc. [Spec. Rapp. 2009].

Chapter 7

# Defining rape under the European Convention on Human Rights

Torture, consent and equality

*Patricia Londono*

The European Convention on Human Rights (ECHR) came into force in 1953. Its implementation was in line with the 'regional integration and the institutionalization of common values' that lay behind the contemporaneous establishment of the Council of Europe and the European Union; and its motivating force lay in the belief, following the atrocities of the Second World War, that nations bound to respecting human rights were 'less likely to wage war on their neighbours' (Steiner and Alston 2007: 933). Article 19 of the Convention established the European Court of Human Rights (ECtHR) with powers to hear both inter-state (Article 33) and individual (Article 34) complaints. Of the various international human rights systems that exist, it is judicially the most well-developed and most extensive generator of jurisprudence (Steiner and Alston 2007: 933).

The Convention was drafted when there was little understanding of women's rights and it was thus not designed with their needs in mind, reflecting their political marginalization at the time (Quinlivian 1997: 11; Charlesworth 1998: 782). Despite this, and notwithstanding the fact that there is a paucity of Europe-wide research into the incidence of rape and sexual violence (Regan and Kelly 2003), the ECtHR has in recent years made some progress in developing human rights jurisprudence in a manner that might assist victims of rape. In addition, there have been moves on the part of the Council of Europe to ensure protection for women from sexual violence (Council of Europe 2002), although studies suggest that average conviction rates have in fact fallen in almost all European countries in recent years (Regan and Kelly 2003: 6, 13).

The development of principles to address rape within international human rights systems have, until recently, tended to focus on times of conflict. Despite recent moves to articulate sexual violence between private actors as human rights violations within Convention jurisprudence, underdeveloped notions of equality mean that the ECHR does not articulate rape or sexual crime as something that is both commonplace, and which substantially impedes women's enjoyment of rights (cf. Edwards, this volume). This is in contrast to the current approach taken by the ECtHR in cases of domestic violence (*Opuz v Turkey* 33201/02, 9 June 2009).

This chapter examines the way that rape is substantively defined and treated in European human rights law focusing on Article 3 of the Convention: the prohibition on 'torture or inhuman or degrading treatment or punishment'. It will take as its basis the perspective advocated by the Committee for the Elimination of Discrimination Against Women (CEDAW) that rape and sexual violence are forms of discrimination, disproportionately affecting women and girls, and which are perpetuated by stereotypical and prejudicial perspectives that permeate all aspects of society, including the home (CEDAW 1992). It is argued here that, given the nature and severity of the harm, rape claims are best characterized as violations of Article 3. If conduct which constitutes torture is governed by the nature of the act, rape would appear to fall within this, the most severe category of ill-treatment recognized by Article 3.

The extent to which discrimination on the grounds of gender constitutes a 'prohibited purpose' for a finding of torture is also considered, as is the developing doctrine of positive obligations. It is argued further that the ECtHR's treatment of consent and coercion reveals much about the way that rape is dealt with under Convention jurisprudence. Finally, the potential for the development of sexual violence as an issue of inequality under Article 14 and Protocol 12 of the Convention will be examined and evaluated.

## DEFINING THE NATURE OF THE VIOLATION

### Sexual violence and state actors

There have been a number of cases that have dealt specifically with the effects of rape and the way it might be articulated within European human rights jurisprudence. The earliest case explicitly to examine rape, *Cyprus v Turkey* ((1982) 4 EHRR 482), was a product of the Turkish occupation of Cyprus, and a number of human rights violations that took place during that occupation. In relation to sexual violence, the applicant government complained of 'wholesale and repeated rape of women of all ages', often accompanied by additional physical violence towards, and the killing of, victims. The Commission in this case found that such treatment violated Article 3 on the basis that it constituted inhuman treatment. In addition, it found violations of Article 14 on the basis that such treatment was directed against members of the Greek Cypriot community. The Commission offered no explanation as to why this was the case, or of why the treatment complained of did not amount to torture. The position in this latter regard might be contrasted with the case of *Ireland v UK*, where the Commission found that the five techniques used for interrogating IRA suspects including wall standing, hooding, deprivation of sleep and being subjected to loud noises, amounted to torture under Article 3. Evidencing the confusion over where the line was to be drawn between torture and inhuman treatment in these early cases, however, the Court then disputed the Commission's finding of torture

((1978) 2 EHRR 25), holding that these techniques amounted only to inhuman treatment.

Putting together abuses such as the five techniques in *Ireland* and mass rape under the heading of 'inhuman or degrading treatment' does not adequately do credit to the distinction between levels of severity which ought to be made within Article 3. It is submitted here that the extent and acuteness of the suffering associated with mass rape is more appropriately classed as torture.

This principle appeared to have been accepted in the subsequent case of *Aydin v Turkey* ((1998) 25 EHRR 251), where a young woman had been raped and subjected to other humiliating acts whilst in custody. The Court held that:

> Rape of a detainee by an official of the state must be considered to be an especially grave and abhorrent form of ill-treatment given the ease with which the offender can exploit the vulnerability and weakened resistance of his victim. Furthermore, rape leaves deep psychological scars on the victim which do not respond to the passage of time as quickly as other forms of physical and mental violence. The applicant also experienced the acute physical pain of forced penetration, which must have left her feeling debased and violated both physically and emotionally... Against this background the court is satisfied that the accumulation of acts of physical and mental violence inflicted on the applicant and the especially cruel act of rape to which she was subjected amounted to torture in breach of Article 3... Indeed the court would have reached this conclusion *on either of these grounds taken separately*.
>
> [Emphasis added] (para. 86)

The Court in this case held that the distinction between 'torture' and 'inhuman or degrading treatment' was made with reference to the *severity of the acts*, with torture being confined 'to deliberate inhuman treatment causing very serious and cruel suffering' (para. 82). As noted by Zilli, this case demonstrates that a single rape can be an act of torture and, in this way, *Aydin* departs from the reasoning in *Cyprus* where incidents of mass rape were classed as inhuman and degrading treatment (2002: 253, 261). Whilst *Aydin* concerned rape in detention and, thus, a situation where the perpetrator 'could exploit the vulnerability and weakened resistance of his victim', the Court's subsequent comments on the lasting effects of rape and its associated debasement appear to refer to rape per se, regardless of the status of the perpetrator.

The ECtHR's sentiments on rape in *Aydin* were recently reiterated by the Court in *Maslova v Russia* ((2009) 48 EHRR 37) although, unlike *Aydin*, the decision that the applicant had been tortured was based here on the cumulative effects of the physical and sexual violence to which she had been subjected whilst in custody (paras 107–8).

Together, it is submitted that these cases indicate a certain willingness on the part of the ECtHR to articulate rape cases as cases of torture with reference to the nature of the act, although to date, the Court has only been willing to make such a finding in cases involving state actors.

## Sexual violence by private individuals

Early cases concerning sexual abuse at the hands of private individuals illustrated further areas of confusion. In *X and Y v Netherlands* ((1986) 8 EHRR 235), the absence of criminal laws protecting the mentally disabled from sexual assaults amounted to a violation of Article 8 of the Convention: 'the individual's right to respect for his or her sexual life'. This, it is argued, demonstrates an absence of understanding of the effects of rape. Sexual violence is primarily an attack on the physical and psychological integrity of the individual and therefore properly protected by Article 3 of the Convention. Whilst it could also be seen as a violation of the privacy interest associated with Article 8, articulating rape as primarily an attack on this interest does not encapsulate the degree of suffering involved. The second area of confusion in relation to the lack of understanding of the effects of rape is that the ECtHR appeared in the early cases to be working under a sharp distinction that was made at the time between acts by public and private actors. This was responsible for the articulation of rape as a violation of Article 3 when perpetrated by a public official, and Article 8 when perpetrated by a private actor. The difference between public and private actors apparently altered the nature of the violation at issue.

Subsequent cases have shown a greater willingness on the part of the ECtHR to recognize the effects of rape perpetrated by non-state actors and, therefore, to articulate it as an attack on physical and psychological integrity protected by Article 3. The beginnings of this could be seen in *SW v UK* ((1996) 21 EHRR 363). Here, the applicants complained that their rights under Article 7 ECHR – the prohibition on retrospective criminal liability – had been breached by the decision in the House of Lords in *R v R* ([1992] 1 AC 599). The defendant had appealed against his conviction for attempted rape of his wife, and the House of Lords removed the marital rape exemption hitherto available under English criminal law. The ECtHR held that here had been no breach of Article 7 because the House of Lords had followed a discernable line of legal development. It then went on to say that '[t]he essentially debasing character of rape is so manifest' that the decisions of the UK courts could not have been said to conflict with the purpose of Article 7. In addition, the removal of the marital rape exemption was deemed to be in line with the essence of the Convention, namely 'respect for human dignity and human freedom' (paras 44, 42).

The references made to 'the essentially debasing character of rape' and to human dignity indicate that the Court viewed rape as a violation of physical integrity. In *E v UK* ((2003) 36 EHRR 31), the applicants had been sexually abused by their stepfather over a considerable period of time. He had been convicted of indecently assaulting two of the children but continued having contact with the family. The Court in this case found that there had been a violation of Article 3. The treatment complained of was inhuman and degrading, and the authorities should have known the children were at risk and taken appropriate measures to prevent further abuse. Similarly, in *MC v Bulgaria* ((2005) 40 EHRR 20), the applicant (who was aged 14 at the time of the alleged attack) complained that she had been raped by two men. The Bulgarian Criminal Code required that a complaint could only be established if 'the victim was coerced into having sexual intercourse by the use of force or threats' (para. 80). The case had been discontinued because there was no evidence of threats or force (para. 64). The Court found that both Articles 3 and 8 had been breached. States were obligated 'to protect the individual's physical integrity and private life and to provide effective remedies in this respect' (para. 109). The Court stated again that obligations under Article 3 did not apply only to State officials and concluded that 'States have a positive obligation inherent in Articles 3 and 8 of the Convention to enact criminal-law provisions effectively punishing rape and to apply them in practice through effective investigation and prosecution' (para. 153).

Both of the decisions in *E* and *MC* involved findings under Article 3. However, as we have seen, case law suggests that rape is regarded as torture when perpetrated by State actors but inhuman treatment when perpetrated by private individuals. This is so even in cases such as *E*, where the number of acts of abuse far exceeded those in *Aydin* and *Maslova* and where the youth of the victims and their relationship to the perpetrator (their stepfather) make it highly likely that those power dynamics, combined with the length of time over which these acts took place, enabled him 'to exploit the vulnerability and weakened resistance of his victim'. In *E* ((2003) 36 EHRR 245), the Court found that prolonged sexual abuse amounted to ill-treatment. No reference was made to the extensive psychological suffering experienced by these children, which must have, at least, equalled the suffering of the applicants in *Aydin* and *Maslova*. It is argued here that thus differentiating rape as torture from rape as inhuman or degrading treatment with reference to the status of the perpetrator (that is, a state or non-state official) as opposed to the nature of the act is problematic (cf. McGlynn 2009).

Although this claim is not uncontroversial, some feminists have argued that all rape per se should be classed as torture (MacKinnon 2006: Ch. 1). At the same time, others have questioned whether it is strategically wise to employ the gender-neutral term 'torture' to crimes that are essentially gendered, given the potential for obfuscation of the gender element that this may bring (McGlynn 2008: 77). Whilst the term 'torture' does appear on the surface to be gender-neutral, it is submitted here that there is some potential for the gendered nature of this crime to be explicitly articulated as one of the 'prohibited purposes' that underlie some ECtHR decisions on torture.

## Torture and discriminatory purposes

In his analysis of ECtHR case law, Cassese argues that torture is regarded as a 'more serious or grave' form of suffering *and* that such suffering is carried out for a *purpose* (1993: 241). The descriptions regarding the nature of rape as a human rights violation articulated in *Aydin* indicate that rape in itself comes within the category of a violation causing particularly serious suffering.

The purposes Cassese refers to can be the extraction of information, punishment or to discriminate against the tortured person (as is the case under Article 1 of the Convention Against Torture). The ECtHR has mirrored this in a number of decisions (*Ilhan v Turkey* (2002) 34 EHRR 36: 85; *Salman v Turkey* (2002) 34 EHRR 147: 114). However, what is less clear is whether the discriminatory purposes encapsulate the discriminatory purpose of rape envisioned by the Convention on the Elimination of Discrimination Against Women (CEDAW) (1992). To adopt the meaning advocated by CEDAW – that rape is a form of discrimination predominantly affecting women and girls – would suggest that rape always has a discriminatory purpose: that of discriminating against women (see further McGlynn 2009: IV). To articulate the issue in this way would mirror the descriptions of rape given by victims of intimate sexual violence who say they feel they have been tortured (Russell 1990: Ch. 20). Further, in *Prosecutor v Delacic* (ICTY-96-21: 941), the International Criminal Tribunal for the former Yugoslavia (ICTY) held that rape was inflicted because the victims were women and this 'constitutes a prohibited purpose for the offence of torture'. However, the explicit recognition of this aspect of 'purpose' in relation to findings of torture – rape as a form of discrimination against women – has been absent from ECHR jurisprudence to date. This failure to articulate the crime of rape as an act of discrimination means that the social prejudice and inequality, which are inherent characteristics of the crime of rape, do not enter EHCR human rights discourse in any meaningful way.

## The effects of positive duties on the processing and prosecuting of rape cases

The ECtHR case law illustrates the importance that the Court attaches to the developing doctrine of positive obligations – a doctrine which applies regardless of whether the perpetrator is a private individual or a state official (see further Londono 2007).

This principle was first stated in the case of *X and Y*, where it was held that positive obligations not only require states to refrain from violating rights, but may also impose a proactive duty to ensure that the rights of individuals are not violated by other private individuals (para. 23). Further development of this principle in the content of sexual offences can be seen in cases such as *E*, where a violation of Article 3 was found because social services knew or ought to have known of the risks to the complainants from their stepfather and ought to have taken steps to protect them.

This has implications not only for children being abused in the home. It also has implications for the way in which the police deal with domestic rape and assault involving adults. The obligation not only includes effective enforcement machinery but also requires that measures to prevent violations be taken in certain circumstances. The ECtHR has also held that the lack of awareness at the time of the extent of victimization by sexual offenders within families was not relevant in cases where authorities knew of the abuse and criminal convictions followed. In contrast, however, in the case of *DC and JC v United Kingdom* ((2003) 36 EHRR 14), the ECtHR held that where children had been repeatedly sexually abused at the hands of their stepfather, and it could not be shown that social services should have been aware of the abuse, the claim under Article 3 will not be successful.

In *MC v Bulgaria*, the Court found that the obligations to protect rights under Article 3 and under Article 8 led to duties to conduct official investigations and effectively punish rape (paras 149–53). In *Maslova v Russia* (2009) 48 EHRR 37), the Court – citing *MC* and *SW* – held that 'the manifestly debasing character' of rape 'emphasises the state's procedural obligation in this context' (para. 91). The Court went on to hold that:

> The effective official investigation should be capable of leading to the identification and punishment of those responsible . . . The minimum standards as to effectiveness defined by the Court's case law also include the requirements that the investigation must be independent, impartial and subject to public scrutiny, and that the competent authorities must act with exemplary diligence and promptness.
>
> (para. 91)

These factors pose a significant challenge to the activities of police and prosecutors charged with enforcing rape laws and through whom most of the complaints are filtered out of the criminal justice system (see, e.g., Kelly 2002; Kelly et al. 2005). Recognition of these positive duties also suggests a need for a redoubling of current efforts to bring perpetrators to justice.

## CONSENT AND THE ECHR: CONSENT v COERCION?

There has been some concern about the concept of consent as key in determining liability for sexual offences, given its perceived limitations in considering the social and contextual factors involved in sexual exchanges (see, further, Munro in this collection; Tadros 2006; Chamallas 1988: 820–30). MacKinnon argues that whilst non-consent focuses on rape 'fundamentally as a deprivation of sexual freedom, a denial of self-acting', coercion as a basis of liability 'sees rape fundamentally as a crime of inequality, whether of physical or other force, status or relation' (2006: 237–8). The most obvious example of circumstances that are coercive is during times of conflict, and this is the context of the cases considered here. However, were coercion as opposed to non-consent to be adopted in European human rights jurisprudence, this would have the effect of enabling domestic criminal law systems to consider inequality, such as economic inequality and disparities of power, as a factor inhibiting genuine agreement in sexual interaction.

A number of the recent cases before the International Criminal Tribunal for Rwanda and the ICTY have moved away from determining rape cases as consent-based sexual intercourse to a broader notion of sexual abuse. In *Prosecutor v Akayesu* (ICTR-96-4-T Ch. 1, 2 September 1998), the Court defined rape as:

> [A] physical invasion of a sexual character committed on a person under circumstances which are coercive. Sexual violence which includes rape, is considered to be any act of a sexual nature which is committed on a person in circumstances which are coercive.
>
> (para. 598)

This case is significant for a number of reasons. First, it was the first case to offer a definition of rape under international law. Secondly, it was ambitious in its definition – a 'physical invasion of a sexual character' is broader than the definition of rape often found in domestic jurisdictions. Thirdly, it represented a move away from consent to coercion as the basis for determining liability.

Whilst the jurisprudence of human rights treaties and the international criminal courts have influenced the decision-making of the ECtHR, the pathbreaking decision of *Akayesu* appears not to have been considered explicitly in *MC v Bulgaria* – the first ECtHR case to consider a definition of rape. Repeated references are made to cases in front of the ICTY in which consent-based definitions return (thus appearing to qualify the broad *Akayesu* perspective) and are used interchangeably with coercion-based definitions in determining liability (see MacKinnon 2006: Ch. 23). The focus on consent-based definitions can be seen as trying to prevent an excessively narrow definition of rape, which requires force or threats (as was the case in *MC v Bulgaria*). The ICTY decisions move away from this and seek to give 'force' a broader meaning. However, they also move away from a definition based solely on coercion articulated in *Akayesu*.

In *MC*, the Court relied on the decision in *Prosecutor v Anto Furundzija* (case no. IT-95-17/1-T, 10 December 1998) in which the Court found that in the jurisdictions surveyed, rape required 'an element of force, coercion, threat or acting without the consent of the victim' with force 'given a broad interpretation . . . [including] rendering the victim helpless' (para. 180). Rape was defined as '[S]exual penetration . . . by coercion or force or threat of force against the victim or a third person' (para. 185). The ECtHR noted that these concepts were not to be narrowly interpreted and went on to consider the decision in *Prosecutor v Kunarac, Kovac and Vukovic* (ICTY-96-23T) where the ICTY found that the basic principle underlying liability within various legal systems was to penalize 'serious violations of sexual *autonomy*'. This is compromised 'wherever a person subjected to the act has not freely agreed to it or is otherwise not a voluntary participant'. The Court in *Kunarac* then went on to focus on 'coercion, force or threat of force' and stated that these concepts should not be interpreted narrowly. The *actus reus* of rape in international law was defined as non-consensual penetration and it was emphasized that 'consent for this purpose must be given voluntarily, as a result of the victim's free will, assessed in the context of the surrounding circumstances'. The *mens rea* was declared to be intention and knowledge that penetration occurs without the consent of the victim (paras 447–60). This was explained further on appeal where the Court reinforced again that force should not be interpreted narrowly and held that:

> A narrow focus on force or threat of force could permit perpetrators to evade liability for sexual activity to which the other party had not consented by taking advantage of coercive circumstances without relying on physical force . . .
> (IT-96-23 & IT-96-23/1-A, Appeal Judgment 12 June 2002)

What emerges from these cases is that *Akayesu* notwithstanding, the international criminal courts have again moved towards consent-based definitions of rape. This is mirrored in many of the jurisdictions surveyed by the ECtHR in the *MC* case, in which rape is characterized by lack of consent. Indeed, the Court also referred to the Recommendation Rec (2002) 5 of the Committee of Ministers of the Council of Europe on the Protection of Women Against Violence, which states that Member States should 'penalise any sexual act committed against non-consenting persons, even if they do not show signs of resistance' (Council of Europe 2002: para. 35). The Court in *MC* appears to cement this position in holding that whilst the applicant was raped because she was taken to a deserted area to create circumstances of coercion, ECHR jurisprudence requires that in investigating and prosecuting rape cases, the central focus must be on 'non-consent' (para. 181).

There are limitations to this approach, namely the extent to which non-consent can be said to encompass non-violent coercion (such as economic pressure) or social inequality in sexual relationships. However, coercive circumstances as the defining principle is even more vague a concept than non-consent and there is thus difficulty translating it into domestic non-conflict systems where the circumstances in which coercion is sufficient to ground liability for sexual offences is less clear (see, further, Munro in this collection).

## BOLSTERING EQUALITY WITHIN CONVENTION JURISPRUDENCE

There are two further mechanisms by which the language of inequality with regard to sexual offences might enter ECHR discourse. The first source is associated with the jurisprudence of Article 14 as a means of securing equivalence between groups in the protection of rights. Article 14 secures Convention rights to all regardless of, inter alia, sex, but one of the other substantive Articles needs to be engaged. The argument here is developed from the idea that the failure to protect women from acts of rape is also an act of discrimination because women are disproportionately victims of sexual violence, and this failure impedes their enjoyment of other rights. It will be shown here that such an approach is consistent with the jurisprudence of the International Covenant on Civil and Political Rights (ICCPR). The second source within Convention jurisprudence is developed from Protocol 12, the freestanding right to equality, which is less well developed. This section examines these sources of what shall be termed 'equality jurisprudence' in terms of their application to cases of rape and sexual violence.

## Article 14 ECHR as a source of 'equality jurisprudence'

The Human Rights Committee (HRC), the independent body which monitors the operation of the ICCPR as well as hearing individual and inter-state complaints, has developed jurisprudence in relation to sexual violence as an issue of equality under Article 3 of the ICCPR (equal enjoyment of rights under the Covenant) and Articles 7 (the prohibition on torture and 'cruel, inhuman or degrading treatment or punishment'), 8 (the prohibition of slavery and servitude) and 9 (the right to liberty and security of person). Giving effect to the provisions of Article 3 ICCPR has meant that states are obligated to report on the ways in which laws or practices may be affecting women's enjoyment of these rights, including their right to protection from torture and inhuman or degrading treatment, slavery and arbitrary deprivations of liberty. To date, the ECtHR has not, however, followed this approach. Indeed, in its recent position on domestic violence in the case of *Opuz v Turkey*, the ECtHR has yet to develop any jurisprudence which would confirm that sexual violence per se is an issue of equality which engages Article 14 ECHR.

Article 14 is lacking on a number of levels when it comes to addressing violations that particularly affect women. First, it is formulated in terms of formal equality and the development of its jurisprudence has been limited (Easton 2002: 22–5). Secondly, of the rape cases cited here, not one was heard as an issue of equality for women. In *Cyprus*, the Court found a violation of Article 3 in combination with Article 14 because Turkey had 'failed to secure the rights and freedoms ... without discrimination on the grounds of ethnic origin, race and religion' (para. 503). In no other case has the ECtHR dealt with sexual violence as an issue of discrimination. The ECtHR did not consider arguments of gender discrimination under Article 14 in the *MC* decision, notwithstanding its references to CEDAW and the Committee's clear position that rape is a form of discrimination against women.

The HRC seems to have adopted the stance of tackling violence against women as an issue under the substantive articles as well as an issue of equality under Article 3 ICCPR. This is to increase awareness amongst states of the ways in which enjoyment of rights is impeded by gender. In this way, the extent to which sexual violence impedes women's equal enjoyment of rights, and the effects that this type of violence has on them socially and politically, can be articulated. Treating rape or sexual violence purely as a violation of a substantive Article – such as inhuman and degrading treatment under Article 3 ECHR – does not reflect the fact that attacks of this nature are attacks on women because they are women. The group dimension is absent (MacKinnon 2006: Ch. 19). The position of the ECtHR in relation to Article 14 limits the articulation of this pervasive, highly gendered type of abuse within the ECHR paradigm. In addition, on the rare occasions that Article 14 is engaged, it is inherently limited by notions of formal equality, inadequate in addressing the structural disadvantages faced by women. The problems with Article 14 result in limits to the potential claims brought under Article 3 ECHR. They also affect the manner in which violations of women's rights under, for example, Articles 4 (prohibition of slavery) and 5 (right to liberty) ECHR might be tackled from an equality perspective.

There is an additional difficulty in that, until recently at least, it has been uncertain whether private individuals can perpetrate acts of discrimination. If Article 14 is read in conjunction with Article 1 of the ECHR, it becomes clear that, like the jurisprudence being developed by the HRC, the securing of rights without discrimination does carry with it positive obligations (McColgan 2003: 160). Support for the proposition that Article 14 carries positive obligations is to be found in the *Belgian Linguistics Case* ((1979–80) 1 EHRR 252), although the principle could be interpreted as, at most, a positive obligation to secure the rights under the Convention without discrimination. As previously stated, Article 14 does not make explicit reference to acts of private individuals, unlike the equality provisions of other international human rights treaties (McColgan 2003: 161–3). However, none of the Articles of the Convention does this. Article 1 (the obligation on states to secure rights to all within their jurisdiction) in combination with the development of the doctrine of positive obligations generally, combined with the fact that violations of Article 14 cannot occur without a violation of another substantive right (that may carry with it positive obligations between private individuals) would tend towards states being required to protect individuals from violations of their rights where the additional dimension of discrimination is involved. Significantly, this seems to have been the approach to Article 14 taken by the ECtHR to domestic violence in the recent case of *Opuz v Turkey*.

## Protocol 12 ECHR as a source of 'equality jurisprudence'

Protocol 12 to the ECHR provides a freestanding right to equality. Article 1 states that:

> The enjoyment of any right set forth by law shall be secured without discrimination on any ground such as sex, race, colour, language, religion, political or other opinion, national or social origin, association with a national minority, property, birth or status.

The Protocol also states that its provisions do not prevent states from taking steps to 'promote full and effective equality'. In providing this freestanding right, the equality jurisprudence of the ECHR is being brought into line with Article 26 ICCPR, which provides for equality before the law, 'equal protection of the law ... and effective protection against discrimination on any ground'. The freestanding right to equality under Protocol 12 and Article 26 ICCPR may provide a mechanism for addressing the structural disadvantages faced by women socially in view of its acceptance of measures to secure de facto equality. However, the Explanatory Report to the Protocol states that whilst the doctrine of positive obligations – including the obligation on states to secure rights between private individuals – 'cannot be excluded altogether, the prime objective of Article 1 of Protocol 12 is to embody a negative obligation for the Parties'. This limits the development of arguments to secure rights to equality between private individuals. Furthermore, the development of jurisprudence in relation to violence against women as an issue of equality has not occurred under Article 26 ICCPR (but rather Article 3), and given the reluctance to date of the ECtHR to articulate sexual (cf. domestic) violence as an issue of equality in the first place, the use of this stand-alone right may well be limited in this context.

## CONCLUSIONS

It is clear from this discussion that whilst considerable progress has been made, there are a number of problems with the way that the ECtHR has developed its jurisprudence in relation to sexual violence. The distinction between acts of rape as torture and acts of rape as inhuman and degrading treatment is difficult to sustain. In addition, what is missing from ECHR jurisprudence is the articulation of sexual violence as an issue of discrimination. Conceptualizing rape in this way might provide a way to articulate the extent to which social inequality and disadvantage impedes genuine agreement in the context of sexual relations. Although the potential exists to develop rights analysis under the ECHR in ways that would benefit women, the will to do this in relation to sexual violence appears to be lacking at present. The Council of Europe is moving further towards adopting measures aimed at tackling violence against women, such as Rec 1847 Combating Violence Against Women (2008), which acknowledges the gendered nature of such violence (including sexual violence), and the recently established Ad Hoc Committee on combating and preventing violence against women and domestic violence. In addition, recent ECtHR jurisprudence has recognized that, in some circumstances, physical forms of domestic violence and inadequate police responses thereto can give rise to discrimination, contrary to Article 14. This gives hope for similar developments in relation to rape and sexual violence in the future.

## Bibliography

Cassese, A. (1993) 'The prohibition on torture or inhuman or degrading treatment or punishment', in R.S.J. MacDonald, F. Matscher and H. Petzold (eds) *The European System for the Protection of Human Rights*, Dordrecht: Martinus Nijhoff, 225–61.

CEDAW (1992) *General Recommendation 19* (11th Session) UN Doc CEDAW/C/1992/L1/Add15.

Chamallas, M. (1988) 'Consent, equality and the legal control of sexual conduct', *South California Law Review*, 61: 777–862.

Charlesworth, H. (1998) 'The mid-life crisis of the Universal Declaration of Human Rights', *Washington and Lee Law Review*, 55(3): 781–96.

Council of Europe Committee of Ministers (2002) Recommendation Rec (2002) 5 of the Committee of Ministers of the Council of Europe on the Protection of Women Against Violence.

Council of Europe (2008) *Recommendation 1847 Combating Violence Against Women: Towards a Council of Europe Convention*.

Easton, S. (2002) 'Feminist perspectives on the Human Rights Act: two cheers for incorporation', *Res Publica*, 8: 21–40.

Kelly, L. (2002) *A Research Review on the Reporting, Investigation and Prosecution of Rape Cases*, London: Her Majesty's Crown Prosecution Service Inspectorate.

Kelly, L., Lovett, J. and Regan, L. (2005) *A Gap or Chasm? Attrition in reported rape cases*, London: Home Office Research Study 293.

Londono, P. (2007) 'Positive obligations, criminal procedure and rape cases', *European Human Rights Law Review*, 2: 158–71.

McColgan, A. (2003) 'Principles of equality and protection from discrimination in international human rights law', *European Human Rights Law Review*, 2: 157–75.

McGlynn, C. (2008) 'Rape as "torture"? Catharine MacKinnon and questions of feminist strategy', *Feminist Legal Studies*, 16: 71–85.

—— (2009) 'Rape, torture and the European Convention on Human Rights: expanding the boundaries', *International Criminal Law Quarterly* 58(3): 565–595.

MacKinnon, C. (2006) *Are Women Human? And other international dialogues*, Cambridge, MA: Harvard University Press.

Quinlivian, K. (1997) 'Women's rights and the European Convention on Human Rights', in C. Bell (ed.) *Women's Rights as Human Rights: a practical guide*, Centre for International and Comparative Human Rights Law: Queens University Belfast, 11–20.

Regan, L. and Kelly, L. (2003) *Rape: still a forgotten issue*, London: London Metropolitan University, Child and Woman Abuse Studies Unit.

Russell, D. (1990) *Rape in Marriage*, Bloomington: Indiana University Press.

Steiner, H. and Alston, P. (2007) *International Human Rights in Context: law, politics, morals*, 3rd edn, Oxford: Oxford University Press.

Tadros, V. (2006) 'Rape without consent', *Oxford Journal of Legal Studies*, 26(3): 515–43.

Zilli, L. (2002) 'The crime of rape in the Case Law of the Strasbourg Institutions', *Criminal Law Forum*, 13: 243–65.

Chapter 8

# Rape law reform in Africa
'More of the same' or new opportunities?

*Heléne Combrinck*[1]

As has been the case elsewhere in the world, several countries in Africa have in recent years embarked on the daunting journey of rape law reform. At the same time, a number of important developments have unfolded in the African regional human rights system, most notably the adoption of the Protocol to the Africa Charter on Human and Peoples' Rights on the Rights of Women in Africa (the African Women's Protocol) and the introduction of two gender-related Protocols in the Great Lakes and Southern African sub-regions.

This chapter assesses the potential of these instruments to expand the normative framework for rape law reform in Africa. It first looks at the contents of the African Women's Protocol and its enforcement mechanisms, and also briefly examines the two sub-regional documents. It then considers how these developments may influence future rape law reform initiatives.

## OUTLINE OF THE AFRICAN[2] CONTEXT

Violence against women is a global phenomenon: it is not limited to any one culture, region or country, or to particular groups of women within a society (UN Secretary-General 2006: para. 66). The United Nations (UN) Secretary-General, reporting on an in-depth study on all forms of violence against women, has identified a number of explanations for such violence, that is, patriarchy and other relations of dominance and subordination, cultural norms and practices and economic inequalities. The report also recognized a number of specific causal factors such as the use of violence in conflict resolution, the doctrine of privacy and state inaction, as well as individual or family behavioural patterns, which create a higher risk of violence (UN Secretary-General 2006: paras 69–91).

At the risk of generalization, it is among the broader systemic factors identified above, such as cultural norms and economic inequalities, prevailing in African societies that one finds the explanation for the high levels of violence against women that have been observed here. For example, 50–70 per cent of Ethiopian women experience gender-based violence in their lifetime, among the highest levels globally (Philpart et al. 2009: 123). A South African study published in 2004 reported the highest rate of intimate femicide noted in international research, amounting to a woman being killed by her intimate partner every six hours (Mathews et al. 2004: 4). While unacceptable anywhere, in developing countries, particularly in sub-Saharan Africa and Asia, gender-based violence has greater negative impacts on human development than elsewhere because of its high prevalence, limited access to legal services, insensitivity of law enforcement and limited constitutional efforts to address gender inequality (Philpart et al. 2009: 122–3).

It has been said that contemporary Africa finds itself 'poised between tradition and modernity' (Viljoen 2007: 268). While important strides have been made across the region in terms of changing the role of women from that of a perpetual minor, restricted to the home with the duties of childrearing, to an independent, equal partner with choices in terms of entering the public sphere, the 'ideology of domesticity' is still in many respects the persistent reality (Tamale 2004: 51–3; see also Viljoen 2007: 268–9).

For example, in 2002, Specioza Kazibwe, then the Vice-President of Uganda, made public the fact that she had, over a number of years, been subjected to physical violence by her husband. While she did receive some support, mainly from women's groups, the majority of people felt that she had been wrong to make public what had happened within the privacy of her home. Her husband responded in public that he had 'only' slapped her and that this was to correct her, because he felt that she needed to know that her public role ended at the gate – when she entered the home, she was his wife and not the Vice-President. In her role as his wife, she had to submit to him and not be impertinent (Banda 2005: 159; Anon. (19 March 2002)).

As Fareda Banda observes, this incident underlines the resilience of the traditional notion of 'the good wife': one who is obedient and who does not challenge accepted gender roles (Banda 2005: 159). It also illustrates how strongly the division between the public and private still operates in African societies – by no means unique to Uganda.

Fitnat Adjetey, cautioning against oversimplification, observes that because traditional African institutions are broadly diverse, women's rights vary from one society to another (Adjetey 1995: 1355–6). However, it can be stated as a general rule that women's sexuality remains a deeply contested area. In some parts of Africa, marriage results in a woman's physical person, including her sexuality, becoming part of her husband's property (Adjetey 1995: 1359–60; Banda 2005: 172; Ebeku 2006: 26). Unsurprisingly, customary law regards all sex within a marriage as consensual. This has resulted in marital rape proving to be a major area of controversy in virtually every Anglophone African country where women's rights activists have advocated for law reform.[3] The conceptual impossibility of a man raping his wife, originating from customary law, has been reinforced by the 'marital rape exemption' from common law.

The confluence of women's inequality with various structural factors implies, in real terms, that women are often coerced into having sex without being in a position to protect themselves against sexually transmitted diseases, including HIV/AIDS. In 2008, sub-Saharan Africa remained the region most heavily affected by HIV. Women, accounting for nearly 60 per cent of

HIV infections in this region, bear a disproportionate burden in the pandemic (UNAIDS 2008: 30–3).

## THE AFRICAN WOMEN'S PROTOCOL

### Background: reasons for drafting the protocol

A major factor leading to the drafting of the African Women's Protocol was concern about the level of protection offered to women by the African Charter on Human and Peoples' Rights (the African Charter), which is the foundational instrument in the African human rights system. Article 18(3) of the Charter calls on states to ensure the elimination of discrimination against women and also to ensure the protection of the rights of the woman and the child as stipulated in international declarations and conventions.

Concern arose from the close alignment of this provision with the preceding sub-articles, which require state protection for the family as 'the custodian of morals and traditional values recognized by the community' (Articles 18(1) and (2)). The emphasis on traditional values in the African Charter (see Preamble, and sections 29(1) and 61) has been identified as troubling from a women's rights perspective (Adjami 2002: 123; Nsibirwa 2001: 41; Onoria 2002: 234; Viljoen 2007: 269; see, however, Chirwa 2006: 69–70 contra). Article 18 therefore appears to contain an inherent contradiction between the duty of the state to protect the family as the custodian of traditional values, at the same time as ensuring the protection of the rights of women (Onoria 2002: 234). A practical difficulty was that there was no jurisprudence from the treaty-interpreting body, the African Commission on Human and Peoples' Rights (the African Commission), to resolve this contradiction (see Karugonjo-Segawa 2005: 6–7).

A further reason for the drafting of the African Women's Protocol was the fact that the African Charter does not explicitly address issues affecting the rights of women such as female genital mutilation, forced marriages and violence against women (Nsibirwa 2001: 41). It was also argued that women in Africa continued to be victims of harmful practices and discrimination, in spite of the widespread ratification of the African Charter and international instruments, such as the UN Convention on the Elimination of All Forms of Discrimination against Women (CEDAW) by African states (Olowu 2006: 81). The Protocol acquired legal force on 25 November 2005. At the time of writing, 27 countries had ratified the Protocol.

### Overview of contents

This section briefly outlines the key articles of the Protocol in the field of violence against women, with reference to international instruments, particularly CEDAW.

Article 1 comprises the definition section of the African Women's Protocol, where the meaning of the terms 'discrimination against women' as well as 'violence against women' are set out (among others). The definition of 'discrimination against women' is almost verbatim to that employed in CEDAW, and it is clear that both 'direct' and 'indirect' forms of discrimination are included. 'Violence against women' is defined as:

> all acts perpetrated against women which cause or could cause them physical, sexual, psychological, and economic harm, including the threat to take such acts; or to undertake the imposition of arbitrary restrictions on or deprivation of fundamental freedoms in private or public life in peace time and during situations of armed conflicts or of war.

This definition is broader than the one contained in the UN Declaration on the Elimination of Violence against Women (the Violence Declaration) in that it includes 'economic harm'. This is important in the African context where, for example, widows may be denied their inheritance through the practice of 'property-grabbing' (Banda 2008a: 18; Limann 2002: 215–7). The definition also includes the phrase 'in peacetime and during situations of armed conflicts or of war' – again a valuable emphasis in the African situation (Karugonjo-Segawa 2005: 16). Furthermore, the section uniquely provides a definition for 'harmful practices', that is, all behaviour, attitudes and practices that negatively affect the fundamental rights of women and girls, such as their rights to life, health, dignity, education and physical integrity (Karugonjo-Segawa 2005: 15).

Similar to CEDAW, Article 2 of the African Women's Protocol imposes a series of obligations on states to combat discrimination against women through appropriate legislative, institutional and other measures, such as the inclusion of the principle of equality between men and women in their national constitutions (Article 2(1)(a)). States also have a duty to 'modify the social and cultural patterns of conduct of women and men' with a view to eliminating harmful cultural and traditional practices, as well as all other practices based on the idea of the inferiority or the superiority of either of the sexes, or on stereotyped roles for women and men (Article 2(2)). In contrast to Article 2(e) of CEDAW, the Protocol does not impose an explicit duty on states to 'take all appropriate measures to eliminate discrimination against women by any person, organisation or enterprise' (Chirwa 2006: 73).

The Protocol provides that every woman has the right to dignity inherent in a human being and to the recognition and protection of her human and legal rights (Article 3(1)). States must take measures to prohibit the exploitation or degradation of women, and to ensure the protection of every woman's right to respect for her dignity. Importantly, this includes the protection of women from all forms of violence, particularly sexual and verbal violence (Article 3(3) and (4)). The link drawn here between the protection from all forms of violence (especially sexual and verbal violence) and the right to dignity is a significant one, given the statement in both the International Covenant on Civil and Political Rights and the International Covenant on Economic,

Social and Cultural Rights that other rights derive from the inherent dignity of the human person (see Preambles to the Covenants; Cowen 2001: 49).

Article 4, which states that every woman is entitled to respect for her life and the integrity and security of her person, is the central clause dealing with violence against women (although this issue is also interwoven into several other articles of the document – see Banda 2008b: 456). States are required to take a range of measures to address violence against women, including enacting and enforcing laws to prohibit all forms of violence against women, 'including unwanted or forced sex whether the violence takes place in private or public' (Article 4(1)(a)). This provision is a key one in respect of jurisdictions where the criminalization of marital rape remains problematic (Banda 2008a: 13).

States are further expected to adopt such 'other legislative, administrative, social and economic measures as may be necessary' to ensure the prevention, punishment and eradication of all forms of violence against women (Article 4(1)(b)). The omission from the Protocol of the so-called 'due diligence' standard, which has in recent years emerged in international human rights law as one of the crucial aspects of state duties in addressing violence against women (see UN Special Rapporteur on Violence against Women 2006: paras 28–9), is noteworthy. Furthermore, the key international documents all impose duties on states to respond to violence against women 'by all appropriate means and without delay'. The language used in Article 4 of the Protocol seems curiously weak by comparison. States are required to 'take appropriate and effective measures' – there is no reference to urgency or responding 'without delay'. Also surprisingly absent from this article of the Protocol is any statement to the effect that violence against women constitutes discrimination.[4]

Having said this, the provisions of Article 4 remain important. States are required, inter alia, to identify the causes and consequences of violence against women and take measures to prevent and eliminate such violence (Article 4(1)(c)). In addition, they should take steps to eradicate elements in traditional and cultural beliefs, practices and stereotypes that legitimize the persistence and tolerance of violence against women (Article 4(1)(d)). They are furthermore expected to establish mechanisms and accessible services for effective information, rehabilitation and reparation for victims of violence against women (Article 4(1)(f)). Importantly, states must provide adequate budgetary and other resources for the implementation and monitoring of actions aimed at preventing and eradicating violence against women (Article 4(1)(i)). The article also addresses specific instances of vulnerability, such as trafficking, medical experiments without women's consent and the situation of women refugees.

### Enforcement mechanisms

The African Women's Protocol does not introduce any 'new' mechanisms to oversee its enforcement (see Articles 26, 27 and 32). Instead, the implementation and interpretation of the document is slotted into the existing arrangements for the African Charter. In this way, the Protocol is unfortunately subject to the same shortcomings that have limited the implementation of the Charter (Murray 2005: 269–70; Banda 2008b: 470–1).

The African Commission is responsible both for monitoring the implementation of the African Women's Protocol – through the system of state reporting – and for its interpretation, until the African Court of Justice and Human Rights (the African Court) becomes fully operational in all respects. The thorny question is whether the Commission has the resources and the commitment to women's rights issues to carry out this task in a vigorous and progressive way (Banda 2008b: 471). Rachel Murray has pointed out that while the Commission has a broad range of mechanisms at its disposal to protect and promote the rights in the Charter, few have historically been used to enhance the rights of women (Murray 2005: 259). On the positive side, considerable gains have been made, as seen, for example, in the adoption of resolutions specific to women by the African Commission since 2004.[5] However, little jurisprudence on women's rights has emerged from the Commission.

Previously, this was partly due to the fact that women's organizations did not fully explore the potential role of this Commission in protecting women's rights (Murray 2005: 259–60). This situation arose from a number of factors including an initial focus on development rather than on human rights among African women's organizations, a lack of awareness about the system on the part of such organizations, and a lack of financial resources (Welch 1993: 557–8; Butegwa 1994: 509–10). Certain of these factors, such as resource constraints, may still currently have an impeding effect. (It is nonetheless interesting to note that even with a greatly increased attentiveness among women's organizations to human rights and participation in the activities of the African Commission, these organizations have not made use of the complaints mechanisms, even now that the Protocol has come into operation). The reasons for this remain to be explored.

## Assessment of the African Women's Protocol

The Protocol has been met with mixed reviews. On one hand, gender activists have referred to the adoption of the Protocol as 'an important event in the history of African women's struggle for the recognition of their rights' (Adjamagbo-Johnson cited in Chirwa 2006: 64). Catharine MacKinnon has also praised the Protocol for putting Africa 'in the lead on women's equality in world law' (2006: 9).

Similarly, Frans Viljoen is of the opinion that the Protocol takes an 'undeniable normative step forward' (2007: 272; Banda 2006: 84; Olowu 2006: 85). However, he expresses concern that the main reasons for the deficiencies in the supervisory procedures under the African Charter (as well as CEDAW) – that is, lack of compliance with reporting obligations, the failure on the part of states to domesticate treaty obligations and implement concluding observations, and the limited use of complaints mechanisms – are also likely to plague the implementation of the African Women's Protocol (Viljoen 2007: 275).

Rachel Murray, on the other hand, has questioned why the decision was taken in the first place to propose an additional Protocol, when existing mechanisms such as the state reporting system and the ability to submit cases before the Commission had not been fully explored (2005: 261). Her assessment of the substantive provisions is that the Protocol is hardly a 'comprehensive restatement of existing obligations', nor is it structured to be an interpretation of the Charter for women (2005: 269). She concludes that one of the underlying aims in drafting the Protocol was to develop a document that would be a promotional tool and over which there would be a sense of ownership on the part of African organizations. What is missing, according to her, is an overall vision of how the Protocol would consolidate existing standards, interpret the African Charter for women or ensure mechanisms for enforcement (Murray 2005: 271).

Looking at the provisions on violence against women, I would have to concur with the commentators who have noted that the Protocol advances the existing normative structure. First, it emphasizes the importance of 'supportive arrangements' (such as the allocation of budgetary resources and the provision of services to victims) that underpin the state's legislative response to violence against women. While it is true that certain of these duties have been set out in other documents, such as the Violence Declaration and the Beijing Platform, the African Women's Protocol now constitutes a *legally binding* document in the African human rights system, which elevates its significance as a standard-setting document. Experience in comparative jurisdictions has shown that it is often the absence of such supportive arrangements that cause the implementation of well-intended rape law reform projects to flounder.

The articles specific to violence against women (or harmful practices, as the case may be) should, secondly, be read with other interlocking provisions, such as Article 25, which requires the state to ensure access to justice for women (including legal aid) and to provide for appropriate remedies where women's rights have been violated.

Another example here is the right to equal access to housing. Article 16 requires the state to grant women, whatever their marital status, access to adequate housing. This recognition is significant, given the links between a lack of access to adequate housing and domestic violence (Centre on Housing Rights and Evictions 2008: 34). In this regard, Article 16 of the African Women's Protocol expands on CEDAW, which only refers to women's right to access to housing in a limited sense, that is, when dealing with the rights of rural women (Article 14(2)(h)).

By thus considering the provisions on violence against women in conjunction with other articles of the Protocol, the progressive potential of the document becomes even more apparent. This reading is in line with the general principle of the indivisibility of, and interrelationship between, rights.

One hopes that the Commission (and, in due course, the African Court) will be presented with an opportunity to consider the provisions of the African Women's Protocol in respect of violence against women, especially since there is now forward-looking jurisprudence from other regional bodies to provide guidance (depending, of course, on the facts and legal question of the particular case).

## Gender-related instruments: advances at sub-regional level

In addition to the adoption of the African Protocol, the African system has lately seen certain developments indicating that sub-regional bodies may in the future play a more prominent role in the protection and promotion of women's rights. For example, the Economic Community of West African States (ECOWAS) Court of Justice recently handed down the first ruling on women's rights by a sub-regional body in *Hadijatou Mani Koraou v Niger* (Judgment no. ECW/CCJ/JUD/06/08 of 27 October 2008).[6] Furthermore, two gender-related instruments have been adopted in the southern and central African sub-regions respectively that should also have an impact on rape law reform in future. A brief discussion of these instruments follows.

## Great Lakes Protocol on the Prevention and Suppression of Sexual Violence against Women and Children

In June 2008, the Protocol on the Prevention and Suppression of Sexual Violence against Women and Children, agreed on by 11 countries in the Great Lakes region in 2006, came into force. The Great Lakes Protocol combines the establishment of a legal framework for the prosecution of perpetrators of sexual violence with measures designed to provide for the medical, material and social assistance of victims. This Protocol, innovative in its combination of international humanitarian law and international criminal law, was developed in the specific context of sexual violence against women and children during and after the protracted armed conflict in the Great Lakes region.

This document has been praised for its 'procedural sensitivity' (Banda 2008b: 458): it specifically demands, for example, that criminal procedures for the prosecution of persons accused of crimes of sexual violence should be sensitive to the emotional state of victims of such crimes (Article 6(5)). The Protocol constitutes an important development in that it is legally binding in respect of ratifying member states of the Great Lakes Pact on Security, Stability and Development.

## SADC Protocol on Gender and Development

The most recently adopted sub-regional instrument is the Southern African Economic Development Community (SADC) Protocol on Gender and

Development, which was accepted and signed at the SADC Summit of Heads of State and Government in Johannesburg on 17 August 2008. At the time of writing, the Protocol has not attracted sufficient ratifications for it to come into force (which is understandable, given the short time period since its adoption). It is encouraging to note that both Malawi and Madagascar, two of the SADC member states that did not sign the Protocol at the time of its adoption, have subsequently added their signatures (Anon (30 October 2009); Zirima (January 2009)), and Namibia and Zimbabwe have taken the further step of ratification.

The SADC Protocol has its genesis in the 1997 SADC Declaration on Gender and Development and an Addendum on violence against women, accepted in 1998, which called for states to consider the adoption of a legally binding instrument on the prevention of violence against women and children.

Part Six of the SADC Protocol (Articles 20 to 25) deals in depth with gender-based violence and state obligations to address such violence. Importantly, it attaches time frames to the duties undertaken by states. The key articles deal with legislative requirements, setting out how states should (by 2015) address gender-based violence in legislation. States must also review and reform their criminal laws and procedures to (inter alia) eliminate gender bias. Further articles address in detail the provision of services to victims of gender-based violence, including police, prosecutorial, health, social welfare and legal services and mandate training for service providers.

This document is potentially the most far-reaching of its kind, with tangible time frames and in-depth provisions relating to the monitoring of its implementation. However, full compliance with the Protocol will undeniably have resource implications for states in contexts where service provision is already imperilled, such as the public health sector. For example, Article 20(2) requires the provision of universal access to post-exposure prophylaxis to victims of sexual offences to reduce the risk of contracting HIV. One therefore hopes that the ambitious nature of the Protocol's contents will not deter states from ratifying the document.

## THE POTENTIAL IMPACT OF RECENT DEVELOPMENTS ON RAPE LAW REFORM IN AFRICA

Given the fact that the application of the African Women's Protocol and other documents is at present wholly untested in the regional human rights arena, it may be instructive to briefly consider how these emerging norms and standards may have an influence at the *national* level. Here one should look at the emerging body of jurisprudence where African courts have relied on human rights instruments in adjudicating challenges to legislation, rules of customary law or other practices constituting discrimination against women. This is of particular importance where the national legal system follows a so-called dualist approach to the reception of international law (Adjami 2002: 108–9; Oppong 2007: 297–8).

While the role and impact of international law on national law varies across jurisdictions, certain trends have emerged from this body of case law, which includes the judgments in *Ephraim v Pastory* ((2001) AHRLR 236 (TzHC 1990)) and *Unity Dow v Attorney-General, Botswana* ((2001) AHRLR 99 (BwCA 1992)). In these cases, national courts found interpretative guidance in the norms and principles of (unincorporated) international and regional human rights law in determining the ambit of the constitutional prohibition of sex-based discrimination. In its oft-cited judgment in *Unity Dow v Attorney-General, Botswana*, the Botswana Court of Appeal took this approach one step further by placing reliance on CEDAW, which Botswana at the time had signed, but not ratified.

It is important to note, therefore, that these cases provide a foundation for arguing that even where a country has not yet ratified the African Women's Protocol, or where a document such as the SADC Protocol is limited to a particular sub-region, the principles set out in these documents may be taken into consideration by courts at the national level to guide interpretation.

Interpretive guidance may be one way in which the newly emergent documents may have an impact on law reform initiatives. In jurisdictions where the law reform process has faltered or remains incomplete, a court challenge to existing (or recently amended) legislation may be the only way to effect changes. For example, in spite of recent amendments to legislation on sexual violence, both Kenyan and Ethiopian law still fails to criminalize marital rape. This is a serious shortcoming, and there can be no doubt that these two countries are falling short of the standards set in the African Women's Protocol, which requires states to ensure the prevention, punishment and eradication of *all* forms of violence against women. This failure should be open to court challenge on the national level, even though both countries at the time of writing are only signatories to the Protocol (they have yet to ratify the document).

Another prospective level of impact is that of advocacy and mobilization. Kaniye Ebeku identifies a number of instances where the African Women's Protocol, even when it was still in draft form, already made its influence felt in law reform initiatives at the national level (2006: 26). The potential of these instruments as promotional tools for the purposes of advocacy and other strategies should not be underestimated, especially when it comes to the 'infrastructure' provisions such as budget allocation, training of police officials and other aspects that are crucial to the successful implementation of rape legislation. In this respect, the effect of the 'interlocking' provisions of the African Women's Protocol and other documents should be taken into consideration. For example, given the intersections between sexual violence and women's disproportionate vulnerability to contracting HIV, the provisions of the Protocol relating to health and reproductive rights (Article 14) should be taken into account when advocating for changes to existing rape laws. Similarly, the provisions on the elimination of harmful practices, read with the guarantee of the rights of widows (Article 20), may be important tools for advocacy in jurisdictions where systematic violations such as 'widow-cleansing' or property-grabbing are still tolerated.

In this capacity, the 'sense of ownership' that Murray mentions, and the credentials of these instruments as 'African' documents, may go a long way to consolidate their power (Murray 2005: 271; see also Ocran 2007: 152). This can imply power in a direct, short-term sense of overcoming instances of lack of political will on the part of governments (for example, to harmonize national legislation with the more progressive model legislation included in the Great Lakes Protocol). But it can also indicate the longer-term transformative power of these instruments – in other words, to change the societal beliefs and norms that underlie unequal gender relations and contribute to violence against women.

## CONCLUSION

It has been argued that the speed with which the African Women's Protocol attracted the required number of ratifications to come into force is an indication of a renewed commitment among African states to address women's rights concerns (Ocran 2007: 152). The African Union (AU), since it replaced the Organisation of African Unity in 2001, has undertaken a number of initiatives aimed at addressing gender inequality and violence against women (Stefiszyn 2007: 19–30). Prominent among these are the adoption of the Solemn Declaration on Gender Equality in 2004, read with its Implementation Framework approved in Dakar, Senegal, in 2005. (An analysis of these initiatives goes beyond the scope of this chapter). These AU projects, while encouraging, are too new for a comprehensive assessment (for a discussion of monitoring mechanisms under the Solemn Declaration, see Banda 2008b: 471–2).

Individual African countries are at present in the process of either reviewing existing or introducing new legislation addressing gender-based violence. Even a country such as Sierra Leone, still reeling in the aftershock of 11 years of armed conflict and currently at the bottom of the UNDP's Human Development Index, recently introduced three crucial laws aimed at combating gender inequalities, including domestic violence (Hanciles 2008). All these developments, together with the adoption of the instruments described above, indicate a gathering of significant cumulative momentum on the continent to address violations of women's rights.

The outcome of the assessment undertaken in this chapter is, ultimately, that recent developments in the African human rights system do represent new opportunities when it comes to the reform of rape law. I have argued elsewhere that it will be up to the energy and creativity of women's rights activists to ensure that the promise bound up in the African Women's Protocol becomes a reality (Combrinck 2003: 26). The contribution of the African Women's Protocol and related sub-regional documents to rape law reform will be evaluated in the future by the hard test of whether or not they make a difference in practice.

## Notes

1 I would like to express my appreciation to the Ford Foundation for its financial support of the work of the Gender Project of the Community Law Centre, which made the research for this chapter possible.
2 Although this chapter makes use of general terms such as the 'African context' and 'African women', this does not imply an assumption that there is a single homogenous African experience or group of African women – differences in socio-economic, cultural and other variables should be considered, especially where these may have an impact on women's rights and gender equality.
3 In Uganda, for example, the inclusion of a provision removing the 'marital rape exemption' in the proposed Domestic Relations Bill was reportedly one of the factors that led to the long-term shelving of the Bill. The passage of the Ghanaian Domestic Violence Act in 2007 was almost derailed by the inclusion of a provision that could criminalize marital rape (see Charnock (24 February 2007); Oye Lithur (2009)).
4 This conceptual connection was drawn by the CEDAW Committee in its General Recommendation No. 19 (paras 1 and 6) and subsequently followed in documents such as the Violence Declaration and the Beijing Platform.
5 See Resolution on the Situation of Women in Africa (ACHPR/Res.66 (XXXV)04 dated 2004); Resolution on the Status of Women and the Entry into Force of the Protocol to the African Charter on Human and Peoples' Rights on the Rights of Women in Africa (ACHPR/Res.85(XXXVIII)05 dated 2005); Resolution on the Situation of Women in the Democratic Republic of Congo (ACHPR/Res.103(XXXX)06 dated 2006).
6 Unofficial English translation of judgment provided by Interights. Online. Available at: <http://www.interights.org/view-document/index.htm?id=533>. The matter dealt with the customary practice of 'wahiya', which entails a man acquiring a young woman to work as a servant (as well as concubine) under slave-like conditions.

## Bibliography

Adjami, M.E. (2002) 'African courts, international law, and comparative case law: chimera or emerging human rights jurisprudence?', *Michigan Journal of International Law*, 24: 103–67.
Adjetey, F.N. (1995) 'Reclaiming the African woman's individuality: the struggle between women's reproductive autonomy and African society and culture', *American University Law Review*, 44: 1351–81.
Anon. (2002) 'Uganda tackles wife-beating taboo', *BBC News*, 19 March 2002. Online. Available at: <http://news.bbc.co.uk/2/hi/africa/1881472.stm>.
—— (2009) 'CHRR applauds Bingu for signing SADC gender protocol, calls for implementation,' *Nyara Times*, 23 October 2009. Online. Available at: <http://www.nyasatimes.com/women/watchdog-applaude-bingu-for-signing-sadc-gender-protocol-calls-for-speedy-implementation.html>.
Banda, F. (2005) *Women, Law and Human Rights: an African perspective*, Oxford: Hart Publishing.
—— (2006) 'Blazing a trail: the African Protocol on Women's Rights comes into force', *Journal on African Law*, 50: 72–84.
—— (2008a) 'Building on a global movement: violence against women in the African context', *African Human Rights Law Journal*, 8: 1–22.
—— (2008b) 'The Protocol to the African Charter on Human and Peoples' Rights on

the Rights of Women in Africa', in M. Evans and R. Murray (eds) *The African Charter on Human and Peoples' Rights: the system in practice, 1986–2006*, 2nd edn, Cambridge: Cambridge University Press, 441–74.

Butegwa, F. (1994) 'Using the African Charter on Human and Peoples' Rights to secure women's access to land in Africa', in R. Cook (ed.) *Human Rights of Women: national and international perspectives*, Philadelphia: University of Pennsylvania Press, 495–514.

Centre on Housing Rights and Evictions (2008) *Sources 5: Women and Housing Rights*, 2nd edn, Geneva: Centre on Housing Rights and Evictions.

Charnock, A. (2007) 'Confusion over marital rape following passage of domestic violence act', *The Statesman*, 24 February 2007.

Chirwa, D.M. (2006) 'Reclaiming (wo)manity: the merits and demerits of the African Protocol on Women's Rights', *Netherlands International Law Review*, 63–96.

Combrinck, H. (2003) 'Reforming laws on sexual violence in Africa: a new approach required', *Africa Legal Aid Quarterly*, 22–6.

Cowen, S. (2001) 'Can "dignity" guide South Africa's equality jurisprudence?', *South African Journal on Human Rights*, 17: 34–58.

Ebeku, K.S.A. (2006) 'Considering the Protocol on the Rights of Women in Africa', *African Review*, 24–34.

Hanciles, E. (2008) 'From frameworks and norms on sexual and gender-based violence to action', *Pambazuka News*, 14 July 2008. Online. Available at: <http://pambazuka.org/en/category/comment/49425>.

Karogonjo-Segawa, R. (2005) *The Protocol to the African Charter on Human and Peoples' Rights on the Rights of Women in Africa*, Copenhagen: Danish Institute for Human Rights.

Limann, L.H. (2002) 'Practices and rites related to widowhood and the rights of women in Africa: the Ugandan experience', *Human Rights Development Year Book*, 217–23.

MacKinnon, C. (2006) *Are Women Human? And other international dialogues*, Cambridge, MA: Harvard University Press.

Mathews, S. et al. (2004) 'Every six minutes a woman is killed by her intimate partner', *Medical Research Council Policy Brief 5*, June 2004.

Murray, R. (2005) 'Women's rights and the Organization of African Unity and African Union: The Protocol on the Rights of Women in Africa', in D. Buss and A. Manji (eds) *International Law: modern feminist approaches*, Portland: Hart Publishing, 253–72.

Nsibirwa, M. (2001) 'A Brief analysis of the Draft Protocol to the African Charter on Human and Peoples' Rights on the Rights of Women', *African Human Rights Law Journal*, 1: 40–63.

Ocran, C. (2007) 'The Protocol to the African Charter on Human and Peoples' Rights on the Rights of Women in Africa', *The African Journal of International and Comparative Law*, 15: 147–52.

Olowu, D. (2006) 'A critique of the rhetoric, ambivalence, and promise in the Protocol to the African Charter on Human and Peoples' Rights on the Rights of Women in Africa', *Human Rights Review*, 78–101.

Onoria, H. (2002) 'Introduction to the African System of Protection of Human Rights and the Draft Protocol', in W. Benedek, E. Kisaakya and G. Oberleitner (eds) *Human Rights of Women: international instruments and African experiences*, London: Zed Books, 231–42.

Oppong, F.R. (2007) 'Re-imagining international law: an examination of recent trends in the reception of international law into national legal systems in Africa', *Fordham International Law Journal*, 30: 296–345.

Oye Lithur, N. (2009) 'See how far we've come', *Modern Ghana News*, 10 March 2009. Online. Available at: <http://www.modernghana.com/news/205809/1/nana-oye-lithur-see-how-far-weve-come-html>.

Philpart, M., Goshu, M., Gelaye, B., Williams, M.A. and Berhane, Y. (2009) 'Prevalence and risk factors of gender-based violence committed by male college students in Awassa, Ethiopia', *Violence and Victims*, 24(1): 122–34.

Stefiszyn, K. (2007) 'The African regional response to gender-based violence', in E. Delport (ed.) *Gender-Based Violence in Africa: perspectives from the continent*, Pretoria: Pretoria University Law Press, 17–30.

Tamale, S. (2004) 'Gender trauma in Africa: enhancing women's links to resources', *Journal of African Law*, 48: 50–61.

UN Secretary-General (2006) *In-Depth Study on All Forms of Violence against Women*, UN Doc. A/61/122/Add.1.

UN Special Rapporteur on Violence Against Women (2006) *The Due Diligence Standard as a Tool for the Elimination of Violence Against Women*, UN Doc. E/CN/2006/61.

UNAIDS (2008) *2008 Report on the Global AIDS Pandemic*, Geneva: UNAIDS.

Viljoen, F. (2007) *International Human Rights Law in Africa*, Oxford: Oxford University Press.

Welch, C. (1993) 'Human rights and African women: a comparison of protection under two major treaties', *Human Rights Quarterly*, 15: 549–74.

Zirima, P. (2009) 'SADC Gender Protocol: from commitment to action', *Southern African News Features*, January 2009.

# Part III

# National perspectives

Chapter 9

# Feminist activism and rape law reform in England and Wales
## A Sisyphean struggle?

*Clare McGlynn*

Rape is a political issue because of feminist activism. Ever since second-wave feminism lifted the lid on the systemic nature of sexual violence, including rape, feminists in the UK have fought to secure the better treatment of rape victims by society generally, and by the criminal justice system in particular. Reforming the law on rape has played a key role in these feminist campaigns partly due to the symbolic power of the criminal law, and most recently because of a government receptive to demands for change. However, while law reform has been successful in eliminating some of the most egregious examples of discriminatory attitudes and practices, rape remains endemic and convictions for rape are unjustifiably low.

To set the analysis of recent reforms to rape law in context, this chapter provides a trajectory of feminist activism and rape law reform in England and Wales over the past 30 years. It then examines three particular aspects of recent reform which are causing considerable controversy, namely changes to the defence of belief in consent, the introduction of a strict liability offence for child rape and the challenges of intoxicated capacity and consent.[1] The aim is to develop an analysis which demonstrates the vitality and achievements of feminist activism and rape law reform, but also the sustained resistance which such efforts meet.

## FEMINIST ACTIVISM AND RAPE LAW REFORM

In England and Wales, as elsewhere, there has been a sustained commitment from feminists to rape law reform over recent decades. Going back to the 1970s, the 'event' which sparked second-wave feminist activism in relation to rape law was the House of Lords' judgment in *DPP v Morgan* [1975] 2 WLR 913. *Morgan* declared that a man could not be found guilty of rape if he had an honest, even if unreasonable, belief that the woman was consenting. Proclaimed as a 'rapist's charter' (Temkin 2002: 119), this judgment crystallized feminist concerns that the legal system did not treat women complainants fairly; indeed that their reports of rape, their evidence and their perspectives on the offence were routinely discredited or ignored. The furore surrounding the *Morgan* judgment led the government to establish an advisory committee on the law of rape, which resulted in the Sexual Offences (Amendment) Act 1976. While the *Morgan* judgment remained good law, and would do so for another 25 years or so, the 1976 Act did respond to other criticisms of rape law which feminists had been making, namely over the misuse of sexual history evidence in rape trials.

The 1976 Act aimed to restrict the use of sexual history evidence and was cautiously welcomed by many feminists (Edwards 1981). However, despite the reforms, evidence continued to mount over the negative way in which complaints of rape were treated in the courts: in one case, for example, the judge castigated the woman victim and held her to have been guilty of a 'great deal of contributory negligence' in accepting a lift from a rapist (Benn et al. 1986: 3). In the early 1980s, a television documentary revealing the brutality of police questioning of rape complainants was also aired in the UK, leading to yet another public uproar (Benn et al. 1986: 3). This, in turn, gave rise to the first of many investigations into police practices, as well as to recommendations for reform and to new, tougher sentencing guidelines for the punishment of rape (*R v Billam* [1986] 1 All ER 986).

This was a pattern which was to continue throughout the 1980s and 1990s; examples of adverse treatment by the police, judiciary and other parts of the legal system were met with outrage, demands for reform, and changes, in response. While piecemeal, the reforms nonetheless often had significant merit in and of themselves. Notable in this regard was the recognition that husbands can perpetrate rape, so held by the House of Lords in the landmark judgment *R v R* ([1992] 1 AC 599). Of similar significance was the 1994 Criminal Justice and Public Order Act's recognition that men too can be victims of rape and the removal of the requirement for judges to warn a jury against convicting on the uncorroborated evidence of a woman. But while such formal changes were welcome, they fell far short of the wide-ranging response required and therefore failed to generate wholesale change. Nearly 20 years after *R v R*, for example, scepticism over the extent and harm of marital rape remains rife (Kelly et al. 2005). Likewise, attitudes of disbelief and stigmatization towards male victims of rape appear to be similarly impervious to legal change (Rumney 2008).

All the while, therefore, demands for significant change were mounting, with activism in England and Wales during the 1980s and 1990s focusing on the reform of rape trials. Successive studies during these decades revealed the harrowing nature of routine questioning of complainants in rape trials (Lees 1996; Adler 1987; Brown et al. 1992). Analysis of the 1976 Act found that not only was it not achieving its ambition to restrict the use of sexual history evidence, in fact the opposite effect was being observed: judges were often granting counsel greater flexibility to introduce sexual history evidence (Temkin 1984, 1993). The focus this encouraged on women's behaviour, dress, mental health, background and, of course, sexual history, though rarely relevant to the issues at trial, was hugely distressing for complainants and impacted negatively on their ability to give their best evidence.

By the end of the 1990s, it seemed that sustained pressure in this regard may have achieved a result. Implementing one of the Labour Party's election manifesto pledges to reform rape trials, the Youth Justice and Criminal Evidence Act 1999 was passed into law. This provided for a blanket ban on the use of sexual history evidence in rape trials, subject only to limited exceptions (Temkin 2003). However, just a few days after the 1999 Act came into force, it was challenged under the Human Rights Act 1998 as contravening a defendant's right to a fair trial. The subsequent ruling of the House of Lords in *R v A (no. 2)* [2001] UKHL 25, which effectively rewrote the legislation to introduce greater judicial discretion to admit sexual history evidence, has largely undermined the potential benefits of this reform. Indeed, a study into the effectiveness of the 1999 Act found that its provisions were being flouted by many judges and barristers who either knew little of the law or were less than keen to implement it in full (Kelly et al. 2006). Procedural requirements were often not followed and while there were examples of positive rulings enforcing the Act's restrictive provisions (*R v White* [2004] EWCA Crim 946), it was also not hard to find examples of judicial rulings which harked back to an earlier era (*R v Mukadi* [2003] EWCA Crim 3765) or where, at best, the legislation was rendered almost futile (*R v Martin* [2004] EWCA Crim 916).

Perhaps more positive results can be found in reforms to the substantive law of rape. At the end of the 1990s, a major review of sexual offences in England and Wales was undertaken, with significant input from feminists and activists, resulting in the Sexual Offences Act 2003 (SOA). The SOA overhauled the archaic laws on several sexual offences, with the explicit aim, among others, of improving rape conviction rates (Home Office 2002: para. 10). The offence of rape was reformed by introducing a statutory definition of consent. In addition, a number of presumptions regarding consent were created, designed to make proving non-consent more straightforward. Oral penetration was included within the *actus reus* of rape, penalties upon conviction were increased and the defence of honest belief, that major bête noire of feminists, was also reformed (Temkin and Ashworth 2004). The latter change, in particular, was reported in the press as the government responding to the concerns of 'women's organisations' (Dyer 2002) and is considered further in the next section.

Nonetheless, and perhaps perspicaciously anticipating the limited impact of the 1999 and 2003 Acts, by the end of the 1990s and into the 2000s, feminists were reflecting on how rape was the 'forgotten issue', as public policy regarding violence against women concentrated on domestic violence (Kelly and Regan 2001; Regan and Kelly 2003). From these reflections, the strategy emerged to focus on attrition in rape cases, that is, the process by which police reports of rape drop out of the criminal justice system and result in few convictions.

Research in the 1990s found a high rate of attrition in rape cases, pinpointing the failings in police investigations and high level of victim withdrawals as the principal causes (Gregory and Lees 1996). However, it was research in the 2000s which brought the issue to public prominence, largely due to the ever-increasing rate of reporting, yet ever-decreasing conviction rate. While in

1980 only 1,225 rapes were reported to the police in England and Wales (Toner 2006), this increased to 14,449 by 2005–06 (Home Office 2006b). Thus, in the decade between 1989/90 and 1999/2000, there was a 150 per cent increase in the number of recorded rapes (cf. an average increase for all offences of around 2.8 per cent (Temkin and Krahé 2008: 15)). While the number of rapes reported to the police was increasing, however, the proportion of convictions for rape was dramatically falling. The conviction rate for rape in 1977 was 32 per cent (Regan and Kelly 2003: 13): that is, of all rapes reported, just under one third resulted in a conviction. By 2002, this had fallen to 5.6 per cent (Kelly et al. 2005). In the last year or so, it has crept up to a meagre 6.5 per cent, but this remains intolerable when compared to the figure of 34 per cent for all crimes (Williams 2009). In relation to male rape, the limited evidence available suggests that there is an even higher rate of attrition (Rumney 2008). Not surprisingly in the light of these figures, England and Wales has one of the lowest rape conviction rates across Europe (Regan and Kelly 2003; Kelly and Lovett 2009).

The focus on attrition, and the low conviction rate, coincided with studies demonstrating the continued high prevalence of rape and sexual violence. The results of successive British Crime Surveys provided renewed impetus for change. These studies revealed that each year between 47,000 (Walby and Allen 2004) and 61,000 (Myhill and Allen 2002) women were the victims of rape. Greeted with alarm and considerable public outcry (for example, Travis 2002), these studies also found that many women (40 per cent) had not told anyone about the sexual assault they had suffered (Walby and Allen 2004: viii).

Beyond the headline figures, the research illustrates that there are problems with every stage of the criminal justice system. Successive investigations have revealed the continuing tendency of the police to treat reports of rape with scepticism, sometimes resulting in inappropriate 'no-criming' of reports, as well as a lack of thorough investigation (Kelly et al. 2005; HMIC and HMCPSI 2007). The conventional wisdom that low conviction rates result from the difficulties of investigating rape has also been challenged with evidence revealing rape conviction rates varying from one in five in some police areas to one in 60 in others (Fawcett 2008).

Difficulties do not just lie with police practices. The Crown Prosecution Service (CPS), which decides whether or not to proceed cases to trial in England and Wales, has been criticized for often focusing on weaknesses in evidence, rather than trying to build a prosecution case (Temkin and Krahé 2008: 19). Further, victim withdrawals are an important feature of the high rate of attrition, with many withdrawing due to police and CPS attitudes, fear of harassment and humiliation at trial and the same feelings of shame, guilt and anguish which give rise to low numbers of reports to the police in the first place (Kelly et al. 2005).

A key policy response to this mounting evidence has been centred on assisting victims, especially through the funding of rape crisis centres and the establishment of Sexual Assault Referral Centres, as well as the creation of a number of 'independent sexual violence advisors' to support victims of rape

(GEO 2009). While the funding of rape crisis centres is by no means secure, and many have closed over the past decade, the fact that 'sustainable funding' is acknowledged as a political issue – proclaimed as a key policy of the Conservative Party as well as the Labour Government – is significant. There are, however, areas of the country with few or no support services, and campaigns around a 'map of the gaps' have been successful in highlighting the need for further services (Coy et al. 2007).

These policy developments recognize that law reform alone cannot meet the challenges of increasing reports of rape and falling convictions. The government's own review of the SOA 2003 found 'little evidence that it had made any significant impact, either in encouraging victims to report the crimes or in terms of securing more convictions' (Home Office 2006a: para. 97). It was perhaps unduly optimistic to think that substantive law reform, especially in such a short period of time, would lead directly to more convictions. Nonetheless, there are indications that the SOA has not been living up to its promise, however limited that might be.

## THE SEXUAL OFFENCES ACT 2003: DEFINING AND UNDERMINING CONSENT

The SOA 2003 in England and Wales was a major reform designed to respond to criticisms that the common law on rape, particularly relating to consent, was vague, confusing and was contributing to low conviction rates. Three particular aspects of this initiative are analysed below, chosen because they each exemplify the challenges facing feminists seeking rape law reform. In each area, the potential of the reforms has not been realized, due to many factors, including both the tenacity of rape myths and judicial attitudes towards legislative reform.

### From honest to reasonable belief: plus ça change?

The SOA's requirement that a defendant's belief in consent no longer just be honest, but also be reasonable, was a leitmotif of the new Act. The reform appeared to constitute a significant feminist victory; such change had been rejected in the preceding *Setting the Boundaries* review (Home Office 2000) and faced strong opposition in parliament (Temkin and Ashworth 2004: 332). However, beyond the symbolic importance of this reform, serious doubts have been raised as to whether the new formulation in the SOA exacts a higher level of accountability from defendants (Temkin and Ashworth 2004: 340–2). The SOA does not require that the defendant's belief be objectively reasonable (as was originally proposed by the government), but that *his* belief be reasonable 'in all the circumstances' (section 1). This changes the standard from that of an 'objective bystander' to one which requires scrutiny of *this* defendant's likely beliefs: for example, what is it reasonable for this defendant to believe where he appears to be very popular with women? This leaves open the possibility of considering the particular personal characteristics of the defendant which may impact on his beliefs and their reasonableness (Cowan 2007: 59–66). It also straightforwardly invites jury scrutiny of the complainant's behaviour (and sexual history) to see whether there is anything that can be said to have induced a 'reasonable' belief. As Andrew Ashworth and Jennifer Temkin warn, the Act therefore provides 'no real challenge to society's norms and stereotypes' and 'leaves open the possibility that those stereotypes will determine assessments of reasonableness' (Temkin and Ashworth 2004: 342).

While some feminists were rightly critical of the *Morgan* defence, and therefore advocated reform towards a reasonableness standard, others have long been more sceptical over the value of such a change on the basis that it still focuses on the defendant's perspective (MacKinnon 1989: 183). To the extent that the focus of the reasonableness enquiry is to be based on 'all the circumstances', these concerns may be borne out by the new formulation. Indeed, successive studies of public attitudes towards rape in England and Wales have demonstrated a particular propensity for victim-blaming views, with strong beliefs in complainant precipitation of rape (Amnesty 2005; Home Office 2009; Temkin and Krahé 2008). Such attitudes are found among the public at large, as well as lawyers and judges (Temkin and Krahé 2008). Similarly, Emily Finch and Vanessa Munro's study investigating how mock jurors interpret the requirements of reasonable belief in 'all the circumstances', found that jurors often took into account a wide range of behaviours and actions which had little temporal correspondence with the sexual activity at issue and which arguably have little relationship to consent (Finch and Munro 2006: 318). Further, many jurors subjectivized the reasonableness standard, determining what that particular defendant might have thought reasonable, even if the juror themselves did not consider it reasonable (Finch and Munro 2006: 317).

It seems, therefore, that while the introduction of a reasonableness standard has an important symbolic value, and its very introduction did indeed represent something of a victory for feminists, it may have little impact in practice. While there remains scope for the reasonableness standard to make a positive difference, this will require attitudinal change among the public and, therefore, juries. This suggests that ultimately, it is changes in attitudes which may bring improvement in the law, rather than the law itself presaging change.

## Child rape: from strict liability to 'implied', 'ostensible' and 'genuine' consent

The SOA 2003 introduced a range of new offences relating to children, the breadth and complexity of which gave rise to immediate criticism (Spencer 2004). Of particular controversy was the creation of the new strict liability offence of 'child rape' (section 5). Intentional penile penetration of a child under the age of 13 constitutes the offence, there being no issue of consent and no defence as to mistaken belief in either consent or age. The offence had been introduced to strengthen the protection afforded to children under 13, particularly by removing the need for invasive questioning about their sexual knowledge, experience and behaviour, which routinely took place to raise issues about consent, belief in consent and mistaken belief as to age. Indeed, the government specifically justified the measures on the basis that there are many cases where it would be 'utterly invidious for a 12-year-old or under to have to give evidence in relation to consent' (Falconer 2003b).

However, it was not long before a challenge was mounted to this new offence under the Human Rights Act 1998, arguing that such a strict liability offence contravenes a defendant's right to a fair trial under Article 6 of the European Convention on Human Rights. The House of Lords, by a three to two majority, upheld the validity of the legislation (*R v G* ([2008] UKHL 37) with Baroness Hale strongly emphasizing that one of the objectives of section 5 is to make any male 'take responsibility for what he chooses to do with' his penis (para. 46).

Even in upholding the legislation, however, the judgments of some of the Law Lords in this case revealed some worrying assumptions and attitudes. The 12-year-old girl who made the allegation of rape withdrew her complaint because, as Baroness Hale noted in her judgment, she was so 'terrified' of the court process (per Baroness Hale paras 51 and 66). Following the withdrawal, the case proceeded on the basis of the defendant's claim that the sexual activity was consensual. While this by no means meant that the intercourse had indeed been consensual, this was apparently accepted by some of the Law Lords. There are references in the judgment to the defendant being 'morally blameless' (para. 17). In addition, Lord Hope was critical of the complainant who had not, at first, admitted to the police that she had told the defendant she was actually older than 12. Hope stated that the 'problem revealed by this case is the familiar one which faces every prosecutor', namely that the complainant's 'account of events may change' (para. 23). This hints at an assumption on the part of some judges that complainants' statements are generally unreliable, and a failure to appreciate the pressure which complainants may feel when reporting rape, especially at such a young age (and as evidenced by the complainant's withdrawal). Lord Carswell also referred to the complainant being unwilling to give evidence, 'even' in a children's hearing (para. 59), compounding the lack of understanding of a victim's fears about reporting rape.

What we see here is the House of Lords upholding the strict liability provisions set out in the SOA 2003, though evidencing some lack of appreciation of the experiences of complainants, the nature of their trauma and the impact this may have on both their willingness to proceed with a complaint and provision of evidence. Nonetheless, it is in the sentencing of child rapists that we see an undermining of this new offence. The Court of Appeal in *R v Corran* ([2005] EWCA Crim 192), which set down general guidelines for sentencing in section 5 cases, reduced the prison sentence of one offender from imprisonment to a conditional discharge (released without any punishment or fine) on the basis that the intercourse between the 12-year-old girl and a man who was 'just' 20 (para. 19) was consensual and the girl had led the defendant to believe that she was 16. The case involved, according to the Court of Appeal, 'every feature of mitigation which could be imagined' (para. 25), aside from the difference in age, including a guilty plea, the defendant's 'good work record' and that he 'came from a respectable family' (para. 22). Strikingly, the Court of Appeal in *R v G* [2006] EWCA Crim 821 described *Corran* as involving a '20-year-old youth who had been deceived by a precocious 12 year old' (para. 49). Absent here is any criticism of the sexual exploitation of a very young girl by a considerably older male.

This is just one case, but it does not stand alone. In 2007, 20-year-old Liam Edgecombe was given a conditional discharge for the rape of a girl aged 10 (O'Neill 2007). The judge referred to the defendant's belief that the girl had been 16 as 'reasonable' and continued that she 'was looking for a man and got what she wanted', while the defendant had been 'visibly traumatised' (O'Neill 2007). In 2008, a 25-year-old man was given a conditional discharge for intercourse with a 12-year-old girl, with the judge concluding that the defendant had been 'deceived' into believing the girl was over 16, especially by revealing photographs on her social networking website and her comments that she liked drinking and having sex (Jeeves 2008). Similar cases are regularly reported in the press (for example, Steele 2009).

While the aims of section 5 of the SOA were to do away with invasive questioning of children under 13 about consent and to emphasize, as a matter of policy, the irrelevance of a defence of belief as to age, we see an emergence of these issues through the language of 'ostensible consent', 'genuine consent', 'complete consent' and 'willing consent' (*Attorney General's Reference (no. 29 of 2008)* [2008] EWCA Crim 2026). At the same time, it should be noted that there have also been examples of strong judicial condemnation of these attitudes. In one Court of Appeal case, Lady Justice Hallet was excoriating in her criticism of a first instance judge who treated the 'forcible rape of a young girl, in the presence of three young men' as a 'childish prank gone wrong' (*R v Black; R v Gowan* [2006] EWCA Crim 2306: para. 30).

My argument here is not that judges are uniformly undermining the aims of the new child rape offence in the SOA; my examples do not purport to be representative of all cases. But what I am suggesting is that the enactment of progressive legislation can often be undermined by prevailing attitudes and assumptions which reform of the substantive law does little to change. In this instance, while there are now individuals being found guilty of the offence of child rape, the value of such convictions is being diluted by derisory punishments, often combined with disparaging and highly critical comments about the young women victims. There are some examples of these attitudes and approaches being challenged, but is it any wonder that the victim in *R v G* was 'terrified' at the thought of proceeding with her case?

## Intoxication, capacity and consent

As Emily Finch and Vanessa Munro report, it is well established that alcohol has been consumed by one or both parties in a high proportion of rape cases (Finch and Munro 2007: 592). Exact estimates vary for complainant consumption, ranging from one third (Kelly et al. 2005: 96) to over three quarters (Scott-Ham and Burton 2005). At the same time, we know from an Amnesty attitudinal study that 30 per cent of those questioned thought that a woman was partially or totally responsible for her rape if she had become drunk beforehand (Amnesty 2005). Research by Finch and Munro similarly establishes the societal disapprobation with which female intoxication is widely viewed and demonstrates the relationship between such censure and juror attributions of responsibility, notably away from the defendant and onto the shoulders of the complainant (Finch and Munro 2007: 607).

This conjunction between intoxication and rape has challenged the efficacy of the SOA's introduction of a statutory definition of consent, namely that a person consents if she or he 'agrees by choice and has the freedom and capacity to make that choice' (section 74). The idea behind a statutory definition was that it would 'provide a clearer legal framework for juries as they decide on the facts of each case' (Falconer 2003a), but cases involving rape and intoxication demonstrate that this has been far from the case. Two particular issues have arisen in a series of high-profile cases, the first being where a complainant has memory loss due to intoxication. This raises the question of whether such loss is fatal to the prosecution case and calls into question the law's stance on whether a complainant is required to say 'no' and unequivocally reject sexual advances, or whether non-consent is presumed unless there is evidence of positive consent. Secondly, the question of capacity to consent is raised where a complainant is extremely intoxicated.

These problems came to public prominence with newspaper headlines reporting a judge's dismissal of a rape jury in *R v Dougal* on the basis that 'drunken consent is still consent' (Roberts 2005; Gibb 2005). In this (unreported) case, the complainant had been so drunk that bar staff had asked a security guard to accompany her back to her student accommodation as she was barely capable of walking (Roberts 2005). Sexual intercourse took place between the security guard and the complainant in the corridor outside her room, but as the complainant could not remember some parts of the evening and sexual activity, due to her intoxication, the judge dismissed the prosecution case. The focus of the judge's ruling appeared to have been solely based on proof of the complainant's non-consent or otherwise and the impossibility, as the judge saw it (and as was accepted by the prosecution), of proving non-consent where the complainant was unable to recall all that happened. As Vera Baird QC noted at the time, this 'seems to reverse the burden of proof . . . requiring her to show that she didn't say yes' (quoted in Dyer and Morris 2005). Accordingly, in terms of debates over positive consent, this case raised the ugly spectre of intoxicated women being presumed to consent to sexual activity unless they could clearly establish that they did not consent. Indeed, this was the message contained in media reports (Roberts 2005; Gibb 2005). Capacity to consent was simply not considered as an issue, despite the evidence of the extreme intoxication of the complainant.

The resultant furore provoked the government to consult on proposals to introduce a statutory definition of capacity, in conjunction with other possible reforms aimed at improving conviction rates (Home Office 2006c). Broadly welcomed by many feminist groups, the proposals were vehemently rejected by the Council of Circuit Judges and the Bar Council (the collective organization representing barristers) (Dyer 2007). In any event, before the government could act, a similar case to *Dougal* presented itself to the Court of Appeal, providing an opportunity for judicial clarification on the issue of intoxication and consent.

Dealing first with the issue of capacity to consent, the judgment in *R v Bree* ([2007] EWCA Crim 256) suggested that the law in this area is, in fact, straightforward. If someone is so drunk that they are incapable of consenting, then there is no capacity to consent. Equally, if someone retains capacity, then they have capacity. Finally, someone can lose capacity even though not unconscious. While this may be an accurate summary of the key principles, it does little to help courts and juries deal with the complexities of these cases as they arise in practice. A significant aspect of *R v Bree* was a determination regarding the stage at which a complainant who is heavily intoxicated loses capacity. In this case, the complainant was intoxicated to the extent that she was vomiting repeatedly, with intercourse following shortly thereafter. The Court of Appeal suggested that the jury in such cases should be given some 'assistance' with the meaning of capacity, but failed to state what that assistance might be.

In relation to the issue of positive consent, the Court of Appeal judgment is exemplary in setting out clearly that consent must be positive and cannot be assumed. It said that it is 'wrong in law' and 'offensive' to suggest or assume that drunkenness deprives a woman of the opportunity whether to choose to have intercourse (para. 33). Further, it noted that what it called 'quiet submission' or 'surrender' are examples of non-consent (para. 22) and it approved the ruling in *R v Malone* ([1998] 2 CAR 447) that there is no consent where a complainant submits to an act of sexual intercourse because through drink she was unable to physically resist (para. 27). Thus, it may be that, as the Court of Appeal suggested, the problems of these cases 'do not arise from the legal principles' (para. 36), but in the 'infinite circumstances of human behaviour' (para. 36). Yet it is exactly how this 'human behaviour' is characterized and judged which makes the difference, as further analysis of the *Bree* judgment reveals.

The first sentence of that judgment tells us that Benjamin Bree is a 'man of excellent previous character' (para. 1) and that when the police arrested him he appeared to be 'shocked and extremely upset and could not believe that an allegation of rape had been made against him' (para. 12). Later, we are informed that the defendant 'looked after' the complainant whilst she was intoxicated (para. 7), 'unselfishly' washing her hair (para. 7).[2] What are the assumptions we are to draw from such statements (not really a rapist then?) and the way in which they contrast against the depiction of the complainant as being 'badly affected by drink' (para. 6) and unable to recall all events clearly?

Phil Rumney and Rachel Fenton suggest that there is a 'positive tone' to the judgment in *Bree*, referring to judicial statements emphasizing that the case was not about judging irresponsible behaviour or criticizing casual sex (2008: 283). This is welcome, as are the principled statements regarding the need for positive consent. However, such statements are difficult to square with the overall tenor of the judgment, discussed above, and its apparent unwillingness to contend with the difficulties of this area of law by providing greater guidance and direction for judges and juries. It is also interesting that the Court clearly rejected the suggestion, made by the government following the *Dougal* case (Home Office 2006c), that further reform of the definition of capacity was required.

Not long after *Bree*, the Court of Appeal was again required to clarify the law in another rape case involving a heavily intoxicated complainant. In *R v H* an extremely drunk 16-year-old girl had sexual intercourse with a man within minutes of meeting him ([2007] EWCA Crim 2056). She was unable to recollect all the events of the evening in question and, as in *Dougal*, the judge dismissed the jury before giving it an opportunity to consider issues of capacity or consent. In relation to capacity, the Court reiterated its statements in *Bree* that this was a decision for the jury to determine. However, what remains troubling from this case, and *Dougal*, *Bree* and others preceding it, is the apparent assumption that so long as someone remains conscious, they have capacity. While the Court in *Bree* stated that capacity can be lost before unconsciousness, this does not appear to be the general assumption. Both prosecution witnesses and defence argument in *R v H* noted that, as the complainant was still functioning, that is, walking and making some decisions, she retained capacity, even though she had serious memory lapses and had drunk what can only be considered an excessive amount of alcohol and taken other drugs. This does not mean that the jury – as arbiters of whether the complainant had capacity – would have agreed. But it is an important area to highlight.

If it is the case that juries consider complainants to retain capacity simply by reason of their being able to move about and take even such simple decisions as crossing roads or taking a bus, despite evidence of memory loss, instability in movement, vomiting and extreme levels of intoxication, then in practice lack of capacity is coterminous with unconsciousness. Indeed, such views were expressed by some of the mock jurors in Finch and Munro's study (Finch and Munro 2006: 314). This means that a heavily intoxicated woman is indeed extremely vulnerable to rape as she will be assumed to have capacity to consent. This is a difficult area; many feminists fear the infantilization of women if they are deemed unable to consent to sex while drunk (Williams 2002). Indeed, the Court of Appeal in *Bree* stated that provisions which might be intended to protect women from sexual assault in this area may be interpreted as a 'patronising interference with the right of autonomous adults' to make their own decisions (para. 35). There is clearly a balance to be struck, but there is, I would argue, a far greater danger here in assuming that women in extreme states of drunkenness retain capacity. As Phil Rumney and Rachel Fenton put it, the Court's endorsement of an apparent liberal non-interventionist approach can also be seen as a 'means by which some men's disregard for the sexual autonomy of women is maintained' (Rumney and Fenton 2008: 289).

The Court of Appeal judgment in *R v H* begins by lamenting that this case is 'yet another sad example of what can happen when young people roam the streets of our cities vulnerable though drink and/or drugs' (para. 1). The iteration of the facts in the case also include judicial statements of disbelief at the actions of the complainant, particularly accepting invitations of lifts with unknown men (paras 6, 10). These cases are indeed tragic examples of situations in which extremely drunk women have found themselves making complaints of rape. It is not the case that their drunkenness precludes a rape conviction, but the sense of incredulity mixed with disapproval with which their behaviour is treated makes successful prosecution far less likely. Unfortunately, it seems improbable that further statutory reform would make any real difference. As Nicola Lacey noted when the SOA was introduced, section 74 on consent points 'in the direction which cogent feminist analyses have argued to be desirable' (Lacey 2001: 12), and we already have principled statements regarding the need for positive consent in *R v Bree*. It is the operationalization of such principles which appears to be elusive.

## CONCLUSIONS

Victoria Nourse suggests that writing about feminist reform of the criminal law is to write of simultaneous success and failure (Nourse 1999–2000). She continues that these failures are a 'normal' part of the law reform process, pitting feminist ideas in a 'perpetual challenge' to old norms. Seen in this way, law reform is not 'futile', but a work in progress which requires 'perpetual vigilance' from feminists (Nourse 1999–2000: 951). Certainly, the story of rape law reform in England and Wales over the past 10 or more years is one which includes tales of progressive changes being met with resistance; often unacknowledged and perhaps unconscious and unrecognized, but resistance nonetheless. And cases such as *R v Bree* do indeed exemplify simultaneous 'success' and 'failure'.

In this way, reforming rape law feels like a Sisyphean task, with constant pressure leading to reforms, only to have such 'successes' neutralized in practice; the boulder falling back down the mountain. Yet to paint a wholly bleak picture would be to do a great disservice to those activists, lawyers, judges and others who have wrought important changes and improvements; who have helped to shape debate such that reform of rape law and policy has been discussed, introduced and implemented. Seen in such a light, perhaps it is the case that, unlike Sisyphus, feminists can slowly, and often imperceptibly, push higher up the mountain and not fall so far back. Incrementally, important improvements to the law on rape can be made, even though the rate of progress is unjustifiably slow.

## Notes

1 This chapter will consider English law which in most respects is the same as the law applying to Wales, though note moves to devolve greater powers to reform the criminal law to the Welsh Assembly (Jones 2008).
2 Rumney and Fenton note that this is pure assumption, and one favourable to the defendant at that. As they suggest, the defendant could have been acting wholly selfishly, by wishing to establish physical contact and/or not wishing to become intimate with someone with vomit in their hair (2008: 284).

## Bibliography

Adler, Z. (1987) *Rape on Trial*, London: Routledge and Kegan Paul.
Amnesty International (2005) *Sexual Assault Research: summary report*. Online. Available at: <http://amnesty.org.uk/uploads/documents/doc_16619.doc>.
Benn, M., Coote, A. and Gill, T. (1986) *The Rape Controversy*, London: National Council for Civil Liberties.
Brown, B. et al. (1992) *Sexual History and Sexual Character Evidence in Scottish Sexual Offence Trials*, Scottish Office Central Research Unit.
Cowan, S. (2007) ' "Freedom and capacity to make a choice": a feminist analysis of consent in the law of rape', in V. Munro and C. Stychin (eds) *Sexuality and the Law: feminist engagements*, Oxford: Routledge-Cavendish, 51–71.
Coy, M., Kelly, L. and Foord, J. (2007) *Map of Gaps: the postcode lottery of violence against women support services* (London: End Violence Against Women Coalition). Online. Available at: <http://www.mapofgaps.org/>.
Dyer, C. (2002) 'Honest belief of woman's consent is dumped as rape defence', *The Guardian*, 20 November 2002.
—— (2007) 'Judges try to block rape trial reforms', *The Guardian*, 23 January 2007.
Dyer, C. and Morris, S. (2005) 'Rape case student "conscious" ', *The Guardian*, 25 November 2005.
Edwards, S. (1981) *Female Sexuality and the Law*, London: Martin Robertson.
Falconer, Lord (2003a) *Hansard*, 13 February, col. 771.
—— (2003b) *Hansard*, 1 April, col. 1177.
Fawcett Society (2008) 'Regional rape conviction rates'. Online. Available at: <http://www.fawcettsociety.org.uk/index.asp?PageID=712>.
Finch, E. and Munro, V. (2006) 'Breaking Boundaries? Sexual consent in the jury room', *Legal Studies*, 26: 303–20.
—— (2007) 'The demon drink and the demonized woman: social-sexual stereotypes and responsibility attribution in rape trials involving intoxicants', *Social and Legal Studies*, 16: 591–614.
Gibb, F. (2005) 'Binge-drinking women may lose right to claim rape', *The Times*, 24 November 2005.
Government Equalities Office (GEO) (2009) 'More money to help rape and sexual abuse victims', 5 August 2009. Online. Available at: <http://www.equalities.gov.uk/default.aspx?page=1401>.

Gregory, J. and Lees, S. (1996) 'Attrition in rape and sexual assault cases', *British Journal of Criminology*, 36: 1–17.

Her Majesty's Inspectorate of Constabulary and Her Majesty's Crown Prosecution Service Inspectorate (2007), *Without Consent – A report of the joint review of the investigation and prosecution of rape cases*, HMIC: London.

Home Office (2000) *Setting the Boundaries: reforming the law on sexual offences*, London: Home Office.

—— (2002) *Protecting the Public*, London: Home Office.

—— (2006a) *The Sexual Offences Act 2003 – a stocktake of effectiveness of the Act since its implementation*, London: Home Office.

—— (2006b) *Crime in England and Wales 2005–06 Home Office Statistical Bulletin 12/06*, London: Home Office.

—— (2006c) *Convicting Rapists and Protecting Victims – justice for victims of rape*, London: Home Office.

—— (2009) 'Violence Against Women Opinion Polling February 2009', London: Home Office. Online. Available at: <http://www.homeoffice.gov.uk/documents/violence-against-women-poll>.

Jeeves, P. (2008) 'Man who raped girl of 12 is freed after she claimed to be 19', *Daily Express*, 19 September 2008.

Jones, J. (2008) 'The next stage of devolution? A (d)evolving criminal justice system for Wales' (2008) 2/1 *Crimes and Misdemeanours* ISSN 1754-0445.

Kelly, L. and Lovett, J. (2009) *Different Systems, Similar Outcomes? Tracking attrition in reported rape cases in eleven countries*, London: CWASU.

Kelly, L., Lovett, J. and Regan, L. (2005), 'A Gap or a Chasm? Attrition in reported rape cases', London: Home Office Research Study 293.

Kelly, L. and Regan, L. (2001) *Rape: the forgotten issue?*, London: Child and Woman Abuse Studies Unit, University of North London.

Kelly, L., Temkin, J. and Griffiths, S. (2006) *Section 41: An evaluation of new legislation limiting sexual history evidence in rape trials*, London: Home Office.

Lacey, N. (2001) 'Beset by Boundaries: the Home Office review of sexual offences', *Criminal Law Review*, 3–14.

Lees, S. (1996) *Carnal Knowledge – Rape on Trial*, London: Penguin.

MacKinnon, C. (1989) *Toward a Feminist Theory of State*, Cambridge, MA: Harvard University Press.

Myhill, A. and Allen, J. (2002) *Rape and Sexual Assault of Women: the extent and nature of the problem – findings from the British Crime Survey*, London: Home Office.

Nourse, V. (1999–2000) 'The "normal" successes and failures of feminism and the criminal law', *Chicago-Kent Law Review*, 75: 951–78.

O'Neill, S. (2007) 'Judge frees man who had sex with girl, 10', *The Times*, 5 April 2007.

Regan, L. and Kelly, L. (2003) *Rape: still a forgotten issue*, London: London Metropolitan University, Child and Woman Abuse Studies Unit.

Roberts, G. (2005) 'Drunken consent to sex is still consent, judge rules', *The Independent*, 24 November 2005.

Rumney, P. (2008) 'Policing male rape and sexual assault', *Journal of Criminal Law*, 72: 67–86.

Rumney, P. and Fenton, R. (2008) 'Intoxicated consent in rape: *Bree* and juror decision-making', *Modern Law Review*, 71: 271–302.

Scott-Ham, M. and Burton, F. (2005) 'A study of blood and urine alcohol

concentration in cases of alleged drug-facilitated sexual assault in the UK over a 3-year period', *Journal of Clinical Forensic Medicine*, 13: 107–11.
Spencer, J. (2004) 'The Sexual Offences Act 2003: (2) child and family offences', *Criminal Law Review*, 347–60.
Steele, J. (2009) ' "Child Rape" teen is saved by bebo', *Metro*, 6 August 2009. Online. Available at: <http://www.metro.co.uk/news/article.html? Child_rape_teen_is_saved_by_Bebo&in_article_id=716227&in_page_id=34>.
Temkin, J. (1984) 'Regulating sexual history evidence – the limits of discretionary legislation', *International and Comparative Law Quarterly*, 33: 942–78.
—— (1993) 'Sexual history evidence – the ravishment of section 2', *Criminal Law Review*, 3–20.
—— (2002) *Rape and the Legal Process*, 2nd edn, Oxford: Sweet and Maxwell.
—— (2003) 'Sexual history evidence: beware the backlash', *Criminal Law Review*, 217–43.
Temkin, J. and Ashworth, A. (2004) 'The Sexual Offences Act 2003 – rape, sexual assault and the problems of consent', *Criminal Law Review*, 328–46.
Temkin, J. and Krahé, B. (2008) *Sexual Assault and the Justice Gap: a question of attitude*, Oxford: Hart.
Toner, B. (2006) 'Inside a rape trial', *The Guardian*, 22 June 2006.
Travis, A. (2002) 'One in twenty women has been raped', *The Guardian*, 23 July 2002.
Walby, S. and Allen, J. (2004) *Domestic Violence, Sexual Assault and Stalking: findings from the British Crime Survey*, London: Home Office Research Study 276.
Williams, R. (2009) ' "This crime ruins people's lives" ', *The Guardian*, 27 March 2009.
Williams, Z. (2002) 'Now yes means no', *The Guardian*, 29 October 2002.

# Chapter 10

# All change or business as usual?
Reforming the law of rape in Scotland

*Sharon Cowan*[1]

Against a backdrop of heightened political and legal attention to the problem of rape, particularly the low rate of conviction for the offence, this chapter will examine the law on rape in Scotland. It will focus principally upon the recently enacted Sexual Offences (Scotland) Act 2009 (the 2009 Act), which completely overhauls the substantive law of rape and other sexual offences in Scotland. The primary issue for discussion will be the reforms to the law of rape, though issues of consent pertain equally to various other sexual offences. Beginning with a brief summary of the common law of rape in Scotland prior to the new Act, the chapter then goes on to consider specific aspects of the new measures and the ways in which much needed changes to the laws in this area have been negotiated. It argues that the reform process was constrained by its remit and that, ultimately, the substantive reforms themselves will have a limited effect.

### THE COMMON LAW OF RAPE IN SCOTLAND

Unlike other jurisdictions, the law on sexual offences in Scotland has historically been primarily common-law based, with a small number of provisions contained within the Criminal Law (Consolidation) (Scotland) Act 1995. Until relatively recently, very little had changed with respect to Scotland's substantive law of rape, which dates back to the time of Baron Hume in the eighteenth century. Other than the provisions contained in Part 3 of the 2003 Draft Criminal Code for Scotland (a document which has effectively been ignored by judges and legislators), and until the proposal by the Scottish Law Commission (SLC) for a new bill on Rape and Other Sexual Offences in 2008, there has been no concerted attempt either to codify the law or introduce new legislation to reform the outdated common law. The changes that have occurred have been slow in coming, have evolved in a piecemeal fashion, and have been realized through judicial activism, rather than legislative reform. Marital rape, for example, was conclusively outlawed in the landmark case of *Stallard v HMA* (1989 SLT 469), but until the 2009 Act, male rape was a linguistic and legal impossibility in Scotland (such offences would have been regarded as indecent assaults). The SLC's recent review of the law of rape and other sexual offences – in the form of a consultation document (2006) and report (2007) – and the subsequent legislative reform is, thus, long overdue.

## The *actus reus*

Until 2002, according to Scots common law, the *actus reus* of rape required that a woman's will be overcome by force, and that there be evidence of resistance 'to the last' (Hume Commentaries on the Law of Scotland I: 302). Force was interpreted to include situations where the woman's will was overcome through threats, drugs or where no force was necessary because the woman was disabled and thus unable to resist (*Charles Sweenie* (1858) 3 Irv. 109: 148). However, since the act of rape required force, intercourse with a sleeping woman was not held to be rape, since the accused did not have to overcome her will; rather this represented the offence of 'clandestine injury', a species of indecent assault rather than rape.[2]

Concern about the very narrow *actus reus* culminated, in 2001, in a reference from the Lord Advocate (Scotland's most senior law officer and the head of public prosecutions) to the High Court (*Lord Advocate's Reference (no. 1 of 2001)* 2002 SLT 466). On a majority of five to two, the court abandoned the historical formulation 'against her will' in favour of a new *actus reus* of rape which was more 'in accordance with a modern view of the rights of women' (para. 40). This was to be 'constituted by the man having sexual intercourse with the woman *without her consent*' (para. 44, emphasis added).

Despite this welcome shift away from a need for force and resistance,[3] the *actus reus* of rape under Scots criminal law remained problematically archaic in other respects. First, sexual intercourse was confined to penetration of the vagina; non-heterosexual and non-reproductive sexual, penetrative acts, if non-consensual, constituted indecent assaults. Second, rape was restricted to non-consensual *penile* penetration of the vagina, thus excluding penetration by objects. Together, these requirements rendered rape a gender-specific crime that could only be committed by men against women. Furthermore, although to date there have been no reported cases involving transgendered perpetrators or victims of rape in Scotland, commentators have suggested that the common law of rape only applied to non-trans men and women (Jones and Christie 2008: para. 9.73). Third, there has been, until now, no statutory or judicial guidance on what amounts to consent. Judges have been reluctant to direct juries on this issue, the notion being that the term needs no explanation, and could only be obfuscated by judicial gloss. Indeed one trial judge, when asked specifically by the jury for such guidance, replied 'the definition of consent is a common, straightforward definition of consent. It's the common English word given its normal meaning. And that I am afraid is it. Consent is consent' (quoted by the Lord Justice-Clerk Ross on appeal in *Marr v HMA* 1996 SCCR 696: 699).

Finally, although Scotland, like other jurisdictions, historically recognized that consent could be fraudulently obtained, the circumstances in which fraud could arise were narrowly defined. Consent was only invalid where the accused had deceived the victim as to the 'nature and purpose' of the act, for example, in the commonly cited English case of *R v Williams*, where a doctor told a patient that he was conducting a medical procedure but went on to sexually assault her ((1923) 1 KB 340), or where the woman had been deceived into believing her sexual partner to be her husband (section 7(3) of the Criminal Law (Consolidation) (Scotland) Act 1995). Misrepresenting oneself as a cohabitee, lover, civil partner or friend did not undermine consent sufficiently to effect a rape charge. Likewise, a mistake on the part of the woman as to the man's identity, as opposed to deception by him, did not constitute fraudulently obtained consent (though see *Allan v HMA* 2004 SCCR 278, where mistake as to identity was in issue, but was not open to judicial debate as the accused pled guilty to rape).

### The *mens rea*

The *mens rea* of rape in Scotland is said to be 'under-developed' (Ferguson and Raitt 2006: 188), but it has been held to be present where the accused either knew of an absence of consent or was reckless as to consent (*Lord Advocate's Reference (no. 1 of 2001)* 2002 SLT 466: 476B). This is not particularly controversial and many other jurisdictions have similar formulations. What critics have found more troubling is the rule on mistaken belief in consent. Despite the fact that mistake in other areas of Scots law, such as self-defence, is assessed by reference to an objective test of reasonableness (*Owens v HMA* 1946 JC 119), under the common law of rape, a man's mistaken belief is assessed subjectively. This test is based on the ruling in the English case of *DPP v Morgan* [1976] AC 182, that the accused's belief in consent need only be honest, as opposed to honest and reasonable. This was defended by the court in *Morgan* on the basis of fairness to the accused, and the fact that juries can take the reasonableness of the belief into account when assessing the accused's honesty (cf. McSherry 1998). In two key cases, the courts in Scotland followed the *Morgan* line of reasoning (*Meek v HMA* 1983 SLT 280; *Jamieson v HMA* 1994 SLT 573), and while Scots law continued to apply the subjective approach, England and Wales, through the Sexual Offences Act 2003, moved towards a more objective test (Cowan 2007; Munro 2008; McGlynn in this collection). Other jurisdictions such as New Zealand and some Australian states have similarly moved from subjective to more objective assessments, and Scotland's continued reliance upon the subjective test of *mens rea* was strongly criticized (Ferguson and Raitt 2006).

### Corroboration

Before proceeding to a detailed discussion of the new reforms, there is one final aspect, unique to Scots criminal law, to note – the corroboration requirement. This demands that every aspect of the offence requiring to be proven by the prosecution must be corroborated. Although this is a rule of evidence, and one that applies to all criminal offences, it has been noted by many commentators, including the current Lord Advocate (Justice Committee Official Report 25: 1407, hereinafter JCOR 25), that the corroboration requirement may well be one obstacle amongst several that results in Scotland's extremely low conviction rate for rape (currently around 3 per cent).[4] More often than not in rape trials, sexual intercourse is not in dispute, but disagreement focuses on whether or not there was consent. Frequently there is little evidence beyond that of the parties to trial, and corroboration is likely to be extremely difficult to achieve, as exemplified recently in *CJLS v HM Advocate* ([2009] HCJAC 57).[5]

## THE SEXUAL OFFENCES (SCOTLAND) ACT 2009

Since the reintroduction of the Scottish parliament in 1999, matters relating to criminal law (other than a few specific areas, such as terrorism and road traffic offences) have been devolved from the UK to the Scottish government, which has been keen to update anachronistic laws and find 'Scottish solutions to Scottish problems' (Dewar 1999). In this vein, in 2004, the government asked the SLC to review the substantive law of rape and other sexual offences, recognizing that the existing laws left much room for improvement. Alongside the SLC review, the Scottish Crown Office and Procurator Fiscal Service (COPFS) also undertook a review of the investigation and prosecution of sexual offences, reporting in 2006. After a period of consultation beginning in 2006, the bill proposed by the SLC in its 2007 Report was subsequently introduced to the Scottish parliament in June 2008, and it received Royal Assent on 14 July 2009.

### A new and improved *actus reus*?

Under section 1 of the 2009 Act, the offence of rape is defined as follows:

1. Rape

   (1) If a person ('A'), with A's penis—

   (a) without another person ('B') consenting, and
   (b) without any reasonable belief that B consents,

   penetrates to any extent, either intending to do so or reckless as to whether there is penetration, the vagina, anus or mouth of B then A commits an offence, to be known as the offence of rape.

Three aspects of the *actus reus* will be now be discussed: penetration *of* what; penetration *by* what; and the definition of consent.

### Penetration of what?

The new statutory definition of rape is substantially broader than its common-law predecessor. Non-consensual penetration (to any extent) of the vagina, anus or mouth can constitute rape. Section 1(4) also makes it clear that the definition includes penetration of a surgically constructed vagina (or vulva). Hence, transgender women are now explicitly brought under the protection of the criminal law.

This is not a particularly contentious reform (although some who responded to the SLC consultation did not consider it necessary to include the mouth). It allows for male (and female) victims of anal rape to be legally recognized as such. It also acknowledges the argument that forced anal and oral penetration is just as degrading and humiliating, and possibly, particularly in the case of anal rape, even more injurious to the victim than non-consensual vaginal penetration. The more controversial question that seems to trouble academics, practitioners and policymakers is not penetration *of* what, but penetration *by* what constitutes rape?

### Penetration by what?

Despite the SLC's explicit commitment to principles of gender neutrality (2007: para. 1.29), according to section 1 only men can be guilty of rape, and rape can only be committed with a penis (including a surgically constructed penis). In both regards, section 1 is controversial.

### Women as perpetrators?

For many, to be raped is to be penetrated by a penis. This reflects the statistically overwhelming fact that the vast majority of sexual offences are committed by men, and recognizes the research (sociological, medical and psychological) that attests to the shame, humiliation, physical and psychological injury and trauma (not to mention pregnancy and sexually transmitted infections) that non-consensual penile penetration can effect. Shifting the definition to include a statistically small number of women perpetrators could 'detract from the core of the crime and its motivations' (Regan and Kelly 2003: 15). However, failure to recognize as rape those cases in which a woman forces a man to penetrate her vaginally, orally or anally suggests that there is something specific about being non-consensually penetrated that is more fundamentally damaging, traumatic or violating than being compelled to penetrate. This approach was supported by the drafters of the *Setting the Boundaries* review in England and Wales, who were unconvinced – based on the little anecdotal evidence that they found on the matter – that forcing a man against his will to penetrate a woman was really 'rape' (Home Office 2000: para. 2.8.2).

The desire to separate non-consensual penile penetration as symbolically different from other offences, including penetrating non-consensually, is, however, in direct tension with a desire to be responsive to concerns about gender neutrality, and to challenge deeply ingrained gendered assumptions about sexuality and victimhood. The inclusion of women as potential perpetrators is arguably progressive in that it challenges the traditional understanding of rape as premised on active male sexuality preying on the passive bodies of women. Rape, confined to non-consensual penile penetration, can be read as grounded in gendered stereotypes of active/passive male/female sexuality. It may also be contrary to human rights principles – men who are forced into penile penetration may contend that unless rape is expanded, the criminal law is not affording them adequate protection from inhuman or degrading treatment, or that they are being discriminated against because of their gender. It is submitted, then, that the question of whether forcing someone to penetrate another constitutes rape is one that deserves more consideration. Yet, it was not discussed in any detail in the SLC review process or during the bill's progress through parliament.[6]

*Rape by an object?*

There are various ways to criminalize non-consensual penetration by an object: every non-consensual penetration that is not penile could simply be grouped with other sexual assaults; alternatively, penetration by an object, or non-penile part of the body, could be defined as rape. A 'middle-way' option is to set out a separate offence of sexual penetration that would sit between rape and more general sexual assaults.

In its 2006 consultation, the SLC considered assault by penetration to be serious enough to merit a distinct and separate offence. However, in its final 2007 report, and in the bill as introduced, the SLC proposed that non-penile sexual penetration should be subsumed within the category of sexual assaults, despite the fact that they considered penetrative assaults to be markedly different from non-penetrative assaults, and distinctively wrong (2007: para. 3.11). Since similar harms should be dealt with similarly, they argued, rape should be a distinct offence, and all other non-consensual sexual offences should be categorized together. However, section 2 of the 2009 Act now provides an offence of sexual assault by penetration of the vagina or anus, by any part of the body or anything else, with a maximum sentence of life imprisonment. Despite the fact that this offence carries the same maximum sentence as rape, it is unclear whether the Scottish courts will follow practice in England and Wales, where sentencing guidelines have indicated a more lenient approach (*R v Garvey; Attorney-General's Reference (no. 104 of 2004)* 2004 EWCA Crim 2672).

Could the 2009 Act have gone further, and been more radical on this issue? As the legislators in Victoria, Australia, have identified, it is arguable that it is the penetration that marks out rape as a distinct offence rather than the fact that it is penile. Many of those giving evidence to the Justice Committee, as the bill proceeded through the Scottish parliament, including Rape Crisis Scotland (RCS), Scottish Women's Aid (SWA) and Victim Support Scotland

(VSS), argued for the distinctiveness of penetrative as opposed to non-penetrative sexual assaults. SWA suggested that violation by 'an object is as distressing as penile penetration ... they are equal in severity' (JCOR 25: 1222). VSS stated that in their experience, victims find it just as distressing, and suffer similar psychological impact, from non-penile penetration as from penile penetration (JCOR 25: 1238). VSS argued in favour of a more expansive rape offence, emphasizing that, as well as the possibility of an object causing serious injury, the victim may not know whether they have been penetrated by an object or a penis because, for example, they have been blindfolded (JCOR 25: 1239). In these circumstances, the victim is likely to be traumatized by the penetration per se, and not knowing whether it was by an object or a penis could exacerbate their anxiety.

Indeed, in *Garvock v HMA* (1991 SCCR 593), a 4-year-old child was vaginally and anally penetrated by an adult man. It could not be established, either by interviewing the victim or through forensic evidence, whether the victim was penetrated by a penis or by an object. On appeal, the conviction for rape and attempted sodomy was quashed, to be replaced by a conviction of 'assault by attempting to penetrate the hinder parts of the complainer's body and penetrating her private parts'; and the sentence reduced from 10 years' to eight years' imprisonment. This is the type of case where the wrong done may be more accurately captured by the offence of rape, rather than a lesser offence of either sexual assault or even a specific sexual penetration offence. Arguably, to focus on the question of the object of penetration in *Garvock* is to miss the proper object of focus – the harm, trauma and violation of bodily integrity suffered by the victim – and to imply that penile penetration is always inherently more harmful and wrongful than other forms of non-consensual penetration.

On the contrary, however, many argue that penile penetration has a symbolic importance in society. Gardner and Shute have suggested that there is a rationale for keeping penile penetration as a separate (and the most serious) level of offence, which we should call rape, since for those who take pleasure in heterosexual sexual intercourse, rape is the antithesis, the inversion, of the moment of intimacy, and for those who do not take pleasure in heterosexual sexual intercourse, rape is the purest example of the act they least desire (2000). Likewise, during the Scottish bill's passage, a representative of the Equality Network suggested that rape should focus on non-consensual penile penetration because 'the penis is a sexual organ, it is in the nature of rape, and it is what people understand rape to be' (JCOR 25: 1301). One might be tempted to see this as perpetuating a rather heterosexist and phallocentric notion about what counts as sexual intercourse. Catharine MacKinnon has argued that women do resent forced penile penetration, but 'penile invasion of the vagina may be less pivotal to women's sexuality, pleasure or violation, than it is to male sexuality' (1989: 172). The wrongness of rape is not necessarily linked to *penile* penetration but characterized by a violation of sexual autonomy and bodily integrity, which may be caused by *any* sexual penetration.

A further and related concern here is the proper protection of women who have sex with women. A representative of Lesbian, Gay, Bisexual and Transgender (LGBT) Domestic Abuse told the Justice Committee that rape of women by women was a significant worry, and that legislation in Scotland could not be gender neutral without taking into account lesbian and bisexual women's experiences (JCOR 25: 1301). However, LGBT Domestic Abuse, as well as the Equality and Human Rights Commission Scotland (EHRC) and the Equality Network, supported a separate offence of sexual penetration that would sit alongside rape. Rather than exemplifying a gender-neutral approach, this view maintains – at least symbolically, and through labelling if not through sentencing – the gendered hierarchy between penile (normal) intercourse and non-penile sexual activity.

The statistical reality of rape is that it is a gendered crime, and as Łoś suggests, law reform based on the tenet that penetrative assaults can be committed by both genders may replace women's experiences of the world as a gendered place with the 'legal construct of the gender-neutral world' (1994: 34). Ultimately, however, Łoś concludes that, though rape is a gendered reality, attempts to deal with the gendered nature of rape through the formal structure of the criminal law may well 'petrify' and hence 'legitimate' inequality itself (1994: 35). Rape as an offence of penile penetration leaves women who have sex with women without the same level of criminal law protection from intimate partner assault as heterosexuals and gay men.

The inclusion of non-heterosexual women as potential victims of rape by other women would bring the sexual behaviour of lesbians and bisexual women under the scrutiny and regulation of the criminal law. While this legal incursion poses its own difficulties, equal protection of such women thus supports the argument for either combining all penetrative offences into one rape offence or adopting a system of grading sexual assaults where penetration is an aggravating factor, as the Canadians have done (Roberts and Mohr 1994).

## Consent

The SLC looked to the Australian State of Victoria law reforms as a model, and the 2009 Act now statutorily defines consent as 'free agreement' (section 12) with a non-exhaustive list of 'circumstances' where free agreement is absent (section 13), such as where the victim is subject to violence, or threats of violence, or where the victim has been unlawfully detained. This is similar to the approach taken in England and Wales, although there consent is made by choice where the person has freedom and capacity to make a choice, with an exhaustive list of 'presumptions' of non-consent (see McGlynn in this collection). A comparable formulation has also been used in other jurisdictions such as Canada, several Australian states, and South Africa, though each jurisdiction has taken a subtly different approach (see Gotell, Rush and Mills in this collection).

The SLC has had the advantage of examining previous attempts at reform. Thus, in some respects, the proposals contained in the bill and in the resultant

Act are more progressive and more open-ended than other provisions. The 2009 Act refers to the victim being 'incapable' because of the effect of alcohol or other substances (section 13(2)(a)). This renders the question of how the victim became incapable legislatively irrelevant, although it remains to be seen, in light of Finch and Munro's research in England and Wales (2005; 2006), how this will be interpreted by juries. There is no legislative guidance on (in)capacity (except in so far as it relates to Part 3 of the bill on 'Mentally Disordered Persons') and this is problematic in light of the judicial tendency to avoid giving guidance in intoxication cases (Cowan 2008). In addition, the 2009 Act fraud provisions include those who impersonate not just husbands, but any individual known personally to the accused (section 13(2)(e) (albeit still focusing on the deception perpetrated by the accused, rather than the mistake made by the complainer) (Chalmers 2006).

Is this approach to consent appropriate? Somewhat surprisingly, the Association of Chief Police Officers in Scotland (ACPOS) raised the issue of whether 'free agreement' followed by a list of circumstances goes far enough. They argued that the new provisions should give more guidance on positive indications of what constitutes consent, through the use of terms such as voluntarily, or with knowledge, and that juries, but also police officers, needed more guidance on terms such as consent and free agreement (JCOR 25: 1333–5). They insisted that this clarity could benefit the accused as well as the complainer, as it might shed light on the reasonable steps part of the legislation (discussed below). This inclination towards clarity and guidance is positive, and juries may well be interpreting terms such as choice and freedom rather narrowly (Finch and Munro 2005), but it is not clear that much judicial contemplation or brow-furrowing will in fact occur over the meaning of 'free agreement'. Arguably courts will continue to operate with the 'common-sense' definition of consent that they have always used, without a philosophical foray into the precise meanings of 'freedom' and 'capacity' (see for example *R v Jheeta* [2007] All ER (D) 164), although there does seem to be huge scope for disagreement about the meaning of capacity as it relates to intoxication (Cowan 2008). At any rate, it is interesting that of all those called to give evidence to the Justice Committee, it was ACPOS that pushed the government to go further than the SLC proposals. No one suggested, as Tadros (2006: 1999) has done, that we could try to define rape without consent, for example by setting out a differentiated set of offences that would specify the wrong in each instance (for example rape through violence, rape through threat, rape through abuse of trust – see also Ferguson and Raitt 2006).

The 'non-exhaustive' list of circumstances where free agreement is absent has also posed some problems. One question relates to the sense in which the list is non-exhaustive. Will judges, over time, be able to construct other grounds where consent is deemed absent? Or will other circumstances simply be dealt with under the section 12 definition of consent? It is difficult not to surmise that courts will treat the list as representing those circumstances where consent is most clearly absent. The general definition may well be seen (for instance by the jury) as a catch-all provision for those cases that do not fit the list. Hence, the framework may be perceived as a hierarchy, where cases that fall within the list are taken to be more persuasive than those that do not (Tadros 2006). In any case, even if the prosecution proves that the circumstances pertain, it has proved only a lack of consent, that is, the *actus reus*, and the accused can always argue lack of *mens rea*, as discussed below.

The content of the non-exhaustive list has also prompted debate. For example, section 13(2)(b) states that free agreement is absent 'where B agrees or submits to the conduct because of violence used against B or any other person, or because of threats of violence made against B or any other person'. It is unclear from this formulation whether the threat or violence has to occur at the time of the non-consensual intercourse. Organizations presenting evidence to the Justice Committee queried whether this provision would properly address situations of domestic abuse and violence, where no explicit threat is made but consent is given in the context of ongoing, if underlying, threats and/or violence. The Committee heard evidence from SWA, for example, who insisted that coerced consent within abusive relationships should be invalid under this provision (JCOR 25: 1225). Consequently there was an attempt at stage two of the bill's passage to amend the section to include the phrase, 'or because a fear that violence *or other harm* may be inflicted upon B or any other person *has otherwise been induced* in B', thereby acknowledging both that threats could include non-physical harm, and that consent might be undermined because of an ongoing abusive relationship. However, the amendment was not adopted since it was perceived to 'inappropriately' extend the scope of the provision (JCOR 25: 1655). An opportunity to give a wider interpretation of harm and fear of violence, one that has been advocated by those working with victims of domestic violence, has thus been lost, as has the opportunity to specifically state that non-violent threats of harm to the complainer, such as loss of employment, would be covered (Ferguson and Raitt 2006: 202).

The other issue that has exercised commentators is the giving of consent while asleep or unconscious. Section 14(2) of the Act reads: 'a person is incapable, while asleep or unconscious, of consenting to any conduct'. Originally, the bill stated that consent would be absent 'where, at the time of the conduct, B is asleep or unconscious, in circumstances where B has not, prior to becoming asleep or unconscious, consented to the conduct taking place while B is in that condition'. Many of those giving evidence to the Justice Committee, such as representatives from Rape Crisis Scotland, expressed anxiety about the proposed section, arguing that a person cannot consent while unconscious: the worry being that if the unconscious person no longer consents, they do not have an opportunity to withdraw consent, and men might thus 'get away with' rape. As the LGBT Domestic Abuse representative stated to the Justice Committee, 'prior consent does not sit sensibly alongside free agreement' (JCOR 25: 1305). The EHRC similarly argued that referring explicitly to prior consent in the bill simply shores up misconceptions about victim responsibility for rape (JCOR 25: 1304).

On the other hand, stating that one can never give advance consent to something that will occur later while one is asleep appears to limit autonomy in some potentially significant ways. To illustrate the problem, the Justice Committee raised the oft-cited question of whether a man sexually touching his wife while she was sleeping, with prior consent, can be guilty of sexual assault (JCOR 25: 1243). VSS sensibly replied that the answer depends on what it would be reasonable to expect in the context of that particular relationship; arguably different issues are raised when this situation arises within a long(er) term relationship than when the couple have just met (Anderson 2005). While the example given by the Committee may show a concern to preserve the privacy of the marital bedroom, and the freedom of parties to engage in consensual sex as they please without the interference of the criminal law, there is a legitimate concern to balance justice for victims alongside fairness to the accused and the autonomy of 'victims'.

Ultimately, section 14 of the Act makes no reference to prior consent, but states that consent while asleep or unconscious is impossible. At one level, this is positive: the possibility of a spurious defence ought not to be explicitly housed within the provision itself, and under the common law, there was at least a starting presumption that those who were unconscious or asleep could not give consent to intercourse. However, Chalmers has expressed the view that section 14 overcriminalizes unnecessarily – the provision renders sexual touching and even kissing a sleeping partner unlawful (2009: 556). Chalmers suggests that the provision can and should be read as meaning that one cannot give consent while in the state of sleep, but that advance consent could have been given. While arguably undermining the spirit of the reworded provision, this approach errs on the side of the autonomy of the genuinely consenting sleeping person (and their partner), while still leaving some criminal law protection for rape victims intact; the accused still has to adduce some evidence of belief in consent despite the complainer's unconsciousness.

## *Mens rea*: recklessness, mistakes and reasonable steps

Section 1 of the 2009 Act makes it clear that rape is committed where there is no reasonable belief as to consent. The question remains as to how a reasonable belief is reached. Section 16 states that 'regard is to be had to whether the person took any steps to ascertain whether there was consent or, as the case may be, knowledge; and if so what those steps were'.

Leaving aside the question of what knowledge means here, and, although the Scottish formulation avoids the problematic reasonable 'in all the circumstances' wording used in the English Sexual Offences Act 2003, this formulation may still pose difficulties. Juries may yet read into this provision inappropriate subjective questions about what it would have been reasonable for the accused to have done (Finch and Munro 2006). One Australian study of potential jurors has shown that while in theory participants accepted that beliefs about consent should be reasonable, when given rape scenarios to discuss, participants tended to excuse honest mistakes (Stewart 2009).

Thus, although it is said that section 16 'objectifies' the issue (JCOR 25: 1241), concerns about the age/mental capacity of the accused to understand the relevant circumstances means that the application of a pure objective test is unlikely (and, unless there is a clear exception for those who have diminished mental capacity, undesirable). In practice, section 16 is likely to result in a 'mixed' test (as suggested by the explanatory notes to the bill itself). The worry is that, despite the language of reasonableness, courts will take into account characteristics (that is, flaws or vices) of the accused that make him less likely to know (or believe) that the victim is not consenting, and thus overly subjectivize the test – in essence, reinstituting the 'honest belief' test (Ferguson and Raitt 2006: 199). In addition, in circumstances where the accused exercises his right not to give testimony, it will be difficult for the reasonable steps assessment to take place. Although some negative inference may be commented upon by the prosecution or even the judge, this has to be carefully crafted, so that it does not contradict the accused's presumption of innocence. There is no guidance on this issue in the 2009 Act. However, it seems important that the Scottish courts should embrace a more objective conception of *mens rea* in rape law, and in doing so 'express an unambiguous commitment to the positive integrity as well as the full humanity of both rape victims and men accused of rape' (Lacey 1998: 122).

## CONCLUDING THOUGHTS: THE ROAD TO REFORM NEVER RUNS SMOOTH...

The Victorian Law Reform Commission Final Report on Sexual Offences (2004) was based on empirical research into the ways in which changes to the laws in 1991 had been implemented, and how the changes were perceived by key legal actors. Since there has been no previous legislative programme of rape reform in Scotland, the SLC did not have a similar opportunity. No empirical research was conducted into the views of key legal actors, and indeed obvious resistance to reform was shown by the Faculty of Advocates in their oral evidence to the Justice Committee, who expressed the view that rape law was not broken and did not need fixing (JCOR 25: 1376). Furthermore, though it may be important to clarify the substantive law, without parallel review of the evidential rules in this area (which have been strongly criticized – see Burman et al. 2007), and the relationship between the two, the SLC evaluation of rape law unhelpfully abstracts it from its complex courtroom context. At the same time, there was also no scope for proper engagement with the socio-legal research on, for example, the ways in which difficulties in defining rape can be compounded by the often (though not always) stereotypical socio-sexual assumptions made by those policing, prosecuting, defending and judging complaints. These limits call into question the appropriateness of this kind of Law Commission review in an area where important issues of social policy are raised (Adler 1986).

As Rape Crisis Scotland acknowledged in their recent public education campaign, changing attitudes rather than substantive law reform is the key to changing the way in which women's claims of rape are dealt with by the criminal justice system.[7] Temkin and Krahé's recent research with members of the legal profession, as well as the general public, found that people tend to rely on their preconceived stereotypical intuitions about gender-appropriate behaviour, which lowers their propensity to blame and convict defendants and increases their inclination to blame the complainant (2008). These prevailing attitudes make it extremely difficult for a defendant to be brought to, and convicted at, trial, regardless of how well crafted the substantive law is. Even where a case goes to trial, Finch and Munro (2005) found that mock jurors tended to blame women and neutralize the behaviour of sexually aggressive men (see also Rumney 2001). While the reforms to the substantive law of rape in Scotland are long awaited and, in the main, progressive, the failure to see that changes to substantive rape laws in themselves do not necessarily change the legal position of rape complainers (Roberts and Mohr 1994) means that, in practice, the reforms may well have a limited effect upon the appallingly low conviction rate for rape in Scotland.

The SLC could have gone further in their original proposals to more creatively reimagine the landscape of sexual offences law, but the process of parliamentary discussion, decision-making and drafting inevitably also impacts upon the way in which such proposals become law. This trajectory of law's becoming demonstrates that some entrenched assumptions about sex/gender and socio-sexual behaviour have been left intact, and that important areas of (non-doctrinal) concern and knowledge have not been taken into account when reviewing and drafting the law. This in turn raises the question of what role we can legitimately expect substantive criminal law reform to play in either improving the conviction rate, or reducing the prevalence of rape.

## Notes

1 Thanks are due to James Chalmers for comments on an earlier draft, and to Vanessa Munro and Clare McGlynn for their encouragement and excellent editing skills.
2 See for example *Charles Sweenie* (1858) 3 Irv. 109. Such cases are arguably aggravated cases but the courts have generally treated them much less seriously than rape; see for example *Paton v HMA* (2002 SCCR 57) where on appeal a two-year prison sentence for clandestine injury was reduced to 300 hours' community service.
3 Some legal practitioners and judges have resisted the changes and the problem of how to corroborate the accused's awareness of 'lack of consent' was brought acutely into focus by the case of *McKearney* (2004 JC 87). For critical comment see Ferguson and Raitt (2006) and Chalmers (2002).
4 http://www.scotland.gov.uk/News/Releases/2008/06/13134810. A recent European study puts the Scottish conviction rate at 3 per cent, the lowest in Europe despite the reporting rate being the fourth highest (Burman, Lovett and Kelly 2009). Since attrition is strongly linked to policing and prosecution practices (Kelly 2009), it is hoped that the newly announced National Sexual Crimes Unit of senior prosecutors will positively impact upon the conviction rate.

5  It is unlikely that the corroboration rule will be abandoned any time soon. Indeed it is seen as a cornerstone of the oft-stated uniquely fair and impartial Scottish criminal justice system.
6  The Draft Criminal Code for Scotland (2003) did propose that women be included as potential perpetrators.
7  See http://www.thisisnotaninvitationtorapeme.co.uk/.

## Bibliography

Adler, M. (1986) 'Social research and legal reform: reflections on the politics of commissioned research', in I. Ramsay (ed.) *Debtors and Creditors: a socio-legal perspective*, Abingdon: Professional Books, 317–46.

Anderson, M. (2005) 'Negotiating sex', *Southern California Law Review*, 78: 101–38.

Burman, M., Jamieson, L., Nicholson, J. and Brooks, O. (2007) 'Impact of aspects of the law of evidence in sexual offence trials: an evaluation study', Scottish Government, 2007. Online. Available at: <http://www.scotland.gov.uk/Publications/2007/09/12093427/0>.

Burman, M., Lovett, J. and Kelly, L. (2009) Scotland Country Report 'Different Systems, Similar Outcomes? Tracking Attrition in Reported Rape Cases in 11 European Countries' (CWASU London Metropolitan University).

Chalmers, J. (2002) 'How (Not) To Reform the Law of Rape' Edinburgh Law Review 6(3), 388–396.

—— (2006) 'Fraud, mistake and consent in rape: some preliminary observations', *Scots Law Times* (News), 29–33.

—— (2009) 'Two problems in the Sexual Offences (Scotland) Bill', *Scottish Criminal Law*, 553–9.

Cowan. S. (2007) 'Freedom and capacity to make a choice: a feminist analysis of consent in the criminal law', in V. Munro and C. Stychin (eds) *Sexuality and the Law: feminist engagements*, London: Routledge-Cavendish.

—— (2008) 'The trouble with drink: intoxication, (in)capacity, and the evaporation of consent to sex', *Akron Law Review*, 41: 899–922.

Crown Office and Procurator Fiscal Service (2006) *Review of the Investigation and Prosecution of Sexual Offences in Scotland: report and recommendations*, Edinburgh: COPFS.

Dewar, D. (1999) 'Legislative Statement', 28 June 1999. Online. Available at: <http://news.bbc.co.uk/1/hi/special_report/1999/06/99/scottish_parliament_opening/379336.stm>.

Ferguson, P. and Raitt, F. (2006) 'Reforming the Scots law of rape: redefining the offence', *Edinburgh Law Review*, 10: 185–208.

Finch, E. and Munro, V. (2005) 'Juror stereotypes and blame attribution in rape cases involving intoxicants: the findings of a pilot study', *British Journal of Criminology*, 45: 25–38.

—— '(2006) Breaking boundaries?: Sexual consent in the jury room', *Legal Studies*, 26: 303–20.

Gardner, J. and Shute, S. (2000) 'The wrongness of rape', in J. Horder (ed.) *Oxford Essays on Jurisprudence* (Fourth Series), Oxford: Oxford University Press.

Home Office (2000) *Setting the Boundaries: reforming the law on sexual offences*, London: HMSO.

Hume, D. (1797) Commentaries on the Law of Scotland Respecting the Description and Punishment of Crimes, in Two Volumes, Edinburgh; Bell and Gradfute; and E. Balfour.

Jones, T. and Christie, M. (2008) *Criminal Law*, 4th edn, Edinburgh: W. Green.

Justice Committee Official Report 25 (2009) 'Sexual Offences (Scotland) Bill'. Online. Available at: <www.scottish.parliament.uk/s3/committees/justice/inquiries/SexualOffences/index.htm>.

Kelly, L. 'Rape Conviction rate can improve if we tackle culture of scepticism', *The Times* May 14, 2009.

Lacey, N. (1998) *Unspeakable Subjects: feminist essays in legal and social theory*, Oxford: Hart.

Łoś, M. (1994) 'The struggle to redefine rape in the early 1980s', in J. Roberts and R. Mohr (eds) *Confronting Sexual Assault: a decade of legal and social change*, Toronto: University of Toronto Press.

MacKinnon, C. (1989) *Towards a Feminist Theory of the State*, Cambridge, MA: Harvard University Press.

McSherry, B. (1998) 'Constructing lack of consent', in P. Easteal, (ed.) *Balancing the Scales: rape, law reform and Australian culture*, Sydney: Federation Press, 26–40.

Munro, V. (2008) 'Constructing consent: legislating freedom and legitimating constraint in the expression of sexual autonomy', *Akron Law Review*, 41(4): 923–56.

Regan, L. and Kelly, L. (2003) 'Rape: still a forgotten issue', London: London Metropolitan University, Child and Woman Abuse Studies Unit.

Roberts, J. and Mohr, R. (1994) 'Sexual assault in Canada: recent developments', J. Roberts and R. Mohr (eds) *Confronting Sexual Assault: a decade of legal and social change*, Toronto: University of Toronto Press, 3–19.

Rumney, P. (2001) 'The review of sex offences and rape law reform: another false dawn?', *Modern Law Review*, 64: 890–910.

Scottish Law Commission (2003) *Draft Criminal Code for Scotland*, Edinburgh: Scottish Law Commission.

—— (2006) *Rape and Other Sexual Offences: discussion paper 131*, Edinburgh: Scottish Law Commission.

—— (2007) *Report on Rape and Other Sexual Offences*, Edinburgh: Scottish Law Commission.

Stewart, L. (2009) ' "It is Rape, But . . ." Issues with definition and implications for the Australian legal system', unpublished PhD Thesis, University of Edinburgh.

Tadros, V. (1999) 'No consent: a historical critique of the actus reus of rape', *Edinburgh Law Review*, 3: 317–40.

—— (2006) 'Rape without consent', *Oxford Journal of Legal Studies*, 26: 515–43.

Temkin, J. and Krahé, B. (2008) *Sexual Assault and the Justice Gap: a question of attitude*, Oxford: Hart Publishing.

Victorian Law Reform Commission (2004) *Sexual Offences: Final Report*, Melbourne, Victorian Law Reform Commission.

Chapter 11

# Rethinking Croatian rape laws

Force, consent and the 'contribution of the victim'

*Ivana Radačić and Ksenija Turković*

Rape laws have been the focus of feminist debates for decades. These debates have instigated a number of rape law reforms in many countries in order to ensure that the laws are fairer and deliver justice to victims. In Croatia, however, literature on rape is still limited and there has been only one major reform of rape laws (when the whole criminal law was reformed). While in many countries (especially those within the common-law legal tradition) a 'no means no' standard has been replaced by (at least in theory) an 'only yes means yes' standard (Munro 2008; Gotell 2008), in Croatia, rape is still defined by force or threat of force. Furthermore, in practice, resistance is often required as evidence of force. As social attitudes on gender relations are changing – pushed both by Croatian participation in international organisations and domestic women's rights activism – Croatian rape laws are, however, currently in the process of reform.

In this chapter, we analyse Croatian rape laws and legal practice in the light of feminist research, international standards and comparative experience. On the basis of our analysis, we propose reforms with the aim of securing more effective protection from rape. Our main argument is that the central element of rape should become non-consent, rather than force or threat of force. We propose an affirmative, communicative model of consent, according to which submission and lack of resistance do not constitute consent; a genuine, free and voluntary agreement is required.

## HISTORICAL AND POLITICAL CONTEXT

Croatia is a young country, having gained independence in 1991. Before that, and since 1945, it was one of the six republics of the Socialist Federative Republic of Yugoslavia (SFRY). Both SFRY and Croatia are civil-law jurisdictions. In the SFRY, since 1974 when the Constitution gave the republics more autonomy, the general part of criminal law and certain crimes, such as crimes against the state or military forces, were under the competence of the federal government, while the republics gained competence to define most other crimes, including that of rape. During the 1977 reforms, consensual homosexual sexual intercourse was decriminalized, as was the crime of seduction (seducing a girl of age 14–16 into sexual intercourse by false promises of marriage). Rape was defined as compelling a female, with whom one is not in a matrimonial relationship, to have sexual intercourse by force or threat of immediate attack upon life or limb (Official Gazette 32/93). This law remained in force until January 1998 when the new Croatian Criminal Code entered into force (Official Gazette 110/97).

The modern period in Croatian history begins in 1990 (first multi-party elections) with the country's change of political and economic system, as well as achieving independence from SFRY. The period between 1991 and 1998 was a difficult period for Croatia and neighbouring countries, as it was affected by war. The armed conflict started in 1991 and remained intermittent and mostly on a small scale until 1995. In 1995, Croatia reconquered most of the territories from the Republic of Serbian Krajina authorities. A peaceful integration of the remaining Serbian-controlled territories was completed in 1998 under United Nations supervision. From an economic point of view, Croatia (as well as the remainder of the former Yugoslavia) experienced a serious depression; transition was not easy. The new government's legal system was inefficient and slow, and the detrimental effects of 'wild' and unrestricted capitalism had become strikingly visible, with more than 400,000 unemployed citizens and a significant drop in the GDP per capita. Indeed, these are problems with which Croatia continues to struggle to this day.

By the end of 1996, Croatia became a member of the Council of Europe. In relation to the European Union (EU), negotiations were formally opened on 3 October 2005. It is expected that they will be closed by the end of 2010 and that Croatia will enter the EU in 2011, though there are some doubts regarding this time frame.[1]

In the first years of independence, violence against women was not at the top of the government's agenda. While some attention had been paid to sexual violence committed by the Serbs against Croatian and Muslim women, wartime sexual violence committed by the Croatian armed forces was neglected, as was the 'peace-time' sexual abuse of women. Priority was given instead to maintaining the territorial integrity of the country and to instituting economic and political changes.

It was mostly women's groups, many of which were also active in the anti-war movement, which provided legal, psychological and other help to the victims of sexual violence (Kesić 2003). Framing the debate in terms of (male) violence and patriarchy, rather than ethnicity, and engaging with women on all sides of the war, they tried to deconstruct the nationalist discourses around rape and inject it with critical feminist thinking. The work of these women's groups, together with the developments in relation to sexual violence in the International Criminal Tribunal for the Former Yugoslavia (Radačić 2005), gradually pushed 'peace-time' sexual violence on to the government's agenda.

The new Criminal Code brought many positive changes in the area of sexual violence, primarily under the influence of German and Austrian law reforms in this field. It defined rape in a gender-neutral manner and criminalized marital rape (although prosecution for this offence, cf. non-marital rape, required a motion by the victim). The *actus reus* of the rape offence was widened to include sexual acts equivalent to sexual intercourse, and the pregnancy and age[2] of the victim were introduced as aggravating circumstances. Since its adoption, the Code has been amended eight times. The most significant changes include the reform in 2000, which eliminated procedural differences in the prosecution of marital and non-marital rape (Official Gazette 129/00), followed by the 2006 reform which extended the time within which proceedings in respect of sexual crimes against minors must be brought and increased the severity of sanctions imposed for almost all sexual crimes (Official Gazette 71/06).

## POLICY CONTEXT

According to the results of the International Crime Victim Survey (ICVS)[3] and official statistics, there has been a small, but constant, increase in the number of sexual offences committed, as well as reported, over the past 11 years (1997 to 2008) in Croatia. However, sexual crimes are among those least likely to enter the criminal justice system. Of all incidents of sexual crime reported in the 1997 ICVS, only one (2.5 per cent) had been reported to the police. By 2000, this rate of reporting had increased – 15.5 per cent of sexual crimes (nine rapes or attempted rapes) had been reported to the police. While still a very low level of reporting, this finding brings Croatia in line with rates in many other industrialized countries (15–17 per cent).[4] To a great extent, this increase in reporting should be credited to various women's groups which, in recent years, have been working to educate women, and the public in general, on issues of sexual violence, especially domestic violence.

Except for these groups, there are no support services for victims of sexual violence. Recently, with the financial assistance of the United Nations Development Programme, the Ministry of Justice started to develop victims' services and an overall strategy for victim assistance, but this is at a very early stage.

## CRITICAL ANALYSIS OF CURRENT LAW

The Croatian Criminal Code criminalizes a number of sexual offences. Head XIII, entitled 'Offences against the Values Protected by International Law', contains wartime sexual violence as a specific category of war crimes against a civilian population, as well as international prostitution and trafficking for sexual exploitation. However, it is in Head XIV of the Code, entitled 'Criminal Offences against Sexual Freedoms and Sexual Morals', that the greatest number of offences can be found. Head XIV sexual offences are commonly divided into a) criminal offences which protect sexual autonomy;

b) criminal offences which protect the sexual integrity of persons under a certain age; c) criminal offences which protect against financial exploitation in relation to sexual acts; and d) criminal offences which protect 'sexual morals' (Turković 2007). Rape, together with the offences of sexual intercourse with a helpless person, sexual intercourse by duress, sexual intercourse by abuse of position and indecent acts, falls under the first category, namely sexual offences which protect sexual autonomy.

### Definition of the *actus reus* of rape

The offence is committed when a person compels another to have sexual intercourse, or an equivalent sexual act, by use of force or threat of immediate attack upon her life or limb, or the life or limb of a person close to her. The *actus reus* of the offence thus contains two elements: use of force or threats of force, and sexual intercourse or an equivalent sexual act. As noted above, the definition is gender-neutral: both a perpetrator and a victim can be female or male (minor and full age), and the existence of marriage is irrelevant.[5]

### *Sexual intercourse or an equivalent sexual act*

Sexual intercourse is defined in practice as the merging of sexual organs of heterosexual persons. A simple touching is not enough: a penile penetration of the vagina is required (Turković 2007). Acts equivalent to sexual intercourse are those which, by their nature, affects and impact on a victim, similar to intercourse. According to judicial practice, the acts that fall into this category are penetration of the body orifices of a victim by the sexual organs of a perpetrator (such as penetration of the mouth of a victim by a penis of a perpetrator) and penetration of the sexual organs of a victim by the body orifices of a perpetrator (such as penetration of the vagina of a victim by a fist, finger or the mouth of a perpetrator) (Turković 2007). Penetration of the bodily orifices of the perpetrator by the sexual organs of a victim (such as putting the penis of a victim into the mouth of a perpetrator) also constitutes an act equivalent to sexual intercourse, as does penetration of the bodily orifices of a victim by objects (such as insertion of the penis of a dog, or a candle, into the vagina of a woman) (Turković 2007).

There is no consensus in practice as regards acts which do not involve penetration. For example, where a perpetrator licked the genitals of a child without his tongue entering the child's vagina, the Supreme Court characterized this as an indecent act rather than rape (VSRH KŽ-870/04). On the other hand, ejaculation in the mouth of a victim without penetration was characterized as an act equivalent to intercourse, rather than an indecent act (VSRH KŽ-726/03). Thus, it is not clear when a certain sexual act short of intercourse will be considered as an act equivalent to intercourse and thus rape; when it will be considered as attempted sexual intercourse and thus attempted rape; and when it will be considered as an act falling short of attempted sexual intercourse or an act equivalent thereto and, thus, an indecent act. Taking into account the different symbolic meaning ascribed to these different acts, and the variable penalties prescribed for each,[6] it is important to demarcate the different acts precisely to ensure both legal certainty and equal application of the laws.

## Force or the threat of force (resistance and consent)

According to the Criminal Code, force is a means of influencing another person, by which that person is compelled to behave against her will. Force as an element of the criminal offence of rape is a means of overcoming resistance, aimed at the realization of sexual intercourse or an act equivalent to it. It has to be targeted towards a person, rather than objects,[7] and there has to be a causal link between the force and intercourse, which in the case of a passage of time has to be specifically proved (Turković 2007).

There is no consensus about what constitutes force. Examples from case law include: holding the victim's hands or neck so she cannot resist, kicking her in different parts of the body, locking her in a room, taking a victim to a deserted place, drugging a victim, pushing a victim, and taking her clothes off (Turković 2007). Whether the driving of a victim to a deserted place in order to have intercourse with her constitutes force is controversial. In one case in which this was considered, the trial court held that these facts did constitute attempted rape. However, the Supreme Court disagreed, considering that it was instead an unlawful taking of liberty, since the use of force was too distant in time from possible sexual intercourse (VSRH, I KŽ 108/91).

The threat of an immediate attack upon the life or limb of a victim, or life or limb of a person close to her, where it is done with the purpose of achieving sexual intercourse or an equivalent sexual act with the victim, constitutes a relevant threat. It is not necessary that words be used to articulate the threat, but the threat does have to be serious: its content and the circumstances in which it is expressed must objectively be perceived as threatening. It has to be targeted at the life or body of a victim, or the life or body of a person close to her. The closeness is assessed in each case, according to the circumstances. In the case of immediate relatives (blood relatives such as parents, children and siblings, as well as a husband or partner) the closeness of the relationship will be presumed, but in other cases it will have to be proved. The threat of some other harm, including the suicide of the perpetrator (even if the perpetrator is a person close to a victim), unlawfully taking of liberty, destroying objects, revealing some information which could harm a person's honour or privacy, does not suffice (Turković 2007). That said, these circumstances will constitute coercion to sexual intercourse, an offence that requires only a serious threat of serious harm. The threat has to be simultaneous with, or immediately precede, the attack; if there is a passage of time, even if only a couple of hours, there will be no rape (Turković 2007).

While the definition of rape does not mention resistance or non-consent as required elements, these are very often discussed in the case law, in determining whether or not a rape took place. The view that rape exists only in situations where the victim exerts the utmost, serious and permanent resistance, or where the force used/threatened is more than simply unpleasant (*vis haut ingrata*), can still be found in the case law (Bačić and Pavlović 2004). Thus, in practice, prosecutors often do not proceed with a case in which there is no evidence of resistance.

The Supreme Court held in one case that there was no rape as 'the victim did not resist in a clear and unambiguous manner because she stopped resisting at a critical moment – when a completely naked defendant pushed apart the legs of a completely naked victim who lay in a car seat – but not too forcefully, finishing soon'[8] (VSRH, KŽ-473/94). In another case, the same court concluded that 'resistance can be lacking only when the fear is stronger than a perception of the harm which will ensue (sexual intercourse)' (VSRH, KŽ-445/92). A recent analysis of the judgments adopted on the basis of the new Criminal Code in Croatia showed that, in 17 out of 27 cases, proof of resistance was sought as evidence of rape.[9] Thus, while the definition mentions only force and threat of force, in practice a force plus non-consent formula is applied.

There is no rape where the victim consented to intercourse or an equivalent act. The consent must be sincere and precede the act. However, in the case law there are views which state that there will be no rape conviction for a non-consensual sexual act, if the victim later consented to another sexual act with the same person (Novoselec 1996).

### Mens rea and a mistaken belief in consent

Rape can only be committed with intent. Intent implies that a perpetrator is aware of the use of force or a threat of force, as well as of the lack of consent on the part of a victim, and that he desires the perpetration of the office (direct intent) or accedes to it (indirect intent). The perpetrator acts with intent when he is aware that the victim does not consent or is aware that non-consent is possible, but continues with the sexual act.

In Croatian law any mistake – reasonable or unreasonable – precludes a finding of the required intent. Unreasonable mistakes are punishable only in connection with crimes which are subject to prosecution on the basis of criminal negligence. Since rape is subject to prosecution only for intentional commission, any mistake which bears upon the intent required for rape, regardless of whether the mistake is reasonable or unreasonable, categorically prevents conviction. Thus if the defendant honestly believes that the victim consented, he cannot be found guilty, even if his belief was unreasonable.

### Penalties, and extenuating and aggravating circumstances

The 1998 Code prescribed one to 10 years' imprisonment for the basic offence of rape. However, an analysis of judicial practice for the period from 1998 to 2002 showed that in 70 per cent of cases, the courts sentenced the perpetrators to a term of imprisonment ranging from three months to five years, and that in 14 per cent of cases they mitigated the sentence (Garačić 2004). Reacting to a disparity between the prescribed and applied sentences, in 2006, the legislature increased the minimum term to three years. Thus, even when the mitigation of sentence is applied, one year of imprisonment is the minimum penalty which can be imposed. This is perceived, especially among some judges, as excessive curbing of judicial discretion and so the minimum will most probably be set to one year again.[10]

The Code recognizes a number of aggravated forms of rape for which the maximum penalty is 10 years (and three years minimum). There are two types of circumstances which will make an offence an aggravated rape. One concerns modalities of the act (rape committed in a particularly cruel or degrading manner, or gang rape: Article 188(2)), and the characteristics of the victim (a minor).[11] The other concerns the consequences of the act (for example death, serious physical injury to the victim,[12] severe impairment of health, or pregnancy).[13] If two of these aggravated forms coincide, an especially grievous form of rape is committed for which a higher sentence is prescribed (5–15 years' imprisonment). Some aggravated circumstances, found in other European legal systems, such as the use of torture, the use of arms, or the fact that the rape was committed by a husband and/or a partner, are missing.

When determining a sentence, as in the case of other offences, the judges examine extenuating and aggravating circumstances. However, in cases of rape, specific circumstances are often examined, such as the behaviour of the victim and her previous sexual life. Where the victim's behaviour does not fit the stereotypical notions of 'proper' female conduct, the judges often conclude that the victim contributed to the rape, which is considered a mitigating circumstance for the defendant. The following circumstances are often considered as relevant: that a victim was sexually active, that she was a prostitute, that she hitchhiked, that she was in a bar or a disco, that she voluntarily left with a perpetrator to go to an isolated place or his flat, that she kissed or flirted with the perpetrator, or that she danced provocatively (Turković 2007). In one recent case, the Supreme Court mitigated the sentence of one year's imprisonment to a 10-month suspended sentence on the ground that the victim contributed to her rape as she hitchhiked (VSRH, I KŽ 596/02). The facts that the defendant was a war veteran and that he had, in the meantime, married were also taken into account as extenuating circumstances. Fatherhood and – in cases of rape of an intimate partner – the victim's sexual affair or the perpetrator's disappointment at the relationship break-up are also often viewed sympathetically. Our experience suggests, however, that these attitudes are amenable to change with judicial training.

## Rights of rape victims during criminal proceedings

Recently, a new Criminal Procedure Code was enacted (Official Gazette 152/08), which came into force on 1 July 2009. It guarantees to victims of sexual crimes some special rights during criminal proceedings, such as the right to protection of privacy and personal data during the investigation and prosecution of crime, the right to demand the exclusion of the public during the trial, the right to consult legal counsel free of charge before giving testimony, the right to be interviewed in the police or public prosecutor's office by a person of the same gender, the right to refuse to answer questions related to one's private life, and the right to ask to be interviewed through a video-link. According to the new law, previous sexual behaviour of a victim and her sexual preferences cannot be used as evidence any longer.[14] However, it remains possible that these issues will play a role in the pre-trial phase as well as at the sentencing stage. It remains to be seen to what extent these rights will actually be effective in practice once the new Criminal Procedure Code starts to be implemented.

## CURRENT ISSUES

### Classification and the central elements of rape

Two ways of conceptualizing rape have traditionally been discussed in feminist literature. Some feminists have advocated defining rape as a violent crime, whereby consent would be irrelevant where force or threat of force is used, while others have suggested a definition based on rape as a crime against sexual autonomy, according to which a central element of rape would be consent, and the force and threat of force would be just an example of non-consent.[15] The question of how consent should be defined has been another central question, and many contemporary feminists have argued for the adoption of a 'consent plus' standard in rape laws, according to which a process of deliberation on, and communication of, agreement would also be analysed, and not a mere presence or absence of consent (Munro 2008; Anderson 2005).

In Croatia, as we have seen, rape is classified as an offence against sexual autonomy, contained under the head of 'protecting sexual freedoms and sexual morals'. Reference to sexual morals is, however, problematic. For one thing, it can be used to curtail sexual freedoms. Further, the classification of sexual offences as crimes against honour may impose shame and stigma upon a victim of sexual abuse. This classification also undermines the seriousness of the offences and the consequences they have on the physical and psychological integrity and autonomy of a person.

Even though rape in Croatian law falls within the subcategory of crimes against sexual autonomy, its definition contains force or threat of force as a central element, rather than a lack of consent. However, in practice, both use of force (or threat of force) and non-consent are required, as sex is thought of as consensual where there is no resistance, unless there are exceptional circumstances. The definition and interpretation of force and threats of force are restrictive, and the Code does not prohibit all non-consensual sex, since sex procured by fear, deceit or fraud is not criminalized in any of the sexual offences.

Feminist critiques, as well as international standards, argue against a restrictive conceptualization of rape. There is widespread agreement among feminists, as well as international human rights lawyers, that 'no means no' and that no resistance should be required. Moreover, there is greater acceptance of an 'only yes means yes' standard. Thus, for example, the European Court of Human Rights held in *MC v Bulgaria* (ECHR 2003-VII) that the central element of rape is not force but consent, and imposed on states an obligation to penalize and effectively prosecute any non-consensual sexual act, including in the absence of physical resistance by the victim (Radačić 2008; and Londono in this volume). The same obligation is contained in the Council of Europe Recommendation to the Member States on the Protection of Women against Violence (2002). Similarly, the Trial Chamber of the International Criminal Court for the Former Yugoslavia (ICTY) in *Kunarac* held that 'sexual penetration will constitute rape if it is not truly voluntary or consensual on the part of the victim' and that force, threat of force or coercion are only some of the examples of non-consent, which should not be defined narrowly (ICTY-96-23 (2001): para. 440). While the Elements of Crime of the International Criminal Court (ICC-ASP/1/3 (2002)) did not follow the ICTY's approach, defining rape as a sexual invasion committed by force or a threat of force or a compulsion, it did define force, threat of force and coercion broadly, giving examples of these as fear, duress, detention, psychological oppression, abuse of power, taking advantage of a coercive environment or incapability to give consent.

In the light of feminist research and international standards, we submit that the definition of rape in Croatian law should be changed so that the central element would no longer be force or a threat of force, but a lack of genuine and free consent. The presence of certain circumstances, such as force, threat of force or other serious harm, abuse of power, incapacity to give consent (which now constitutes other sexual acts), as well as fear, compulsion, fraud and deceit (which are not mentioned in the Code) should give rise to a presumption of a lack of consent. Some of them might also represent aggravated forms of rape. Contrary to the current practice of the Croatian courts, consent should be operative at the time of the sexual act. In addition, in order for an 'affirmative standard' to be adopted, as will be discussed below, the current standard of *mens rea* in relation to the mistaken belief in consent needs to be changed.

## Mens rea and the mistaken belief in consent

*Mens rea* requirements, and the defence of mistaken belief in consent, have been among the most controversial areas of rape laws. Historically, mistaken belief in consent negated *mens rea*, however unreasonable it was. This was justified on the basis that those who are not morally culpable should not be convicted of a criminal offence. However, a defence of mistaken belief may lead to the acquittal of many blameworthy defendants whose 'moral culpability ... lies in a deliberate choice to engage in a sexual act with subjective awareness of one or more facts that are rationally inconsistent with the voluntary communication by the other person of valid capable consent' (Vandervort 2004: 658).

To respond to these concerns, many jurisdictions now qualify this defence, stipulating that unreasonable belief, or a belief that arose from the self-intoxication of the accused, recklessness or wilful blindness, will not negate responsibility. In such frameworks, the accused is often required to take reasonable steps to ascertain whether there was consent, and circumstances that give rise to a presumption of lack of consent also give rise to a presumption of a lack of reasonable belief therein. To adopt a similar framework in Croatia would, however, require significant reform. In Croatian law, unreasonable mistakes negate responsibility for an intentional crime, but not for offences that can be committed negligently. Thus, the only way to apply an 'affirmative consent standard' to a full extent would be to subject rape to prosecution on the basis of negligence. Then, the perpetrator would be held to a higher standard of accountability, benefiting only from faultless or reasonable mistakes in consent.

## The act of rape: 'acts equivalent to sexual intercourse'

Historically, only penile penetration of the vagina was considered to constitute an act of rape. With time, however, many jurisdictions have also included oral and anal sex/penetration, while some have criminalized all non-voluntary acts of a sexual nature in a general category of sexual assault. The ICC Elements of Crime defined rape as penetration, however slight, of any part of a body of the victim or of the perpetrator, with a sexual organ, or of the anal or the genital opening of the victim, with any object or other part of the body. A similar definition was adopted by the ICTY Appeals Chamber in the *Kunarac* case (ICTY-96-23 (2002): para. 127).

As seen above, in practice, the definition of rape in Croatia is not restricted to such penetrative acts. While not engaging here in a discussion as to the gravity and meaning of penetrative versus non-penetrative sexual acts, for the sake of legal clarity and equality before the law, we would propose that only penetrative acts, as defined in the Elements of Crime, should constitute rape.

## Rape myths, 'victim contribution' and the rights of victims in the proceedings

The victim's behaviour has long been a central element of the rape trial, most often when assessing whether she consented, as well the reasonableness of the accused's belief in consent. There is often reliance on erroneous beliefs that it is women, rather than the perpetrators, who are responsible for rape (Torrey 1991). Gender stereotypes and rape myths – such as that only 'bad' women are raped, that women mean 'yes' when they say 'no' and that women often fabricate rape – have often inhibited the delivery of justice and have contributed to the humiliation and stigmatization of victims (Vandervort 2004). Moreover, research has shown not only that rape myths have an impact on a low level of reporting of rape, but also on its prevalence (Vandervort 2004).

In order to challenge these myths, many jurisdictions have enacted rules aimed at protecting the dignity and equality of victims, such as a non-corroboration requirement, the prohibition of evidence of sexual history, limitations on cross-examination of a victim and special means of testifying, the right of victims to free legal assistance, the right to be interviewed and examined by a person of the same gender and the introduction of rape trauma syndrome (RTS) expert testimony. As seen above, the new Croatian Code of Criminal Procedure has incorporated many of these rules. However, there is no mention of the possibility of using expert testimony to explore the various reactions that rape might inspire, other than RTS, nor is there any limitation on the number of interviews that prosecutors and judges could have with a rape victim, as is the case in some jurisdictions in relation to other vulnerable witnesses.

As our analysis shows, in Croatia, gender stereotypes and rape myths are most visible in the development of the concept of the 'contribution of the victim'. The concept itself, and the way it is applied in practice, have serious negative effects. These effects extend not only to victims, but to women generally and to society as a whole. It legitimizes gender stereotypes and thus the subordination of women. The highest Croatian courts should send a clear message that rape myths are not allowed in the courtroom and that it is the behaviour of the accused, and not that of the victim, which should be on trial. Rather than suggesting that women should limit their freedom and avoid 'risky' situations, the courts should send a message that it is inappropriate to take advantage of a person in a vulnerable situation. In order for these changes to be affected, judges, prosecutors, police and other legal practitioners should be educated on women's rights and gender equality, and in particular, on the realities of rape. Gender equality and sexual education should also be a part of the school curriculum.

## REFORM AND THE FUTURE

There remain a number of problems with Croatian rape law and its application.[16] First, the characterization of rape as a crime against honour does not reflect the true nature of the offence and has problematic connotations. The title of the head dealing with sexual offences should thus be renamed, so that no reference to honour is made.

The legal definition of rape should be changed to reflect the fact that the main protected value is the sexual autonomy of a person. Lack of consent, rather than force or a threat of force, should become a central element of rape, and resistance should be irrelevant. Consent should not mean an absence of a physical resistance, silence or submission: only positive, freely given consent, by a person who has freedom and capacity to give it, should suffice. The presence of certain circumstances, such as force, threat of force or other serious harm, abuse of power, incapacity to give consent (which now constitute other sexual acts) as well as fear, compulsion, fraud and deceit (which are not mentioned in the Code) should constitute presumptions of a lack of consent in relation to the offence of rape. While acknowledging the failure of the affirmative consent standard to address the low rate of reporting, high attrition rates and presence of rape myths and stereotypes in the courtroom (Gotell 2008; Munro 2008; Temkin and Ashworth 2004), we believe that this standard would represent an advance on the current situation in Croatia where both force or threat of force and resistance are required.

Moreover, the *mens rea* of rape should be changed. A standard of negligence should be adopted, in order to be able to punish negligently made mistakes (that is unreasonable – even if honest – belief in consent). Where circumstances create a presumption of lack of consent, and the perpetrator is aware of these circumstances, this should give rise to an accompanying presumption of the unreasonableness of a belief in consent. In cases where a person has information which could put him on notice that there might not be consent, he should take steps to ascertain whether there is consent and failure to do so should give rise to culpability. In such cases, the perpetrator should be responsible for rape committed by negligence.

In addition, the distinction between a sexual act equivalent to sexual intercourse and an indecent act needs to be clearly defined. The critical criterion for deciding when a sexual act constitutes an act equivalent to rape should be penetration, however slight, of any part of a body of the victim or of the perpetrator, with a sexual organ, or of the anal or the genital opening of the victim, with any object or other part of the body.

These definitional changes should be supported by procedural changes that will ensure that the focus of the rape trial shifts from the victim's to the perpetrator's behaviour. To minimize the presence of rape myths and prejudices in rape prosecutions, legal practitioners (and the wider public) should be educated on gender equality and women's rights. In particular, rape awareness programmes should be conducted in which experts on rape trauma and women's rights would be involved.

## Notes

1 By summer 2009, Croatia had concluded negotiations in respect of only four acquis chapters of the EU Treaty, while negotiations are on the way in respect of the remaining 17. See www.delhrv.ec.europa.eu.
2 If the victim is a minor (a person between 14 and 16 years of age).
3 The first ICVS was conducted in 1997, the second in 2000 and the pilot for the third one was completed in 2008.
4 For the results of the ICVS in various countries see www.unicri.it/wwd/analysis/icvs/publications/php.
5 In this chapter, we usually refer to potential or actual rape victims as female and

to potential or actual rapists as male. We do not employ this nomenclature to reinforce the gender roles of male sexual aggression and female sexual victimization, but to reflect the reality of rape.
6 Indecent acts are punished by imprisonment for three months to three years only.
7 In cases where the force is targeted at objects it shall be considered as a threat, and if it is of a serious nature, it shall constitute coercion into sexual intercourse, since this criminal offence does not require that the threat be targeted at a person, as does the criminal offence of rape.
8 The authors' translation.
9 This research was a part of the project of analysis of Croatian rape laws and judicial practice conducted by B.a.B.e, a women's rights group in Zagreb, in which both of the authors participated. Twenty Supreme Court judgments and 20 judgments of various county courts were analysed. The results are not yet published.
10 This view has been expressed in the Ministry of Justice Expert Group which is tasked with drafting a new Criminal Code and of which one of the authors, Turković, is chair.
11 However, if the perpetrator is mistaken in respect of age, he will not be responsible for aggravated rape, but the basic form: Art. 188 (4).
12 Art. 188(3). In respect of the consequence (death, serious physical injury), the *mens rea* requirement is negligence and not intent.
13 Art. 188(3). In respect of the consequence (severe impairment of health, pregnancy) the *mens rea* requirement is either intent or negligence.
14 Exceptionally, it is possible to prove that sperm, and other material evidence or injuries described in medical documentation, derive from a person other than the defendant (Art. 422).
15 Yet others have argued that forced sex and non-consensual sex are distinct crimes: McGregor 1996; West 1996.
16 The Ministry of Justice has appointed an expert group to review the Criminal Code of which one of the authors, Ksenija Turković, is chair.

## Bibliography

Anderson, M.J. (2005) 'Negotiating sex', *South California Review*, 78: 1401–38.
Bačić, F. and Pavlović, S. (2004) *Komentar kaznenog zakona*, Zagreb: Organizator (Commentary of Criminal Law).
Garačić, A. (2004) 'Zakonska i sudska politika kažnjavanja županijskih sudova u Republici Hrvatskoj za kaznena djela silovanja i zlouporabe droga', *Hrvatski ljetopis za kazneno pravo i praksu*, 2: 475–16 ('Legislative and judicial policy of sentencing by the county courts in the Republic of Croatia for the criminal offences of rape and drug abuse', *Croatian Summer Book of Criminal Law and Practice*).
Gotell, L. (2008) 'Rethinking affirmative consent in Canadian sexual assault law: neoliberal sexual subjects and risky women', *Akron Law Review*, 41: 865–98.
Kesić V. (2003) *Žene obnavljaju sjećanja*, Zagreb: Centar za žene žrtve rata (*Women Recollecting Memories*, Zagreb: Center for Women Victims of War).
McGregor, J. (1996) 'Why when she says no she doesn't mean maybe and doesn't mean yes: a critical reconstruction of consent, sex, and the law', *Legal Theory*, 2: 175–208.
Munro, V. (2008) 'Constructing consent: legislating freedom and legitimating constraint in the expression of sexual autonomy', *Akron Law Review*, 41: 923–56.

Novoselec, P. (1996) 'Pojam sile kod silovanja (sudska praksa)', *Hrvatski ljetopis za kazneno pravo i praksu*, 2: 935–38 ('Concept of Force in Rape (Judicial Practice)', *Croatian Summerbook for Criminal Law and Practice*).

Radačić, I. (2005) 'The status of women and treatment of sexual violence in international criminal law', *Zbornik Pravnog fakulteta Sveucilista u Rijeci*, 26: 1041–62 (*Rijeka Law School Law Review*).

—— (2008) 'Rape cases in the jurisprudence of the European Court of Human Rights', *European Human Rights Law Review*, 3: 357–75.

Temkin, J. and Ashworth, A. (2004) 'The Sexual Offences Act 2003: rape, sexual assault and the problem of consent', *Criminal Law Review*, 328–46.

Torrey, M. (1991) 'When will we be believed? Rape myths and the idea of fair trial in rape prosecutions', *University of California Davis Law Review*, 24: 1013–71.

Turković, K. (2007) 'Kaznena djela protiv spolne slobode i spolnog ćudoređa', u: P. Novoselec (ed.) *Posebni dio kaznenog prava*, Zagreb: Sveučilišna tiskara ('Criminal offences against sexual freedoms and sexual morals', in: *Special Part of Criminal Law*).

Vandervort, L. (2004) 'Honest beliefs, credible lies and culpable awareness: rhetoric, inequality and mens rea', *Osgoode Hall Law Journal*, 42: 625–60.

West, R. (1996) 'A comment on consent, sex and rape', *Legal Theory*, 2: 233–51.

Chapter 12

# Rape in Italian law
## Towards the recognition of sexual autonomy

*Rachel Anne Fenton*[1]

The 1996 Italian reform of sexual offences was hailed as a victory for women and a cultural turnaround in its symbolic recognition and protection of sexual autonomy. The lynchpin of the reform is that the law now classifies sexual offences as 'offences against personal freedom', whereas previously they were classified as simply 'offences against public morality'. Under the 1930 Rocco code, sexual autonomy and bodily integrity had not been protected as interests in themselves, but rather as part of the public good. This was symptomatic of the fascist ideology underpinning the code and the historical legacy of the Italian legal tradition that conceptualized sexual activity as tied to legitimate procreation. The symbolic potential of law has been used to promote the axiological value of the right to sexual autonomy – the reform has been lived by women as a strategic and symbolic legitimization and recognition of their existence as political subjects (Manna 2005). The new law has thus been used to send an ideological message to society about the status of women and the right to sexual self-determination. This is particularly important in view of the fact that sexual violence takes place within culturally and sociologically defined parameters (Ponti and Merzagora Betsos 2008).

The main features of the law are: the abolition of the distinction between penile penetration and other sexual acts accompanied by graduated sentencing; an increase in the minimum sentence from three to five years whilst retaining the maximum sentence of 10 years; a list of aggravating circumstances which increase the sentence; some recognition of the sexual autonomy of minors and people with learning disabilities and an autonomous provision and higher sentence for gang rape. There are also some interesting procedural provisions such as mandatory prosecution by the state in some circumstances. This chapter will explore rape in contemporary Italian society, the background to the 1996 reform and the substance of the new law. It will also question whether the symbolic recognition of sexual autonomy reflected therein has had any effect in practice.

The 1996 law (L. 15.2.1996, n. 66) marked the beginning of an onslaught of legislation (L. 3.8.1998, n. 269; L. 6.2.2006, n. 38; D.L. 23.2.2009, n. 11) in related areas, particularly regarding the (sexual) protection of minors, prostitution, paedophilia, pornography, sex tourism, paedo-pornography, internet offences and, most recently, stalking. The offence of rape does not appear in itself to be singled out for particular attention. Rather, the Ministry for Equal Opportunities has violence against women at the forefront of its agenda and sexual violence is part of this more general concern. Indeed, the most recent report by the Italian Statistics Office on violence and maltreatment of women inside and outside the family (ISTAT 2007) combines the study of sexual and physical violence. This study reveals interesting data about contemporary Italian women's experience of sexual violence. In fact, of the 24 per cent of women who have experienced sexual violence in their lifetime, 5 per cent had experienced rape or attempted rape. Of these rapes, almost all (92 per cent of rapes and 94 per cent of attempted rapes) went unreported. Sixty-eight per cent of rapes and 38 per cent of attempted rapes were committed by the woman's current or ex-partner, as compared to 6 per cent by a stranger and 17 per cent by someone known to the victim. Current or ex-partners were also responsible for 94 per cent of unwanted sexual relations experienced by the victim as violence and 100 per cent of cases where the victim was forced to undertake a sexual act they considered humiliating. These statistics illustrate Italy's conformity with patterns elsewhere, which challenge common myths about the preponderance of stranger (cf. acquaintance/intimate) rapes. Of those victims of rape, or attempted rape, by a current or ex-partner, only 26 per cent considered it to be a crime, 46 per cent considered it to be 'a wrong but not a crime', and 25 per cent as 'just something that happened', demonstrating the propensity of Italian women not to categorize rape as a crime and to self-blame (Merzagora Betsos 2006).

However, the 2007 statistics do not individuate a specific conviction or attrition rate for rape. Although ISTAT reports give the numbers of crimes reported for which proceedings have been initiated and convictions obtained in a given year, this precludes tracking of crimes across different annual reports, since the time lapse between initiating proceedings and verdicts is two to three years for most sexual violence cases (Merzagora Betsos 2006). Some studies into specific courts have, however, produced illustrative results. For example, the criminal court in Rome had a conviction rate of 53 per cent for those crimes of sexual violence for which proceedings were initiated between 1975 and 1985 (Merzagora Betsos 2006). In addition, a rough estimate, derived from averaging the number of proceedings initiated in Italy over a three-year period (2001–03) and comparing against the number of convictions in 2004, indicates a lower conviction rate of 35 per cent, mirroring the experiences of other European jurisdictions whereby increased reporting has not resulted in increased convictions (Merzagora Betsos 2006). It should be noted that this figure includes all crimes of sexual violence (and thus, the less serious offences as well as rape), which makes it difficult to discern whether proceedings for rape are more or less successful than those for offences such as sexual molestation.

## THE HISTORY OF REFORM

### The previous law: the Rocco code of 1930

The 1930 code divided sexual offences into two types. These were the serious offence of *congiunzione carnale* ('joining of the flesh') (A.519 *codice penale* (criminal code) (c.p.)) constituted by vaginal, anal and oral penetration (Cadoppi 2006) and a less serious offence of *atti di libidine* ('acts of lust') (A.521 c.p.) defined simply as acts *different* from *congiunzione carnale* (Fenton 2009).

The way in which these offences were set out meant that the only way to distinguish between them was to establish whether there had been penile penetration. This naturally led to extensive and invasive questioning of the victim as to the exact nature and extent of the act. Such questioning was said to be one of the main reasons for victims not reporting rape (Ponti and Merzagora Betsos 2008; Farinelli 1996). Furthermore, this distinction did not recognize that acts not involving penetration may be more offensive and degrading to the victim (Padovani 1989 and 2006).

Sexual offences were concerned with public morality and not with the rights of women as individuals. This was consistent with the role of marriage in 1930s Italian society: women were regarded as property and not as the bearers of rights. Indeed, in criminal law, adultery by the wife (but not the husband) was a criminal offence and a marital rape exception existed. In addition, the offence of rape could be extinguished simply if the victim married the rapist. Thus, marriage was seen to provide legitimate reparation for the damaged honour of the woman and her family (*matrimonio riparatore* (A. 544 c.p.)).

### Italian feminism

The reform of sexual offences owes much to the Italian woman's movement. Changes in Italian society regarding the role of women became apparent in the 1970s, leading to the formation of feminist consciousness-raising groups and subsequent legislative change. Events such as the Circeo Massacre of 1975 (in which three young men abducted, raped and tortured two 17-year-old girls, killing one of them) and a 1979 prize-winning documentary *Processo per Stupro* (Trial for Rape), which followed court proceedings (filmed for the first time) against four men for the abduction and rape of an 18-year-old, heightened awareness of rape in the public consciousness (Lagostena Bassi 1993). Prevalent social attitudes and rape myths were illustrated, including victim-blaming by the mothers and wives of the defendants, and the use of invasive questioning of the victim in the courtroom was documented. With the changing role and emancipation of women in Italian society, the Rocco code of 1930 became increasingly unacceptable.

The start of the parliamentary reform process was marked by women's groups mobilizing to draft a rape law in 1979. This law, which became known as 'women's law', proposed that sexual violence become a crime against the person and not against public morality and that the distinction between *congiunzione carnale* and *atti di libidine* be abolished. The woman's movement favoured using the criminal law and its symbolic-expressive function to send a message to society that women are human beings, not objects of pleasure to be used by men (Fiandaca 1993). Indeed, the campaign's leaders asserted that the primary purpose 'was first and foremost to proclaim women as equal citizens' (Everhart 1998). In the 1980s and 1990s, reform remained on the political agenda. In these debates, many women members of parliament (MPs) identified explicitly with the feminist movement, regardless of their party politics, illustrating the extent to which feminism had been influential both inside and outside of Parliament (Bono and Kemp 1991). This period also saw further high-profile media coverage of brutal rape cases, leading to increased public outrage. The Vatican spoke out about the onslaught of sexual violence and sociologists warned about the increase in gang rape as a social phenomenon (Everhart 1998). In 1995, women MPs from all parties drafted a bill which drew heavily on the 'women's law' and this was finally passed by parliament in 1996 (Everhart 1998).

## THE NEW OFFENCE OF *VIOLENZA SESSUALE* (SEXUAL VIOLENCE)

The cornerstone of the 1996 reform was to unify the offences of *congiunzione carnale* and *atti di libidine* under one offence. The offence of sexual violence under A. 609 *bis* c.p. now reads:

> Whosoever, by violence or threat or by abuse of authority coerces another to commit or submit to sexual acts is punished by imprisonment of five to 10 years.
> The same punishment is applicable to he who induces another to commit or submit to sexual acts:
>
> 1. abusing the physical or psychological inferiority of the victim at the time of the offence
> 2. deceiving the victim as to the identity of the perpetrator
>
> In less serious cases the punishment is reduced by not more than two thirds.

A. 609 *ter* c.p. contains a list of aggravating circumstances which increase the sentence to between six and 12 years. These include the victim being a minor, use of arms, alcohol, narcotics or stupefying substances, commission by a person in disguise or pretending to be a public official and commission on a person whose personal liberty is curtailed.

The unification of the offences may represent a paradigm shift but the offence continues to be based upon coercion, as opposed to consent, and predicated upon the historical components of violence and threat. Coercion is thus the causal nexus – the passive subject must do, or submit to, the sexual act *because* of the coercion. This was a specific legislative choice, to which Italian *dottrina* (academic writing) contributed greatly (Pavarini 2002). The legislator ignored some authoritative *dottrina* (Padovani 1989 and 2006), which argued that, as the reform is centred upon harm done to the victim, incrimination should be measured in terms of the victim's dissent. The focus on lack of consent in the 'women's law' was also not adopted. Coercion has its origins in the historic 'duty to resist' placed on women, meaning that coercion (or induction) would need to be shown to have overcome this 'natural' resistance (*vis grata puellae*). In this sense, the conception of sex is still based upon the notion of 'conquest of the prey' (Padovani 1989 and 2006). To retain a coercion-based definition would, therefore, appear to contradict legislation specifically aimed at protecting sexual autonomy: self-determination includes the recognition of a woman's capacity to freely consent and the need for resistance is anathema to such capacity.

The criticism is that effective sexual autonomy can only be achieved, or at least be seen to be achieved, by a consent-based definition. The argument may appear, however, to be somewhat academic. Although non-consent does not figure in the legal definition, it features extensively in the interpretation of the law (Pavarini 2002). The Italian Supreme Court (*Corte di Cassazione* – the highest appeal court (Fenton 2000)) has declared that 'the new law is aimed at a more modern concept of personal liberty, which in principle is equally offended by non-consensual relations as it is by violent relations' and that 'the material element of the offence coincides with the committal of any sexual act without the consent of the partner' (Cass III 3.12.1999 n. 13829; Pavarini 2002). In order for coercion to be present, the act must have occurred against the will of the passive subject, that is, the victim must have dissented. Consent thus appears to be the reality of how coercion is measured. Indeed, according to recent *giurisprudenza* (case law), consent must be present continuously throughout the sexual encounter and consensual relations will become an offence if one party withdraws consent at any time or the encounter goes beyond what was originally agreed to (Cass III 24.2. 2004, Guzzardi, RV 228687, CP 2005: 25). Thus, even where there is consent to the intercourse itself, ejaculation into the vagina without consent is sufficient to constitute the offence (Cass III 10.5.1996 RV 205292, CP 1997: 1739).

Put simply, consent will negate coercion. Despite the official focus on coercion, the Supreme Court talks consistently in terms of the consent of the victim. It is thus arguable that the protection of sexual autonomy does, in the Court's mind, equate with non-consent. However, the fact that consent will negate the causal nexus of coercion suggests that there will be as much scope for focus on the victim's behaviour in the courtroom (if the defendant argues that he/she consented) as there would be in a jurisdiction employing a consent-based definition.

The new offence requires simply that *atti sessuali* be committed against or submitted to by the passive subject. The active subject can coerce the passive subject to do things to himself/herself, to the active subject or another person. The focus is thus on the victim and the offence is gender-neutral. *Atti sessuali* is a potentially all-encompassing category whose limits remain undefined by the legislator. The aim of using this phrase was to emphasize that any act which invades the sexual sphere and compromises the bodily sexual autonomy of the victim will be an offence. The rhetoric has certainly been embraced by the Supreme Court, which has pronounced that: 'included in the notion of *atti sessuali* are all acts apt to compromise the victim's free determination of his own sexuality and enter into his sexual sphere' (Cass. III 27.4.1998, Di Francia, RV 210975, CP 1998: 3281). This phraseology, which has been repeated consistently in subsequent case law, recognizes the potentially equally degrading and harmful nature of sexual acts whether penetrative or not. This has also been recognized by the Supreme Court: 'acts other than *congiunzione carnale* can have more serious connotations than penetration itself' (Cass. III 15.11.1996, Coro, RV 207298, RP 1997: 147).

The debate as to the precise meaning of the phrase 'sexual acts' has centred on what constitutes a 'sexual' act at the lower end of the spectrum (Fenton 2009). Having an all-encompassing definition means that sexual acts do not need to be categorized as 'rape' or 'assault' or 'penetrative' – any sexual act which meets the definition will be *violenza sessuale*. This, however, is problematic in terms of analysing the varying types of sexual offence and, collating statistics, and may raise difficulties in terms of fair labelling, since a vicious rape at knifepoint will carry the same title as a fleeting touching of the buttocks.

One of the primary objectives of the new law was to reduce the need for invasive questioning of the victim and thus to encourage more women to report rape. By placing less emphasis upon the actual act and more emphasis upon the quantum of violence used upon, and trauma caused to, the victim (Cadoppi 2006), the need for invasive questioning should theoretically be diminished. The problem with this approach is not the unification of the two offences per se, but that the formula enacted for determining sentencing is to distinguish between serious and less serious acts. This means that a fairly detailed examination of the sexual act must be carried out by the trial judge in order to determine whether the act is 'less serious' and thus to decide on the appropriate sentence. The victim cannot, it seems, avoid invasive questioning and the aim of the legislator in this regard has arguably been thwarted.

Furthermore, the provision for 'less serious' cases which attract a reduced sentence gives a great deal of discretion to the trial judge. The Supreme Court has stated that an offence is 'less serious' 'when it is possible to assert that the personal sexual liberty of the victim has been suppressed in a non-serious way' (Cass. III n. 5646/2000; Palumbieri 2006). In making this assessment, it is clear that the whole context of the offence should be considered, including psychological damage caused to the victim. This is completely in tune with the aim of protecting sexual autonomy and, correlatively, the psychological well-being of the victim (Cadoppi 2001). However, such judicial discretion leaves legitimate space for subjective stereotyping, reliance on rape myths and victim precipitation factors to influence the categorization of the offence (Padovani 2006). For example, it appears that the relationship between the accused and victim will be considered when assessing the psychological damage (or perceived lack thereof) to the victim. In several cases, rapes have been deemed less serious when there has been a loving relationship between the victim and accused, including the rape of a girlfriend who was seven months pregnant (Cass. III 24.2.1999, p.m. in c. C., RP 1999: 445) and statutory rape of an under-14-year-old in which the defendant was praised by the court for his 'considerate', 'caring' and 'courteous' behaviour (Trib Vicenza Sent., 8.1.2008, FD, 2008: 11,1046). Yet the fact that the outcome of this latter case contradicts an earlier judgment of the Supreme Court (note that Italy does not have a formal doctrine of precedent), in which intercourse with a 'fully consenting' and proactive minor in an affectionate relationship was not found to be less serious (Cass. III 28.4.2006, n. 34120, DeG 2006: 40, 66), illustrates the scope of the discretion afforded to the judiciary and the potential for different outcomes depending on the persuasion of the individual judge.

## Constituent elements of the offence: sexual violence by coercion

The first part of A.609 *bis* c.p. requires that the perpetrator coerce the victim to commit or submit to sexual acts. The coercion can take three forms, namely, violence, threat or abuse of authority. These will be examined in turn.

Interestingly, what constitutes violence for this purpose has decreased over time from actual physical force being needed to overcome determined resistance by the victim, to the situation today where violence appears to be anything, physical or psychological, which overcomes consent. The *giurisprudenza* has also created a type of violence where the perpetrator acts with a 'surprise' element and, thus, with presumed dissent. In such situations, it is the suddenness and rapidity of the act which overcomes consent and constitutes violence – for example, where a doctor suddenly penetrates the vagina fully with his finger during a gynaecological examination (Cass. III 16.4.1999, p.m. in c. Lorè, RP 1999: 967). In reality, however, this type of violence is a judicial fiction: if the act happens before the victim has time to accept or reject it, then there is no consent that can be overcome by this form of 'surprise' violence.

It has been emphasized that violence will exist 'even where the victim yielded to put an end to an unbearable situation, because that is not free consent, it is coerced consent' (Cass. 16.11.1988, *Mass.uff.*, 1988, m.179752), thus, the victim need not actively resist. There will be violence even where the perpetrator takes advantage of a difficult situation that the victim finds herself in (Cadoppi 2006). The court has also held that it is not necessary for the violence to continue up until the moment of the intercourse; nor need it completely eliminate the capacity of the victim to resist. It is sufficient that there is a causal nexus between the psychological state of the victim and the act. What matters is the effect of the violence on consent, not what method is used.

In light of the above, one might wonder what the nature of the difference is between a violence-based and consent-based definition. It is arguable that the requirement that violence and coercion be present means that the court must pay attention to what the perpetrator actually did to overcome consent, rather than simply concentrating on whether the victim consented. The distinction may be subtle, but is exemplified by the following case: the victim was locked in a car in deserted countryside and held by the wrists. Threats were made against her and her family. She then undressed herself and submitted to intercourse. There was no violence at the actual time of the intercourse. The court focused entirely on the defendant's behaviour which annulled any possibility of genuine consent, rather than examining whether she had consented at the time of intercourse. The court dismissed the fact that she had undressed herself and did not try to stop him as unimportant. The defendant had already perfected his moral coercion before the act took place (Cass. III 15.11.1999, Lutterotti, *Dir. Pen. e proc.*, 2000: 1612).

The second form of coercion is by threat. As with violence, the threat must operate to overcome the victim's consent. This ground has been invoked very infrequently. Examples from the case law are threats to inform a husband of a wife's previous infidelity and the threat to send compromising photos to the victim's parents (Cadoppi 2006).

Finally, *violenza sessuale* can be committed by abuse of authority. The preparatory works indicate that the legislator was keen to protect the sexual freedom of anyone in a weak position in the workplace and/or the family (Palumbieri 2006). The authority in question can be both public and private: private authority covers teachers, parents, healthcare workers, but is aimed particularly at employers and bosses. The offence can thus be used to regulate serious workplace sexual harassment. In the workplace, the Supreme Court has ruled it sufficient that the employer has used his authority over and above its limits to put the worker in a position of being unable to refuse sexual acts (Cass. III 17.3.2004 n. 22786, DPL, 2004, 1993).

## Sexual violence by induction

The second part of A.609 *bis* c.p. has induction as its causal nexus – here the defendant must *induce* (as opposed to coerce) another to commit or submit to sexual acts. The word *induzione* implies suggestion, moral/psychological pressure or persuasion. It is something less than the coercion required to make out the offence in the first part of A.609 *bis* c.p., presumably because the victim is already perceived to be less able to give genuine consent – the victim only need be induced to consent and such consent is vitiated by the induction. Induction can take two forms. The first is by abusing the physical or psychological inferiority of the victim. Physical inferiority means paralysis or serious weakness, including pregnancy. However, the new wording is potentially problematic in cases where the victim is stupefied or unconscious and thus is neither coerced nor induced into sex (Cadoppi 2006). As regards psychological inferiority, under the previous law, having carnal relations (without any coercion) with a mentally disabled person (*malato di mente*) was an offence. Thus, the mentally disabled were deemed unable to consent to sexual activity and had no sexual autonomy. The new law affords sexual autonomy to those with learning difficulties, in that they may engage in sexual relations as long as they are not induced. Simultaneously, the law endeavours to protect such vulnerable people from abuse if they are indeed induced.

The second form that induction can take is by deceiving the victim as to the identity of the perpetrator (*inganno di persona*). The deception must induce the sexual act. This formula is unproblematic where the victim thinks the perpetrator is another person, but becomes problematic where the perpetrator assumes a false quality. The Supreme Court (Cass. III 21.11.2000 n. 250/2001; Cadoppi 2006) has further illustrated its readiness to protect the sexual autonomy of the victim by extending the provision to cover the situation where a 'photographer' deceived young aspiring soubrettes that he would get them work and induced them into sexual acts. Again the reasoning was consent-based: 'the substitution of person which invalidates consent includes a vast array of offences which do not always have a legal form . . . but have the common characteristic of deceiving the victim vitiating consent'. Italian *dottrina* is, however, not in agreement – there is no deception as to the sex act or identity of the perpetrator in this type of situation (Cadoppi 2006).

Finally, the offence of *violenza sessuale* must be committed intentionally. Intention (*dolo*) is defined under A. 43 c.p as when the result is foreseen and desired as a consequence of the perpetrator's action or omission. As seen above, the case law has diluted the concepts of violence and threat so that the offence is made out even where there is a simple lack of consent. However, this diminishing need for violence or threat leads to increasing difficulty for the perpetrator in realizing the dissent of the other party. According to the Supreme Court (Cass. III 4.2.2004 n. 14789, RP, 2004: 608), the victim may be silent or submissive due to the coercion used, but it is still a requirement of the offence that the defendant knows that the victim is not consenting (Palumbieri 2006). Where the perpetrator cannot be aware of the victim's dissent because of lack of reaction or where no real threat or violence has been used, then there will be no intention (Cadoppi 2006). Thus, there will be no intention where the defendant makes a mistake as to consent. There is no formal requirement that any mistake be reasonable, but the defendant must prove his honest mistake. Whilst operation of rape myths and stereotypes cannot be underestimated, any perceived weakness of the Italian system in this regard can be to some extent counteracted by the fact that rape cases will be tried by a panel of professional judges (*tribunale in composizione collegiale*) and that the standard of proof is the free evaluation of the evidence by the judge (*libero convincimento del giudice*), which is accompanied by full reasoning (*motivazione*). Thus the defendant would have to be fully credible and any suggested mistake would have to stand up to judicial scrutiny.

## Gang rape

The 1996 law contains a new and autonomous provision for gang rape in response to the fact that this appears to be a particular social problem in Italy, often being committed by under-18s. A. 609 *octies* c.p. defines gang rape as *violenza sessuale* by persons together (two people are enough (Donini 2006)). The provision is grounded in the protection of personal sexual liberty because gang rape is perceived as being even more degrading and dangerous for the victim than sexual violence by one person. The Supreme Court has clarified that little is expected in the way of dissent from a victim in these circumstances: the victim need only voice her lack of consent once, at the beginning of the attack. This offence carries a higher sentence, of six to 12 years. According to the Supreme Court, this is due to the disappearance of any semblance of analogy to 'normal' sexual relations (Cass. III. 3.6.1999, Bombaci, RV 215149). Such reasoning might be criticized for reinforcing notions of 'real rape' in that gang rape more clearly fits the 'real rape' script, problematizing 'other' rapes which look like consensual sex.

## Minors

There is a new regime regulating non-coerced sexual acts with minors. Under A.609 *quater* c.p. statutory rape is retained (although feminists had argued for its abolition) at varying ages depending on the relationship with the adult. Under-14s cannot consent, under-16s cannot consent where there is a parental, cohabitation or educative relationship with the adult, and under-18s cannot consent where there is an abuse of the power inherent in the relationship. This regime appears predominantly paternalistic. The law is not interested in determining whether an under-14 may have the emotional or sexual maturity to freely determine the expression of their sexuality in relation to an adult. The legal goal is no longer sexual autonomy and liberty but rather the protection of the psycho-physical integrity of the minor's sexual development (Cass. III 13.5.2004, p.m. in c. Sonno, RV 229358). However, some sexual autonomy is recognized for those aged 13 or over who have consensual sexual relations with another minor, as long as there is no more than a three-year age gap. In this situation, the minor is not afforded a positive right to express his/her sexuality. Rather, the law provides that such circumstances are exempt from punishment. The 13-year-old is thus in a state of 'limbo' (Veneziani 2006) in that he/she can consent to sex with a 16-year-old, but not with a 17-year-old. The legal focus is on the age of the recipient of the consent, rather than on whether the giver of consent does so with the relevant maturity and capacity.

## Procedural provisions

The principle of mandatory prosecution is typical of civil-law jurisdictions. Italy is no exception, the principle being contained in A.112 of the Italian

Constitution. The procedural rules for all crimes differentiate between offences for which the prosecutor must act *ex officio* and those for which a complaint by the victim, *querela*, is required. Whether sexual violence should require a *querela* or not attracted some debate during the reform process and it is suggested by Virgilio that the value afforded to the victim's self-determination is embodied by the choice between *querela* and *ex officio* prosecution (Virgilio 2006). To make the prosecution *ex officio* would be to proclaim that sexual violence is not just a crime against the victim but against society and would protect the victim from pressure to not complain or later retract their complaint. Yet such a regime would potentially expose the victim to further harm in terms of a trial they may not desire to undergo and thus limit their autonomy. Women would arguably be characterized as weak, victimized and in need of protection from the law. The new A. 609 *septies* c.p. embodies a compromise: prosecution requires a *querela* by the victim, which once made is irrevocable, but with some exceptions (minors, gang rape, commission by a public official) where prosecution will be *ex officio*. The usual time limit for the *querela* to be made has been extended from three to six months, intended to increase the number of complaints made, but criticized by Virgilio (2006) as differentiating women victims, portraying them as different, weak and indecisive.

## CONCLUSION

According to Picotti, the 1996 law has performed a profound cultural revolution (2001). It embodies a new right to sexuality and sexual autonomy on the part of adults, particularly women, those with learning difficulties and, to some extent, minors. Although unable to shake the historical concepts of coercion and violence, the Supreme Court has diluted them and talks consistently in terms of consent. The Supreme Court has also embraced the right to sexual autonomy and when it has not appeared to do so, female politicians and mass media have been quick to vociferously object (Fenton 2000). Thus, in terms of its desired symbolic expressive function, the 1996 law can be said to have been successful.

In terms of doctrinal evaluation, the conclusion that a profound cultural revolution has taken place appears grounded. Yet in terms of Italian socio-cultural mores, such a conclusion is more difficult to sustain. The difficulty arises in that research conducted in Italian law schools is predominantly doctrinal and little attention has been paid to the extra-legal factors which permeate this area of law and society. Although some criminologists have conducted research, socio-legal empirical work is not yet conducted on a large scale in Italy. Furthermore, whilst the Ministry of Equal Opportunities is currently interested in physical violence against women, rape only figures as a part of this wider concern rather than as a serious issue per se. The most detailed funded research since the 1996 reform appears to have been carried out in a conference held at the University of Parma in 2000 and not since repeated on any similar scale (Cadoppi 2001). Recent statistics indicate an increase in the reporting of sexual violence but that convictions do not mirror this increase (Merzagora Betsos 2006). Virgilio points out, however, that reporting rates were increasing *before* the 1996 law and thus it is questionable whether the 1996 law in itself has affected this trend (2001). The unavailability of ongoing empirical studies and detailed statistical evidence makes it almost impossible to discern whether indeed a cultural revolution has taken place. In addition, the fact that recent surveys (ISTAT 2007) indicate that many Italian women continue to endorse the rape myths and stereotypes that abound in other jurisdictions suggests that Italy still has a long way to go in changing its rape culture and that, in practice, the symbolic recognition of sexual autonomy has not had any profound effect.

## Note

With grateful thanks to Alberto Cadoppi and Malaika Bianchi, University of Palma.

## Bibliography

Bono, P. and Kemp, S. (1991) *Italian Feminist Thought*, Basil Blackwell.
Cadoppi, A. (2001) 'Presentazione', in A. Cadoppi (ed.) *La Violenza Sessuale a Cinque Anni dalla Legge, N.66/98*: Cedam.
—— (2006) 'Commento Art. 609 *bis* c.p.', in A. Cadoppi (ed.) *Commentario delle Norme Contro la Violenza Sessuale e Contro la Pedofilia*, 4th edn, Cedam.
Donini, M. (2006) 'Commento Art. 609 octies c.p.', in A. Cadoppi (ed.) *Commentario delle Norme Contro la Violenza Sessuale e Contro la Pedofilia*, 4th edn, Cedam.
Everhart, A.J. (1998) 'Predicting the effect of Italy's long-awaited rape law reform on "the land of machismo" ', *Vanderbilt Journal of Transnational Law*, 671–718.
Farinelli, R. (1996) 'Aspetti Forensi', in A. Cadoppi (ed.) *Commentario delle Norme Contro la Violenza Sessuale*, 1st edn, Cedam.
Fenton, R.A. (2000) 'Separating law from facts: the difficulties faced by the Italian *Corte di Cassazione* in an appeal for illogicality of reasoning', *International and Comparative Law Quarterly*, 49: 709–19.
—— (2009) 'The meaning of the word "sexual": a comparative analysis', on file with the author.
Fiandaca, G. (1993) 'Voce Violenza Sessuale', in *Enciclopedia del Diritto*, Giuffrè.
ISTAT (2007) 'La violenza e i maltrattamenti contro le donne dentro e fuori la famiglia'. Online. Available at: <www.istat.it/salastampa/comunicati/non_calendario/20070221_00/testointegrale.pdf> (accessed 13 October 2008).
Lagostena Bassi, T. (1993) 'Violence against women and the response of Italian institutions', in M. Cicioni and N. Prunster *Visions and Revisions Women in Italian Culture*, Berg, 199–212.
Manna, A. (2005) 'La Donna nel Diritto Penale', *L'indice Penale*, 3: 851–87.
Merzagora Betsos, I. (2006) *Criminologia della violenza e dell'omicidio dei reati sessuali dei fenomeni di dipendenza*, Cedam.
Padovani, T. (1989) 'Violenza Carnale e Tutela della Libertà', *Riv. It. Dir. Proc. Pen.*, 1301–12.

—— (2006) 'Commento Pre-Art 609 *bis* c.p.', in A. Cadoppi (ed.) *Commentario delle Norme Contro la Violenza Sessuale e Contro la Pedofilia*, 4th edn, Cedam.
Palumbieri, S.R. (2006) 'Violenza Sessuale', in A. Cadoppi (ed.) *Reati Contro la Libertà Sessuale e lo Sviluppo Psico-Fisico dei Minori*, UTET.
Pavarini, C. (2002) 'Il Mero *Dissenso* della Vittima nella Violenza Sessuale: Profili di Diritto Italiano e Anglosassone', *L'indice Penale*, 771–802.
Picotti, L. (2001) 'Profili Generali di Diritto Penale Sostanziale', in A. Cadoppi, (ed.) *La Violenza Sessuale a Cinque Anni dalla Legge N.66/98*, Cedam.
Ponti, G. and Merzagora Betsos, I. (2008) *Compendio di Criminologia*, 5th edn, Raffaello Cortina.
Veneziani, P. (2006) 'Commento Art.609 *quater* c.p.', in A. Cadoppi, (ed.) *Commentario delle Norme Contro la Violenza Sessuale e Contro la Pedofilia*, 4th edn, Cedam.
Virgilio, M. (2001) 'Nei Dintorni della Legge Contro la Violenza Sessuale: un Bilancio Oltre la Giurisprudenza', in A. Cadoppi (ed.) *La Violenza Sessuale a Cinque Anni dalla Legge N.66/98*: Cedam.
—— (2006) 'Commento Art. 609 *septies* c.p.', in A. Cadoppi, (ed.) *Commentario delle Norme Contro la Violenza Sessuale e Contro la Pedofilia*, 4th edn, Cedam.

Chapter 13

# Rethinking rape law in Sweden
Coercion, consent or non-voluntariness?

*Monica Burman*

During the last 30 years, rape has been the subject of more government and official investigations and legislative changes than any other criminal act in Sweden. However, there have been very few *policy* initiatives that have explicitly addressed rape and other forms of sexual abuse. In addition, the underlying dimensions of gender, power, sexuality and equality have barely been recognized in law and policy-making processes. This is somewhat peculiar in a Swedish context, where equality and issues of gender and power have generally been highly influential in framing legal and policy responses to men's violence against women.

This chapter deals with the main aspects of current law, policy and feminist legal research in Sweden regarding the rape of adults (when the victim is 15 or older), focusing particularly on the latest reform of 2005. In that reform, the government decided *not* to replace coercion with consent as the criminal element in rape, while simultaneously extending the definition of rape to include cases where there was no coercion, as further discussed below. However, a new reform process is already under way. An important contribution brought to that process will be a feminist-inspired attempt to reconstruct rape law with a provision in which non-voluntariness replaces coercion as the criminal element.

## HISTORICAL AND POLITICAL CONTEXT

When the Swedish Penal Code was enacted in 1965, the most significant change regarding rape was the penalization of rape within marriage. However, an intense parliamentary debate about the feared consequences of this penalization led to the creation of a new offence besides rape – a provision of *violation*, which carried a much lower penalty. This was mainly to be applied when the man and the woman had an intimate relationship or when the behaviour of the woman was regarded as causing the man's sexual act (Sutorius and Kaldal 2003: 40).

Coercion was, as in earlier provisions, the main criminal element in rape. The coercion required was equivalent to that in cases of robbery. It comprised assault, an overpowering of freedom of movement or threat. As also in earlier provisions, the perpetrator had to be a man and the victim a woman, and only heterosexual, vaginal intercourse could constitute rape.

The first comprehensive public and political discussions about men's violence against women started in Sweden at the end of the 1970s. Feminist critique was directed at case law and at a report arising out of an official inquiry which blamed women for building up a 'sexual atmosphere' presumed to provoke men's sexual abuse (Elman 1996). There was a large-scale reform in 1984, the purpose of which was to discard objectionable conceptions that women were responsible for sexual abuse. The offence of violation was replaced with a provision for less aggravated rape according to which the woman's relationship to the man or her behaviour before the abuse should be of no relevance. Furthermore, with the aim of including same-sex abuse within the definition of rape, the offence was made sex-neutral and the criterion of the sexual act extended to include sexual acts comparable with vaginal intercourse, that is, anal and oral penile penetration (Prop. 1983/84: 105).

At this time, gender equality politics were well established in Sweden, but it was not until the beginning of the 1990s that men's violence against women was politically defined as a specific gender-equality issue (Wendt Höjer 2002). New perspectives on men's violence against women, as related to gender, power and women's human rights were introduced in a government Bill on gender equality in 1994. Recognizing its close connection to wider, social power relations between men and women, men's violence against women was described in this Bill as one of the most serious limitations on the achievement of gender equality (Prop. 1993/94: 147). At the same time, the Commission on Violence against Women was appointed with the task of reviewing several areas of law and policy concerning men's violence against women, from the perspective of women (Directive 1993: 88). A government Bill in 1998, entitled 'Women's Peace', following the work of the Commission, was a comprehensive and gender-sensitive reform, which comprised several legislative and policy measures (Prop. 1997/98: 55). Thus, the criminal law became an instrument for promoting gender equality, while gender equality was simultaneously formulated as a relevant aspect of criminal policy (Burman 2010).

Rape was included within the new conceptualization of violence against women. However, in contrast to other issues dealt with in the Women's Peace reform in 1998, such as the new crime of 'gross violation of a woman's integrity' aimed at providing better treatment of domestic violence and criminalizing the purchase of sex, this new perspective had little impact on the rape provisions and very few policy initiatives specifically targeting rape were undertaken in the Women's Peace reform. Attention was, however, paid to the definition of rape. It was broadened by extending the criterion of the sexual act to include sexual acts not directly comparable with intercourse, but nevertheless constituting a serious violation of the sexual integrity of the victim, that is, digital vaginal or anal penetration. The only reason given by the government for the extension was that it was 'motivated' to do so, without explaining why (Prop. 1997/98: 55: 91). Nonetheless, the government did decide to initiate a review of all sexual crimes (Prop. 1997/98: 55: 95). Regarding rape, this new enquiry, in 1998, considered, first, whether coercion should be replaced by a criterion of non-consent or whether the degree of coercion constituting rape should be adjusted. Secondly, the review set out to identify possible gaps in the protection of sexual integrity in cases where women were sexually abused but not raped, according to the law. This would arise in circumstances where the perpetrator(s) did not have to coerce them into sex – for example, due to their alcoholic intoxication (Directive 1998: 48).

The focus in the resulting 2005 legislative reforms was on the damaging and violating nature of sexual abuse for the individual victim. The violation of bodily integrity was seen as the aspect common to all sexual crimes (Prop. 2004/05: 45). But this underlying rationale was not openly feminist, concerned with a woman's perspective or with sexual abuse as a gender-equality or human rights issue. In the reform, the government decided not to replace coercion with consent as the main criminal element. After analysing the possible impact of the judgment in *MC v Bulgaria* ((2005) 40 EHRR 20), where the European Court of Human Rights held that rape laws must criminalize all non-violent sexual violations, the Swedish government concluded that maintaining a requirement for violence or threat was not in opposition to the European Convention. Instead, the government chose to reduce the level of violence and threat required to that which is sufficient for the offence of unlawful coercion. Furthermore, the scope of the offence of rape was widened to include cases that were previously regarded as the less serious crime of *sexual exploitation*, that is, when the perpetrator inappropriately exploits the victim who, for various reasons, is in a helpless state. This was found to be reasonable because the sexual violation was considered to be as serious as when the victim is coerced into a similar sexual act (Prop. 2004/05: 45: 48).

## POLICY CONTEXT

The first Swedish prevalence study concerning men's violence against women was published in 2001. It showed that 34 per cent of all women had experienced sexual violence at the hands of a man since their fifteenth birthday and that 7 per cent had been subjected to such violence in the preceding year (Lundgren et al. 2002). According to the 2008 national survey on exposure to crime, safety and confidence in the criminal justice system, 1.3 per cent of women reported that during 2008 they had been exposed to sexual violence. Young women (16–24 years old) reported the highest level of sexual victimization during 2008, namely 3.4 per cent (BRÅ 2009).

Sweden has the highest level in Europe of rapes reported to the police per capita (Diesen et al. 2009). Rapes reported to the police have increased by more than 100 per cent since the mid-1990s. The most significant increase concerns rapes involving more than one perpetrator, date-rapes and where the victim and perpetrator are recently acquainted (BRÅ 2008a). This increase might be the result of enhanced gender equality, that is, that more often than before women assert their right to sexual self-determination, even in the kinds of cases that are known to seldom get through the criminal justice system (Diesen and Diesen 2009). However, the proportion of rapes not reported to the police is still high (estimated at approximately 80–90 per cent) and the statistics point to a possible increase in actual rapes, especially of young female victims (BRÅ 2008b; Diesen and Diesen 2009).

The calculated rate of prosecution, that is, cases reported to the police brought to trial, since 2000 is 10–12 per cent, a decrease of almost 50 per cent compared to 1996. Furthermore, the number of convicted perpetrators is almost the same as in 1965, in spite of the increasing number of reports to the police, while the proportion of prosecuted cases in which the defendant is acquitted has increased from below 10 per cent in the 1980s to 22 per cent in 2006 (Diesen and Diesen 2009). Based on an analysis of all preliminary investigations of sexual crimes in Stockholm County in 2004 and 2006, Diesen and Diesen concluded: first, that too many investigations are poorly conducted and are closed even if a decision regarding prosecution could be potentially reached; and, secondly, that too many cases are closed before all adequate investigative measures have been undertaken (Diesen and Diesen 2009). From a European perspective, the Swedish prosecution rate is lower than in some other western European countries and the conviction rate one of the lowest in Europe (Diesen et al. 2009).

The victim has a strong procedural position in Sweden and can be a party to the trial alongside the prosecutor. Rape victims are also entitled to a legal counsel appointed by the court with competence to act from the start of the preliminary investigation. During trial the counsel can, for example, call new witnesses and question the defendant. Even though these victim rights do not seem to have any noticeable impact on attrition, they are regarded as promising practices from a European perspective (Kelly and Lovett 2009).

Specialized services for rape victims in the public, private and voluntary sectors are scarce in Sweden (Ju 2004: 1). The Women's Shelters do provide support, but they are more explicitly engaged in giving support to women exposed to domestic violence and few have the opportunity to offer specialized assistance to rape victims. Public rape victim services are only available in a few of the largest cities. Regarding the general public welfare sector, for example the health care and communal social services, studies indicate that the quality of services and competence among staff varies substantially over the country (NCK 2006 and 2007). At the national level, there is a telephone support line funded by the government for women who have been subjected to threats, violence or sexual abuse. It was established in December 2007 and has not been evaluated, so there is no knowledge yet about how, and to what extent, it functions as a support for raped women.[1]

The only policy initiative undertaken during the last five years addressing rape, in a comprehensive manner and from an explicit gender and crime-victim perspective, is a 2005 report from a special commissioner appointed by the government. In the report, measures encouraging victims of sexual crimes to report to the police are suggested, such as the establishment of local specialized health care services and legislative changes aimed at providing the victim with free legal advice before reporting to the police and a legal counsel at an earlier stage of the criminal procedure than normally is the case (Ju 2004: 1). Only two measures have been carried through by the government to date: an education programme for staff in the criminal justice system on better treatment of rape victims and national 'good practice' guidelines for the health care sector. Further, rape is almost invisible both in the latest government Bill on gender equality (Prop. 2005/06: 155) and in the latest government action plan on men's violence against women (Government Communication 2007/08: 39).

## THE CURRENT LAW OF RAPE

The boundaries of rape in the statutory definition are determined by coercion or exploitation. In the first version (coercion), it is a crime to force a person – by assault, other forms of violence or threats – to have intercourse or to engage in a sexual act that, with reference to the character of the violation and the circumstances of the crime, is comparable to intercourse. In the second version (exploitation), the criminal element is defined as inappropriately exploiting the helpless state of another person. Each version will be discussed in more detail below.

The political and legal point of departure is that rape should be reserved for sexual acts that are considered to constitute the most serious violations (Prop. 2004/05: 45: 45). Consequently, the main division between rape, and sexual crimes secondary to rape, relates to the nature of the sexual act. If the violation is not judged to constitute rape, other provisions such as *sexual coercion* or *sexual exploitation of a person in a dependent position* might be applicable.

### The sexual act

Only heterosexual vaginal intercourse is included in the concept 'intercourse'. Penetration is not required; bodily contact between a penis and a vagina is sufficient. Other sexual acts can constitute rape if the violation involved is judged to be as serious as the violation resulting from forced intercourse. Oral and anal intercourse and the introduction of fingers or objects into the victim's anus or vagina are examples of such sexual acts (Prop. 2004/05: 45: 136).

Sexual acts are represented as expressions of 'natural' male heterosexual sexuality. Heterosexual vaginal intercourse is automatically regarded as 'sexual' (Asp 2008–09). Other behaviours must be considered as either having the purpose of sexually exciting the perpetrator or be related to the perpetrator already being in such a condition and wanting to satisfy his needs

(Prop. 2004/05: 45: 140). It is the character and seriousness of the sexual violation that is to be decisive concerning which sexual acts constitute rape, not the sexual act as such (Prop. 1997/98: 55: 135). However, heterosexual vaginal intercourse is still the paradigm and relevant reference point in assessing if other sexual acts constitute rape. The starting point, according to the Supreme Court, shall be that forced intercourse or other penetrations of the victim's body are typically the most violating forms of sexual abuse (NJA 2008 s. 482I).

Thus, even though rape presents the perpetrator and victim as genderless 'persons', hetero-normativity is reflected in the criterion of the sexual act. This became obvious in a Supreme Court case about male same-sex abuse when the perpetrator masturbated the victim's penis. The hetero-normative structure and penetrative focus of the law contributed to the Supreme Court making no effort to specifically judge the sexual violation of the actual act, which was not considered serious enough to constitute rape (NJA 2008 s. 482II).

## Coercion, consent and the legal treatment of victims

Even though the perpetrator's force is the constitutive element in this version of rape, the criminal element of violence is interpreted in the light of, and thus transformed into, the victim's will. Predominant criminal legal discourses concern the victim's expression of will and impose an obligation on the victim to express her or his attitude towards the perpetrator's actions. In the judicial context, the victim's will is mostly expressed in terms of the presence or absence of consent. So, in practice, it seems that consent and the victim's will constitute the legal boundary (Andersson 2004). As in many other Western countries, criminal legal discourse in Sweden is thus compatible with the norm of passive and submissive female sexuality; and it produces the body of the victim mainly as open and sexually accessible (Andersson 2004).

Violence and threat are said to be 'proof' of non-consensual sex (Prop. 2004/05: 45: 41). This leads to the presumption that when consent (operationalized in terms of passivity and lack of physical resistance) is present, coercion is absent (Andersson 2001). Even under a test that focuses formally on coercion, then, discovering whether the victim consented or acted in a way that might be seen to communicate consent to the defendant remains crucial. This continues to invite a thorough scrutiny of the woman and her sexual behaviour.

It is very common in Sweden for the defendant to argue, in his defence, that the woman consented to the sexual act, or that he concluded that she consented because there was no significant resistance (Leijonhufvud 2008). Such objections – and predictions that such objections will be lodged by the accused – play a key role in many rape cases being closed without prosecution. Police and prosecutors in Sweden, it seems, hold a strong belief that it is almost impossible to counter this consent-based defence (Diesen and Diesen 2009).

Swedish law is based on the principles of free presentation and free evaluation of evidence. There are provisions in the Code of Judicial Procedure which oblige the court to reject irrelevant questions, that is, when the information sought through the question can be supposed to be without importance, or undue questions, for example when the only purpose of the question seems to be to insult or humiliate the victim in order to make it more difficult for the victim to give a clear and sensible statement. However, these provisions are seldom applied. An important reason seems to be the difficulties in foreseeing the evidentiary relevance or value of the questions asked and the themes they touch upon (Diesen 2008–09). Owing to the way the law is interpreted, evidence relating to the victim's behaviour and character is often still seen to be relevant to some degree, particularly when it comes to judging both her own trustworthiness and the *mens rea* of the perpetrator. Therefore, while the government has stated (Prop. 2004/05: 45: 23) that the courts must be more active in rejecting undue or irrelevant questioning of the victim (including questions relating to her former sexual experiences), this has not had any considerable impact in practice and old fashioned conceptions of women and sexuality continue to go unchallenged in the courtroom.

## Exploitation

Rape as exploitation is defined as inappropriately exploiting a person in a helpless state, where that state is the result of unconsciousness, sleep, intoxication or other drug abuse, illness, physical injury or mental disturbance, or other general circumstances. The concept of a 'helpless state' is defined, in the government Bill, as lacking either the ability to defend oneself or the ability to control one's own actions (Prop. 2004/05: 45: 137).

In the political discourse, including exploitation within the definition of rape is considered to be a progressive measure, enhancing the legal protection of sexual integrity. However, it seems to be difficult to sustain the principle of exploited victims being equally violated as coerced victims. This is due to the provision for less aggravated rape, according to which lack of coercion continues to play an important role as a mitigating element in judging the blameworthiness of sexual abuse. The main purpose of this provision is, in fact, to capture within the terms of exploitation those rape cases that are not deemed to be as blameworthy as 'ordinary' rape and, therefore, should attract a lower sentence for the perpetrator (Prop. 2004/05: 45: 53). The provision for less aggravated rape has so far been applied by the Supreme Court in two cases in which the accused penetrated their sleeping female victims with a couple of fingers. In both cases, the accused halted their actions when the women woke up and clearly demonstrated that they did not consent to the sexual behaviour (NJA 2008 s. 482I and N 61). The Supreme Court applied the provision on less aggravated rape with reference to a statement in the government Bill about the applicability of the provision in situations where the victim is asleep, but the perpetrator stops his sexual act when the victim wakes up and protests, and there has been no penile penetration (Prop. 2004/05: 45: 53).

The ambition to enhance the protection of sexual integrity that formally animates the Swedish legislative response to rape is also counteracted by a requirement to regard intoxicated women as being in a helpless state. In practice, this has developed to require a woman to establish a total lack of memory of the abuse in order to prove that she was sufficiently intoxicated. Yet, even if this requirement is fulfilled, it can be counter-productive, since Supreme Court jurisprudence indicates that in cases where the woman has no memory, it is the account given by the perpetrator(s) that provides the evidentiary starting point (Leijonhufvud 2008).

## CURRENT ISSUES, REFORM AND THE FUTURE

Since the legislative reforms of 2005, political and legal debate has been continuing in Sweden regarding both coercion/consent as the main criminal element and the interpretation of the concept of a 'helpless state'. The main critique is concerned with the common situation where sexual acts are performed without coercion, but in violation of the victim's will and integrity. These cases, due to the statutory definitions of both 'coercion' and 'helpless state', cannot be considered as rape, or any other kind of sexual abuse, because women in vulnerable situations are not regarded as lacking the ability to defend themselves. As noted earlier, this has proved particularly problematic in relation to intoxicated women. Arguments against reforming rape law often consider rape an inherently difficult crime to investigate and prove, especially in situations where it occurs in the context of prior vulnerability or intimate relations (Halfwordson et al. 2007; Wersäll and Johansson 2007). Unfortunately, this reinforces the view that abuse in private settings is out of reach for criminal intervention and justice, and affords criminal justice agencies a convenient excuse for not trying to improve their skills and methods of investigation and evidence-gathering.

The reforms made to the scope of the sexual act are important because they ensure that the sexual violation is acknowledged from the perspective of the victim. But these reforms have, for the most part, been discussed without acknowledging the presuppositions about gender and sexuality that underlie them and without taking into consideration broader power relations between women and men. Swedish feminist criminal legal scholars argue, therefore, that a reconstruction of rape law must involve a much more serious and sustained engagement with these issues. The feminist critique has so far mostly been involved in deconstructing rape law to reveal its underlying notions concerning gender, sexuality and subjectivity. There has also been some critical engagement, at the theoretical level, about its reconstruction. However, so far only one detailed suggestion concerning what a feminist rape provision might look like has been presented in Sweden. This was presented in 2008 by Leijonhufvud, as a result of an assignment from the Swedish Green Party specifically to review current rape law provisions.

## Feminist legal critique

A common feminist legal critique is that rape law should abandon its liberal conception of an autonomous subject and the attendant focus on will, freedom to act and self-determination, replacing this with a focus on sexual integrity and the body. Andersson, for example, takes as the starting point the fact that the Swedish crime of rape differs from the binary criminal legal division of mind (*mens rea*) and body (*actus reus*) in that it includes a mental element, the victim's lack of consent, in the *actus reus*. Yet, according to Andersson, when the courts decide whether lack of consent is at stake, they are not exploring the rational will of the victim. Instead, the victim's bodily and verbal expressions are decisive. Ideally, Andersson argues that this division between mind and body should be replaced by an integrated thinking which challenges the construction of the modern subject of criminal law. Failing that, she insists that the starting point for rape provisions should focus upon the subject's bodily integrity rather than her will/self-determination (Andersson 2004). This is an interesting theorization, but it has not yet developed into a more concrete proposal of a reconstructed rape law.

Berglund and Niemi-Kiesiläinen too have argued that the starting point for rape law should be the violation of sexual integrity. Berglund suggests that rape law should be anchored in the bodily and sexualized experience of abuse, while acknowledging that these are gendered phenomena given meaning in a socio-cultural context (Berglund 2009). Similarly, Niemi-Kiesiläinen argues that an approach grounded in violation of sexual integrity requires an understanding of the context in which the actions take place – a context in which women's experiences are made relevant. She suggests that rape law should facilitate an understanding of gender, sexuality and subjectivity in relational terms. This would, she argues, enhance the possibility of viewing the victim as an acting subject worthy of protection, even when her ability to exercise sexual self-determination is impaired but not altogether eliminated. It would also ensure that the power relations between the parties, and within the gender system of society, are included in the analysis of rape, which in turn – she argues – will prevent a relational approach to sexuality evolving into victim-blaming (Niemi-Kiesiläinen 2004). No detailed suggestions on reform have yet been presented by Berglund or Niemi-Kiesiläinen.

But not all Swedish feminist criminal legal scholars are convinced that putting sexual integrity at the centre of rape law will, in fact, bring about significant progress. Sutorius and Kaldal fear that it would lead to individualized judgments of the victim and her worthiness of protection. Further, they argue that women's sexual self-determination remains the most logical starting point. However the provision for rape is constructed, in many rape cases involving threats, less violence or no violence at all, it is the woman and her behaviour that will be in focus. What is really needed, according to them, is to abandon the understanding of non-consent as active resistance and shift the focus on to the perpetrator, his actions and his ignoring of, or intention to disregard, the woman's non-consent (Sutorius and Kaldal 2003).

## A feminist proposal

Leijonhufvud suggests a new provision, *sexual exploitation*, which would penalize a person who undertakes a sexual act against, or obtains such an act from, a person who does *not voluntarily participate* in the act (Leijonhufvud 2008). The proposed provision is meant to replace the current rape offence as the basic penalization of sexual abuse. By abandoning current divisions related to the sexual act and the perpetrator's method, it brings together several provisions that are seen to be secondary to rape in the current legal response. Partly in recognition of this, the proposed penalty is lower than the current law allows for rape. A provision for aggravated sexual exploitation is, however, also suggested, which would carry the same minimum penalty as today's rape law and a higher maximum penalty than today's aggravated rape. In assessing whether the crime is aggravated, it is proposed that special consideration be given to circumstances that are already recognized in the current provisions for rape and aggravated rape, that is, whether more than one person assaulted the victim or in any other way took part in the abuse. But it is also suggested that new circumstances be taken into account, such as whether the victim has been in a particularly vulnerable situation. In addition, if the perpetrator in pursuing, or as a consequence of the sexual abuse, is also liable for crimes such as assault, threat or unlawful coercion, he would be sentenced for these crimes together with sexual exploitation and the crimes altogether would be named as rape.

Leijonhufvud argues that the law must be reconstructed in order to meet the requirement of penalizing *any non-consensual sexual act* as laid down in the European Court of Human Rights case of *MC v Bulgaria*. She takes a feminist position by emphasizing that the violation of sexual integrity is not dependent upon the methods used. On this account, it is the element of *forced sexuality*, not the coercion used to be forced into sex, that violates sexual integrity. Leijonhufvud also argues that the suggested provision would more adequately reflect how women behave, react and perceive the situation during an event of sexual violence.

The proposal takes *lack of voluntary participation* as its point of departure. This concept is meant to represent something similar to the Swedish concept 'unlawfully', which is used in criminal law to describe a situation in which another act is undertaken without permission. Leijonhufvud has two main arguments for using non-voluntariness instead of non-consent. First, she argues that, while a focus on non-consent may render a woman's earlier behaviour relevant in determining whether the man had a reasonable belief in her consent to the subsequent sexual act, the concept of non-voluntariness clarifies that the relevant point for judging the crime is *precisely at the moment of the sexual act*. Secondly, she argues that the concept of non-voluntariness, unlike non-consent, emphasizes that sex is a mutual act, not something one person performs against another or uses another person's body to perform.

Leijonhufvud's proposal has so far been met with positive responses from feminist legal scholars (Berglund 2009; Diesen and Diesen 2009). Diesen and

Diesen especially appreciate that the provision enforces new demands on men to consider whether their behaviour might be a misuse of power and a violation of women's integrity. The purpose behind the suggested provision is also to get to grips with the ease with which flat objections about consent lead to rape cases being closed or the defendant being acquitted. The suggested provision is not intended to solve all current difficulties in investigating and proving sexual abuse in cases where there has been no violence, but it is expected to reduce attrition rates in cases where victims were very drunk or in vulnerable situations. The new construction is also expected to encourage a critical consideration of what the perpetrator did to make sure that the sexual act was something that the other person wanted to take part in (Leijonhufvud 2008).

I understand Leijonhufvud's proposal as an attempt to integrate sexual integrity and sexual self-determination and to dissolve the consent–coercion dichotomy, a dichotomy which is presumed to be unaffected by a regulation based on non-consent (Andersson 2001; Sutorius and Kaldal 2003). Importantly, her proposal – in being less burdened by hetero-normative concepts – may be better equipped to deal with same-sex abuse. Implementing these reforms will not solve all the current problems. For one thing, notions of gender and sexuality will probably find new ways of influencing legal practice. But as Sweden, in order to comply with European human rights law, ought – in my view – to abandon coercion by force as the only criminal element in rape, Leijonhufvud's proposal provides a clear step in the right direction.

## CONCLUSION

Following the election of a new government in 2006, and the continued debate in parliament regarding the use of coercion as the basis for rape law, in July 2008 the government appointed a special commissioner to review, once again, whether coercion should be replaced by non-consent in rape law. The application of the contentious concept of 'helpless state' is also to be reviewed (Directive 2008: 94). Rape is, thus, definitely back on the public and political agenda. While this is to be welcomed, the absence of a progressive policy, coupled with an apparent lack of interest in implementing a gender and/or human rights perspective and the ongoing failure to acknowledge the problematic aspects of contemporary constructions of male heterosexuality are alarming. These aspects must be dealt with urgently if Sweden's aspirations to evolve in a gender-equal direction are to be realized in the context of rape law.

### Note

1 The Women's Peace Telephone Support Line is administered by the National Centre for Knowledge about Men's Violence Against Women at Uppsala

University, which also hosts one of the few specialized health care services for female rape victims: see http://www.nck.uu/node40.

## Bibliography

Andersson, U. (2001) 'The unbounded body of the law of rape – the intrusive criterion of non-consent', in K. Nousiainen, Å. Gunnarsson, K. Lundström, and J. Niemi-Kiesiläinen (eds) *Responsible Selves. Women in the Nordic legal culture*, Aldershot: Ashgate, 331–51.

—— (2004) *Hans (ord) eller hennes? En könsteoretisk analys av straffrättsligt skydd mot sexuella övergrepp*, Lund: Bokbox förlag (His (word) or hers? A gender theoretical analysis of criminal legal protection against sexual abuse).

Asp, P. (2008–09) 'Grader av kränkning – våldtäkt eller sexuellt tvång?', *Juridisk tidskrift*, 20: 75–85 (Degrees of violations – rape or sexual coercion?).

Berglund, K. (2009) 'Samtyckesutredningen', *Juridisk tidskrift*, 20: 701–19 (The inquiry concerning consent).

BRÅ (2008a) *Våldtäkt mot personer 15 år eller äldre. Utvecklingen under åren 1995–2006*, Rapport 2008: 13 (Swedish National Council of Crime Prevention – Rape against persons 15 years or older. Development 1995–2006).

—— (2008b) *Brottsutvecklingen i Sverige fram till år 2007*, Rapport 2008: 23 (Swedish National Council of Crime Prevention – the development of crime in Sweden up to 2007).

—— (2009) *NTU 2008. Om utsatthet, trygghet och förtroende*, Rapport 2009: 2 (Swedish National Council of Crime Prevention – National survey 2008 on exposure to crime, safety and confidence in the criminal justice system).

Burman, M. (2010) 'The ability of criminal law to produce gender equality – judicial discourses in the Swedish criminal legal system', *Violence Against Women*, 16(2): 173–88.

Diesen, C. (2008–9) 'HD tillåter karaktärsbevisning', *Juridisk tidskrift*, 20: 86–99 (The Supreme Court permits evidence on personal character).

Diesen, C. and Diesen, E. (2009) *Övergrepp mot kvinnor och barn – den rättsliga hanteringen*, Stockholm: Norstedts Juridik AB (The legal handling of sexual abuse against women and children).

Diesen, C., Diesen, E., Lovett, J. and Kelly, L. (2009) *Different systems, similar outcomes? Tracking attrition in reported rape cases in eleven countries. Country briefing: Sweden*, London: Child and Woman Abuse Studies Unit. Online. Available at: <http://www.cwasu.org/publication_display.asp?type=1&pageid=PAPERS&pagekey=44>.

Directive 1993: 88.

Directive 1998: 48.

Directive 2008: 94.

Elman, A. (1996) *Sexual Subordination and State Intervention: comparing Sweden and the United States*, Oxford: Berghahn Book, Providence.

Government Communication 2007/08: 39, *Action plan for combating men's violence against women, violence and oppression in the name of honour and violence in same-sex relationships*.

Halfwordson, A., Hillegren, R., Pettersson, A., and Sundholm, A. (2007) *Extra svårt att bevisa sexualbrott*, DN Debatt, 15 September 2007 (It is particularly difficult to prove sexual crimes).

Ju 2004: 1 *Anmälan och utredning av sexualbrott. Förslag på förbättringar ur ett brottsofferperspektiv*, Ministry of Justice (Reporting and investigating sexual crimes. Suggestions for improvements from a crime-victim perspective).
Kelly, L. and Lovett, J. (2009) *Different systems, similar outcomes? Tracking attrition in reported rape cases in eleven countries. European briefing*. Online. Available at: <http://www.cwasu.org/publication_display.asp?type=1&pageid=PAPERS&pagekey=44>.
Leijonhufvud, M. (2008) *Samtyckesutredningen*, Stockholm: Thomson Förlag AB (An Inquiry concerning Consent).
Lundgren, E., Heimer, G., Westerstrand, J. and Kalliokoski, A.M. (2002) *Captured Queen – Men's violence against women in 'equal' Sweden – a prevalence study*, Stockholm: Fritzes.
NCK (2006) *Den svenska hälso- och sjukvårdens arbete inom kompetensområdet våld mot kvinnor*, Uppsala: The National Centre for Knowledge about Men's Violence against Women (The work in the health care sector regarding violence against women).
NCK (2007) *Varannan kommun saknar information på internet till våldsutsatta kvinnor*, Uppsala: The National Centre for Knowledge about Men's Violence against Women (Half of Swedish communes lack internet-based information for women exposed to violence).
Niemi-Kiesiläinen, J. (2004) 'The reform of sex crime law and the gender-neutral subject', in E.M. Svensson, A. Pylkkänen, and J. Niemi-Kiesiläinen (eds), *Nordic Equality at a Crossroads: feminist legal studies coping with difference*, Aldershot: Ashgate, 167–94.
Prop. 1983/84: 105 *Om ändring i brottsbalken m.m. (sexualbrotten)* (Changes in the Penal Code (sexual crimes)).
Prop. 1993/94: 147 *Jämställdhetspolitiken: Delad makt – delat ansvar* (Gender Equality Politics: shared power – shared responsibility).
Prop. 1997/98: 55 *Kvinnofrid* (Women's Peace).
Prop. 2004/05: 45 *En ny sexualbrottslagstiftning* (New legislation on sexual crimes).
Prop. 2005/06: 155 *Makt att forma samhället och sitt eget liv – nya mål i jämställdhetspolitiken* (The power to shape society and one's own life – new goals for the politics of gender equality).
Sutorius, H. and Kaldal, A. (2003) *Bevisprövning vid sexualbrott*, Stockholm: Norstedts Juridik AB (Evaluation of evidence in cases of sexual crimes).
Wendt Höjer, M. (2002) *Rädslans politik. Våld och sexualitet i den svenska demokratin*, Malmö: Liber AB (The Politics of Fear. Violence and Sexuality in Swedish democracy).
Wersäll, F. and Johansson, L. (2007) *Förvänta er ingen ökning av våldtäktsåtal*, DN Debatt 19 October 2007 (Do not expect an increase in rape prosecutions).

Chapter 14

# Canadian sexual assault law

Neoliberalism and the erosion of feminist-inspired law reforms

Lise Gotell

In April 2009, Prime Minister Stephen Harper warned the President of Afghanistan that critical Allied support for the mission could diminish if the Afghan government did not change a law that would 'make it legal for men to rape their wives' (*Vancouver Sun*, 4 April 2009). Drawing upon and restating the now familiar gendered rationalization of the 'War Against Terror', the assumed sexual autonomy of Canadian women is posed as an important symbol of Western democracy and progress. Obscured beneath this brief flurry of political and media attention to rape (in Afghanistan) is, ironically, the very disappearance of sexual violence as a critical and systemic problem affecting Canadian women. Over the past decade, sexual violence has been increasingly depoliticized and erased from political agendas.

In this chapter, I analyse Canadian sexual assault law, focusing most closely on the feminist-inspired changes to the Criminal Code enacted in 1992 that moved Canada in the direction of an affirmative consent standard. While significant in enshrining protections for complainants and in clarifying the law of consent, these revised provisions have been inconsistently interpreted. Despite doctrinal developments supporting sexual autonomy and positive consent, there is also a dramatic gap between the thrust of Canadian law and a reality characterized by continued high prevalence rates, low police reporting rates and high attrition rates. Analysing the implications of Canadian sexual assault law against the backdrop of neoliberalism, I demonstrate how the embrace of an affirmative model of consent consolidates the individualizing frame of criminal law and produces normative sexual subjects who actively manage the risk of sexual assault. In this process, new forms of victim-blaming are created and some categories of women are excluded from the protections of law. Tying the impact and fate of 1990s reforms to the elaboration of neoliberal governance, I conclude with an analysis of key features of the current political context that mitigate against the emergence of new reform initiatives.

## HISTORICAL AND POLITICAL CONTEXT OF FEMINIST-INSPIRED SEXUAL ASSAULT LAW REFORMS

As in many other countries, Canadian second-wave feminist activists succeeded in 'breaking the silence' around sexualized violence and, for a brief period, inserted sexual assault onto the political agenda as a pervasive social problem requiring government intervention. As part of a broader agenda that saw the establishment of independent women-controlled rape crisis centres, protests (such as Take Back the Night marches) and consciousness-raising activities, feminists pushed for legal reforms in order to constrain the influence of rape myths on the practice of law. Activists hoped that the elimination of sexist bias in law would deter rape by reducing men's expectation of immunity and women's expectations of unjust treatment by the criminal justice system.

In the 1980s, feminists campaigned for a new gender-neutral offence of sexual assault that would shift the way in which the Criminal Code conceptualized sexual violence – as a crime of violence, rather than as a crime of sex. Underlying this campaign was the belief that desexualizing rape would diminish opportunities for victim-blaming. By redefining rape as violence, Canadian feminists hoped to convey the seriousness of this crime and to emphasize the similarity between sexual assault and the criminal assaults that men typically experience (McIntyre 2000; Los 1994). But as critics argued even then, while drawing attention to the harms of sexual violence, this strategy misrepresents the problem of rape by removing it from its deeply gendered context and obscuring the relationship between male power, violence and sex (Los 1994: 34; McIntyre 2000).

The Canadian federal government's interest in rape law reform in the early 1980s was tied to concerns that gender-specific sexual offences could offend the equality rights guarantee of the newly entrenched Charter of Rights (Los 1994: 27). In 1983, and in response to a vocal feminist lobby led by the National Association of Women and the Law, Parliament replaced the rape provision with the current three-tier structure of sexual assault offences (distinguished by degrees of violence), criminalizing all forms of non-consensual sexual touching (Los 1994). This redefinition expanded the narrow view of sexual aggression denoted by rape, making criminally punishable sexual acts that do not involve penetration and, for the first time, explicitly criminalizing sexual assault within marriage. The amendments also addressed the unique evidentiary rules that had characterized the prosecution of rape, abolishing the corroboration requirement and the doctrine of recent complaint. Finally, in an effort to reduce the humiliation experienced by complainants and the sway of rape myths in trials, new provisions restricting cross-examination on sexual history and banning the publication of victims' names were included in the Criminal Code.

In the early 1990s, sexual violence re-emerged on the political agenda as the federal government responded to the Montreal Massacre. In 1989, 14 young women engineering students were shot at the Ecole Polytechnique, precipitating attention to the problem of violence against women. This deliberate act of gendered terror brought into stark relief feminist claims about the extreme consequences of violence against women, provoking a national debate about male violence. While the Massacre produced a new and often highly symbolic political emphasis on gendered violence, the specific and almost exclusive framing of the problem as a criminal justice matter must be understood in relation to the rise of neoliberal governance (Gotell 2007). By the early 1990s, the erosion of post-war notions of social citizenship had diminished political spaces for feminists and other social justice movements. Social and political problems were being redefined as individual problems, best managed through responsibility and self-regulation. During this period, governmental actors began to mount a steady attack on the Canadian women's movement, delegitimizing feminist voices and dismantling programmes designed to enhance women's equality (Brodie 2008; Gotell 2007). As I have argued elsewhere, during this period gendered 'victimization' became one of the last few gender-specific bases for claims to social entitlement, tied intimately to an enhancement of the state's coercive powers (Gotell 1997: 67). Governmental attention to sexual violence, defined primarily as an object of criminal law, is related to the development of the leaner, meaner neo-liberal state.

If shifting rationalities of governance and the fallout from the Montreal Massacre provided the broad context for attention to sexual violence as a criminal justice issue, the Supreme Court of Canada's (SCC) decision in *R v Seaboyer* [1991] 2 SCR 577 placed sexual assault law reform squarely on the political agenda. In this, the first SCC Charter decision dealing with sexual assault, sexual history evidence restrictions enacted in 1983 were struck down as a violation of defendants' fair trial rights. The majority ruled that because the restrictions failed to provide scope for judicial discretion, they potentially excluded relevant evidence. What the majority ignored, however, was how sexual history evidence relies upon and reinstalls rape myths, discrediting claimants by sexualizing them and undermining the fairness of the trial process through introducing discriminatory myths.

The broad-based sexual assault law reform enacted in 1992 was a direct response to the *Seaboyer* decision. Bill C-49 was drafted after an unprecedented series of consultations with national feminist organizations and resulted in a set of fundamental changes to the definition and criminal regulation of sexual assault (McIntyre 2000). This legislation re-enacted restrictions on sexual history evidence, but in a weakened form that complied with the Supreme Court's insistence on scope for judicial discretion (Criminal Code, section 276). At the same time, the amendments went far beyond the recodification of guidelines for sexual history evidence. Sheila McIntyre, a participant in the reform process, explains that the feminist strategy was 'to amend the substantive law of sexual assault to define consent and non-consent so as to narrow the range of "evidence" capable of being relevant to the determination of guilt or innocence' (McIntyre 2000: 76). For the first time, and as a result of feminist pressures, a statutory definition of consent as 'the voluntary agreement to engage in the sexual activity in question' (section 273(1)2) was embedded in the Criminal Code, transforming consent into 'something that a woman does and freely chooses to do, not something that men fantasize or choose for her' (McIntyre 2000: 76). The revised Code also enumerated a non-exhaustive set of situations where no consent is presumed to exist (including when agreement is expressed by another person, when the complainant is 'incapable of consenting', when the accused abuses a position of power, trust or authority, and when the complainant expresses a lack of agreement to engage or continue to engage in the sexual activity) (section 273(1)3). According to McIntyre, this provision was intended to 'convert self-serving rape-myths and rationalizations proffered as honest, but mistaken beliefs in a woman's consent, into errors of law' (2000: 76).

Finally, the defence of mistaken belief was specifically limited by a new requirement that the accused must have taken 'reasonable steps' to ensure consent and by explicitly specifying that there can be no such defence when this belief arises through 'recklessness' or 'willful blindness' (section 273(2)b). The 'reasonable steps' provision was a Canadian innovation; it modified what had been a purely subjective *mens rea* standard by introducing a quasi-objective fault element, such that the belief in consent need not be reasonable, but the accused must have taken reasonable steps in the circumstances to ascertain consent. Popularly referred to as the 'no means no' amendments, the positive definition of consent as a voluntary agreement, as well as limitations on the defence of mistaken belief, had the effect of distinguishing consent from submission, challenging a version of normative heterosexuality founded on feminine acquiescence (Gotell 2008).

Subsequent rounds of sexual assault law reform in the 1990s, though more limited in scope, shared similarities with Bill C-49. Shaped by consultations with women's organizations, amendments were explicitly framed as measures to address the pervasiveness of sexual violence in women's lives and to improve the treatment of complainants and low rates of police reporting. And like Bill C-49, subsequent reforms were provoked by judicial decisions that privileged defendants' legal rights. In 1995, the common-law bar on the defence of intoxication was found to violate the defendant's legal rights in *R v Daviault* [1994] 3 SCR 63, an SCC case involving the sexual assault of an unconscious disabled woman. This ruling prompted a national outcry and caused Parliament to enact a legislative ban on the intoxication defence (Criminal Code, section 33(1)). In 1997, the government created a legislative regime strengthening the weak common-law test for disclosure of third-party records that had been established by the SCC in *R v O'Connor* [1995] 4 SCR 411 (section 278), thereby responding to long-standing feminist concerns about the widespread defence tactic of discrediting complainants through the contents of their therapy, medical and other confidential records (Gotell 2002).

By the end of the decade, the Criminal Code contained strong provisions recognizing sexual autonomy, placing an onus on defendants asserting mistake of fact defences to have taken steps to secure agreement and restricting the opportunities for discrediting complainants based upon their sexual history and the contents of their private records. In fact, Canadian legislation is widely viewed as expressing a communicative model of consent (Pineau 1996: 92–3) and its Criminal Code provisions have influenced law reform in other jurisdictions (see, for example, Criminal Justice Sexual Offences Taskforce 2006).

Yet these feminist-inspired sexual assault law reforms unfold in a context distinct from that of the early 1990s, where the recognition of sexual violence as a social problem requiring governmental intervention has all but disappeared. By the end of the 1990s, feminist anti-violence activists were recast as 'special interest groups' and excluded from policy networks (Gotell 2007; McIntyre 2000). The policy field signified by 'violence against women' was evacuated and replaced with degendered and individualized policy frameworks. One crucial institutional mechanism by which this has occurred is the elaboration of victims' services bureaucracies. Now preoccupied with the rights of individualized 'victims', new policy discourses avoid systemic constructions linking 'crime' to context, signalling the disappearance of gendered policy discourses of sexual violence. The withdrawal of funding from feminist front-line and activist work is a crucial aspect of this reconfigured context. With the decline of federal support for Canadian women's organizations, funding for anti-rape activism and front-line work has been decentralized to the provinces. Because new funding arrangements are increasingly contingent on the provision of services to generic victims of crime, feminist front-line organizations have had to redefine themselves as social service delivery agencies, affecting their capacity to intervene in national debate and to combat the pervasive reprivatization and individualization of sexualized violence (Beres et al. 2009). The clever disappearing act embedded within these interrelated moves does not signal a victory over sexual violence, merely its disappearance as an object of policy and public discourse.

In stark contrast to the post-feminist tenor of current political discourse, sexual violence persists as a deeply gendered social problem. Only 3 per cent of persons charged with sexual assault in 2007 were women, while 87 per cent of those assaulted were women and girls (Johnson 2009: 2). The Canadian Violence Against Women Survey, conducted by Statistics Canada in 1993, found that 39 per cent of Canadian women had experienced sexual assault since the age of 16 (Johnson and Sacco 1995). Approximately 460,000 (3 per cent) of Canadian women were sexually assaulted in 2004, though just 8 per cent reported to the police (Johnson 2009: 13). Holly Johnson, the leading Canadian empirical researcher on violence against women and principal investigator on the Violence Against Women Survey, has recently reviewed the statistical evidence on criminal justice responses to sexual assault. As she documents, even though police-reported sexual assaults have declined since 1993, the estimated incidence of sexual assault has remained relatively constant (3). The rate at which sexual assaults are reported to police has also remained consistently low, never rising above 10 per cent, suggesting that confidence in the criminal justice system affects women's willingness to make police complaints (4). Given the extremely high attrition rate for sexual assault, this caution seems warranted. Because of low reporting rates, high rates of police 'unfounding' or 'no-criming' and low charging and conviction rates, attrition rates based upon estimated incidence are astronomically high, with an overall conviction rate of 0.3 per cent, rising slightly to 1.6 per cent for sexual attacks accompanied by threats or physical attack (13). This evidence leads Johnson to conclude that 'rape law reform and the efforts of grassroots feminist organizations to raise awareness and challenge widespread discriminatory stereotypes have not resulted in improvements in women's willingness to come forward, or in the response of the criminal justice system to those who come forward' (17).

Other feminist critics have also expressed scepticism about the utility of sexual assault law reform as strategy, emphasizing that feminists do not determine the mobilization or enforcement of the law (Snider 1990: 161). Because law is a disunified and contradictory field, we cannot expect law reforms to produce uniform, predictable effects (Smart 1995: 144, 212). What Canadian feminists achieved in rewriting sexual assault legislation was complex, inserting recognition of sexual autonomy and gender equality into a criminal legal framework defined by individual responsibility and punishment. Though revised Criminal Code provisions provide the architecture of an affirmative consent standard, their interpretation by a wide variety of actors in the criminal justice system occurs in the context of an official silence. Without external political discourses recognizing sexual assault as a systemic problem, the tendency of criminal law toward decontextualization and individualization holds sway.

## CONSENT IN CANADIAN LAW: INDIVIDUALIZATION, DECONTEXTUALIZATION AND THE UNEVEN DEVELOPMENT OF LAW

As Smart has insisted, law develops unevenly, operating simultaneously as a site of, and an obstacle to, change (1995: 154–6). Canadian sexual assault law reforms have had complex effects, demonstrating the uneven development of law and the gap between what Smart refers to as 'law as legislation' and 'law as practice' (1995). Studies analysing the effectiveness of evidentiary provisions governing sexual history and access to complainants' records reveal the permeability of statutory restrictions (Gotell 2002 and 2007). Decisions have weakened and narrowed the tests introduced by legislation, downplaying the need to undertake a full analysis of the implications of sexual history evidence and personal records disclosure for complainants' rights and very often privileging defendants' rights. Despite protections embedded in the Criminal Code, complainants have remained vulnerable to being cross-examined on their sexual histories and to having a wide array of their personal records disclosed at trial. Some categories of complainants, including those who allege historical assaults, those who have histories of mental illness, those who have made previous complaints of sexual assault and/or those whose lives have been extensively documented under conditions of multiple inequalities and institutionalization (for example, aboriginal women, women with disabilities or women who have been imprisoned or involved with child welfare authorities), are especially vulnerable to these defence tactics (see also Benedet and Grant in this volume).

Unlike the sexual history and records case law where an erosion of the 1990s reforms is evident, recent decisions have built upon the foundation of affirmative consent laid through Bill C-49. *R v Ewanchuk* [1999] 1 SCR 330 is the leading authority for trial and appellate judges as they attempt to apply these revised statutory provisions. In this important decision, the SCC articulated a standard for sexual consent that approaches 'only yes means yes' (Ruparelia 2006). The court unanimously found that there is no defence of 'implied consent' in Canadian law, defining the *actus reus* of sexual assault as non-consensual sexual touching where consent is determined from the subjective position of the complainant (paras 30–1, 34–5). While insisting that intent is a crucial element of the crime of sexual assault, the decision emphasized that the defence of mistaken belief is not available when tainted by recklessness or wilful blindness (paras 42 and 52). Moreover, gesturing towards the 'reasonable steps' requirement, the court emphasized that triers of fact must consider whether the accused took active steps to establish consent (paras 58 and 60). Clear agreement to continue to engage in sexual contact must be obtained after someone has said no: '[t]he accused cannot rely on the mere lapse of time or the complainant's silence or equivocal conduct to indicate that . . . consent now exists, nor can he engage in further sexual touching to "test the waters" ' (para. 52). Finally, the SCC emphasized that consent must be positive, arguing that 'the mens rea of sexual assault is not only satisfied when it is shown that the accused knew that the complainant was essentially saying "no", but is also satisfied when it is shown that the accused knew that the complainant was essentially not saying "yes" ' (para. 45). Silence and ambiguous conduct thus do not constitute consent. In effect, *Ewanchuk* shifted the starting point in Canadian law from the assumption that women exist in a state of consent to a requirement that there be some positive evidence of agreement (Benedet and Grant 2007: 261; Gotell 2008: 869).

Important appellate-level decisions since *Ewanchuk* have continued to consolidate an affirmative consent standard by giving teeth to the requirements that consent must be voluntary and active and by holding that consent-seeking must comprise positive steps to secure agreement. Rulings have emphasized that to be legally valid, consent must be 'freely given'. In *R v Stender* [2005] 1 SCR 914, the SCC upheld a conviction in a case where the complainant had participated in sex in order to stop a former boyfriend from disseminating sexual photos. As *Stender* affirmed, the presence of pressure and extortion meant that no consent was given because consent must be voluntary. In a significant decision clarifying the defence of mistaken belief, the Manitoba Court of Appeal determined that active steps to secure agreement are required when circumstances exist that would cause a 'reasonable man to inquire further', raising the *mens rea* standard close to an objective standard (*R v Malcolm* 2000: para. 21).¹ The Court argued that some circumstances, such as entering a complainant's bedroom while she was sleeping, after a night of drinking and knowing that she was married to a close friend, require conversation and verbal consent, rather than a mere reliance on physical responses.

Even in situations where complainants are intoxicated, drug-affected and/ or unconscious, Canadian courts are increasingly convicting (Gotell 2007: 146–7). On the basis of an extensive review of written decisions involving intoxication, Benedet has found that judges are now more likely to rule that complainants lacked capacity to consent, especially when unconscious or asleep when the sexual activity began, or, if not unconscious, when they have been rendered intoxicated involuntarily (2009: 10–19). Judges also appear less willing to apply the claim of mistaken belief when a complainant is intoxicated, finding that the duty to take reasonable steps is elevated and often determining that proceeding with sex in such situations constitutes recklessness or wilful blindness (see, for example, *R v Cornejo* (2003) 68 OR (3d) (Ont. CA); Benedet 2009: 20–25; Gotell 2008: 870). In addition, the Alberta Court of Appeal ruled out the possibility of a defence of 'prior consent' to sexual activity when asleep or unconscious because, as the majority emphasized, consent must be operative at the time sexual contact takes place (*R v Ashlee* [2006] AJ no. 1040 (CA); Gotell 2008: 894–7). Clearly, cases involving intoxication continue to be contentious as complainants are often unable to completely remember what happened. Yet, in some key decisions, judges have relied on indirect evidence (for example, that the complainant would be unlikely to have had unprotected intercourse with two men) to find a lack of consent against defendants' claims to the contrary (*R v JR* (2006) 40 CR (6th) 97 (Ont. SCJ): para. 38).

The elaboration of an affirmative consent standard in Canadian law means that it is now far less likely that acquiescence will be transformed into consent. What Smart has labelled the 'pleasurable phallocentric pastime' of pressing a woman until she submits is clearly disrupted through emerging legal standards (1989: 45). And yet, reflecting the way in which the systemic nature of sexual violence has been increasingly erased in a context of neoliberal governance, Canadian judicial discourses consolidating an affirmative consent standard reinforce a decontextualized construction of sexual assault. Emphasis is placed on discrete sexual transactions, consent-seeking actions and the quality of agreement. And while valuable in focusing attention on the demonstration of positive consent, sexual violence is atomized; its manifestations and consequences are never collected, never considered in a context where sexual assault is a mechanism for sustaining gendered power relations. Recent Canadian decisions recognize sexual autonomy, but in a form that is consistent with individuated norms of criminal law. Normative sexual interaction is reconceived as being like an economic transaction and good sexual citizens are reconfigured to resemble rational economic actors assuming responsibility for their actions and the risks that they take. Tied to this decontexualized framing, the production of risk-managing subjects who diligently practise sexual safekeeping becomes privileged as a governmental technique for managing the once 'social' problem of sexual violence.

Alongside the shift to an affirmative consent standard in Canadian law, the line between the ideal victim and the incredible complainant has also shifted (Gotell 2007, 2008). When standards for consent are raised to 'only yes means yes' and when responsibility is placed on those initiating sex to take active steps to secure agreement, sexual virtue is eroded as the essential prerequisite of good victimhood. Indeed, this was the conscious intent of feminist law reformers. Yet, in post-*Ewanchuk* Canadian sexual assault law, the idealized (read credible) victim does not simply disappear. Instead, the contours of good victimhood shift to reflect the privileged logic of risk management. The performance of a diligent and cautious femininity grants some women access to the protections of law, while those who fail to follow the rules of sexual safekeeping can be denied protection. Victim-blaming constructions emerge repeatedly when complainants fail to behave as responsible risk managers. Even as convictions are entered, complainants are described as having 'questionable judgement', as being 'careless' as displaying 'youthful naiveté' and are criticized for failing to respond quickly and assertively in the face of sexual threats (Gotell 2008: 879–80). In a particularly striking recent example of this revised form of victim-blaming, a trial judge, convicting two men of drugging and sexually assaulting a young woman whom they had met in an internet chatroom, emphasized the reckless nature of the complainant's behaviours:

> J.M. communicated with a stranger who contacted her out of the blue on the internet. She flirted with him and foolishly agreed to meet, giving him her name, address and telephone number. She knew that he had mentioned bringing alcohol and drugs and she did contemplate the possibility of a sexual encounter with him. When he showed up at the residence with his friend, she voluntarily got in the car ... J.M.'s continued attempts to minimize her provocative and foolish behaviour stemmed from her intense embarrassment that she allowed herself to get into the situation in the first place.
> (*R v Sadaatmandi* 2008 cited in Benedet 2009: 8)

Here the complainant is constructed as flirting with risk. The normalized risk-avoiding behaviours of the ideal victim can function as a standard for assessing the credibility of complainants. In *R v AJS* (2005) 192 Man. R. (2d) 4 (Man. CA), for example, the Manitoba Court of Appeal explicitly considered how 'bizarre' (para. 17) behaviours undermine credibility. In this case, an aboriginal woman living in poverty in a remote northern community alleged that she had been repeatedly sexually assaulted by her sister's husband. Her 'abnormal' behaviours, highlighted in this decision as raising concerns about her credibility, included being alone with the accused and borrowing his lawnmower. As the court asked, 'Why would she put herself at risk of being raped for the sole reason of borrowing a lawnmower to cut the grass?' (para. 17).

The characterization of this complainant's actions as unusual enough to undermine her credibility demonstrates a decontextualized view of 'risk management' that ignores constraints on action arising out of situations of social marginalization, including the necessity of continuing to interact with a violent man. As other feminist critics have also argued, while clearly confirmed by doctrine, the affirmative consent standard has been inconsistently applied by trial judges and many sexual assault decisions continue to be infused by myths and stereotypes that prevent legal recognition of unwanted sexual intrusions (Ruparelia 2006). In part, this gap between 'law as legislation' and 'law as practice' occurs because the legal discourse of affirmative consent enacts a separation between discrete events and the power relations constructing vulnerabilities. Sexual assault is reconstructed as the outcome of failed responsibilization and the power relations that define sexual violence are obscured. Extremely disadvantaged women, especially those who can be viewed as inhabiting spaces of risk, may be most likely to fall through the cracks of an affirmative consent standard.

Systemic relations of race, class and gender, silenced in judicial discourses of affirmative consent, interact to construct some women's bodies as violable. The Native Women's Association of Canada (2009) has drawn attention to a culture of extreme racialized, sexualized violence against aboriginal women and girls. In the last 25 years, 520 aboriginal women have been murdered or have gone missing in circumstances involving violence (88). Research suggests that Canadian aboriginal women face rates of physical and sexual assault that are many times higher than the average for all Canadian women (Dylan et al. 2008). As Razack (2000) contends, sexual violence against aboriginal women is an ongoing repetition of the colonial encounter that is sanctioned by law. While there have been no systematic reviews of sexual assault decisions involving aboriginal complainants since the entrenchment of an affirmative consent standard, some analyses suggest that racist stereotypes, long deployed to discount aboriginal women's claims and render them 'unrapeable', persist and are being recoded under norms of risk management (Gotell 2008; Jiwani and Young 2006). The discourse of 'high-risk lifestyle' has framed criminal justice and investigatory responses to the national tragedy of missing and murdered aboriginal women (Gotell 2008: 884). This framing locates aboriginal women in a space of risk. High-profile cases have demonstrated how the culpability of white men enacting sexual violence against aboriginal women is often minimized, while complainants and victims are held responsible for their own violation because they engaged in 'risky' actions such as sex work, drinking and hitchhiking (Razack 2000; Gotell 2008).

The decontexutalized lens of affirmative consent, and the manner in which choice and responsibility are highlighted, pose problems for other highly vulnerable groups of Canadian women. Although women with mental disabilities face extremely high rates of sexual violence, Benedet and Grant contend that the substantive law of sexual assault is inadequate to meet their needs (2007; and in this volume). Based upon their analysis of more than

100 Canadian cases, they demonstrate how the courts rarely acknowledge the specific vulnerability of women with mental disabilities and very often use the language of autonomy in order to justify acquittals. Legal attention is focused on complainants' participation in the sexual activities as an indication of consent, ignoring how high levels of control over the lives of women with mental disabilities produce compliant behaviour. Benedet and Grant are critical of the overemphasis on complainants' conduct in these cases and the corresponding failure to scrutinize defendants' actions in inducing compliance, actions that undermine the voluntariness of consent. Moreover, exacting demands of accuracy, consistency, rationality and psychological coherence placed upon all sexual assault complainants work against the legal recognition of sexual violence against women with mental disabilities. The focus in *Ewanchuk* on what the complainant was thinking creates difficulties where the complainant was unable to tell the court what was going on in her mind at the time of the alleged assault. Benedet and Grant argue that the substantive law of sexual assault is premised on the assumption that complainants do not have disabilities. The decontextualized lens of affirmative consent creates a fiction of sexual autonomy, while failing to acknowledge how agency is constrained in situations of disadvantage and dependency.

## CURRENT ISSUES: NEOLIBERAL GOVERNANCE, THE DECLINE OF LAW REFORM AND THE EMPHASIS ON ENFORCEMENT

The movement towards an affirmative consent standard can be seen as a positive outcome of feminist-inspired law reforms enacted in the 1990s. Important decisions consolidating this standard function as symbolic public testimonies of law's claim to justice. At the same time, judicial discourses affirm an individualized and narrow understanding of sexual consent. The case law has been marked by inconsistent judicial interpretations and by decontextualized understandings of sexual assault that reinforce individual responsibility and new forms of victim-blaming. Moreover, the statistical evidence strongly suggests that the important objectives of increasing women's confidence in the criminal justice system, improving reporting rates and reducing attrition have yet to be realized.

Despite this much unfinished agenda, the problem of sexual violence has dropped from the Canadian political landscape. In the face of persistent evidence of gender inequalities, including high rates of sexual violence against Canadian women, spaces for the articulation of gender-equality claims-making on the state have closed. While committed to 'a get tough on crime agenda', the Harper Conservative government cut the budget of Status of Women Canada (the core interdepartmental agency responsible for promoting women's equality within the federal state) by 40 per cent, removed the word 'equality' from its mandate and fundamentally altered the funding criteria for women's organizations, making research and activities related to activism ineligible for funding (Brodie 2008: 146). Within this climate of entrenched neoliberalism, a conception of sexual assault law reform tied to the advancement of gender equality has been rendered increasingly unintelligible. The most recent amendments to sexual offence provisions, passed in 2008 with the support of a vocal social conservative lobby, increased the age of consent from 14 to 16, while maintaining 18 as the age of consent for anal sex (Desrosiers 2009). Sexual health, youth and LGBT organizations critiqued this amendment, arguing that it would reduce access to sexual health services. Critics argued that addressing the lack of enforcement of existing sexual offence provisions would be a more effective strategy in combating the sexual exploitation of young people; raising the age of consent is a largely symbolic initiative that would do little to reduce sexual exploitation. Feminist organizations were, however, notably absent from the list of witnesses appearing before the legislative committee on this bill. National women's groups that were centrally involved in consultations that produced sexual assault reforms in the 1990s have been increasingly silenced as a result of federal funding cuts.

In a context where neoliberal political rationalities frame politics as if gender no longer matters, opportunities for future law reforms that might address the persistent gendered realities of sexual violence have diminished. At present, attention is increasingly shifting to the question of how to ensure the enforcement of existing law. One emerging project involves the strategic use of civil and constitutional litigation to compel police to thoroughly investigate complaints of sexual assault, adhering to the existing legal standard for consent. Mounting evidence points to the existence of systemic unfounding (no-criming) by police, a practice that has extremely damaging impacts for survivors who feel that they have been labelled liars by the state. Dubois (2009) has highlighted evidence that confirms that police officers are trained to approach sexual assault investigations with the suspicion complainants are lying. Some categories of complainants, including aboriginal women and women with mental health problems, may be particularly vulnerable to being disbelieved (Dylan et al. 2008; Hattem 2007: 33). In 2000, police across Canada declared that there was 'no crime' in 16 per cent of sexual assault complaints, compared to 9 per cent of assaults (Johnson 2009: 10–11). Although Statistics Canada no longer publishes rates at which complaints of sexual assault are determined unfounded, recent studies covering four jurisdictions have found rates of between 7 and 32 per cent (Hattem 2007; Dubois 2009). According to one study that examined police files, unfounding was determined to be more prevalent in cases that involved non-strangers and no force and victims who did not clearly say 'no', demonstrating how the doctrinal consent standard fails to guide police decision-making (Hattem 2007).

Using the recently confirmed tort of negligent investigation and building on a significant decision that found police negligence in the conduct of a sexual assault investigation a violation of Charter sexual equality (*Jane Doe v Metropolitan Toronto Police* (1998) 39 OR (3d) 487 (Ont. Ct. Gen. Div.)), a group of feminist law professors and students from the University of Ottawa have begun to lay the foundation for claims against police for 'wrongful unfounding' (Crew 2009). The concept 'wrongful unfounding' refers to the wrongful clearing of sexual assault complaints by police and intentionally draws an analogy with negligent investigations producing 'wrongful convictions', now easily and popularly understood to be a violation of justice. The reconceptualization of the widespread practice of unfounding sexual assault complaints aims to ensure the enforcement of existing law by using litigation and the threat of financial damages to challenge discriminatory police practices. Strategic interventions such as this, using law against itself, open possibilities for reducing the gap between 'law as legislation' and 'law as practice' in a political climate that is resistant to feminist claims.

## CONCLUSION

Law reform efforts were only one component of a broad-based Canadian feminist strategy that sought to de-individualize sexual violence and place it firmly in the social and political arena as a legitimate object of governmental intervention. As I have argued here, even though statute and doctrine have moved Canadian law in the direction of an 'only yes means yes' standard, the transactional logics of affirmative consent operate to decontextualize sexual violence from the social power relations that define it. The atomized frame of criminal law is accentuated in a context of neoliberalism where risk management discourses hail women as hyper-cautious victims of sexual violence and reconstruct vulnerability as a failure of responsibilization.

In a context in which sexual violence as a gender equality issue has disappeared from political agendas, the opportunities for law reform have closed. This temporary closure of political spaces has produced a productive strategic emphasis on ensuring enforcement and altering police practices. Restricted opportunities for law reform should also promote critical reflection and prompt a reminder that criminal law reform, even in its most progressive guises, is a limited strategy. As Marcus (1992) has insightfully argued, an emphasis on vindication in the courts has limited effectiveness for a politics of rape prevention. This strategy conceives of sexual violence as a taken-for-granted occurrence, with only post-rape events offering possible occasions for intervention. In the present context, a renewed focus on prevention, including cultivating women's resistance to their assigned role as safety-conscious victims-in-waiting and engaging men in anti-rape education and politics, constitute promising extra-legal strategies.

## Note

1  In the absence of an SCC ruling, appellate court rulings like *Malcolm* are not binding outside their own state jurisdiction. Nonetheless, such rulings will be of persuasive authority and may influence interpretations in other jurisdictions.

## Bibliography

Benedet, J. (2009) 'The sexual assault of intoxicated women and Canadian criminal law', presented at the conference *Sexual Assault Law, Practice and Activism in a post-Jane Doe Era*, 6–7 March, University of Ottawa, Ottawa.

Benedet, J. and Grant, I. (2007) 'Hearing the sexual assault complaints of women with mental disabilities: consent, capacity and mistaken belief', *McGill Law Journal*, 52: 243–89.

Beres, M., Crow, B. and Gotell, L. (2009) 'The perils of institutionalization in neoliberal times: results of a National Survey of Rape Crisis and Sexual Assault Centres', *Canadian Journal of Sociology*, 34: 135–64.

Brodie, J. (2008). 'We are all equal now: contemporary gender politics in Canada', *Feminist Theory*, 9: 145–64.

Crew, A.B. (2009) 'Striking back: the viability of a civil action against the police for the wrongful unfounding of reported rapes', presented at the conference *Sexual Assault Law, Practice and Activism in a post-Jane Doe Era*, 6–7 March, University of Ottawa, Ottawa.

Criminal Code, RSC 1985, c. C-46.

Criminal Justice Sexual Offences Taskforce (2006) *Responding to Sexual Assault: the way forward*, Sydney: Attorney General's Department of New South Wales.

Desrosiers, J. (2009) 'La hausse de l'âge du consentement sexuel: renouveau du moralisme juridique', presented at the conference *Sexual Assault Law, Practice and Activism in a post-Jane Doe Era*, 6–7 March, University of Ottawa, Ottawa.

Dubois, T. (2009) 'A critical analysis of police investigations: the "wrongful unfounding" of sexual assault complaints', presented at the conference *Sexual Assault Law, Practice and Activism in a post-Jane Doe Era*, 6–7 March, University of Ottawa, Ottawa.

Dylan, A., Regehr, C. and Alaggia, R. (2008) 'And justice for all? Aboriginal victims of sexual violence', *Violence Against Women*, 14: 687–96.

Gotell, L. (1997) 'A critical look at state discourse on "violence against women": some implications for feminist politics and women's citizenship', in M. Tremblay and C. Andrew (eds) *Women and Political Representation in Canada*, Ottawa: University of Ottawa Press, 39–84.

—— (2002) 'The ideal victim, the hysterical complainant, and the disclosure of confidential records: the implications of the Charter for sexual assault law', *Osgoode Hall Law Journal*, 40: 251–95.

—— (2007) 'The discursive disappearance of sexualized violence: feminist law reform, judicial resistance and neo-liberal sexual citizenship', in D.E. Chunn, S.B. Boyd and H. Lessard (eds) *Feminism, Law and Social Change: (re)action and resistance*, Vancouver: University of British Columbia Press, 127–63.

—— (2008) 'Rethinking affirmative consent in Canadian law: neoliberal sexual subjects and risky women', *Akron Law Review*, 41: 865–98.

Hattem, T. (2007) 'Highlights of a preliminary study of police classification of sexual assault cases as unfounded', *JustResearch*, Department of Justice, Ottawa 14: 32–6. Online. Available at: <http://www.justice.gc.ca/eng/pi/rs/rep-rap/jr/jr14/toc-tdm.html> (accessed 10 April 2009).

Jiwani, Y. and Young, M.L. (2006) 'Missing and murdered women: reproducing marginality in news discourse', *Canadian Journal of Communications*, 31: 895–917.

Johnson, H. (2009) 'Limits of a criminal justice response: trends in police and court processing of sexual assault', presented at the conference *Sexual Assault Law, Practice and Activism in a post-Jane Doe Era*, 6–7 March, University of Ottawa, Ottawa.

Johnson, H. and Sacco, V. (1995) 'Researching violence against women: Statistics Canada's National Survey', *Canadian Journal of Criminology*, 37: 281–305.

Los, M. (1994) 'The struggle to redefine rape in the early 1980s', in J.V. Roberts and R.M. Mohr (eds) *Confronting Sexual Assault: a decade of legal and social change*, Toronto: University of Toronto Press, 20–56.

McIntyre, S. (2000) 'Tracking and Resisting Backlash Against Equality Gains in Sexual Offence Law', *Canadian Woman Studies*, 20: 72–83.

Marcus, S. (1992) 'Fighting bodies, fighting words: a theory and politics of rape prevention', in J. Butler and J. Scott (eds) *Feminists Theorize the Political*, New York: Routledge, 285–403.

Native Women's Association of Canada (2009) *Voices of Our Sisters in Spirit: a report to our families and communities*, Native Women's Association of Canada, Ottawa. Online. Available at: <http://www.nwac-hq.org/en/index.html> (accessed April 10 2009).

Pineau, L. (1996) 'A response to my critics', in L. Francis (ed.) *Date Rape*, University Park, Pennsylvania: Pennsylvania State University Press, 63–107.

Razack, S. (2000) 'Gendered racial violence and spatialized justice: the murder of Pamela George', *Canadian Journal of Law and Society*, 15: 91–130.

Ruparelia, R. (2006) 'Does "no" mean reasonable doubt: assessing the impact of *Ewanchuk* on determinations of consent', *Canadian Woman Studies*, 25: 167–72.

Smart, C. (1989) *Feminism and the Power of Law*, London: Routledge.

—— (1995) *Law, Crime and Sexuality*, London: Sage.

Snider, L. (1990) 'The potential of the criminal justice system to promote feminist concerns', *Studies in Law, Politics and Society*, 10: 143–72.

*Vancouver Sun* (2009) 'Harper says "rape law" could hurt allies' support for Afghan mission', 4 April 2009. Online. Available at: <http://www.vancouversun.com/news/Danish+named+NATO+boss/1465001/story.html> (accessed 10 April 2009).

Chapter 15

# Rape, law and American society

*Donald Dripps*

## GENERAL FEATURES OF THE US CRIMINAL JUSTICE SYSTEM

Despite sweeping increases in the power of the central government relative to the 50 states, the United States remains a federation in form. For violent crimes not connected to organized crime, including rape, offences are reported to, and investigated by, city or state police. Charging decisions are made by state prosecutors, who are usually organized into regional offices at county level. When charges are filed, cases are decided in felony trial courts, again organs of the particular state and again typically organized at the county level. Those convicted may appeal to higher courts within the state, and, if the accused asserts a claim under the federal constitution, to the Supreme Court of the United States. For crimes committed in US territory not under the jurisdiction of any state, such as the District of Columbia or tribal reservations, cases are investigated, prosecuted and tried by federal officers.

The United States thus does not have a single set of rape laws or a single system for enforcement, but instead 51 different rape statutes and 51 different procedural systems. The US Supreme Court's pervasive regulation of police and trial procedures under the federal constitution's Bill of Rights imposes a degree of uniformity on the procedural systems, since all states must comply with the federal constitution. So in every US jurisdiction, the police are bound not to enter private homes without warrants absent consent or emergency, and bound to comply with the *Miranda* rules when interrogating suspects in custody (*Miranda v Arizona*, 384 US 436 (1966)).

Such restrictions on the police are now fairly common throughout the world. The US constitution, however, imposes two less common procedures on all US jurisdictions. The Sixth Amendment requires trial by jury, and gives the accused the right to cross-examine the complaining witness through defence counsel. The Fifth Amendment double-jeopardy provision prohibits both retrial and appeal if a jury acquits, even against the manifest weight of the evidence.

The Supreme Court, however, has exercised no such unifying influence on the substantive criminal law. State legislatures are free to change the definition of offences, and sexual assault has been a topic on which state legislatures have been very active for the last 25 years. As a result, rape law in the US varies significantly among the states.

Two other features of the US system deserve preliminary remark. The first is that, by the standards of other wealthy democracies, US sentences are distinctively harsh. For example, the maximum penalty for forcible rape in Massachusetts, a liberal jurisdiction, is 20 years' imprisonment (MGLA 265 §22(b)).

Finally, the US system is highly discretionary. The police are not required to believe reports of offences. Prosecutors are not required to pursue cases referred by the police. Offenders are punished only after victims convince first a police officer, and then a prosecutor, of the truth of the charge, and the prosecutor persuades either defence counsel to recommend a guilty plea, or a jury that the evidence shows guilt beyond reasonable doubt (Fairstein 1993: 55–7).

Absent a claim of discrimination based on race or political viewpoint, there is no judicial regulation of prosecutorial charging decisions. Many, perhaps most, criminal incidents involve the violation of multiple statutes. For example, the forcible rape of a juvenile can be charged as forcible rape, statutory rape, or both. Forcible rape often may support related but separate charges such as kidnapping or false imprisonment. Under the modern statutes, the most aggravated forms of sexual assault include many lesser offences.

As a result, US prosecutors have great discretionary power over case outcomes. Most convictions result from pleas rather than from trials. Plea bargaining avoids the costs of trial, and reduces the liability the accused might otherwise face. The determinants of plea bargaining are the prosecutor's discretion and the credibility of the defence chances at a trial by jury. A guilty plea by the innocent can be perfectly rational, just as the prosecution may rationally conclude that a plea to a minor charge is a better outcome than an acquittal at trial in a case that is in fact very aggravated.

## HISTORICAL AND POLITICAL CONTEXT

Identity politics have influenced the development of US rape law in dramatic ways. Obviously enough, rape law will reflect a society's norms about gender roles and sexual morality; and the United States is no exception. Race and class have also played important roles. Fears of predation by blacks on white women were (and remain) a common preoccupation, especially but by no means exclusively in the South (Crenshaw 1991: 1271–4; Taslitz 1999: 28). For example, in the notorious case of the 'Scottsboro boys', Alabama officials cozened two poor white women into fabricating rape charges against nine black youths (Goodman 1994). As late as 1955, a black youth was lynched, by torture, in Mississippi for whistling at a white woman (Crowe 2003). Until 1977, when the Supreme Court declared the practice unconstitutional (*Coker v Georgia*, 433 US 584 (1977)), some Southern states still provided the death penalty for rape.

In America, as in England, the legal system recognized unusual procedural safeguards to prevent false accusations by lower-class women against upper-class men. Indeed, from Independence in 1776 until late in the nineteenth century, US rape law generally followed the familiar English definition of carnal knowledge of a woman by a man not her husband, by force and without consent. This definition was coupled with requirements, unique to the rape context, of resistance to the utmost, chastity, prompt complaint and admissibility of both reputation testimony and past-act evidence to show propensity to consent. The courts began to modify the resistance requirement to mean that reasonable resistance only was required (Klein 2008: 987–8). Otherwise, the substantive definition and the unusual procedure remained in place until the second half of the twentieth century.

In 1961, Illinois became the first US jurisdiction to adopt a comprehensive criminal code based on the American Law Institute's renowned and influential Model Penal Code (MPC). The MPC became the basis for the codes of two-thirds of the American states, while the rest retain nineteenth-century codes based on the English common law of crimes, as reflected in the writings of Blackstone, Hawkins and Hale.

The MPC made major changes in the criminal law's general part, by clearly setting out a graduated range of culpable mental states, predicating liability on subjective mental states, and generally rationalizing doctrine across the board. The MPC rape provision, however, broke little new ground, providing:

> A male who has sexual intercourse with a female not his wife is guilty of rape if:
>
> (a) he compels her to submit by force or by threat of imminent death, serious bodily injury, extreme pain or kidnapping, to be inflicted on anyone; or
> (b) he has substantially impaired her power to appraise or control her conduct by administering or employing without her knowledge drugs, intoxicants or other means for the purpose of preventing resistance; or
> (c) the female is unconscious; or
> (d) the female is less than 10 years old.
>
> (MPC §213.1(a))

Section (a) still requires penetration, force, and the absence of consent.

The resistance requirement masked two great mysteries implicit in the traditional definition. One is the meaning of consent, a concept which continues to perplex philosophers and academic lawyers (Wertheimer 2003; Westen 2004). The other is the *mens rea* required for the offence. If the accuser must physically resist the defendant before he is liable, the defendant must know perfectly well that there is no consent. The cases in which the accuser's behavior is either passive or ambivalent could not be prosecuted.

In the 1970s and 1980s, the US jurisdictions repealed the traditional procedural safeguards, including the per se requirements of proving resistance, prompt complaint and good repute (Klein 2008: 983–7). Absence of resistance and reporting delay were made admissible in evidence but given only such weight as the jury might give them.

So-called 'Rape Shield Laws' were also adopted in all US jurisdictions save Arizona (Anderson 2002: 81–2). These laws prohibit the defence from questioning the complaining witness, or calling other witnesses to testify, about the complaining witness's propensity to consent, whether the testimony is elicited in the form of opinion, reputation or past-act evidence. The shield laws typically include exceptions for past-act evidence offered to explain physical evidence or injury, and for past-act evidence of sex between the accused and the complaining witness when relevant to a claim of consent. The laws vary substantially, but they share a common central application: barring proof of the accuser's actual or rumored consensual sex with X, Y and Z to show consent to sex with the defendant. This central application has survived constitutional challenge, although the US Supreme Court has held that the defendant's right to a fair trial requires admitting evidence of a sexual relationship with a third party offered to prove a motive to fabricate a charge against the accused (*Olden v Kentucky*, 488 US 227 (1988)).

Whether by court decision or by statute, most US jurisdictions allow the prosecution to make some use of expert testimony about rape trauma syndrome (RTS) (Kanusher 2004: 293). The precise rules vary among the jurisdictions, but a fairly typical arrangement is to permit the expert to describe RTS and explain how behaviour, such as failure to report or recantation of an accusation, can be explained by the syndrome; but not to give an opinion about the truth of the charge or the veracity of the complaining witness.

It is fair to label these sweeping changes the first wave of rape law reform. This first wave was the product of two powerful social forces, namely the movement for equal rights for women and intense public hostility to increasing levels of violent crime. Susan Brownmiller's book, *Against our Will* (Brownmiller 1975), was perhaps the most prominent call to treat the criminal law of sexual assault as a feminist issue. Researchers and law enforcement officers helped make the case for reform by pointing out that rape was the most under-reported serious crime, as well as the most likely charge to be lost at a trial by jury. Reformers hoped that repealing the old procedural rules would encourage victims to report and to testify, and reduce the frequency of irrational acquittals by juries. Although generally contemporaneous with the widespread adoption of the MPC, the major changes were procedural. Even jurisdictions that retained the common-law definition of rape adopted such changes as rape shield laws and the admission of RTS testimony. The first wave of reform generally did not change the basic crime/force/non-consent definition of the substantive offence.

During the first reform period, it is probably fair to say that victims (and potential victims) benefited more from administrative and technological changes than from doctrinal changes. While these changes varied widely across jurisdictions, it became quite common for both police departments and prosecutors' offices to establish specialized sex-crimes units, with officials trained to deal with the special needs of victims and the special difficulties of prosecution. The development of DNA identification evidence revolutionized the prosecution of sex crimes. In stranger-rape cases, identification was often problematic, permitting both the prosecution of the innocent and the escape of the guilty. Police worked with hospitals to collect forensic evidence following emergency room visits by rape victims. Victims came to have access to social workers or psychologists, either through the hospital or by contacting a rape crisis centre.

The hoped-for consequences of reform, by and large, did not materialize (Schulhofer 1998: 38; Bryden and Lengnick 1996–7: 1199). It is generally agreed that rape remains the most under-reported major offence. Persuading victims to testify at trial remains a major challenge for prosecutors. A rape charge defended on consent is still the most likely accusation to be rejected by a jury although apparently well-founded in fact (see further, Ellison and Munro in this collection). Rape myths remain prevalent. Substantial portions of the public continue to regard a woman who agrees to go into a man's home, or invites a man into her home, as either consenting to sex or being morally responsible for her own rape. Similar attitudes remain common with respect to women who look for sex, as men commonly do, by drinking at singles bars or by placing or answering online personal advertisements. Prostitutes are both particularly vulnerable to rape and targets of especially strong negative prejudice (Bryden 2000: 425; Pillsbury 2002: 876–7; Taslitz 1999).

In addition to continuing prejudice against adult women who transgress traditional gender roles or sexual mores, some victims are indeed very hard for the criminal justice system to reach at all. Children, the mentally disabled (see further, Benedet and Grant in this collection) and prisoners face different obstacles to pressing charges, but each of these populations is both especially vulnerable and especially difficult to reach.

The frustrating failure of the first wave of legal reform, however, spurred fresh discussions (which we may label the second wave of reform) about how to address the troubling persistence of under-reporting and excessive case attrition. Cases that formerly would have been blocked by the resistance requirement raised difficult questions about the meaning of 'force' and 'consent'.

For example, in *Commonwealth v Berkowitz* (641 A.2d 1161 (Pa. 1994)), the victim and defendant were college students who had met in a course on human sexuality. The victim stopped by the defendant's room to see his roommate, who was not present. The defendant asked the victim to stay and she remained, although she refused physical overtures and sat on the floor rather than the bed. The defendant locked the door (it locked only from the inside, so if the victim had attempted to leave, the lock would not have prevented her). He shoved her onto the bed before penetration, but the victim described it as neither a hard shove nor a gentle shove but as an 'in-between shove'. The victim said 'no' repeatedly but made no attempt to leave. A divided court reversed the jury's conviction for rape and substituted a misdemeanor conviction for the lesser offence of indecent assault, for which force is not an element of the offence (although consent remains a defence). The decision was disapproved of by the Pennsylvania legislature, which created a new felony offence for engaging in sex without consent.

Sixteen states now have statutes recognizing sex without consent as a lesser-included offence of forcible rape (Anderson 2005: 631–2). Several other jurisdictions that have not created separate crimes of sex without consent have upheld convictions based on very slight evidence of force. Only one state, New Jersey, has equated sexual penetration with force by judicial decision (*In re MTS*, 609 A.2d 1266 (NJ 1992)). When, however, the victim is very young, or mentally disabled, many courts have upheld convictions based on 'psychological force', 'constructive force', or by treating modest physical contact extrinsic to penetration as legally sufficient force (Dripps 2008: 966–1).

The general trend of the law in the US is clear, even if the jurisdictions are very far indeed from unanimity. When consent is clearly absent, the defendant should be criminally liable, either under a special statute or a wide reading of the traditional rape statutes. There are at least two troubling features of this trend. First, it is doubtful that this second phase of legal reform will achieve the object of increasing the likelihood that rapists of adult women will be punished. The reluctance of victims to report and testify, and the sympathy of juries for male sexual aggression against women perceived as promiscuous, are the greatest challenges to fuller enforcement. Broadening the paper coverage of the criminal code does not directly address either challenge. Secondly, pure consent formulations at least arguably apply to many sexual encounters that ordinary people do not recognize as rape. For example, if the defendant, a manager, threatens to deny the victim, an employee, a deserved promotion unless she has sex with him, it is reasonable to regard the victim's decision to have sex with the defendant as without consent in the normatively relevant sense. Yet neither citizens, nor legislatures, nor prosecutors appear to regard this type of sexual harassment as either rape or a violation of the pure-consent statutes. Reported cases under the pure-consent statutes have not pushed these statutes to the limits of their logic. Instead, they seem to be applied primarily to deal with near-miss charges under the traditional sex/force/non-consent rubric. This is entirely understandable, given the difficulty of persuading juries to convict even in acquaintance-rape cases. Criminalizing very common conduct and then leaving it to the executive to select a few cases for prosecution nonetheless compromises important principles of legality and transparency.

This type of delegation, however, is not likely to be ended through ordinary political processes. Elected representatives certainly will not cast votes in defence of sex without consent. Nor are they likely to make hard decisions about the meaning of consent. For example, the California legislature adopted the following definition of consent: 'positive cooperation in act or attitude pursuant to an exercise of free will. The person must act freely and voluntarily and have knowledge of the nature of the act or transaction involved'

(Cal. Penal Code §261.6). This language does not even attempt to address the difficult issue of what inducements make sexual co-operation not 'free' or 'voluntary'. What of the drug addict who has sex with her source to ensure a continued supply, the abused spouse who initiates sex to pre-empt a feared beating, the *quid pro quo* employment cases, and so on? The language chosen here commands wide support precisely because it avoids such thorny questions.

Although some US jurisdictions recognize reasonable mistake about consent as a defence, the majority position continues to reject any mistake defence. The statutes and cases are thoughtfully surveyed in a recent Massachusetts case adhering to the majority, no-defence position (*Commonwealth v Lopez*, 745 NE 2d 961 (Mass. 2001)). Under the dominant view, rape remains a general intent crime, i.e. the defendant need only intend penetration. Cases in which the acts alleged to constitute force are unintentional are likely to be rare. Cases in which the defendant may plausibly claim ignorance of their threatening character to the accuser are not uncommon, as are cases in which the defendant claims to have believed the accuser consented.

The mistake defence appeals to the principle that serious criminal liability should not be imposed absent subjective awareness of wrongdoing (Cavallaro 1996). Pragmatic considerations support the traditional view. Juries might believe the defence in many cases where it is unfounded, especially given the government's burden of proving guilt beyond reasonable doubt. Moreover, the mistake defence potentially opens a loophole in the rape shield laws. The defendant may testify that he believed that the accuser consented in part because of what he has heard about her sexual history. Such testimony is easy to fabricate and clearly prejudicial, but when offered to support a mistake defence it is relevant to the defendant's belief (and so also not barred by the hearsay rule, as the rumors defendant has heard are not, strictly speaking, offered for truth). The mistake defence therefore enables a stronger constitutional challenge to the shield rules than does the majority position.

The government's ongoing victimization survey showed a significant decline in incidence of rape during the period 1993–98, but it is doubtful that legal changes had much to do with the trend inasmuch as violent crime across categories declined during the same period (Bureau of Justice Statistics 2008: 3). Moreover, the latest data shows the victimization rate for rape rising from 0.8 to 1.0 victimizations per thousand in the general population, even though other serious offences continued to decline (Bureau of Justice Statistics 2008: 1). The victimization survey data indicates that 42 per cent of rapes are reported to the police (Bureau of Justice Statistics 2008: 6).

Other official statistics indicate a clearance rate by arrest for reported forcible rapes of 40.9 per cent (Bureau of Justice Statistics 2009: Table 4.19.2006). Coupled with the reporting data, this suggests that only 16 per cent of rapes result in an arrest. There is some evidence that convictions are at last becoming easier to obtain. In 2004, 56 per cent of those arrested for rape in the state systems were convicted, a lower rate than for homicide and drug trafficking but a higher rate than for robbery and burglary (Bureau of Justice Statistics 2009: Table 5.57.2004).

Taking the figures at face value suggests that any given rape in the US runs a risk of felony conviction slightly smaller than one in 10. The official statistics do not distinguish stranger from acquaintance rapes. Advances in DNA evidence and record-keeping, which have dramatically strengthened the position of the prosecution in cases of stranger rape, and continued anecdotal evidence of juror prejudice in acquaintance rape cases (see further, Ellison and Munro in this collection), make it plausible to speculate that the prospect of conviction in an acquaintance rape case is considerably less than one in 10.

Speaking very generally, the first wave of reform replaced the common law's special, pro-defense procedures in rape cases with a new set of special, pro-prosecution procedures. The second wave of reform, by no means spent, has broadened the definition of the substantive crime. Much can be said for or against any individual change in the law on the books. There is widespread agreement that reforms so far achieved in the US have fallen short of their proponents' hopes. Given that the law on the books both reflects and influences evolving social attitudes, we can expect to see continuing, relatively rapid, change in legal doctrine and administrative practice, and continuing, relatively slow, changes in social attitudes.

## CRITICAL ANALYSES OF THE CURRENT LAW

The variations among the US jurisdictions can be categorized, at least in a rough and ready way, into three major groups. Some states still retain the classic formulation of sex by force without consent. Even in these jurisdictions, forcible sodomy and marital rape are now criminalized, either by eliminating prior exemptions from the rape statute or by statutes creating separate offences. For example, the Massachusetts code provides that:

> Whoever has sexual intercourse or unnatural sexual intercourse with a person and compels such person to submit by force and against his will, or compels such person to submit by threat of bodily injury, shall be punished by imprisonment in the state prison for not more than twenty years; and whoever commits a second or subsequent such offense shall be punished by imprisonment in the state prison for life or for any term or years.
>
> (MGLA 265 §22(b))

There are enhanced penalties for the use of weapons or infliction of extrinsic injuries and the like, but in Massachusetts (and several other states) the core of the definition of rape has not changed for centuries.

Many state statutes are based on the MPC's 'forcible compulsion' formula. For example, the Pennsylvania code provides:

A person commits a felony of the first degree when the person engages in sexual intercourse with a complainant:

(1) By forcible compulsion.
(2) By threat of forcible compulsion that would prevent resistance by a person of reasonable resolution.
(3) Who is unconscious or where the person knows that the complainant is unaware that the sexual intercourse is occurring.
(4) Where the person has substantially impaired the complainant's power to appraise or control his or her conduct by administering or employing, without the knowledge of the complainant, drugs, intoxicants or other means for the purpose of preventing resistance.
(5) Who suffers from a mental disability which renders the complainant incapable of consent.

(18 Pa.CSA 3121(a))

The Michigan statute illustrates a third approach. Michigan abandoned the 'rape' terminology altogether, in favor of defining separate degrees of sexual assault. The most serious – First Degree sexual assault – can be committed in violation of any of eight different subheadings, including sex with a child below the age of 13, sex with a child between 13 and 16 when aggravating circumstances are present, etc. (Mich. Pen. C. §750-520(b)). The traditional offence, however, did not disappear. When '[f]orce or coercion is used to accomplish the sexual penetration', the actor commits Criminal Sexual Assault in the Third Degree (Mich. Pen. C. §750-520(d)(1)(b)), which may be aggravated to Second or First Degree if aggravating factors such as the use of a weapon are present.

New Jersey still apparently stands alone in equating sex with force, so as to define forcible rape as sex without consent. As previously discussed, however, 16 states recognize a lesser crime of sex without consent, and several other jurisdictions have read the force requirement broadly against defendants whose disregard for consent is particularly patent, or in some other way odious.

As previously discussed, almost all US jurisdictions have a rape shield law, and almost all allow some use of RTS evidence. The jurisdictions do differ significantly with respect to evidence of prior conduct by the defendant. As a matter of general evidence law, the US jurisdictions uniformly prohibit proof of past crimes to show a character predisposed to commit crimes of the type charged. For example, at trial of a charge of robbing one bank, the government may not prove that the defendant previously robbed another bank. The reasons given for the rule include the difficulties of ascertaining the truth of charges of collateral crimes, that propensity is only a weak predictor of behavior and that juries will be hostile to parties they know have done wrong in the past. A significant number of US jurisdictions modified the rule in rape cases in the aftermath of the Kennedy-Smith case (*Florida v Smith*, 91 case no. 005482CFA02, Circuit Court of the 15th Judicial Circuit in and for Palm Beach Country Florida Criminal Division (1992)). The prosecution in that case offered to prove that the defendant had attacked several other women in the past, but this evidence was excluded, as required by the then-prevailing law. Smith's acquittal provoked popular umbrage, leading the federal Congress and 10 states to permit proof of past sexual assaults to prove the sexual assault on charge (Lombardi 2004: 116).

Perhaps the most radical change afoot is the increasing reliance on civil proceedings to regulate or restrain sexual offenders. Prompted by federal legislation, every state now has a sex offender registration system (Klein 2008: 1036), and 19 states authorize indefinite civil commitment of sexually violent offenders. The Supreme Court has rejected constitutional challenges to such a statute, even when commitment was predicated on conduct which the state had prosecuted and punished as a criminal offence prior to commitment (Klein 2008: 1043–4).

## CURRENT ISSUES

The law of sexual assault confronts a wide range of very difficult issues, including these:

1  What does consent mean?
2  Are there any cases of sex without consent that should not be treated as rape?
3  Should there be a reasonable mistake of consent defence?
4  When, if ever, should past sexual history be admitted for the defence?
5  Should past-act evidence be admitted against the defence?
6  What can public policy do to dispel rape myths?
7  What can be done to protect the innocent against false charges?

Each of these issues could be a chapter unto itself (indeed, whole books have been written about the meaning of consent). Perhaps the best way to approach the range of issues in short compass is by reviewing two prominent recent cases, the Kobe Bryant case (*People v Bryant*, Co. Eagle Cty. Dist. Ct. case no. 03CR204 (2003)) and the Duke lacrosse case (the first indictment was *State v Finnerty*, N.C. Super. Ct. Durham Cty. case no. 06 CRS 4332 (2006)). A 19-year-old, Caucasian hotel clerk accused Bryant, an African-American, and a wealthy and famous professional basketball star, of raping her in his motel room (Haddad 2005). Bryant did not deny having sex with her, and she did not deny consenting to preliminary flirting and kissing. The case brings together many of the issues summarized above. Does a woman who voluntarily flirts with a man and goes to his motel room thereby consent to sex? The law is clear that she does not; but it is very difficult to persuade a jury to agree with the law (LaFree 1989: 217–25). Should the law permit a man in such a case to claim that he believed the victim consented even if she did not consent in fact? The law here is less clear, with a mistake defence being recognized only by a minority of US jurisdictions.

Traditionally rape was a general intent crime: the defendant need only intend the intercourse to be guilty. That understanding reflected the resistance requirement, which effectively required unequivocal indicia of non-consent. If Bryant thought his accuser consented, he lacked the subjective culpability generally required for serious criminal liability. What, then, if he was negligent or reckless in his belief?

Whatever fairness demands for the accused in such a case, the prevalence of rape myths have been a factor inhibiting recognition of any mistake defence. Jurors are all too prone to look at a case like Bryant's as 'justified rape'. A woman who makes advances on a celebrity and then accepts an invitation to his motel room, in a very common view, is asking for trouble and should not be heard to complain about the consequences. In all probability, if the evidence shows a white woman who came on to a black man, racial prejudices would hurt the prosecution at least as much as the defence. One way to understand the reluctance to recognize a mistake defence is to characterize the substantive-law rule as a way to reduce the influence of rape myths. Juries given a signal to acquit when 'there was a rape but there wasn't a rapist' might often turn a blind eye to bona fide rapists.

The US has an adversary system, and defence lawyers are under a professional duty to zealously represent the client. If this requires character assassination of the state's star witness (the complainant), so be it. In the Bryant case, the defence sought to prove that the physical evidence showed that the accuser had sex with other men as well as Bryant either the day before or the day after the alleged offence. The trial judge ruled that this evidence would be admissible. It could not be used to prove a promiscuous propensity, but it was relevant to two other issues: to question whether another man might have caused the vaginal lacerations, which the prosecution said were probative of forced sex, and to impeach the credibility of prosecution witnesses who were alleged to be sexually involved with the accuser. The judge's ruling was a reasonable application of Colorado's rape shield law, but it had the effect of causing the accuser to refuse to co-operate further with the prosecution, causing the dismissal of the case.

By then, the accuser's identity, and many alleged, unflattering details of her biography were available on the internet. T-shirts and coffee mugs with her likeness under such labels as 'lying bitch' were widely available (Haddad 2005: 186). If Hollywood screenwriters had set about inventing an incident to discourage rape reporting, they could scarcely have improved on the Bryant script. After dropping the criminal case, Bryant settled a civil suit by the accuser for an undisclosed sum, a turn that to some degree compensated her for her ordeal, but that also suggested the possibility of impure motives and a troubling capability of the wealthy to buy immunity.

The identity politics of the Duke lacrosse case were close to the reverse of the Kobe Bryant case. A black woman, who worked as an exotic dancer while attending a low-status state university, was paid to dance at a party held by members of the Duke University lacrosse team (Mosteller 2007). Duke is a prestigious private university, and the accused players were all white (in the

US, lacrosse is a sport commonly played at private colleges and prep schools, but rarely played at public institutions). The accusation sounded a powerful chord of sexual predation privileged by gender, wealth and race. Prior to trial, Duke University suspended the two charged players who had not graduated. The accusation, however, turned out to be false. The accuser never had sex with any of the players, and pursued the case either as a deliberate hoax or under the influence of delusions. The police investigation was marred by a suspects-only photo identification procedure, and the prosecutor was eventually disbarred for misconduct that included withholding exculpatory evidence. Duke University settled lawsuits brought by the two suspended players.

In a sense, the Duke case was a success of the adversary system. The unusual wealth of the defendants enabled them to retain first-rate counsel, whose diligence exposed deceit by the accuser and overreaching by the authorities. Had the evidence proved sexual contact between accuser and accused, however, these same first-rate lawyers would have devoted themselves to exploiting rape myths just as counsel for Bryant did. They likely would have painted the accuser as a prostitute who agreed to entertain a party of hooligans-cum-playboys for money, and then showed up intoxicated. It is a picture that many jurors would not see as the portrait of a rape victim, regardless of other facts and circumstances.

The law's objectives in the sexual assault field include increasing reporting, reducing the prevalence of rape myths, fairness to the accused and prevention of fabrications. These goals, unfortunately, conflict. The vigorous defence enjoyed by the Duke defendants is one few indigent defendants receive. It is also a defence capable of exploiting rape myths to pressure victims to abandon prosecution or, failing that, to persuade juries to blame the victim rather than the accused.

A mistake defence seems only fair given the serious consequences attending conviction, and the Supreme Court's recognition that private adult sex, when consensual, is protected by the constitution. A mistake defence, however, would, as discussed above, widen the opportunity for exploiting rape myths.

Procedural fairness seems to require permitting proof of sex between the victim and X to show an alternative explanation for injuries alleged to prove assault by the defendant. But that proof also plays to rape myths and will discourage reporting. These difficult dilemmas pervade the field, and help to explain the considerable variation in legal doctrine from one jurisdiction to the next.

The DNA technique has greatly advanced the prosecution of stranger rape cases, by enabling – in a great many cases – a conclusive identification, implicating the guilty and exonerating the innocent. There is no similar techno-fix for acquaintance rape cases. At a very general level, the legal treatment of acquaintance rape in the United States reflects a tension between elite opinion, which sympathizes with sexual autonomy and gender equality, and popular opinion, which continues to harbour considerable sentiment for male sexual aggression and against female sexual freedom. Elite opinion has controlled the law-on-the-books, but legal doctrine depends on human beings for execution. So far, popular opinion has had more influence on the law-in-action.

## Bibliography

Anderson, M. (2002) 'From chastity requirement to sexuality license: sexual consent and a new rape shield law', *George Washington Law Review*, 70: 51–162.
—— (2005) 'All-American rape', *St. John's Law Review*, 79: 625–44.
Brownmiller, S. (1975) *Against Our Will: men, women and rape*, New York: Simon & Schuster.
Bryden, D. (2000) 'Redefining rape', *Buffalo Criminal Law Review*, 3: 317–512.
Bryden, D. and Lengnick, S. (1996–1997) 'Rape in the criminal justice system', *Journal of Criminal Law and Criminology*, 87: 1194–384.
Bureau of Justice Statistics (US) (2008) 'National Crime Victimization Survey', BJS Bulletin December 2008 (NCJ 224390).
—— (2009), 'Sourcebook of Criminal Justice Statistics'. Online. Available at: <www.albandy.edu/sourcebook/pdf>.
Cavallaro, R. (1996) 'A big mistake: eroding the defense of mistake of fact about consent in rape', *Journal of Criminal Law and Criminology*, 86: 815–60.
Crenshaw, K. (1991) 'Mapping the margins: intersectionality, identity politics, and violence against women of color', *Stanford Law Review*, 43: 1241–300.
Crowe, C. (2003) *Getting Away with Murder: the true story of the Emmet Till case*, New York: Dial.
Dripps, D.A. (2008) 'After rape law: will the turn to consent normalize the prosecution of sexual assault?', *Akron Law Review*, 41: 957–80.
Fairstein, L. (1993) *Sexual Violence: our war against rape*, New York: William Morrow.
Goodman, J.E. (1994) *Stories of Scottsboro*, New York: Pantheon.
Haddad, R.I. (2005) 'Shield or sieve? *People v Bryant* and the rape shield law in high profile cases', *Columbia Journal of Law and Social Problems*, 39: 185–222.
Kanusher, C. (2004) 'PTS, RTS, and Child Abuse Accommodation Syndrome: therapeutic tools or fact finding aids', *Pace Law Review*, 24: 293–300.
Klein, R. (2008) 'An analysis of thirty-five years of rape reform: a frustrating search for fundamental fairness', *Akron Law Review*, 41: 981–1058.
LaFree, G. (1989) *Rape and Criminal Justice: the social construction of sexual assault*, Florence, Kentucky: Wadsworth.
Lombardi, J. (2004) 'Because sex crimes are different', *University of Baltimore Law Review*, 34: 103–30.
Mosteller, R.P. (2007) 'The Duke Lacrosse case, innocence, and false identifications: a fundamental failure to "do justice" ', *Fordham Law Review*, 76: 1337–412.
Pillsbury, S.H. (2002) 'Crimes against the heart: recognizing the wrongs of forced sex', *Loyola (Los Angeles) Law Review*, 35: 845–960.
Schulhofer, S.J. (1998) *Unwanted Sex: the culture of intimidation and the failure of law*, Cambridge, MA: Harvard Press.
Taslitz, A. (1999) *Rape and the Culture of the Courtroom*, New York: New York University Press.
Wertheimer, A. (2003) *Consent to Sexual Relations*, Cambridge: Cambridge University Press.
Westen, P. (2004) *The Logic of Consent*, Aldershot: Ashgate.

Chapter 16

# Criminal law and the reformation of rape in Australia

*Peter D. Rush*[1]

The tradition of criminal law in Australia is constituted by a plurality of jurisdictions, all of which speak to the crime of rape or sexual assault. The power and authority of Anglo-Australian criminal law resides in the several states and territories of the Commonwealth of Australia, with each state and territory creating its own penal legislation. Victoria, New South Wales (NSW), South Australia (SA) and the Australian Capital Territory are conventionally referred to as common-law jurisdictions, in contrast to Queensland, Western Australia (WA), Tasmania and the Northern Territory, which are referred to as code jurisdictions. The common-law jurisdictions use general criminal legislation which is then interpreted in the light of the articulations of common-law principles and practices by the judicial courts. This scheme of general legislation – or *restatement* of the common law of crime – was generated in each of the states in the early decades of the twentieth century. At the end of the nineteenth century, however, what have become known as the code jurisdictions took a different legislative path. The common law of crime was abolished and placed on a *codified* statutory footing, which then becomes the sole source of authority – albeit with some reference to its founding fathers – for the judicial construction of crime and its narratives of legal liability and moral responsibility.

In short, Anglo-Australian criminal law is composed of a plurality of state jurisdictions with differentiated relations to the common-law tradition. Nevertheless, there are clear similarities in terms and structure between the various state jurisdictions when it comes to the juridical attribution of liability for rape. At the same time, there is a federal criminal jurisdiction created by the Commonwealth Parliament. Contemporary forms of sexual violence have provided some of the subject-matter for its construction. Since the 1990s, sex trafficking, international sex tourism and debt bondage have been the subject of commonwealth legislation (*R v Tang* [2008] HCA 39). Similarly, the Commonwealth Government engaged in a project of codification of the entirety of the subject-matter (rape law included) of substantive criminal law in the 1990s (MCCOC 1999).

What can be discerned in this plurality of jurisdictions is that criminal law begins in Australia as a project of reform – the disavowal of indigenous laws of crime, the legislative condensation of the common law of England in some states and territories, the codification and consequent displacement of common law in yet others. Rape law – like criminal law more generally – exists in an isomorphic relation with its reform: each new law calls forth its criticism, each criticism documents the failure of law and its reform, and each failure calls forth yet more laws of rape and their allied sexual offences.

The concern of this chapter is to provide a description – and at times a redescription – of the shape and salience of the enterprise of rape law reform in contemporary Australia. In the first part, my concern is with the *overall* shape of the discourse and its practices. This is provided by a brief history of the project of rape law reform from the 1970s onwards, as well as a consideration of the rise of the languages of social science and of policy advocacy which have come to define the enterprise of reform. In the second part, the concern gets more detailed and looks to *specific* topics and issues of rape law which have engaged the energies of reform. Along the way, the established if not quite settled definition of rape in Australia is presented. But my aim here is to bring out a shift in the object of reform – from substantive law to the procedural institutions of the criminal law of rape. The chapter then concludes that one way forward in the continuing enterprise of rape law reform may be to return to the task of reconstructing the legal definition of rape.

## THE SHAPE OF LAW REFORM

Three critical periods can be sketched in the contemporary history of rape law reform. That history begins in Australia in the 1970s. Rape law is placed within a discourse of political, cultural and social change. The jurisdictions of NSW and SA provide illustration. In the latter, the 1976 Criminal Law and Penal Methods Reform Committee (the Mitchell Committee) presented the first substantial review of rape law by a law reform body in Australia. It marked out rape law as holding a distinctive place and urgency in any reform of criminal law. However, the Mitchell Committee did not advocate significant change to the substantive law of rape. While recognizing that rape is a crime legally composed of an uneasy and inevitable amalgam of sex and violence, that the marital immunity provided for husbands needs to be at least partially abolished, and that the age of the victim as well as the cognitive impairment of the victim demand special treatment in the law of sexual offences, it nevertheless failed to register explicitly the fact that rape is a gendered crime (CLPMRC 1976). Rather, it continued to structure the juridical ordering of sexual relations in terms of individual rights: an approach which it claimed, with some justification, was embodied in the common-law standard of consent. Specifically, liability for rape obtained its legal character from the fact that it was an interference with the sexual rights of individuals rather than from the social fact that it was an offence of violence against the rights of women.

The NSW enterprise of rape law reform provides a stark contrast. In 1981, the state government introduced the Crimes (Sexual Assault) Amendment

Act 1981 (NSW), following substantial community consultation with women's rights activists (Scutt 1980, for illustration). Such activism had taken place throughout the preceding decade, with the first Rape Crisis Centre in Australia being opened in Sydney in 1974. The tenor of this activism was to reconstruct rape as a crime of violence akin to assault. It was argued that sexual assault was primarily an instance of violence and the substantive law of rape (together with some procedural amendments) should reflect that social fact. On this basis, the standard of consent was largely removed from the substantive law of rape and replaced by definitions which reconstructed rape as the infliction of harm with intent to have sexual intercourse.

This initial moment of rape law reform was thus dominated by two prominent concerns. First, the reform enterprise represented law as an instrument of social policy and ideological change. While there was vigorous debate about how to design the reformed laws, law was understood as the means of repairing the social fabric torn by violence against women. Related to this instrumental and restorative presentation of law, the second concern directed the understanding of rape away from a representation of sexual relations and towards an accounting of rape as a social and political problem of violence – and, for some, violence against women. In all this, rape and rape law become a cipher through which to document the place of women in society and, specifically, the administrative and ideological limits which structure women's participation in civil society.

The final decade of the twentieth century signals a second period. By the end of the 1980s, a new round of legislative reforms began to emerge in several state governments. At this time, the discourses of rape law reform began to reorient criminal law towards registering the legal problem of rape in 'gender-neutral' terms. Gender-neutrality was embodied in the substantive legal definition of rape in a number of ways, including the use of terminology such as 'sexual penetration', the expansion of the modes of penetration to include the introduction of the penis into the vagina, anus or mouth of another and the introduction of a bodily part (other than the penis) or a non-human object into the vagina or anus of another. This clinical definition provided a reverse-image of the empirical reality of rape. Or, as Regina Graycar and Jenny Morgan remarked, the legislation provided 'equality with a vengeance' (1990: 340). Apart from such feminist ironies, the extension of sexual conduct captured by the reformed definition of rape was also perhaps one of the unintended side-effects of the movement to decriminalize homosexuality in Australia. With the removal of the crime of buggery in the various states and territories, acts which had been legally identified as 'homosexual acts' were subsequently incorporated into definitions of rape by way of their gender-neutrality.

Gender-neutrality was also embodied in rape law reform by way of the norm of consent. The 1990s saw an increasing emphasis on structuring the *entire* legal regime of sexual offences around the standard of consent – consent became the justification of the law and of its reform. Thus, the standard of consent increasingly dominated each of the definitions of a sexual offence, to the exclusion of standards of violence and coercion. As I have already noted, the approach of the Mitchell Committee in SA was to maintain and consolidate the role of consent in rape law, whereas the NSW approach was to put consent to one side and, as one official and influential commentary put it, 'to the maximum extent possible, place primary emphasis on the violence factor in sexual assault' (Woods 1981: 12). Yet, just under a decade later, NSW *reintroduced* the standard of consent – the prosecution were required to prove absence of consent for each of the gradations of sexual assault. Since then, and until now, all criminal jurisdictions require proof of absence of consent. It remains the case, however, that while gender-neutrality is embodied in the formal element of consent, the ways in which this standard is used by criminal justice institutions in responding to survivors of rape and sexual assault are differentiated along the lines of gender and sexual orientation (Young 1998).

In overall terms, then, this second period in the enterprise of rape law reform continues to situate law within a problematic of social and political change; but it does so in the idiom of the *vulnerable* (Brown 1995: Ch. 3; CDJSC 2008: xi). This enables the discourse of law reform to register both the differential effects of rape and sexual violence on the various segments of the community, while at the same time promoting the protection of the vulnerable in gender-neutral terms. The *experiences* of survivors of sexual violence are increasingly presented in the fragmented but juridical terms of *status* – gender, sexual orientation, class, ethnicity, age, cognitive disability, and so on in a proliferating series of group identities. Yet, as Laura Hengehold has demonstrated in her analysis of a woman's decision to define an event as rape, 'this decision places her at the crossroads of conflicting popular and expert attitudes regarding the meaning of sexuality and justice' (2000: 191).

The third critical period is constituted by the contemporary politics of rape law reform. It takes up the increasing fragmentation of survivor experience and reiterates it. This is done in the language of *the rights of the victim*. The justification of the need for, and objectives of, rape law reform is now phrased in terms of a discourse of public health and human rights.

Consider the most recent legislative reform of sexual offences in Victoria. The first objective is stated to be 'to uphold the fundamental right of every person to make decisions about his or her sexual behaviour and to choose not to engage in sexual activity'. A second objective is stated as: 'to protect children and persons with a cognitive impairment from sexual exploitation' (Crimes Act 1958 (Vic.), section 37A). On its face, there is clearly some tension here between the declaration of fundamental rights and the declaration of victims' rights. This is symptomatic of a more widespread tension between the universality of human rights and the concreteness of the legal practices in which it emerges, as well as the embedded quality of the social practices it wants to manage (Douzinas 2000). But what can be noted is the way the discourse of fundamental rights functions to subsume the factual heterogeneity of survivors under the *general* category of the vulnerable. The new legislative regime in Victoria not only enacts 'objectives' but also what it calls 'guiding principles' for the interpretation of the legislation. These guiding principles are presented as condensations of social scientific facts: there is a high incidence of sexual violence, an underreporting of sexual offences, a significant number of offences are against women, children and people with a cognitive impairment, and so on (section 37B). These facts have been amply demonstrated in the existing research and reform literature. What can be noted in this legislative context, however, is that women are positioned as one more instance of the vulnerable – of a piece with children and those with cognitive impairment – which the language, policy and legislation promises to protect. Fundamental rights appear as the rights of the vulnerable human, but not quite as the rights of women as such (MacKinnon 2006).

In addition to, and alongside, this discourse of fundamental human rights, there has emerged a discourse of public health. Sexual violence is presented as a problem of the costs to the community. It places a burden on health services, as well as criminal justice agencies. Thus, regulation and prevention are said to reduce the institutional and communal burden of rape in a social situation of competing demands for scarce financial and human resources. This has a number of effects on rape law reform, most particularly the increasing dominance of the function of *auditing*. The task of reform is presented as the administration of bureaucratic institutions: managing and co-ordinating the heterogeneous institutions that concern themselves with the treatment, care, counselling and protection of victims. All that remains to be done by the practice of reform is to smooth out the gaps and overlaps between these institutions. As one recent Victorian report put it, the aim is to create 'a single unit providing victims with a consistent and seamless service' (Heenan and Murray 2006: 9; see also CDJSC 2008).

What can we take from this brief history? The contemporary discourse of rape law reform proceeds with a pragmatic amalgam of formal gender-neutrality and the empirically differentiated statuses of the vulnerable victim – be she gendered or otherwise. Instead of a vindication of the rights of women and their participation in the communal life of Australia, what has emerged as dominant in contemporary projects of rape law reform is a discourse of public health and human rights, which construes the task of reform as a managerial one of auditing social facts and co-ordinating institutional heterogeneity. In all this, the gendered ordering of sexual relations is presented as external to law, albeit that law has an impact on the social facts of rape. More worrying still, perhaps, survivors of sexual violence can only be heard in law and in reform campaigns if their experiences as survivors can be rephrased in the juridical language of vulnerable victims.

The shape of rape law reform in Australia is not only a matter of its history, but also of the forms of knowledge which it uses or authorizes. As is to be expected in a country where there are some nine criminal jurisdictions, the authorized forms of knowledge are plural. However, in the context of rape law reform, two related discourses of knowledge are prominent – increasingly since the 1980s, the social scientific registration of rape, as well as policy discourses and advocacy, have come to dominate the field.

The methods and assumptions of social science have provided reform with a powerful instrument through which to document the incidence and prevalence of rape, and to hold the legal institution to account for its response thereto. The current statistics on the incidence and prevalence of rape and sexual violence in Australia show nothing particularly remarkable in global terms. Official crime statistics display low rates until the 1970s, when there is a sharp increase. From the 1980s onwards, the incidence of rape recorded in official statistics and victim surveys has increased in leaps and bounds. Moreover, the number of victims of sexual assault has steadily increased over the last decade (AIC 2009: 24). The actual number of sexual assaults reported has also increased over the same period. Since 1995, the annual increase has been 4 per cent each year; the total increase being 51 per cent. The primary jurisdictions responsible for the reported sexual assaults are Victoria, NSW, SA, Queensland and WA. In 2006, these states – both common-law and code jurisdictions – accounted for some 95 per cent of all reported assaults (AIC 2009). Victims of sexual assault and the survivors of sexual violence are overwhelmingly female – albeit that, as the Personal Safety Survey indicates, sexual assault against men is significant. Some 42,300 men aged 18 and over experienced sexual assault in one year; some 44 per cent of these men experienced sexual assault by a family member or friend; 35 per cent by a person who was known to them (but not family or friend) and 33 per cent by a stranger (ABS 2006).

Social scientific research has not only documented the incidence or prevalence of sexual assault, it has also audited the institutional response of criminal justice agencies and services. Numerous investigations of the attrition process have been conducted by independent researchers as well as by the various Law Reform Commissions. It remains the case in Australia that the institutional and public meaning of rape continues to be structured by a process of *filtering out* at all stages of the criminal justice process: survivors are discouraged from reporting, complainants are encouraged to withdraw their complaints, charges are unauthorized, prosecutions are not brought, acquittal rates are high, and appeals are often unsuccessful. While there are problems with the ways in which the studies of attrition represent the relations between legal institutions in a largely linear and pyramidal fashion (Bluett-Boyd et al. forthcoming), one effect on the enterprise of rape law reform has been that the more attrition is noted, the more the objective of reform is represented as being to *increase conviction* rates. This sets the agenda, and all too frequently the counter-response has been to devalue the reforming effort by restaging the demand of rape law reform in terms of a polemical dispute in which it is argued by opponents of reform that the rights of the victim are being claimed at the expense of the rights of the accused.

In sum, the form of knowledge which has ordered the enterprise of rape law reform has shifted. Initially, what was required of the reformer was a knowledge of the legal rules and their place within modern cultures of criminal responsibility. As the above indicates, however, this has receded, and what occupies the foreground is a social scientific accounting of the incidence, prevalence and institutional responses which shape the observable facts of sexual violence. The doctrinal categories and classifications of the criminal law of rape have receded into the background and what sets the scene of rape law reform is the social scientific understanding of law and of rape.

The results of social scientific research on sexual violence have provided a powerful voice for policy discourse and the demands of advocacy. Government-funded research institutions such as the Australian Institute of Criminology and the Australian Centre for the Study of Sexual Assault have engaged in social science research with a view to shaping public policy on sexual violence. At the same time, policy advocacy has formed part of the remit of women's activism around sexual violence. Rape Crisis Centres, Centres Against Sexual Assault and women's refuges were amongst a patchwork of women's and feminist institutions concerned with increasing the participation of women in civil society. The gains of this institutional movement cannot be overestimated and remain a central feature of contemporary projects of law reform. What can be noted, though, is that the turn to policy advocacy has required feminist activists to engage with official governmental discourses in order to get things done for the benefit of women and the survivors of sexual violence. Thus, rape law reform has increasingly been framed by the facility with which feminist activists could constructively dialogue with the various state and federal governments, as well as the plural institutional arms of the criminal justice system. In turn, feminist activism – in the guise of rape law reform – has increasingly been subjected to governmental objectives of cost-effectiveness and efficiency (VLRC 2003: xii; see also Gottell in this collection).

## FROM SUBSTANTIVE LAW TO PROCEDURAL LAW

In this part of the chapter, I turn from the *overall* shape of the enterprise of rape law reform to a redescription of the *specific* issues of rape law which have engaged the attention of reform and its advocates. At this level, a tension can be discerned, I suggest, between reforming the substantive law of rape and altering the procedural laws which govern the institutional attribution of responsibility for rape. While this tension remains unresolved, and many of the specific reform efforts remain controversial, nevertheless the reforming enterprise now sees its task as primarily changing the procedures of rape law. The promise – not yet fulfilled – is that such changes can succeed where past efforts failed, as well as respond with respect to the plight of the vulnerable survivors of rape.

Let me begin with the substantive criminal law of rape. Much of the history of rape law reform in the various jurisdictions of Australian criminal law has focused its attention on the substantive law of rape and its allied sexual offences. The controversies are many. For example, some take up the language within which the law of crime is constructed. In some jurisdictions, sexual violence is named as 'rape' and in yet other instances as 'sexual assault'. This is more than a matter of semantics. Rather, it addresses the symbolic importance of the language of law, as well as seeks to register what is at stake in the legal regulation of sexual relations and social norms of sexual comportment. This attention to law's symbolic function has also led to reform attempts to recast the language of legal definition and justification in gender-neutral terms. The justification of the reformed laws of rape has been phrased in terms of protecting the autonomy and sexual choice of individuals. But while reform has succeeded in erasing the gender of rape from the *terms* of the legislative definitions, both the *syntax* of the statute (evident in the requirement of sexual penetration) as well as the language of judges and the legal profession generally continue to display a gendered approach to the substantive law of rape.

Reordering the way in which legal offences are put together has been the further concern of the reforming project. Remaining with the substantive law of rape, this has proceeded along at least two vectors: one, the divisions internal to the substantive law and, two, the definition of the offence of rape itself. Consider the divisions that internally structure the law of sexual offences. In overall terms, rape and indecent assault have provided the general offences. These have been supplemented by more specific offences – such as incest, administering a drug for the purposes of sexual penetration, abduction of a child and so on. This approach still informs some jurisdictions. However, the move of reform – especially when it takes the protection of victim's rights as its justification – has been to adopt an overarching division between general offences applicable to all (for example, rape and indecent assault) and offences specific to particular types of victims (for example, sexual offences against children and the cognitively impaired). These reforms have been informed by cultural debates around child (sexual) abuse and the prevalence of sexual abuse in educational, religious and welfare institutions. In this respect, the primary substantive division between offences of general application and offences of specific application is now drawn between 'lack of consent' as the gravamen of the offence and 'breach of trust' as the offence condition.

The substantive offence of rape remains as a general offence and its offence condition is the absence of consent. Nevertheless, reform has exercised considerable energy in contracting and expanding the *scope of the definition* of rape. Some reforms have concerned the act requirement. All jurisdictions in Australia have extended the prohibited acts beyond the common law's concern with 'carnal knowledge' (now: 'penile penetration of a vagina') so as to include anal, digital and oral penetration. While this was part and parcel of the move to formal gender-neutrality, it has had some unintended consequences. For example, the substantive distinction between rape and indecent assault is put under pressure. Procedurally, it has seen those charged with rape having the prosecution accept their plea of guilty to the lesser offence of indecent assault.

Attention has, however, mainly focused on the definitional requirement of non-consent. This has related to both the *actus reus* requirement and the *mens rea* requirement. In all Australian jurisdictions, the *actus reus* of rape presently requires proof that the sexual act of the accused took place without the complainant's consent. In this context, the reform of the substantive law has proceeded in two countervailing directions. One direction presumes that the complainant *was* consenting and then goes on to elaborate the observable circumstances which will be recognized by law as rebutting the presumption. Here, dispute has been engaged over which circumstances should be identified as vitiating consent – for example, whether consent must be by word or by conduct, and whether economic harm or coercion should be specified as a circumstance negating consent to sex. A countervailing direction in the reform of the *actus reus* of consent has used a positive standard of consent which presumes the complainant *was not* consenting to the particular sexual conduct of this particular accused. This positive standard of consent was introduced by reforming legislation in various jurisdictions (Victoria being at the forefront of this reform) and has generated what many have called a 'communicative model' of sexual relations. This model is registered in the statutory language of 'free and voluntary agreement'. But it remains to note that, in either direction, the *actus reus* of non-consent is construed as a prohibited *circumstantial* harm rather than as the prohibition of a *consequential* injury. The effect is that any reforms to the procedural law governing the prosecution and trial of rape have been shaped by this definitional structure. In fact, it is at least arguable – as suggested in the conclusion below – that this circumstantial orientation of substantive law goes some way to explaining the continued low rates of conviction for rape, despite the repeated reforms of the definition (for further discussion, see Rush and Young 1997, 2002). It can also go some way to giving an account of the experience, oft-remarked by survivors, that they had no voice, no space of expression, within which to register in the legal process their experience of rape.

The *mens rea* of rape has also provided a significant focus for the effort at reforming the substantive law. In the common-law jurisdictions, in contrast to the code jurisdictions, the prosecution must prove the indicia of a guilty mind, that is, either that the accused knew that the complainant was not or might not be consenting, or more recently in some jurisdictions, that the accused gave no thought to whether the complainant was consenting. In the Australian code jurisdictions, this requirement of a guilty mind is not required. Nevertheless, in both common-law and code states, a 'defence' of honest but mistaken belief in consent is available to the accused and it is this defence which has provided so much of the focus of law reform initiatives concerned with the *mens rea*. Reform advocacy has generally moved towards some modified form of 'objective' standard, with some success it must be said. In most instances now, the relevant state legislation requires that the honest belief be held on 'reasonable grounds' or, in some jurisdictions, that it be proven that the accused took 'reasonable steps' to ascertain the accuracy of his belief. Nevertheless, it has been repeatedly emphasized that these requirements do not permit an evaluation of the accused's belief by reference to the standard of the 'reasonable man'; the honest belief remains fully subjective. In this respect, and despite the reforms, the defence of honest belief in the circumstance of consent embeds in the very syntax of criminal law the narrative that 'no means yes' – or, in a technical idiom: 'I know now she was not consenting but at the time I believed that she was consenting and so for the purposes of the trial's determination of my mental liability the complainant must be taken as consenting.'

These, then, are some of the specific issues which have been broached in the reform of the substantive law of rape, and specifically its offence definition. None of the reforms to date have been an unparalleled success. In fact, each new change was prompted in the main by renewed evidence that, despite the reforms, the attrition rates for rape were unchanged, the experience of complainants in the hands of the criminal justice system was much the same, and the conviction rates for rape were not increasing to an extent comparable with non-sexual crimes. Faced with this evidence, the trend of the rape law reform project in recent years has been to give up on the substantive law: it might be part of the problem, but it is not seen to offer the solution to the failings of the criminal justice system. Rather, reforming the *procedural* practices of rape law is increasingly held out to be the main way to ameliorate the abuse of the rights and interests of the vulnerable victim that takes place every day in the institutions of law and of the community.

Procedural reform has addressed both the formal rules of evidence and the regulation of the occasion and manner of giving evidence, as well as the policies and practices of criminal justice institutions. The evidential rules of corroboration, recent complaint and admissibility of sexual history have been the subject of considerable efforts at reform. Perhaps less familiar have been those concerned with the manner of giving evidence. These have included the adverse impact of requiring the complainant to submit to witness examination twice – during committal proceedings and during trial. The well-documented problem here is that these examinations amount to gruelling – not to say vigorous – interrogations of the survivor which give rise to a second victimization. And it is along these lines that reform proposals have taken up and promoted – with some degree of success – the use of CCTV and other forms of video-assisted technology in order to lessen, if not erase, the trauma of police questioning as well as court examination. A third dimension of procedural reform takes up the ever-expanding remit of institutional engagement. There has emerged a thoroughgoing movement to address all criminal justice, medical and therapeutic services responding to sexual violence. This has been a matter of increasing co-ordination between heterogeneous agencies, as well as ensuring that individual institutions have models of 'best practice' in place. Programmes for ongoing education have been implemented, as have mechanisms for policy development and for auditing the implementation and effectiveness of the various changes. One procedural issue, however, that continues to create considerable difficulty is the confidentiality of therapeutic records of counsellors of sexual violence – and in particular, the right of defence lawyers to obtain and use these records to discredit the testimony of survivors during court hearings.

In sum, then, a shift can be discerned within Australian projects of rape law reform – from an emphasis on the substantive law of rape to the procedural and institutional arrangements that the incidence of rape sometimes triggers. Where the reform of substantive law was primarily directed at expanding the scope of the legal definition with a view to increasing the reach of the legal prohibition, by contrast, the objective of procedural reform has been to ameliorate or improve the experience of the rape survivor when she is brought before the law and its institutions of criminal justice. While this distinction between substantive legal definition and procedural reform makes considerable sense of the current situation and mood of the rape law reform project, it needs to be remembered that both dimensions – the substantive and the procedural – will at some point be joined, if not precisely identified, with each other. As such, the reform enterprise will have to deal with the fact that procedural reforms that are instituted will be shaped and limited by the framework of substantive law and its definitions of rape – just as the earlier prominence of substantive law reform has in many respects been wrecked on the shores of procedure.

In fact, it is this very necessity of relating the legal definitions of rape to the institutional procedures of rape law that is recognized by one of the more innovative reforms of rape law in Australia. This reform concerns the trial procedure of charging the jury, also known as the institution of the judicial direction to the jury. Initiated in Victoria in the 1990s by way of section 37 of the Crimes Act 1958 (Vic.), it provided a legislative statement of what a judge should and should not say – concerning evidence of consent – when charging the jury with its task. Although they are phrased as directions on the *substantive* law of rape, their legal model is derived from the reforms and debates concerning the *evidential* directions on corroboration and recent complaint. The justification for this reform was that the legislative form of these directions would send a message to the general public that 'it is not acceptable for men to cling to outdated myths about seduction, sexual conquest and female sexuality' (VLRC 1991: 16). However, the jury and general public are not the only addressees of this reform. It is legislation which, like the legislative and common law definitions of rape, is first and foremost directed to the speech of judges: its aim is to shape and limit the exercise of judicial discretion in both interpreting the legislated definition of rape and in charging the jury with its task. This is only confirmed by the most recent development in this vein: in Victoria again, sections 37A and 37B were introduced in 2006 to add further directions to judges (called 'objectives' and 'guidelines') which would once again restrict the exercise of judicial discretion in interpreting the meaning and effect of the reformed legislation.

This innovative strand of the reforming enterprise has not been without its failures and continuing controversies, not least because there have been judicial rulings on the meaning of key phrases in the legislated judicial directions. But what *is* recognized by this initiative is that substantive law (in the form of definitions of rape) and the laws of procedure *shape and limit each other* in fundamental ways in criminal law. Reforming rape law must be Janus-faced: looking both to the substantive law and to the laws of procedure. In this respect, the current shift in reform, which has resulted in a focus on the laws of procedure to the exclusion of almost all else in rape law, is fraught with peril. In fact, many of the current and continuing controversies in rape law in Australia are situated at the crossroads of the definitional and the institutional, the substantive and the procedural. Thus, reform turns away from substantive law at a price – a price which, arguably, will be exacted on, and paid for by, the experiences of survivors of rape once again.

## CONCLUSION

This chapter has been written in response to a sense that there has been a change in the form and idiom – what I have here called the 'shape' – of the enterprise of rape law reform. This has been evident in national as well as international jurisdictions. But my primary sense of a change has been in the Australian context, and specifically in the Victorian context, which is where I have participated most – or at least most recently – in the enterprise of rape law reform.

As this chapter has demonstrated, the main transformations in the Australian enterprise of rape law reform have been twofold. The oldest, in terms of gestation, has been the rise to prominence of social scientific forms of knowledge and research. This has given a voice of authority and legitimacy to many of the reforming efforts in Australia, and sometimes to the claims of the vulnerable survivors of rape. A second, and more recent, transformation has, I would suggest, emerged out of the reorientation of rape law reform around the authority of social science. This I identified as the turn away from the reform of substantive law of rape and towards the laws of procedure that impact on the survivor's encounter with the criminal justice system. Neither of these transformations has been without its controversies, its successes and its failures. Rather, they remain as the very condition of contemporary rape law reform in Australia. In this respect at least, my argument has been modest: namely, to the extent that current efforts at reforming rape law *abandon* the substantive law of rape in favour of the much-needed vagaries of procedural reform, then the controversies will continue to play themselves out in much the same way. And if the measure of the success of any rape law reform is the survivor's experience of the institutions of criminal law – which I believe it should be – then procedural reforms will be at best a partial success if they have not addressed and reformed the substantive law of rape in fundamental ways.

A conclusion is not the place to lay out in any detail what this might mean for making a way through the thickets of controversy that is rape law reform. But one suggestion that might provide further direction in rape law reform would be to reconstruct the syntax of the substantive definition of rape. The current syntax – not only in Australian law, but all common-law countries – is one which predicates the liability for the harm of rape on proof of the circumstances (lack of consent, and sometimes violence) in which the accused acted and his cognitive mental state as to that circumstantial lack of consent (or violence). This is in contrast to all the other serious offences against the person, where the law predicates the harm on proof of the consequences of the accused's actions (death, serious injury, and so on) and his mental state thereto. In short, rape is a crime of circumstance, whereas the offence structure of all other crimes of comparable seriousness (and even less gravity) constitute them as crimes of consequence (for elaboration of this argument and a reformed statutory definition of rape, see Rush and Young 1997, 2002). The effect is that the injury done by the accused to the victim of rape and experienced by the survivor appears nowhere in the substantive legal definition of rape. And it is, I suggest, this syntactical disappearance in law which continues to shape the enterprise of rape law reform, even and perhaps especially when the reforms abandon the law of definition in favour of working with the laws of procedure.

## Note

1  Acknowledgements are due to the editors for their comments on this chapter, as well as to the participants at the *Rethinking Rape Law* conference at Durham University. Thanks to Alison Young for her creative insights over many years and Nicole Bluett-Boyd for her research assistance.

## Bibliography

ABS (2006) *Personal Safety, Australia, 2005*, Canberra: Australian Bureau of Statistics.
AIC (2009) *Australian Crime: facts and figures 2008*, Canberra: Australian Institute of Criminology.
Bluett-Boyd, N., Rush, P. and Young, A. (forthcoming) 'The institutional life of sexual assault: attrition and the brief of evidence within the decisional field'.
Brown, W. (1995) *States of Injury: power and freedom in late modernity*, Princeton: Princeton University Press.
CDJSC (Community Development and Justice Standing Committee) (2008) *Inquiry into the Prosecution of Assaults and Sexual Offences*, Perth: Legislative Assembly, Parliament of Western Australia.
CLPMRC (Criminal Law and Penal Methods Reform Committee of South Australia) (1976) *Special Report: rape and other sexual offences*, Adelaide: Government Printer.
Douzinas, C. (2000) *The End of Human Rights: critical legal thought at the turn of the century*, Oxford: Hart Publishing.
Graycar, R. and Morgan, J. (1990) *The Hidden Gender of Law*, Sydney: Federation Press.

Heenan, M. and Murray, S. (2006) *Study of Reported Rapes in Victoria 2000–2003 (Summary Research Report, Statewide Steering Committee to Reduce Sexual Assault)*, Melbourne: Office of Women's Policy, Department for Victorian Communities.

Hengehold, L. (2000) 'Mapping the Event: institutional discourses and the trauma of rape', *Signs*, 26(1): 189–214.

MacKinnon, C. (2006) *Are Women Human? And other international dialogues*, Cambridge, MA: Belknap Press of Harvard University Press.

MCCOC (1999) *Chapter 5: Sexual Offences Against the Person, Final Report*, Canberra: Model Criminal Code Officers Committee of the Standing Committee of Attorneys-General.

Rush, P. and Young, A. (1997) 'A crime of consequence and a failure of imagination: the sexual offences of the model Criminal Code', *Australian Feminist Law Journal*, 9: 100–33.

—— (2002) 'Submission to VLRC in response to its reference on Sexual Offences; criminal law and procedure (2002)', unpublished (on file with authors).

Scutt, J. (ed.) (1980) *Rape Law Reform: a collection of conference papers*, Canberra: Australian Institute of Criminology.

VLRC (1991) *Rape: Reform of the Law and Procedure, Report No. 43*, Melbourne: Victorian Law Reform Commission.

—— (2003) *Sexual Offences: Law and Procedure, Interim Report*, Melbourne: Victorian Law Reform Commission.

Woods, G. (1981) *Sexual Assault Law Reform in NSW: a commentary on the Crimes (Sexual Assault) Amendment Act 1981 and Cognate Act*, Sydney: Department of the Attorney General and of Justice.

Young, A. (1998) 'The waste land of the law, the wordless song of the rape victim', *Melbourne University Law Review*, 22: 442–65.

Chapter 17

# Reforming the law of rape in South Africa

*Shereen W. Mills*

South Africa has amongst the highest levels of sexual violence in the world (Baden et al. 1998: 34; Albertyn et al. 2007: 301). The devastating effect of sexual violence on women and children has been recognized by the state, and in 1996 the South African Law Reform Commission (SALRC) was mandated to investigate sexual violence against children. This mandate was later extended to adults, with a complete overhaul of the criminal justice system envisaged, and much attention given to the substantive definition of rape (Naylor 2008: 42). This 11-year law reform process resulted in the Sexual Offences Act (Criminal Law (Sexual Offences and Related Matters) Amendment Act 32 of 2007) (hereafter 'the Act'), which was passed into law at the end of 2007.

Although somewhat limited in terms of the protections it offers to survivors of sexual violence, the Act introduces wide-ranging definitional changes, which are discussed below. The most important changes to the definition of rape can be found in the redefinition of consent and in the introduction of coercive circumstances, the existence of which negates consent. This chapter sets out the main changes to the definition of rape affected by the Act. It then examines the implications of this redefinition of rape, which both retains consent and simultaneously creates an area of presumed non-consent. In analysing the provisions of the Act with regard to consent, it is argued that the list of 'coercive circumstances' do not comprehensively reflect one of women's and girls' most common encounters with sexual coercion, which is rape by a perpetrator known to them, often in dating and marital relationships, and nor do they adequately take account of women's vulnerability to sexual exploitation in the face of extreme poverty (Jewkes and Abrahams 2002: 1232, 1234; Rasool et al. 2002: 52; Albertyn et al. 2007: 302; Vetten et al. 2008: 34). It is argued that the circumstances prescribed can (and should), however, be interpreted to take account of these contexts.

This argument is made in a context in which South African women are particularly vulnerable to sexual violence. As will be discussed further below, there is an extremely high incidence of rape, a high rate of under-reporting, low conviction rates, extreme poverty and unemployment, and high levels of sexual coercion in heterosexual relations. In addition, once women have been raped, they are vulnerable to secondary victimization and victim-blaming, because of the extent to which coercion has been normalized and the level of acceptance of rape myths (Jewkes and Abrahams 2002: 1232).

This chapter thus argues that in taking the new law forward, a more nuanced, contextual approach is needed, one that takes account of the imbalance resulting from unequal gender power relations in South African society (SALRC, *Discussion Paper 85*, 1999: para. 3.4.7.3.14). It is submitted that South Africa's constitutional commitment to gender equality, both as a right and as a value, makes it imperative that this is done.

## CONTEXT OF RAPE IN SOUTH AFRICA

### Context and prevalence

The nature and extent of gender-based violence in South Africa must be understood in its historical, political and social context. South Africa is a young democracy, having achieved liberation from the oppressive racial regime of apartheid in 1994, with one of the most progressive Constitutions (Act 108 of 1996) in the world. Despite a peaceful transition to democracy, the levels of gender-based violence in South Africa are extremely high. The impact of the joint legacies of colonization and apartheid on black women has been to increase their vulnerability to gender-based violence (Bonthuys et al. 2005: 342). However, the intersection of patriarchal traditions, with cultural and religious customs, has tended to subordinate women of all race and class groups, with violence embedded in sexual relationships (Albertyn et al. 1999: 112).

Official statistics on reported rapes stand at 55,000 for the year 2005/06, with it being estimated that only one in nine rapes involving physical force are reported to police (Jewkes and Abrahams 2002: 1236; Smythe and Waterhouse 2008: 200). This does not take account of incidents involving other forms of sexual coercion. Thus, the vast majority of rapes never come to the attention of the criminal justice system (Jewkes and Abrahams 2002: 1232–4; Vetten et al. 2008: 16; Smythe and Waterhouse 2008: 199–200). The very high prevalence of rape largely reflects a high level of social tolerance of the crime, as well as high acceptance of rape myths in communities and in society generally (Jewkes and Abrahams 2002: 1232, 1240). South Africa thus fits the definition of a 'rape-prone' society (Albertyn et al. 2007: 300–1). Notions of male sexual entitlement feature strongly in the dominant social constructions of masculinity in South Africa. Both sexual and physical violence against women form part of 'a repertoire of strategies of control' (Jewkes and Abrahams 2002: 1238). Perceptions of 'ownership' of female sexuality by men are pervasive. Studies show a high level of coerced sex in intimate partnerships, and that sexual violence has become so normalized that women have come to accept a level of coercion in their relationships (Jewkes and Abrahams 2002: 1237–8). The effect of poverty on rape adds to the complexity. Poverty increases the likelihood that women will engage in subtle forms of transactional sex. An exchange element in sexual relationships is very common, particularly amongst young people, with a heavy premium placed on having a partner with economic resources (Jewkes and Abrahams 2002: 1239). In circumstances of economic dependency, women find it very difficult to protect themselves from sexual exploitation and very often have to tolerate abuse. Finally, popular ideas of rape as being a violent attack by a stranger or gang are reflected in only a very small proportion of women's experiences of coerced sex. Most rape is by a perpetrator known to the victim (Jewkes and Abrahams 2002: 1232-4; Rasool et al. 2002: 52; Albertyn et al. 2007: 302; Vetten et al. 2008: 34).

## Attrition in the criminal justice system

Not only does South Africa have a high rate of underreporting, it also has high rates of attrition when women encounter the criminal justice system (Artz and Smythe 2007: 166-71; Vetten et al. 2008: 14-23; Smythe and Waterhouse 2008: 204-7). The first point at which cases are lost is when the victim decides whether or not to report the rape. The actual moment of reporting is the second point, when police turn away complaints and complainants that they do not regard as credible (Vetten et al. 2008: 16). High acceptance of rape myths in South African society means that police are particularly prone to believing that women lie easily about rape, and that where there are no signs of violence it is unlikely that rape has occurred (Smythe and Waterhouse, 2008: 199). Vetten et al.'s 2008 study on attrition rates in Gauteng province shows, from a survey of studies done in South Africa and other jurisdictions, that there are a number of factors that affect a victim's credibility before the police, most commonly prior consensual sex (Vetten et al. 2008: 22-3). There is some evidence to suggest that the nature of the relationship with the accused affects police willingness to accept and investigate rape reported by women against their former boyfriends (Francis 2000: 9-11). The use of a weapon and/or the use of force and the amount of resistance shown by the victim are also important indicators of the likelihood of arrest in rape cases (Artz and Combrinck 2003: 90).

Vetten et al.'s 2008 study shows that of the total number of rape complaints reported to the police in Gauteng, 17 per cent proceeded to trial and only 4 per cent resulted in a conviction for rape. This is in comparison to a national average conviction rate of 7.7 per cent for rape. The majority of rape cases are lost during police investigation, with 82 per cent of complaints 'falling out' of the system when cases are closed by the police (Vetten et al. 2008: 46).

## Government policy and civil society responses

In contrast to the period prior to the transition to democracy, in which violence against women was not a policy priority, post-transition, the South African government has expressed, and continues to express, its commitment to dealing with the problem. Section 12(1)(c) of the Bill of Rights in the Constitution of the Republic of South Africa 108 of 1996 explicitly guarantees the right to freedom from all forms of violence from either public or private sources (Combrinck 2005: 172). The government established the Commission on Gender Equality as well as the Office for the Status of Women as part of its national gender machinery. Parliament made violence against women a particular focus of concern in both the Portfolio Committee of Justice and the Committee on the Quality of Life and Status of Women. In 1996, the government drafted the National Crime Prevention Strategy which also gave priority to the issue. An array of policy and legislation has since been formulated by the State to provide services in the criminal justice system and health sector to victims of sexual offences. Lamentably, however, these have not been entirely effective (Albertyn et al. 1999: 112; Vetten 2000b: 92–4). Implementation remains a problem for a number of reasons, including victim-blaming attitudes (Smythe and Waterhouse 2008: 210). The continued high levels of sexual violence attest to the fact both that the law is not doing enough to prevent such violence, and that while the law can set new standards, more is needed to change entrenched social norms (Vetten 2000a: 75)

In civil society, NGOs (particularly women's organizations) and the government formed a partnership via the National Network Against Violence Against Women (Baden et al. 1998: 35). Not only did women's organizations create and sustain networks on violence against women, they were also active in organizing public awareness campaigns, assisting victims, litigating and engaging in advocacy and lobbying for new legislation. Such large-scale mobilization around the problem of violence against women was a new phenomenon in South Africa (Vetten 2000b: 102). As a result, women's organizations have been influential in shaping the law on violence against women, both domestic violence and sexual violence, around a feminist agenda. For example, in 2003, women's organizations and other NGOs came together to form the National Working Group on Sexual Offences, to campaign around, and raise awareness of, the Sexual Offences Bill, bringing rape to the forefront of public consciousness. The 2007 Sexual Offences Act was at least in part a result of the engagement of the Working Group with the SALRC and with parliament (Vetten 2009). Despite these gains, the controversial 2006 rape case of *S v Zuma* ((2006) 3 All SA 8), which involved South Africa's then Deputy-President, now President of the country, illustrated to feminists that, while much had changed in law, not much has changed in society. The so-called 'common-sense' approach to law espoused in the *Zuma* judgment relied on a number of dominant social attitudes and myths about male and female sexuality (Kelly 2001: 32), to the extent that the rape was rendered invisible. Public discourse was heavily influenced by notions such as that the complainant was 'asking for it' by wearing a kanga (a sarong-like wrap), or that the perpetrator could not be expected to restrain himself (Mills 2007: 2).

## CURRENT LAW

Until the Sexual Offences Act came into force in 2007, the crime of rape was defined in the common law as 'unlawful, intentional sexual intercourse with a woman without her consent' (Burchell 2006: 162). Sexual intercourse was defined as vaginal penetration by a penis. The actor was thus conceived of as male. No other form of sexual activity, no matter how invasive or degrading, qualified as rape. Penetration by other body parts or objects – or oral or anal penetration, which are often the reality of rape for women – were excluded. Forced anal penetration of a man was classified as a form of indecent assault (Naylor 2008: 24–5). This reflects the fact that the offence of rape was historically formulated to protect the economic interests of husbands and fathers, and hence the value placed on the chastity of a woman. The patriarchal interest in controlling women's sexuality dominated over an interest in protecting the sexual autonomy of women per se (Artz and Combrinck 2003: 79).

A stated aim of the 2007 Act is to criminalize all forms of sexual abuse and exploitation. In relation to rape, the Act repealed the common law and replaced it with an expanded statutory offence that encompasses a number of penetrative acts, including oral and anal penetration and penetration by objects, thereby moving away from the archaic notion of rape as penetration of a vagina by a penis. The Act is more inclusive in that it now recognizes rape of men and boys. It can also be said to reflect more accurately the reality of rape for many women and girls, and thus to increase victims' access to the criminal justice system (Artz and Combrinck 2003: 84). The Act also created a range of other sexual offences with great specificity, particularly with regard to children (CALS and Tshwaranang 2009: 8–12).

## Constitutional framework

These reforms of the law of rape have taken place within a particular constitutional context (Constitution of the Republic of South Africa Act 108 of 1996). The right to equality (section 9), the right to dignity (section 10) and the right to freedom and security of the person, including specifically freedom from violence from both public and private sources (section 12(1)(b)), have informed the law reform process. The understanding of equality developed by the Constitutional Court is that of substantive equality, which takes account of the context of women's lives (Albertyn and Goldblatt 1998 and 2008: 35–6). Relatively early on in its adjudication, in a groundbreaking case involving the duty of the state to protect women from sexual violence, the Constitutional Court recognized the gravity of sexual violence and its effect on women's rights: 'sexual violence and the threat [thereof] goes to the core of women's subordination in society. It is the single greatest threat to the self-determination of South African women' (*Carmichele v Minister of Safety and Security, Minister of Justice (Centre for Applied Legal Studies intervening)* 2001 (4) SA 938 (CC): para. 45). It has, however, proved difficult to translate women's rights into practice in a society that continues to devalue women's right to be free from sexual coercion.

## Law reform process

The original intention of the SALRC, in initiating its review of the law of rape, was that consent would no longer be an element of the crime (although still a defence) and that the focus would be instead on coercive circumstances (Albertyn et al. 2007: 316–17). The Commission noted in this regard that:

> A shift from 'absence of consent' to 'coercion' represents a shift of focus of the utmost importance from the subjective state of mind of the victim to the imbalance of power between the parties on the occasion in question. This perspective also allows one to understand that coercion constitutes more than physical force or threat thereof, but may also include various other forms of exercise of power over another person: emotional, psychological, economical, social or organisational power.
> (SALRC Sexual Offences: Substantive Law *Discussion Paper 85* 1999, 114: para. 3.4.7.3.14)

The list of coercive circumstances that was envisaged included the use of force, threat of harm and abuse of power or authority, as well as unlawful detention and circumstances pertaining to fraud and capacity (Naylor 2008: 43). Significantly, the notion of abuse of power or authority that the Commission identified and supported is wider than in the preceding case law, as it envisages a range of contexts where abuse of power can be found to have taken place other than in an institutional setting.

In the draft Bill appended to the Commission's 2002 discussion paper (SALRC Sexual Offences: Practice and Procedure *Discussion Paper 102*, 2002), and in the first draft Sexual Offences Bill (B50-2003), three broad categories of coercive circumstances were set out in detail, namely, use of force, threat of harm and abuse of power or authority. These were labelled as coercive circumstances which rendered the act of penetration prima facie unlawful. Unlawful detention was thus omitted. Alongside this, fraud and incapacity were also deemed circumstances that rendered the act prima facie unlawful. It was taken as given that consent would not be an element of the definition of rape (Albertyn et al. 2007: 317; Naylor 2008: 46–8).

However, when the 2003 draft Bill was tabled in parliament, much debate ensued about the necessity to move from a consent model to one grounded in coercive circumstances. The Chairperson of the Parliamentary Portfolio Committee held the strong view that there was no need to make this move. In a context in which the SALRC had so thoroughly canvassed the issue of consent, working together with women's organizations on this proposed definitional shift, this turn of events had not been anticipated by campaigners and activists (Naylor 2008: 49).

In 2006, a revised draft of the Bill (B-2006) was tabled in parliament. In drafting it, the Parliamentary Portfolio Committee decided to retain the common-law position with regard to consent and to draw all the different circumstances which would not amount to consent into one single provision, as circumstances which would vitiate consent – a trend which it held was reflected internationally (Naylor 2008: 48) Under this formulation, if any of the coercive circumstances are proven, the act will amount to rape. The element of consent is retained in the definition of rape and other sexual offences, together with a list of coercive circumstances, which are designed to take account of the power imbalance between the parties. Thus, the Act defines rape as 'an act of sexual penetration without the consent' of the complainant (section 3), and consent is understood to involve 'voluntary or uncoerced agreement' (section 1(2)). Alongside this, the Act also identifies, in section 1(3), a non-exhaustive list of circumstances 'in respect of which a person does not voluntarily and without coercion agree to an act of sexual penetration', that is, coercive circumstances where consent is vitiated, namely:

(a) Where B (the complainant) submits or is subjected to such a sexual act as a result of – i) the use of force or intimidation by A (the accused person) against B, C (a third person) or D (another person) or against the property of B, C or D, or (ii) a threat of harm by A against B, C or D or against the property of B, C or D;
(b) where there is an abuse of power or authority by A to the extent that B is inhibited from indicating his or her unwillingness or resistance to the sexual act, or unwillingness to participate in such a sexual act;
(c) where the sexual act is committed under false pretences or by fraudulent means, including where B is led to believe by A that – (i) B is committing such a sexual act with a particular person who is in fact a different person; or (ii) such a sexual act is something other than that act; or
(d) where B is incapable in law of appreciating the nature of the sexual act, including where B is, at the time of the commission of such sexual act – (i) asleep; (ii) unconscious; (iii) in an altered state of consciousness, including under the influence of any medicine, drug, alcohol or other substance, to the extent that B's consciousness or judgment is adversely affected; (iv) a child below the age of 12 years; or (v) a person who is mentally disabled.

The Act in its final form retains the 'use of force, threat of harm and abuse of power' formulation of previous drafts. However, 'coercive circumstances' now subsumes all categories under it, including fraud and incapacity. The ground of 'abuse of power or authority' is the most innovative. It covers situations where the perpetrator abuses a position which inhibits the victim from indicating her or his unwillingness. It recognizes that women and young girls and boys, and in certain circumstances, men, may find it hard to say 'no' in situations where there is an imbalance of power. The most obvious examples are institutional settings such as school, work and prison. However, it is clear that it was the intention of the SALRC that abuse of power or authority be interpreted widely to include 'various other forms of exercise of power', namely, 'emotional, psychological, economic, social, and organizational power', as set out above (SALRC Sexual Offences: Substantive Law Discussion Paper 85 1999, 114: para. 3.4.7.3.14).

### Interpreting consent and coercion

The implications of this legislative model, which retains consent voluntarily given and, at the same time, creates an area of presumed non-consent, are potentially far-reaching. The offence of rape was historically construed narrowly, confined to situations where the woman's resistance was overcome by physical force or violence, and non-consent was proved by physical resistance. It was later widened to include fraud and deception, and force was no longer required (Artz and Combrinck 2003: 79; Burchell 2006: 708). Although in theory physical resistance or expressly stated or shouted opposition was not required in law, force and resistance requirements were often used to interpret whether the act was consensual (Naylor 2008: 26). At common law, circumstances that rendered consent invalid included fear induced by violence or threats. Even in the absence of threat, consent would be deemed to be invalid where there was the apprehension of power to harm in a manner other than physical. This was so in *S v S* (1971(2) SA 591 (A)), where a woman agreed to a policeman's demand for sexual intercourse because she believed he had the power to hurt her (Burchell 2006: 709–10; Snyman 2008: 447–8). To succeed as a defence, consent had to be consciously and voluntarily given (Snyman 2008: 447).

The new Act codifies the existing common law and develops it further by deeming certain specified circumstances to be coercive. First, by the specific inclusion of 'voluntary [free] agreement' the Act emphasizes sexual autonomy rights and allows a move towards a wider understanding of rape which incorporates a positive consent standard whereby only 'yes means yes'. Affirmative permission, through words or conduct, requires that any person who engages in intercourse shows full respect for the other person's autonomy (Kelly 2001: 40; Wright 2001: 177; see also Munro in this collection). This assists in giving effect to the right of South African women to be free from all forms of violence from either public or private sources (section 12(1)(c)). While this approach takes us far, it is submitted that it does not take us far enough. As Catharine MacKinnon points out, 'until equality exists not even "yes" can reliably mean "yes". "Yes" can be coerced. It can be the outcome of forced choices, precluded options, constrained alternatives, as well as adaptive preferences conditioned by inequalities' (MacKinnon 2005: 246).

Secondly, by requiring that the agreement be, in the alternative, 'uncoerced', and by setting out a non-exhaustive list of the circumstances in which voluntary agreement will be absent and coercion will be deemed to have occurred, including use of force, threat of harm and abuse of power or authority, the Act recognizes that there are circumstances where consent is vitiated, where even 'yes' cannot be said to mean 'yes'. This focus on context has the potential to allow us to redefine rape to take account of the reality of women's lives on an individual level and on the level of systemic inequality, giving effect to the right to gender equality. An example of this would be to look at the ways in which poverty increases women's vulnerability to sexual violence – how their economic dependence in relationships or their economic need generally may compromise them in sexual relations (Jewkes and Abrahams 2002: 1239–40).

Thirdly, in interpreting coercive circumstances, our starting point is that South African law currently recognizes that 'coercion' goes beyond the listed grounds of 'use of force' or 'threat of harm'. With regard to the latter, criminal law scholars in South Africa have argued that the listed ground of 'threat of harm' can be interpreted to include emotional harm or economic hardship (Artz and Combrinck 2003: 89). For example, it is argued that threat of violence against another in a close relationship or threat of the loss of a job should be recognized as duress that negates consent (Burchell 2006: 709–10; Snyman 2008: 448).

South African courts have also recognized that abuse of power or authority can vitiate consent. There are a number of early Appeal Court cases in the Appellate Division where the accused, instead of relying on physical force or threat thereof, abused an imbalance of power between himself and the victim in order to force the victim to submit to sexual intercourse (*S v Swiggelaar* 1950 1 PH H61 (A)). In *S v Volschenk* ([208] 1968 2 PH H283 (D)), the threat to lay a criminal charge by a policeman vitiated consent. In *S v S* (1971 (2) SA 591 (A)), the policeman made no threat but the woman believed he had the power to harm her. In this case, the court went so far as to take account of the racial power dynamics at play (Artz and Combrinck 2003: 89) in assessing whether or not her consent should be deemed to be genuine.

As the courts have already recognized the effect of an imbalance of power on consent in an institutional or organizational context, the development of a broader interpretation of abuse of power, as envisaged by the SALRC to include emotional, psychological, economic and social contexts is the next step. It is argued that the SALRC formulation of abuse of power or authority can – and should – be interpreted to take account of unequal power in relationships, as well as systemic power imbalances, in particular those generated by the economic vulnerability of women in situations of poverty and inequality. It entails developing an approach that takes account of the many ways in which women, especially young women in South Africa, are rendered vulnerable to sexual violence. A significant proportion of sexual coercion is committed in dating and marital relationships (Jewkes and Abrahams 2002: 1238). While women are in theory protected from these acts of sexual violence by the law, in practice police and other players in the criminal justice system are reluctant to believe such claims (Smythe and Waterhouse 2008: 199; Vetten et al. 2008: 22–3; Francis 2000: 9–11).

It is up to the courts to recognize that the dynamics of unequal power, and especially economic dependency, may prevent women from saying 'no' in these situations. Further, in situations of poverty, women are more likely to put themselves at risk by submitting to sexual interaction out of desperation. In the case of *Egglestone v S*, decided before the implementation of the Act, in which teenage women from impoverished communities were recruited as escort agency prostitutes, the court explicitly took account of how poverty rendered the women vulnerable to sexual exploitation ([2008] 4 All SA 207 (SCA) 216).

Finally, it is worth noting that the list of coercive circumstances is not exhaustive, leaving room for the development of other circumstances that may take account of the larger context of the systemic vulnerability of girls and women to rape, given their unequal status in society.

As to the relationship between consent and coercion, the positive formulation of the Act, which lists circumstances 'in respect of which a person does not voluntarily and without coercion agree to an act of sexual penetration', provides support for the proposition that where the state proves the existence of coercive circumstances, absence of consent should not be an issue at trial. It can, however, still be raised as a defence, leading South African commentators to argue that the new formulation will do little to take the focus away from consent. This is because in jurisdictions where law reform has attempted to shift the focus of the trial to coercive circumstances, consent has remained an issue (Artz and Combrinck 2003: 88; Naylor 2008: 27).

## CONCLUSIONS

The challenge for feminist lawyers in South Africa is huge. Now that the substantive law of rape has been reformed, it is necessary to ensure the development of the definitions of consent and coercion by the courts, in a way that transforms rape law to protect women's sexual autonomy and give effect to their constitutional rights. Without the will to make the substantive law truly transformative, the new Act is likely to be applied in the old way. South Africa's new legislative regime symbolizes a shift in how we understand rape in the South African context. By deeming certain circumstances (wider than set out in case law) to be coercive, and thus evidence of non-consensual sex, the new Act recognizes that an imbalance of power between the parties can operate to vitiate consent, so that the victim submits rather than consents (Artz and Combrinck 2003: 88). What is envisaged here is that the court would be required to interrogate the circumstances in which the rape occurred, taking account of the wider context of unequal power relations, gender inequality, poverty and vulnerability. This context should inform the courts' understanding of the individual circumstances of each case. This would conceivably allow the court to find coercion in circumstances of rape where there was an intimate relationship, the unequal dynamics of which prevented the complainant from saying 'no'. In addition, courts would be able to take account of situations where economic dependency or the desperation of poverty prevented the complainant from saying 'no'. Particularly given its social and economic context, it is important that South Africa adopts an approach to rape law that has as its starting point the need to redress the inherent inequality of women. Exploring whether consent was voluntarily obtained forms part of the broader enquiry into coercion and context.

If one accepts that the role of rape law is to define the conduct of sexual relations, not simply to perpetuate the status quo (Estrich 1986: 1180), then it is clear that the courts need a nuanced understanding of the complexity of the context of rape and inequality in South Africa in order to understand the circumstances in which women may submit through coercion. The imperative of substantive equality requires an interpretation and development of the law that reflects the reality of women's experiences – including the pernicious effect of rape, and how it reinforces women's unequal position in society (Albertyn and Goldblatt 2008: 35–60). Such an interpretation will also help to shape our understanding of the right to freedom and security of the person, specifically the right to freedom from violence from public and private sources, and to give effect to the obligation of the state to protect women from sexual violence.

## Bibliography

Albertyn, C., Artz, L., Combrinck, H. et al. (2007) 'Women's freedom and security of the person', in E. Bonthuys and C. Albertyn (eds) *Gender, Law and Justice*, Cape Town: Juta, 295–381.

Albertyn, C. and Goldblatt, B. (1998) 'Facing the challenge of transformation: difficulties in the development of an indigenous jurisprudence of equality', *South African Journal of Human Rights*, 14 (2): 24–76.

—— (2008) 'Equality', in S. Woolman, T. Roux, and M. Bishop (eds) *Constitutional Law of South Africa*, Cape Town, 2nd edn, Vol. 2: Juta, 35-1 – 35-85.

Albertyn, C., Goldblatt, B., Hassim, S. et al. (1999) *Engendering the Political Agenda: a South African case study*, Johannesburg: Centre for Applied Legal Studies, 1–140.

Artz, L. and Combrinck, H. (2003) 'A wall of words: redefining the offence of rape in South African law', in J. Burchell and A. Erasmus (eds) *Criminal Justice in a New Society*, Cape Town: Juta, 72–91.

Artz, L. and Smythe, D. (2007) 'Case attrition in rape cases: a comparative analysis', *South African Journal of Criminal Justice*, 20(2): 158–81.

Baden, S., Hassim, S. and Meintjes, S. (1998) *Country Gender Profile; South Africa*, Brighton: Institute of Development Studies, 1–125.

Bonthuys, E., Field, T.L., Mills, S., Pieterse-Spies, A. and Wolhuter, L. (2005) 'Gender', in W.A. Joubert (ed.) *The Law of South Africa*, Durban: LexisNexis Butterworths, 277–386.

Burchell, J. (2006) *Principles of Criminal Law*, Cape Town: Juta.

Centre for Applied Legal Studies and Tshwaranang Legal Advocacy Centre (2009) *A Summary of the Criminal Law Sexual Offences Amendment Act 32 of 2007*, Johannesburg: Centre for Applied Legal Studies, 1–32.

Combrinck, H. (2005) 'The dark side of the rainbow: violence against women in South Africa after ten years of democracy', in C. Murray and M. O'Sullivan (eds) *Advancing Women's Rights: the first decade of democracy*, Cape Town: Juta, 171–99.

Estrich, S. (1986) 'Rape', *Yale Law Journal*, 95: 1087–184.

Francis, V.A. (2000) *Rape Investigation in the Western Cape: a study of the treatment of rape victims at three police stations in the Cape Flats*, 1–20 (unpublished).

Jewkes, R. and Abrahams, N. (2002) 'The epidemiology of rape and sexual coercion in South Africa: an overview', *Social Science and Medicine*, 55: 1231–44.

Kelly, L. (2001) *Routes to Injustice: a research review on the reporting, investigation and prosecution of rape cases*, London: University of North London, Child and Woman Abuse Studies Unit, 1–48.

MacKinnon, C. (2005) *Women's Lives, Men's Laws*, Cambridge, MA: Harvard University Press.

Mills, S. (2007) 'Telling stories: metaphors, myths, and stereotypes in the *Zuma* Rape Trial', unpublished book project on *Zuma Rape Trial*, Pretoria: Human Sciences Research Council (HSRC), 1–14.

Naylor, N. (2008) 'The politics of a definition', in L. Artz and D. Smythe (eds) *Should We Consent: rape law reform in South Africa*, Cape Town: Juta, 22–51.

Rasool, S., Vermaak, K., Pharoah, R., Louw, A. and Stavrou, A. (2000) *Violence Against Women: a national survey*, Pretoria: Institute for Security Studies.

Smythe, D. and Waterhouse, S. (2008) 'Policing sexual offences: policies, practices and potential pitfalls', in L. Artz and D. Smythe (eds) *Should We Consent: rape law reform in South Africa*, Cape Town: Juta, 198–223.

Snyman, C.R. (2008) *Criminal Law*, Durban: LexisNexis.

Vetten, L. (2000a) 'Gender, race and power dynamics in the face of social change: deconstructing violence against women in South Africa' in Jung Park, Y., Fedler, J., and Dangor, Z. (eds) *Reclaiming Women's Spaces: new perspectives on violence against women and sheltering in South Africa*, Johannesburg: Nisaa Institute for Women's Development, 47–80.

—— (2000b) 'Paper promises, protests and petitions: South African state and civil society responses to violence against women' in Jung Park, Y., Fedler, J., and Dangor, Z. (eds) *Reclaiming Women's Spaces: new perspectives on violence against women and sheltering in South Africa*, Johannesburg: Nisaa Institute for Women's Development, 83–117.

—— (2009) personal e-mail communication to author, 6 July, on file with author.

Vetten, L., Jewkes, R., Sigsworth, R., Christofides, N., Loots, L. and Dunseith, O. (2008) *Tracking Justice: the attrition of rape cases through the criminal justice system in Gauteng*, Johannesburg: Tshwaranang Legal Advocacy Centre, the South

African Medical Research Council and the Centre for the Study of Violence and Reconciliation, 1–60.

Wright, J. (2001) 'Consent and sexual violence in Canadian public discourse: reflections on Ewanchuk', *Canadian Journal of Law & Society*, 16(2): 173–204.

Part IV

# New agendas and directions

Chapter 18

# Independent legal representation for complainants in rape trials

Fiona E. Raitt[1]

This chapter explores the potential for independent lawyers to provide advocacy and representation services for complainants of rape and other sexual offences. My focus is primarily on legal representation in adversarial systems drawing on examples from the UK, in particular Scotland. The issues are considered in the context of international concern about the problems associated with the investigation and prosecution of rape, including universally low reporting rates and high attrition rates for rape compared with other serious offences. Could legal representation for rape complainants have a positive impact on their treatment and on the prosecution of rape generally?

Over recent decades, the need for far greater consideration for victims of crime has dominated the international criminal justice agenda. In Western countries much political energy has been channelled into the project to 're-balance the criminal justice system' away from the perpetrator and towards victims (Doak 2008). In regard to the prosecution of rape, politicians point to substantial legal reforms to support and protect complainants. Policy documents, official guidelines, and protocols are awash with general reference to victims' 'rights', raising expectations of improved conditions, but this does not necessarily signify that these rights are substantive, enforceable or otherwise meaningful for rape victims. On the contrary, they may foretell profound disappointment and confusion once such complainants discover the nature of their 'rights' in a rape trial.

The outcomes are markedly poorer for rape victims within criminal justice systems that follow an adversarial tradition compared to those within inquisitorial systems. European countries with adversarial legal systems have higher attrition rates, and it is notable that the three exclusively adversarial systems in Europe – England and Wales, Scotland and Ireland – have the lowest conviction rates of all (Regan and Kelly 2003: 13). The features of the adversarial process that complainants experience as especially problematic include their lack of 'standing', the emphasis on orality, the rejection of narrative testimony, the focus on cross-examination as the apex of 'truth-seeking', the sense of detachment from the prosecutor and the non-interventionist role of the judge (for example Pizzi 1996; Temkin 2002a; Doak; 2005). In particular, complainants in adversarial systems are usually shocked to discover that they have no entitlement to separate representation (Adler 1987; Burman et al. 2007). Complainants describe the marginalization they experience – they are bit players in the drama of the trial while their private life and trauma are on public display at the bidding of lawyers whose primary interests lie either with the accused or with the wider public (Estrich 1987; Sebold 1999). This sense of alienation discourages complainants' engagement with the legal process and fuels their scepticism regarding the prospects of securing justice. It also reduces the possibility of securing best evidence from them. Although there is recognition that 'victims of violent crime have a stake in the trial that is different from that of the general public or even the prosecutor' (Pizzi 1999: 349), for victims in the adversarial system this does not translate into much that is concrete or adequate in terms of their ability to participate effectively.

One strategy adopted by some countries to compensate for the particular pressures placed upon rape victims has been to introduce some form of independent legal representation for complainants. Numerous models are in place, offering varying levels of intervention, from information and advice at the police station, to status as a secondary prosecutor during the trial (Bacik et al. 1998; Brienen and Hoegen 2000). This chapter is concerned with models of support that entitle independent lawyers to intervene on behalf of complainants to oppose actions by either the prosecution or the defence that may be disadvantageous to the complainant. The more obvious of these include applications for release from custody pending trial, plea bargaining, applications for recovery of personal records, or applications to introduce sexual character evidence. Such models are often viewed as a direct threat to the rights of the accused as their purpose is to challenge the conduct and tactics of the defence (Mosteller 1999), unlike the type of support provided by rape crisis centres and similar bodies, which is largely therapeutic and practical (Wilson 2005). I refer here to these legal models of support by the generic term independent legal representation (ILR).

I argue that ILR, if available from the point of reporting until the conclusion of the case, could make the single most significant contribution to the ability of rape complainants to withstand the legal process and give their best evidence at trial. Best evidence from witnesses is a central policy objective for every prosecution service and in itself is uncontroversial. However, the mechanisms by which prosecution authorities seek to secure best evidence will attract controversy when they appear to clash with accepted theoretical and procedural readings of due process (Young 2005). The received wisdom, at least from criminal bar practitioners in adversarial jurisdictions, is that the principles of equality of arms and the right of the accused to a fair trial are inimical to the extension of third-party legal representation for complainants (for example Greenspan 2001). The objection is that third-party representation elevates private interests to a par with those of the state, which contravenes criminal justice norms of public prosecution (Ashworth 1986). Space does not permit me to engage with the extensive debates concerning the threat victims' rights pose to due process. Suffice to say, the examples of third-party representation already functioning within adversarial jurisdictions have punctured that conceptual barrier. (For a more detailed account see Raitt, forthcoming.) In this chapter, I prefer to turn the tables to examine the role of the prosecutor in the rape trial and consider its compatibility with aspirations to assist the complainant to achieve best evidence. Before doing so, however, it is necessary to explore in a little more detail what is meant by ILR.

## THE FORM AND CHARACTERISTICS OF ILR

In those jurisdictions that grant complainants of sexual offences constitutional or statutory rights to legal assistance, it is evident that ILR comes in many diverse guises. In its most ambitious and arguably most effective form, proponents of ILR see its purpose as providing a complainant with a comprehensive source of legal advice, support, advocacy and representation from the initial decision to report a sexual assault through to any trial, appeal, parole considerations and compensation (Wilson 2005). However, few, if any, jurisdictions actually provide such a comprehensive service, not least because of the costs that would be incurred.

ILR is integral to the prosecution of violent crimes in continental European jurisdictions that largely adopt a judge-led inquisitorial approach. Some countries, such as Germany and Austria, confer upon the victim's lawyer the formal status of a second prosecutor (*Nebenklager*). In other jurisdictions, such as Belgium and France, the victim has *partie civile* status, which entitles them to a lawyer to pursue their civil claims, heard as part of the trial proceedings. The complainant's lawyer possesses similar rights of participation at trial as the prosecution and defence counsel. These include pre-trial rights of access to the evidence, the right to be present in court throughout the trial, the right to cross-examine the defendant, to make submissions on the law, and to address the court on the guilt or innocence of the defendant, compensation and sentence.

Much of the evolution of ILR in Europe has occurred following the Council of Europe's Recommendation 85(11) The Position of the Victim in the Framework of Criminal Law and Procedure (1985). Two major empirical studies have evaluated this Recommendation. The larger study involved 22 European jurisdictions and was principally concerned with reporting on progress for victims generally (Brienen and Hoegen 2000). The smaller study involved the (then) 15 member states of the EU. Five of these states were in-depth participants: Belgium, Denmark, France, Germany and the Republic of Ireland, with the other countries responding to a questionnaire. With the exception of England and Wales and the Republic of Ireland, *every* country gave complainants some form of entitlement to legal representation (Bacik et al. 1998, from here on 'the Irish study').

The Irish study found compelling evidence of the potential benefits for complainants of ILR. The researchers' conclusions are worth repeating in full here:

A highly significant relationship was found to exist between having a lawyer, and overall satisfaction with the trial process. The presence of a victim's lawyer also had a highly significant effect on victims' level of confidence when giving evidence, and meant that the hostility rating for the defence lawyer was much lower. Participants also found it easier to obtain information on the investigation and trial process when they had a lawyer, but were less satisfied with the state prosecutor, perhaps because they had higher expectations of the prosecutor as a result of their positive experience with their own lawyer. Overall, the impact of the legal process on the family of the victim was also lessened where the victim was legally represented. Where participants had a victim's lawyer, their lawyer was the main source of information concerning bail, trial process etc. Some problems were experienced in relation to state-funding of lawyers, since in some countries the qualification threshold for the means test is very high. Finally, the victim's lawyer was the legal officer with the highest satisfaction rating among the sample.

(Bacik et al. 1998: 17–18)

As these two studies largely concerned countries with a civil-law tradition, the proposition that ILR could be imported to a different legal culture might be received with scepticism by some common-law scholars (for example Chase 1997). But that response belies the complexities and nuances of the forms of ILR that have developed in adversarial jurisdictions and that could evolve further. While it is correct to say that ILR is rare in common-law jurisdictions, nonetheless it does exist, and in effect grants legal standing to victims at certain procedural stages. For example, since the publication of the Irish study, the Republic of Ireland now offers complainants legal representation to oppose the introduction of sexual history evidence (section 34 of the Sex Offences Act 2001). In Canada, complainants can invoke section 7 of the Charter of Rights and Fundamental Freedoms and the Criminal Code to defend their privacy and equality rights and oppose discovery applications by the defence for the disclosure of their personal records (Cameron 2003: 24–39; McDonald and Wobick 2004). A significant number of US states have 'chiseled victims' rights into their respective constitutions, though there is ferocious opposition to creating a constitutional amendment embracing such rights (Beloof 1999: 289). Admittedly, each of these forms of legal representation has its limitations, but the principle has taken root – ILR can be accommodated within an adversarial framework.

These 'incursions' from the inquisitorial model into the adversarial one are part of a growing assimilation of procedures within Europe and the Commonwealth. The traditional divisions between adversarial and inquisitorial models are increasingly permeable. Commentators acknowledge that the divisions are artificial (McEwan 1998), blurred (Pizzi 1999) and even obsolete (Jung 2004). Most legal systems have a mixed heritage with features of each system identifiable within the other. Four of the Nordic countries – Denmark, Iceland, Norway and Sweden – specifically adopt elements of adversarialism in their criminal procedure (Temkin 2002a; Strandbakken 2003). This chapter is not an exercise in comparative criminal procedure, but for our purposes the emerging porosity within existing justice models opens up new opportunities for jurisdictions to explore and import ideas from other jurisdictions that might enhance their domestic rape law practices.

## THE STRATEGIC PROPERTIES OF ILR

I want to argue that the most cogent potential for ILR is as a proactive strategy designed to improve the performance and outcomes of the rape investigation and prosecution procedures. ILR would represent another strategy to counter the relentless focus on the character and behaviour of rape complainants within the adversarial trial. It would serve a similar purpose to other proactive strategies designed to support the complainant, including case-building (Ellison 2005), expert witness testimony to educate the jury (Cunliffe 2006; Ellison and Munro, this volume) and witness preparation through closer prosecutorial involvement (Ellison 2007). Such proactive strategies are quite distinct from the host of special measures available in most countries to support vulnerable witnesses, the purpose of which is more to compensate for an individual's lack of resilience in the witness box than to address the wider problems of rape prosecutions associated with lack of corroboration, proof of *mens rea* and narrow interpretations of rape shield legislation.

Proponents of the adversarial trial argue that victims are simply witnesses to an alleged crime, and have no inherent claim to any special status, rights or representation (Greenspan 2001). However, to characterize the rape complainant as merely a provider of testimony mocks the fundamental objective of modern criminal justice systems to enable witnesses to 'give their best evidence' (for example, Home Office 2002: 1). In adversarial systems, the responsibility for assisting complainants to give their best evidence rests with prosecutors, who also have a constitutional duty to act independently of any other person and only to prosecute if satisfied it is in the public interest to do so (Marshall 1984; Jackson and Hancock 2006). In Scotland, this principle is constitutionally enshrined in section 4(5) of the Scotland Act 1998. Although in assessing the public interest, prosecutors must *take account* of the interests of both the complainant and the accused, ultimately, the prosecutor 'represents the wider public interest and not an individual victim of crime' (Crown Office 2006: 1.7). One cannot presume that a complainant's interests are aligned with the public interest, and one cannot conceivably argue that a complainant's interests are aligned with those of an accused. This creates a zone of perpetual friction and acutely curbs the capacity of prosecutors to protect complainants from harsh or undignified treatment.

Prosecutors cannot offer the comfort and support of legitimate partisanship that is vital for complainants' self-confidence when negotiating the legal process and giving evidence effectively. The competing responsibilities that are (quite properly) imposed upon prosecutors serve to marginalize complainants, and leads to their sense of abandonment and disempowerment. The neutrality the law desires of prosecutors has been the focus of sustained criticism (Chambers and Millar 1983; Chambers and Millar 1986; Brown et al. 1992; Garkawe 1994; Young 2005). As the first Scottish review of the prosecution of sexual offences recorded:

> Many women contrasted the fiscal's [prosecutor's] impartial position with the interventionist role of the defence agent or advocate. It has been argued that the prosecutor's impartiality left complainers open to attack and created an imbalance in the conduct of trials and in the way the evidence was presented.
>
> (Chambers and Millar 1986: 131)

The alienation of the complainant, whose confident co-operation is so critical to a successful prosecution, starts at the earliest stages of investigation of a rape complaint. Prosecutors have complete discretion on crucial issues including whether to pursue a prosecution, whether to plea-bargain, whether to oppose applications for release from custody pending trial, or whether to abandon the prosecution at any stage. When consent is at issue, the defence strategy generally rests on the systematic destruction of the complainant's self-confidence and bodily integrity in a manner that no other victim confronts (Matoesian 1993; Ehrlich 2001). To expect a complainant to withstand such onslaughts, with only the possibility of discretionary intervention from a prosecutor, is to assure failure for the goal of achieving best evidence. As one commentator notes, '[c]riminal justice professionals have little incentive to act in accordance with the wishes and needs of victims, since they are not directly accountable to them, either legally or organizationally' (Karmen 1990: 212). In exercising their discretion the notion that public prosecutors can discharge their duties to the court, the state and the accused, while simultaneously looking after the complainant's interests, is simply not realistic. Yet that is precisely the expectation placed upon prosecutors across the common-law world (Garkawe 1994; Warren 2003; Crown Office 2006). Failure to protect complainants' interests is most often rooted in these conflicting duties.

The response to the prosecutor's dilemma requires a greater imaginative shift in emphasis towards participatory rights for complainants than has to date been attempted. The introduction of ILR could make a significant difference to the current prosecutorial deficit. The next section explores this deficit in two areas where currently the prosecutor's responsibilities, stretched as they are across four separate constituencies – to the court, accused, public and complainant – leave the unrepresented complainant without agency. In common-law jurisdictions these two areas are rape shield legislation and the recovery of personal records.

## RAPE SHIELD LEGISLATION

Rape shield legislation has been the favoured response in most countries to regulate the use of irrelevant character evidence, but it has produced very mixed results. Most critical commentators would agree with the following conclusion from US researchers: 'the ability of rape reform legislation to produce instrumental change is limited. In most of the jurisdictions we studied, the reforms had no impact' (Spohn and Horney 1992: 173). Complainants are entirely dependent upon the attitude of the prosecutor and the interpretative discretion of the trial judge for effective opposition to applications that seek to introduce sexual or other character evidence. Scotland provides a typical example of a common-law jurisdiction that has used rape shield provisions to control the evidence admitted into the courtroom. Despite the lessons from past failings of such legislation, the Scottish Parliament opted for another attempt at regulation as recently as the Sexual Offences (Procedure and Evidence) (Scotland) Act 2002.

The 2002 Act was intended to redress the problems of the existing legislation where researchers had found that neither judges nor prosecutors were likely to intervene in cross-examination of the complainant, not least because they were unconvinced of the need for the rape shield legislation in the first place (Brown et al. 1992: 40–2). The researchers suggested that non-intervention was due to deeply shared cultural understandings as to what constituted 'relevant' sexual history evidence, such that there was little resistance by the lawyers on either side to its introduction. This is a phenomenon noted elsewhere. Andrew Karmen, commenting on the position in Australia, observes that when legal personnel are unconvinced of the need for law reform, the retention of the status quo may be difficult to disturb because of the 'latitude and discretion (i.e. "the turf") of these criminal justice decision makers' (Karmen 1992: 165).

Section 8 of the 2002 Act attempts to focus 'criminal justice decision makers' on the purpose of the Scottish legislative reform by placing a specific duty on the trial judge to ensure 'appropriate protection of a complainer's [complainant's] dignity and privacy'. One might therefore anticipate a greater level of judicial intervention post 2002. However, a recent evaluation of the Act, confirmed by the case law, found that 'objections by the other party and/or interventions by the court occurred infrequently' (Burman et al. 2007: para. 7.8).

These findings affirm that the complainant's Convention rights under Articles 3 and 8, respectively to protection from humiliating and degrading treatment, and to privacy, will struggle to influence the balancing tasks fundamental to rape prosecutions. Both prosecutors and judges have to take account of the complainer's interests in the context of the wider public interest, while also upholding the rights of the accused to a fair trial. When faced with such 'an irresolvable conflict', Londono has argued that because Article 3 is a non-derogable right, it is more important in the hierarchy of Convention rights than Article 6. However, she also argues that, in practice, in UK rape prosecutions, judges pay scant attention to Article 3 (2007: 165–6). In addition, prosecutors sometimes confound complainants by applying for permission to lead sexual history or other character evidence where they perceive a strategic necessity to do so. In some instances it will be to provide essential context, for example the rape of a prostitute, and in others it will be to retain control over how the evidence is presented. This is easier to achieve if the prosecutor raises it first in the examination-in-chief of the complainant rather than wait for the issue to be raised by the defence in cross-examination (Burman et al. 2007: paras 4.47–4.52). However, prosecutors rarely explain this to complainants for fear of being accused of coaching. For their part, judges may be loath to intervene to prevent or restrict cross-examination in case it leads to grounds of appeal (*Black v Ruxton* (1998) SLT 1282).

Complainants in adversarial jurisdictions have regularly voiced their concern about what they need in order to give their best evidence without fear or humiliation (Chambers and Millar 1986). For example, they expect a vigorous response to defence applications – unhampered by conflicting interests – and in virtually every other European country they would be entitled to have their views represented through their own lawyer. A recent Home Office study confirmed that the prosecution of rape demands 'courtroom advocacy that does justice to the complainant's account' (Kelly et al. 2005: xii). However, without a radical shift in the prescribed role of the adversarial prosecutor it is difficult to see how they can 'do justice' to the complainant's account while remaining faithful to their other constituents.

## RECOVERY OF PERSONAL RECORDS

The personal records of a complainant are generated from obvious sources such as from medical, mental health, counselling, educational and social work professionals, as well as less obvious ones such as rape crisis centres and private diaries (*R v Shearing* [2002] 3 SCR 33). Potentially, these records could go back decades, and are of value to the defence as they might reveal information on past sexual experiences. The tactic of seeking recovery or disclosure of personal records is the latest in an armoury of tactics to intimidate complainants and discourage them from continuing to co-operate with a prosecution (Gotell 2001). Most jurisdictions grant the defendant certain rights to recover the personal records of the complainant that are in the hands of a third party. This right of recovery can be distinguished from the duty on the prosecutor to disclose to the defence relevant material that is in their hands as a result of the police investigation of the crime.

The equality of arms principle is integral to the right to a fair trial contained in Article 6 of the European Convention on Human Rights 1950 (ECHR). It entitles the defence to have access to the same documentation that is available to the prosecution if it is material to the preparation of the defence (*Edwards v United Kingdom* [1992] 15 EHRR 417). This is so even if the prosecution does not intend to rely upon the documentation as evidence.

While the defence will always wish to examine all available documents for any exculpatory benefit they may have for the accused, many of these documents are ones that the complainant will consider private and confidential. What therefore constitutes 'material' documents may need to be disputed emphatically in order to protect the complainant's privacy. Given the conflicting constraints under which prosecutors operate, it is difficult to see how they can discharge this responsibility satisfactorily.

Experience in various jurisdictions demonstrates that a very robust framework has to be put in place to sift applications for disclosure as defence counsel tend to pursue a range of strategies, many of which are effectively 'fishing expeditions' (Temkin 2002a). Although some Scottish prosecutors claim they resist inappropriate disclosure applications, it is clear that decision is entirely a matter for their discretion (Burman et al. 2007: para. 4.65). Moreover, given that these prosecutors cannot provide legal guidance to a complainant, as they are not acting for her in an advisory capacity, there is no dedicated legal representative able to pursue her interests in opposing applications.

ILR is more readily accommodated in common law countries such as Canada and the US, whose citizens have constitutionally protected rights of privacy and equality. In Canada, the high-water mark of protection against disclosure of sexual assault records was reached in the Supreme Court decision in *R v Mills* ([1999] 3 SCR 688: para. 94) which noted that:

> A complainant's privacy interest is very high where the confidential information contained in a record concerns the complainant's personal identity or where the confidentiality of the record is vital to protect a therapeutic relationship.

Records recovery in rape cases automatically gives rise to equality issues because '[w]omen are disproportionately more likely to generate medical and therapeutic records due to the high rates of sexual assault against them' (Roberts, cited in McDonald and Wobick 2004: para. 3.5).

To defend their privacy and equality rights under the Canadian Charter, complainants can instruct their own legal counsel to oppose defence applications for recovery of medical and therapeutic records and other confidential papers (for example *R v Shearing* 2002). Interestingly, Canadian Crown counsel interviewed in one research study made the revealing admission that when independent counsel were instructed by the complainant, 'everyone takes it more seriously' (Mohr 2002: 16–17). This comment implies that there is indeed a prevailing cultural consensus, which the presence of independent legal counsel at least challenges. How effective they are at defeating recovery applications is uncertain as such applications are often unopposed (though ILR is available in Canada, few provinces fund it). Gotell (2008) argues that the judicial approach in the cases since *Mills* has subverted the legislative intent to restrict disclosure obligations. Even if the recent trend is negative, there remains a solid dissenting jurisprudence in support of privacy and equality rights. L'Heureux Dubé J. exemplified this when she argued passionately in *O'Connor* that complainants' Charter rights must be placed 'on an equal footing with those of accused persons' (*R v O'Connor* [1995] 4 SCR 411: para. 154). If anything, the Canadian experience confirms the importance of state-funded ILR to ensure the possibility of consistent and reliable legal services.

## Compatibility of ILR with human rights

Despite growing international prominence for victims' rights, some commentators argue that the victims' rights movement has stalled before it has achieved its major goal of delivering substantive rights to victims (Young 2005). Recognition of substantive rights for complainants within human rights law is tenuous, but gradually strengthening. As ILR would constitute substantive rights for complainants, it will mobilize considerable resistance from those who see it as incompatible with defendants' rights. Until that debate is settled there is no possibility of ILR establishing any greater foothold in adversarial systems than at present.

Although the ECHR does not specifically constitute the welfare of a victim in terms of a formal 'right', their interests are articulated in several articles. In particular, Articles 3, 8 and 13 respectively protect against 'inhuman or degrading treatment'; 'respect for ... private and family life, ... home and ... correspondence'; and the provision of 'an effective remedy against treaty violations'. Each of these articles is capable of an interpretation that protects complainants in rape and sexual assault cases, notably in guarding against inappropriate cross-examination or recovery of personal records. Even if these articles are still being interpreted cautiously, a growing body of academic opinion argues that the ECHR does place some positive obligations on the state to protect victims, in effect acknowledging that victims *do* have rights (de Than 2003; Klug 2004). The case law of the European Court of Human Rights accepts that in certain circumstances the constituent elements of Article 6 have to yield to victims' rights. It can therefore be compatible with a fair trial for vulnerable or intimidated witnesses to give evidence shielding them from the accused, for example, from behind a screen or by CCTV link (*Doorson v The Netherlands* [1996] ECHR 14), or even anonymously (*Van Mechelen v The Netherlands* [1997] ECHR 22). These decisions are bolstered by the affirmation in *MC v Bulgaria* ([2005] 40 EHRR 20) that there is an inherent positive obligation upon states, derived from Articles 3 and 8, to ensure rape cases are investigated and prosecuted effectively (Conaghan 2005; Londono 2007). These small inroads encourage greater challenges (Londono, this volume).

## CONCLUSION

The problems facing rape complainants are universal, though undoubtedly exacerbated in countries with an adversarial system. The Irish study provided compelling evidence of the benefits of ILR available to complainants in countries with an inquisitorial model, but this has not precluded its emergence in common-law systems, as the Canadian and Irish experiences illustrate. ILR deserves serious consideration as a reform strategy, not least because of the lack of success of other strategies. The traditional duties expected of prosecutors in fulfilling multiple roles belong to an era where there was little demand for transparency, clarity of function or recognition of victims' rights. In modern conditions, it is not sustainable to perform the role of public prosecutor as well as promote the best interests of the complainant, as these demands are fundamentally in tension. To achieve a genuine rebalancing of these competing demands would require a step change of a magnitude not yet witnessed, at least not in the UK. It would mean a transformative shift in approach on the part of the prosecution service in relation to basic issues endemic to rape trials such as the relevance of character evidence, the privacy of personal records and the affronts to dignity tolerated in the name of due process.

The pace of change in criminal justice systems tends to be slow and deeply cautious. There are, though, a few indicators of fresh visions and changing practices, many of which are driven by international initiatives in response to global problems such as terrorism, war crimes and organized crime. The constitutional framework contained in the Rome Statute for the International Criminal Court, which adopts a blend of adversarial and inquisitorial practices, is an illustration of these initiatives. It has signalled that victims' rights are an essential dimension of the process by insisting that the Registrar of the Court aid victims 'in obtaining legal advice and organizing their legal representation, and providing their legal representatives with adequate support, assistance and information' (Rule 16 of the Rules of Procedure and Evidence). For those committed to improving the status and treatment of rape complainants, this model demonstrates that new strategies can be designed for obdurate problems. ILR will not provide all the answers to prosecuting rape. However, given the evidence of its success in many jurisdictions, and the working models that demonstrate its scope for compatibility within the adversarial process, there is no rationale for continuing to ignore its potential.

## Note

1  I am grateful to Rape Crisis Scotland for financial assistance for the research project on independent legal representation for complainants in rape trials from which this chapter has emerged, and to the editors for their insightful and helpful comments on an earlier draft.

## Bibliography

Adler, Z. (1987) *Rape on Trial*, London: Routledge and Kegan Paul.
Ashworth, A. (1986) 'Punishment and compensation: victims, offenders and the state', *Oxford Journal of Legal Studies*, 6: 86–122.

Bacik, I., Maunsell, C. and Gogan, S. (1998) *The Legal Process and Victims of Rape*, Dublin: Dublin Rape Crisis Centre and School of Law, Trinity College, Dublin.

Beloof, D. (1999) 'The third model of criminal process: the victim participation model', *Utah Law Review*, 289–330.

Brienen, M.E.I. and Hoegen, E.H. (2000) *Victims of Crime in 22 European Criminal Justice Systems: the implementation of Recommendation (85) 11 of the Council of Europe on the position of the victim in the framework of criminal law and procedure*, Nijmegen, The Netherlands: Wolf Legal Productions.

Brown, B., Burman, M. and Jamieson, L. (1992) *Sexual History and Sexual Character Evidence in Scottish Sexual Offence Trials*, Edinburgh: Scottish Office Central Research Unit.

Burman, M., Jamieson, L., Nicholson, J. and Brooks, O. (2007) *Impact of Aspects of the Law of Evidence in Sexual Offence Trials: an evaluation study*, Edinburgh: Scottish Government Social Research.

Cameron, J. (2003) *Victim Privacy and the Open Court Principle*, Ottawa, Canada: Department of Justice.

Chambers, G. and Millar, A. (1983) *Investigating Sexual Assault*, Edinburgh: Scottish Office Central Research Unit.

—— (1986) *Prosecuting Sexual Assault*, Edinburgh: Scottish Office Central Research Unit.

Chase, O. (1997) 'Legal processes and national culture', *Cardozo Journal of International and Comparative Law*, 1: 1–39.

Conaghan, J. (2005) 'Extending the reach of human rights to encompass victims of rape', *Feminist Legal Studies*, 13: 134–57.

Crown Office (2006) *Crown Office and Procurator Fiscal Service Review*, Edinburgh: Crown Office.

Cunliffe, E. (2006) 'Without Fear or Favour? Trends and possibilities in the Canadian approach to expert human behaviour evidence', *International Journal of Evidence & Proof* 10: 280–315.

de Than, C. (2003) 'Positive obligations under the European Convention on Human Rights: towards the human rights of victims and vulnerable witnesses?', *Journal of Criminal Law*, 67: 165–82.

Doak, J. (2005) 'Victims rights in criminal trials: prospects for participation', *Journal of Law & Society*, 32(2): 294–316.

—— (2008) *Victims' Rights, Human Rights and Criminal Justice*, Oxford: Hart Publishing.

Ehrlich, S. (2001) *Representing Rape: language and sexual consent*, London: Routledge.

Ellison, L. (2005) 'Closing the credibility gap: the prosecutorial use of expert witness testimony in sexual assault cases', *International Journal of Evidence and Proof*, 9(4): 239–68.

—— (2007) 'Promoting effective case-building in rape cases: a comparative perspective', *Criminal Law Review*, 691–708.

Estrich, S. (1987) *Real Rape*, Cambridge, MA: Harvard University Press.

Garkawe, S. (1994) 'The role of the victim during criminal proceedings', *University of New South Wales Law Journal*, 17: 595–616.

Gotell, L. (2001) 'Colonization through disclosure: confidential records, sexual assault complainants and Canadian law', *Social and Legal Studies*, 10: 315–46.

—— (2008) 'Tracking decisions on access to sexual assault complainants' confidential records: the continued permeability of subsections 278.1–278.9 of the Criminal Code', *Canadian Journal of Women and the Law*, 20: 111–54.

Greenspan, E. (2001) 'The new truth: victims never lie', *Supreme Court Law Review*, 14: 89–95.

Home Office (2002) *Achieving Best Evidence in Criminal Proceedings*, London: Home Office.

Jackson, J. and Hancock, B. (2006) *Standards for Prosecutors, An Analysis of the United National Prosecuting Agencies*, Nijmegen, The Netherlands: Wolf Legal Productions.

Jung, H. (2004) 'Nothing but the truth? Some facts, impressions and confessions about truth in criminal procedure', in A. Duff, L. Farmer, S. Marshall and V. Tadros (eds) *The Trial on Trial*, vol. 1, *Truth and Due Process*, Oxford: Hart Publishing, 147–56.

Karmen, A. (1990) *Crime Victims: an introduction to victimology*, 2nd edn, Florence, KY: Brooks/Cole Publishing.

—— (1992) 'Who's against victims rights?', *St John's Journal of Legal Commentary*, 8: 157–75.

Kelly, L., Lovett, J. and Regan, L. (2005) *A Gap or a Chasm? Attrition in reported rape cases*, London: Home Office Research Study 293.

Klug, F. (2004) 'Human rights and victims', in E. Cape (ed.) *Reconcilable rights? Analysing the tensions between victims and defendants*, London: Legal Action Group.

Londono, P. (2007) 'Positive obligations, criminal procedure and rape cases', *European Human Rights Law Review*, 2: 158–71.

McDonald, S. and Wobick, A. (2004) *Bill C-46: Records Applications Post-Mills, A Caselaw Review*, Ottawa, Canada: Department of Justice.

McEwan, J. (1998) *Evidence and the Adversarial Process*, 2nd edn, Oxford: Hart Publishing.

Marshall, G. (1984) *Constitutional Conventions: the rules and forms of political accountability*, Oxford: Oxford University Press.

Matoesian, G. (1993) *Reproducing Rape – Domination through talk in the courtroom*, Chicago: Chicago University Press.

Mohr, R. (2002) *Words are not Enough*, Ottawa, Canada: Department of Justice.

Mosteller, R. (1999) 'The unnecessary victims' rights amendments', *Utah Law Review*, 443–7.

Pizzi, W. (1996) 'Crime victims in German courtrooms: a comparative perspective on American problems', *Stanford Journal of International Law*, 32: 37–64.

—— (1999) 'Victims' rights: rethinking our "adversary system" ', *Utah Law Review*, 349–68.

Raitt, F. (forthcoming) *Independent Legal Representation for Complainers in Sexual Offence Trials*, Glasgow: Rape Crisis Scotland.

Regan, L. and Kelly, L. (2003) *Rape: still a forgotten issue*, London: London Metropolitan University, Child and Woman Abuse Studies Unit.

Roberts, J. and Benjamin, C. (1998) *Prevalence of Sexual Assault and Therapeutic Records: research findings*, Ottawa, Canada: Department of Justice.

Sebold, A. (1999) *Lucky*, New York: Scribner.

Spohn, C. and Horney, J. (1992) *Rape law reform: a grassroots revolution and its impact*, New York: Plenum.

Strandbakken, A. (2003) 'A fair trial for the suspect?', in *Criminal Justice between*

*Crime Control and Due Process*, Colloquium Proceedings, Freiburg: Max Planck Institute, 241–51.

Temkin, J. (2002a) *Rape and the Legal Process*, 2nd edn, Oxford: Oxford University Press.

Warren, G. (2003) 'Due process – prosecutorial implications of a victim's right to be heard', *Rutgers Law Journal*, 34: 1173–88.

Wilson, L. (2005) 'Independent legal representation for victims of sexual assault: a model for delivery of legal services', *Windsor Yearbook of Access to Justice*, 23: 249–312.

Young, A. (2005) 'Crime victims and constitutional rights', *Criminal Law Quarterly*, 49: 432–71.

Chapter 19

# Jury deliberation and complainant credibility in rape trials

*Louise Ellison and Vanessa E. Munro*

Amongst the most commonly cited problems facing prosecutors in rape cases is the tendency of defence lawyers to portray the normal behaviour of women as 'unusual' or inconsistent with a genuine complaint (Ellison 2005; Jordan 2004; Freckelton 1998). Delay in reporting an assault is often presented as suspicious (Adler 1987; Bronitt 1998; Brereton 1997; Raitt 2004), as is a complainant's lack of physical resistance or injury during an attack (Ehrlich 2001; Lees 1996; Temkin and Krahé 2008). In addition, it has been suggested that complainants who appear calm while recounting events at trial may fail to convince jurors of their victimization (Frazier and Borgida 1988; Buddie and Miller 2002; Taylor and Joudo 2005). But to the extent that such case characteristics act as automatic triggers for disbelief, they are problematic. In reality, many sexual assault victims never report offences, and many more will delay reporting, often for significant periods (Jordan 1998; Fisher et al. 2003; Clay-Warner and Burt 2005). Many victims – for a number of reasons – offer no physical resistance and suffer no serious physical injury (Bowyer and Dalton 1997; Sugar et al. 2004; Du Mont and Whyte 2007); and many will react to sexual assault by exhibiting extreme calm, often as a conscious – or unconscious – coping strategy (Burgess and Holmstom 1974; Petrak and Hedge 2002).

Reforms under the Sexual Offences Act 2003 notwithstanding, in rape trials in England and Wales, it is largely a matter for the jury – applying their combined good sense, experience and knowledge of human nature and modern behaviour – to determine the absence of complainant consent and to assess the reasonableness of any belief in consent harboured by the defendant, which constitute the key grounds for criminal liability. In other jurisdictions where the jury plays a similarly central function, most notably the United States, prosecutors have sought to overcome the questionable defence strategies outlined above by introducing evidence designed to 'educate' jurors on the impact of rape and the complex, disparate reactions of victims both during and post-assault (Massaro 1985; Fischer 1989; Boeschen et al. 1998). In 2006, the Office for Criminal Justice Reform proposed the introduction of something similar in England and Wales (Home Office 2006). The fate of these proposals is still being debated, but the initiative appears to be based on two core assumptions: (i) that certain behavioural cues on the part of the complainant (including courtroom demeanour, delayed reporting and failure to resist) adversely impact upon jurors' perceptions of credibility; and (ii) that expert testimony offers a useful vehicle for addressing these shortcomings in jurors' understandings.

There is a substantial body of work, in the UK and elsewhere, that has explored both broader attitudes to gender roles and so-called 'rape myth acceptance' (for a recent discussion, see Temkin and Krahé 2008). However, there is limited empirical evidence regarding the factors that influence jurors' assessments of credibility in rape cases, and even less examination of the impact of educational guidance thereon. In the present study, we sought to explore each of these issues, and also to examine whether providing educational guidance via an extended judicial instruction at the end of the trial would, as some have argued (Criminal Bar Association 2006; Wolchover and Heaton-Armstrong 2008), offer an equally – if not more – effective alternative to the use of expert evidence.

A series of mini-trial scenarios were scripted and reconstructed, with roles played by actors and barristers in front of an audience of mock jurors. Each reconstruction lasted approximately 75 minutes and was observed simultaneously by 24, 25 or 26 participants, who – after receiving judicial instructions – were separated into three different juries to reach their verdicts. These deliberations, which lasted up to 90 minutes, were recorded and analysed. In total, nine different scenarios were presented – across these, key facts and role-players remained constant, but variables were introduced upon two axes – one substantive and the other procedural. In three of the trials, the complainant displayed signs of bruising and scratching and reported the attack immediately, but was emotionally flat and calm during testimony. In another three of the trials, the complainant again displayed signs of bruising and scratching post-assault – this time, she was visibly upset during testimony but waited three days after the incident before reporting to police. In the final set of three trials, the complainant reported the assault immediately and was visibly upset during testimony but displayed no signs of physical injury, and sought to explain her lack of resistance on the basis that she had 'frozen' during the attack. Alongside these substantive variables, procedural variables were also introduced so that in each sub-set of three scenarios, the extent to which jurors were provided with educational guidance differed. Aware of objections, grounded in unfair prejudice to the accused, which have been raised against proposals to introduce such guidance into rape trials, care was taken to ensure that the comments made were general in nature, thoroughly supported by research literature, and balanced in tone, as per the guidance set out by the Court of Appeal in *R v Doody* [2008] EWCA Crim 2394. In some of the trials, an extended judicial instruction informed jurors about the different emotional reactions that victimization might elicit, the frequency with which complainants delay reporting, or the feasibility of a complainant freezing during an attack. In other trials, this information was provided by an expert called by the prosecution and cross-examined by the defence. In both education conditions, the possibility was acknowledged that the complainant's calm demeanour, delayed reporting or non-resistance could also be attributable to her having fabricated the rape allegation. In the remaining trials, no such guidance was provided.

In this chapter, a brief summary of the key findings arising out of these deliberations will be provided (for further discussion, see Ellison and Munro 2009a, 2009b and 2009c). In the first section, we will explore the tone and substance of participants' discussions in relation to demeanour, delay and resistance in the absence of educational guidance. In a context in which our findings in this regard support the hypothesis that members of the public currently lack an adequate understanding of the various possible (and credible) victim responses to rape, we turn in the second section to examine the impact – if any – attributable to the introduction of targeted expert testimony/judicial instruction on this issue. Having identified a positive influence in regard to two of the three substantive variables under review, we consider possible explanations for the inefficacy of education in relation to non-resistance, and put forward a case for the careful introduction of well-crafted and measured educational guidance in rape trials. In a context in which the low conviction rate remains a matter of ongoing concern, we argue that the introduction of educational guidance into rape trials may help to ensure access to justice for victims.

The limits of the experimental context that frame this research are significant. Despite our efforts to increase verisimilitude by scripting detailed trial stimuli, ensuring appropriate legal direction and requiring group deliberation, mock jurors knew that, ultimately, nobody's fate was held in the balance. While this makes uncritical extrapolation to 'real' courtrooms problematic, studies testing for the existence of a verdict impact from role playing have produced inconclusive results. In addition, in a context in which the Contempt of Court Act 1981 prohibits research with 'real' jurors in England and Wales, we maintain that simulation studies offer a valuable method by which to generate some insight into what may go on behind the closed doors of the jury room (for a fuller defence of this method in the context of this study, see Ellison and Munro 2009a; also Finch and Munro 2008).

## DELIBERATION IN THE ABSENCE OF EDUCATIONAL GUIDANCE

### Complainant demeanour

Rape victims may display a variety of emotional styles when communicating their experiences – ranging from being outwardly distraught and tearful to being composed and/or emotionally 'numb' (Wessel et al. 2006; Littleton and Radecki Breitkopf 2006; Konradi 1999 and 2007). Despite this, and in line with previous research which has shown that popular expectations of emotional distress/anger can undermine the perceived credibility of a calm rape complainant (Calhoun et al. 1981; Krulewitz 1982; Kauffman et al. 2003), mock jurors in the present study were clearly perplexed by what they described as the complainant's 'very, very calm', 'extremely calm' or 'unemotional' appearance. The majority of jurors expected a visible display of emotion, and for the defendant's presence in the courtroom, in particular, to provoke a more pronounced reaction.

While 'calm' was the adjective most commonly employed, some jurors used descriptors with more negative connotations, referring to the complainant as 'cool' and 'cold', implying a lack of feeling, and 'calculating' suggesting deliberate connivance and a lack of honesty. This latter observation appeared to be based not only on the complainant's emotionality – or lack of it – but to relate, in part, to the complainant's style of delivery which was measured in terms of pace and rather 'flat' in terms of intonation. A number of jurors referred to the complainant's responses as being 'too precise', again implying a lack of sincerity, while their deliberate quality denoted careful, and suspicious, pre-trial planning to others. Significantly, the complainant gave the same basic account of the alleged rape in each of the trial scenarios, describing events in the same level of detail, but such comments were generally confined to those trials in which her demeanour was deliberately manipulated in order to make her appear less tearful or visibly distressed.

Only one of the three juries who observed the calm demeanour trial under the no-education condition directly discussed the significance of the complainant's courtroom appearance. One female juror observed that some people are naturally emotional while others are 'just very blank', while a male juror offered as an alternative explanation the possibility that the complainant had been advised by police to avoid being 'too emotional'. Only one juror offered an explanation that related in any way to the trauma of rape, suggesting that the complainant may have tried to remain detached as a way of dealing with the situation, aiming instead to recount events in a 'factual way'. In sum, then, the jurors here appeared to have little understanding of the psychological effects and external pressures that could influence a rape complainant's demeanour in court.

Interestingly, while jurors routinely indicated that they would have expected the complainant to exhibit a more emotional style of self-presentation, this co-existed in the deliberations alongside a sceptical appraisal of the relevance attributable to demeanour more generally. In trials in which the complainant was visibly tearful during testimony, this was clearly an influencing factor for some, with one male juror stating 'I can't imagine someone that's actually lying through her teeth would actually be that emotional at that point'. At the same time, though, where the complainant's demeanour was thus remarked upon, others were often quick to caution that this could have been part of a 'performance'. The possibility that the complainant was simply a 'good actress' was advanced by a number of jurors, who, for example, drew attention to her 'dowdy' dress in court as further evidence that appearance was open to strategic manipulation.

## Delayed reporting

Despite being relatively short, the three-day delay between assault and report presented in some of our scenarios proved to be a significant stumbling block for many jurors, who were quick to state that it had seriously weakened the prosecution case. Jurors were often adamant that their instinctive reaction in the complainant's situation would have been to phone the police immediately – and they were unwilling to countenance any other response. Observations from trials involving an immediate police report reinforced the significance attached to timing, as this information was evidently used when evaluating the veracity of the complainant's account. In the words of one juror 'she phoned the police straight away so she'd been raped', while another referred to the prompt complaint as 'supporting evidence'. Comments here indicated a strong belief that it would have taken the complainant some time to fabricate an allegation and that the speed of her reaction undermined a key element of the defence case, which suggested that the complainant was out for revenge, having had her affections spurned.

While the importance of a prompt complaint was repeatedly emphasized it would, however, be misleading to suggest that delayed reporting uniformly raised suspicion. Some jurors maintained that it was impossible to predict how anyone would respond in the wake of a traumatic event. Specific comments indicated a broader awareness of factors that might contribute to delay, including self-blame and fear of others' judgment or disbelief. The impact of shock and embarrassment was also mentioned, as was the possibility that the complainant may have made a concerted effort to 'block out' the memory of the assault, which ultimately proved unsuccessful. Having rationalized the complainant's reaction in these terms, some jurors were willing to accept that it would have taken her time to 'weigh up all her options' and decide on the best course to take.

It was also clear that the issue of timing would be viewed differently depending on the circumstances. In trials in which the complainant claimed to have 'frozen' as a result of shock and fear, her action in immediately contacting the police often prompted consternation. Jurors also questioned whether a woman in this position would turn to the police as a first point of contact or would be more likely to seek comfort and reassurance from a family member or friend – a point which had not previously been raised in discussion. Thus, one set of assumptions seemed to replace another here, suggesting that complainants could be unfairly discredited for making an immediate report where this conflicted with jurors' views of conceivable post-assault behaviour.

## Resistance/injury

Despite the fact that the use of force is not a requirement under the English law of rape, in scenarios in which the complainant showed no signs of physical injury, our jurors routinely emphasized the significance of this to their not guilty verdicts. Their commitment to the belief that a 'normal' response to sexual attack would be to struggle physically was in many cases unshakeable. As one juror put it, 'even in a paralysed state, isn't it the body's natural reaction to put up some kind of defence?' Notably, it was female jurors who took a prominent role here, asserting that had they been in the complainant's situation, they would have resisted more forcefully. Such comments were often accompanied by unrealistic expectations regarding a woman's capacity to inflict defensive injury. As one put it, for example, 'no matter how big the guy, even if she's 8 stone and he's 16 stone, at some point she can scratch, she can hit, she can knee'.

Significantly, while there were some jurors who were more receptive, in principle, to the idea that a woman might freeze during an attack, for many, the credibility of this only held up in cases in which the perpetrator was unknown to the victim. As one put it, if it was 'someone she didn't know that would be (different), you can believe someone could be paralysed by fear because you don't know what they're capable of'. Though enthusiastically supported by many jurors, this claim contradicts research establishing that there are no reliable differences, in terms of strategies for resistance, between women raped by strangers and those raped by acquaintances (Koss et al. 1988). Moreover, for those jurors who were willing to accept that a woman might freeze, even where the perpetrator was an acquaintance, the upshot was often simply that expectations transferred from physical injury to signs of internal trauma. Although it is not uncommon for sexual assault to occur without generating vaginal injury, jurors insisted that 'if she really froze, there would have been physical damage down there'.

In addition, in those scenarios in which there *was* some evidence of bruising and scratching upon the complainant, a large number of jurors continued to expect higher levels of injury in order to be convinced. While some accepted that bruising and scratching were inconsistent with what they perceived to be 'normal' sex (Ellison and Munro 2009b), several maintained that they would only be swayed by injuries that were more serious. At the same time, while some accepted that bruising may be sufficiently convincing, they lamented the fact that there were not more bruises on this particular complainant to support her version of events – as one juror put it, 'if he pushed her to the floor, why hasn't she got bruising on her head ... he must have pushed her and she should have fallen and hurt herself a lot more than what she's saying'.

A number of jurors went to considerable lengths to provide alternative explanations for how such bruising might have been inflicted. One suggested that 'it might be that she had a necklace on that was hard ... that could have imprinted on her', and another hypothesized that 'she might have been doing some sailing ... or could have been going to aerobics' prior to the incident. Others suggested that the bruising may have been the consequence of consensual sexual activity, while some intimated that the bruising could have been deliberately self-inflicted to support the fabricated rape allegation. Though it was appropriate for jurors to consider such alternative explanations, the persuasive sway held by these accounts, despite being grounded in conjecture, suggests that there were many participants who, in order to be convinced of the complainant's account, would rather unrealistically require her to exhibit injuries that were not only severe but unambiguously attributable to the deliberate infliction of unwanted violence.

## THE IMPACT OF EDUCATION

Together, then, these findings support concerns about the limits of current public understanding as to what constitutes a 'normal' reaction to sexual attack, and its possible implications in terms of juror assessments of complainant credibility in rape cases. While jurors in the no-education condition paid considerable lip service to the notion that 'different people will react differently' to traumatic experiences, a number of assumptions regarding the instinct to fight back, the compulsion to report immediately and the inability to control one's attendant emotions continued to influence their deliberations. In turn, this raises the question of whether introducing additional guidance in court proceedings, designed to disavow jurors of these preconceptions, would have any positive impact, in terms of either increasing their understanding of what rape looks like or fostering less prejudiced evaluations of complainant credibility.

In seeking to track any influence associated with the introduction of educational guidance in the present study, it is important to bear in mind that, since differently composed juries observed each trial scenario, shifts may be attributable, in part, to different initial attitudes and expectations harboured by participants. It is also necessary to recall that the number of participants involved in any one trial was relatively small, and so findings must be treated with caution. That said, by exploring the tone and substance of jurors' comments across the deliberations, it is possible – we argue – to identify certain shifts as between the no-education and education conditions.

### Complainant demeanour revisited

Overall, jurors exposed to educational guidance detailing the reasons why a rape victim may appear calm and controlled when communicating her experience to third parties made fewer references to the complainant's demeanour. Moreover, there were marked differences in the way the participants approached this issue when it was raised. In the absence of guidance, as noted above, jurors typically appeared puzzled by – and took issue with – the complainant's composure, but rarely debated the significance of the complainant's reaction in the course of their discussions. By contrast, jurors who received educational guidance were far more likely to offer thoughts on what could possibly account for the complainant's lack of emotionality. In so doing, they often appeared to draw directly on the information that they had been given in the course of the trial, even though they made notably few direct references to the expert or judge.

Having been advised that rape could leave some victims feeling emotionally detached from events, several jurors suggested that 'emotional numbness' was a feasible explanation for the complainant's calmness in court. Recalling the complainant's own testimony, one juror, for instance, observed 'she said she feels ... detached and stunned since the incident and that is in line with trauma'. Offering a similarly benign reading, others speculated that the complainant may have remained calm and collected in order to present her case effectively – 'to get her point across' – seemingly taking on board information given that some victims of rape make a conscious effort to remain composed when recounting events publicly in order to avoid being emotionally overwhelmed. Following this line, further comments acknowledged the possible impact of stress and embarrassment on the complainant's demeanour as well as the potentially inhibiting presence of the accused in court, with female jurors notably prominent in suggesting that a victim of rape would probably want to keep her guard up. To quote one female juror, 'with him being in the same room surely she'd absolutely want to blank him out and just focus on what she's got to do and I'm sure I'd be the same'.

It is true that, even with this guidance, a fair number of jurors (approximately one-sixth) continued to make comments which indicated a more negative assessment of the complainant's demeanour – the most notable example coming from a male juror who pronounced that the complainant 'was so emotionless on the stand she could be a bit of a bunny boiler'. However, for the most part, the overall range and tenor of the deliberations suggests that jurors who received education displayed a greater understanding of emotional reactions to rape and were more willing to accept that a 'genuine' victim could exhibit few signs of visible distress whilst testifying in court.

## Delayed reporting revisited

In the context of delayed reporting, jurors who received educational guidance were significantly more likely to state that they were untroubled by the three-day delay in our trial scenario and to question, more generally, the significance that could reasonably be attached to the timing of a rape complaint, given the range of emotions rape could inspire [which jurors variously identified as shock, shame, self-doubt, fear of disbelief and fear of the court and investigative process]. While, as discussed above, jurors in the no-education condition had shown some appreciation of these factors, a significant number nevertheless indicated that the complainant's delay had negatively influenced their assessment of her credibility, tagging her response as 'odd', 'strange' and 'disturbing'. By contrast, there were very few jurors in the education condition who expressed either surprise or consternation that the complainant had reacted in the way she alleged in trying to initially 'block out' the incident. As one juror put it, 'the fact that she went three days is neither here nor there to me. I'm sure that varies from victim to victim.' Meanwhile, another insisted 'whether she waited three days, three months or three years you can't use that to say that it was or wasn't rape', reflecting the guidance given that some victims wait months or years before confiding in a third party.

In sum, then, bearing in mind that there was already some apparent appreciation of this issue in the no-education condition, guidance in this context did appear to raise jurors' awareness of the potential obstacles to reporting rape and correspondingly broadened the range of responses that jurors were willing to see as 'normal' or credible.

## Resistance/injury revisited

Rather than uncovering any changes in deliberations in regard to non-resistance, we found marked similarities in comments made by jurors in the guidance and no-guidance conditions. While there were some jurors who claimed to understand why a woman in the situation described by the complainant could be so overwhelmed by shock or disbelief that she would be unable to fight back physically, it was clear that most jurors continued to expect the complainant to offer some sort of resistance, even if it was only to slap, scratch or knee her alleged assailant – and to have sustained some injury as a result. Female jurors remained the key protagonists here, adamantly insisting that their own intuitive response would have been to fight back, despite being informed that some rape victims have the opposite response, due to a combination of shock, fear of further violence and a sense of helplessness. As one female juror put it, 'it's instinct, if you've got a hand free you'd grab for his eyes or his face or anything'.

Significantly, while jurors seemed to understand the content of the guidance on non-resistance, they often failed to make any connection between the 'freezing' response described and the type of acquaintance rape under review. Jurors commented – as they did in the no-education condition – that they would have found the complainant's reaction more credible if she had been attacked by a stranger, threatened with a weapon or approached in a 'dark alley'. As one female juror put it, 'this is going to sound terrible, but I don't know how much shock you would go into where there had been no violence prior . . . in rape cases where women don't know their attackers and they've got a knife or they are very violent, that's where women go into shock and freeze'.

Even accepting the possibility that the complainant had not engaged in physical resistance, as she maintained, there was a clear expectation on the part of many educated jurors – in common with their uneducated counterparts – that a victim of rape would inevitably suffer physical injury as a result of an assault. There was a strong belief – expressed in comments such as 'it's very easy to bruise a lady' – that a man would leave marks or scratches on a woman if he held her by the wrists, pushed her to the floor, or used his weight to pin her down. Jurors also speculated that the defendant would have had to use considerable force in overpowering the complainant, reasoning that it would have been difficult to manoeuvre a woman to the floor, remove her underwear and penetrate her if she was not fully co-operating and consenting. As one juror insisted – despite having been advised in the trial that the medical examiner's failure to find internal damage was neither consistent nor inconsistent with rape – 'if she wasn't up for sex, then there should've been some trauma from a forced entry'.

A number of possible explanations might be offered to account for the apparent inefficacy of the guidance on the issue of non-resistance. It is possible that expectations of force, injury and resistance are just so deeply ingrained within the popular imagination that attempts to disavow jurors of them through education within the rape trial are likely to meet with limited success. At the same time, it is possible that there were other inadequacies in the scope or wording of our guidance on this point which, if rectified, would have ensured a more marked impact. Previous research has suggested that a positive influence in regard to non-resistance requires evidence/instruction that links general claims drawn from the research literature to the case at hand via a hypothetical example (Brekke and Borgida 1988). In contrast, we would argue that there is reason to hope that general guidance emphasizing the feasibility of the 'freezing' reaction in situations of acquaintance or intimate, as well as stranger, rape may offer productive scope (Ellison and Munro 2009c); and it may do so, importantly, without giving rise to the risks of a 'battle of experts' (Temkin and Krahé 2008; Council of Circuit Judges 2006), improper 'oath-helping' (Friedland 1989) or usurping of the jury's function (Vidmar and Schuller 1989), which are associated with more expansive models.

## CONCLUSION

The above discussion summarizes key findings emerging out of our recent mock jury study, and sheds valuable insight into both the need for, and the potential value of, providing educational guidance to jurors in rape trials. While the research was initiated prior to the Solicitor-General's decision to convene an expert panel to consider the Office for Criminal Justice Reform's proposals in more detail, its outcomes have the potential to directly inform that evaluation process. In addition, in a context in which the prognosis for trial conviction clearly influences victims' decision-making in regard to police reporting, as well as any subsequent investigative and prosecutorial progression, its significance extends beyond the immediate confines of the courtroom. Introducing educational guidance represents a pragmatic, defensible and efficient means of redressing at least some of the unfounded assumptions and biases that prevent too many victims of sexual assault from accessing justice, but it does not – and should not – preclude wider educational initiatives designed to target social attitudes outside, and prior to, the courtroom. Ultimately, dispelling myths at the social (and institutional) level may render the role of juror education redundant. For the foreseeable future, however, we would argue that carefully implemented and well-crafted guidance has a vital role to play in ensuring more enlightened assessments of complainant credibility in rape cases.

Just as importantly, moreover, evidence from the present study suggests that this can be done without sacrificing the rights of the accused. Indeed, while our jurors in the trials involving demeanour and delay routinely reported in post-deliberation questionnaires that they found the expert/judicial guidance to be 'helpful', 'useful' and 'interesting', there was no suggestion that they interpreted it as indirectly vouching for the credibility of the complainant. Thus, some participants reported that the expert was 'totally impartial' on delay and 'non-committal either way' on demeanour, while others intimated that the judge's extended instruction had been 'unbiased', 'balanced' and 'neutral' throughout.

## Bibliography

Adler, Z. (1987) *Rape on Trial*, London: Routledge and Kegan Paul.

Boeschen, L., Sales, B. and Koss, M. (1998) 'Rape trauma experts in the courtroom', *Psychology, Public Policy & Law*, 4: 414–32.

Bowyer, L. and Dalton, M. (1997) 'Female victims of rape and the genital injuries', *British Journal of Obstetrics and Gynaecology*, 104: 617–20.

Brekke, N. and Borgida, E. (1988) 'Expert psychological testimony in rape trials: a social cognitive analysis', *Journal of Personality and Social Psychology*, 55: 372–86.

Brereton, D. (1997) 'How different are rape trials? A comparison of the cross-examination of complainants in rape and assault trials', *British Journal of Criminology*, 37: 2242–61.

Bronitt, S. (1998) 'The rules of recent complaint: rape myths and the legal construction of the "reasonable" rape victim', in P. Easteal (ed.) *Balancing the Scales: rape, law reform and Australian culture*, Sydney: Federation Press, 41–58.

Buddie, A. and Miller, A. (2002) 'Beyond rape myths: a more complex view of perceptions of victims', *Sex Roles*, 45: 130–60.

Burgess, A. and Holmstom, L. (1974) 'Rape Trauma Syndrome', *American Journal of Psychiatry*, 131: 981–6.

Calhoun, L., Cann, A., Selby, J. and Magee, D. (1981) 'Victim emotional response: effects on social reaction to victims of rape', *British Journal of Social Psychology*, 20: 17–21.

Clay-Warner, J. and Burt, C. (2005) 'Rape reporting after reforms: have times really changed?', *Violence Against Women*, 11: 150–76.

Council of Circuit Judges (2006) *Convicting Rapists and Protecting Victims: A consultation response of the Council of Her Majesty's Circuit Judges*.

Criminal Bar Association (2006) *Response to Consultation Paper: 'Convicting Rapists and Protecting Victims'*.

Du Mont, J. and White, D. (2007) *The Uses and Impacts of Medico-Legal Evidence in Sexual Assault Cases: a global review*, Geneva: World Health Organization.

Ehrlich, S. (2001) *Representing Rape: language and sexual consent*, London: Routledge.

Ellison, L. (2005) 'Closing the credibility gap: the prosecutorial use of expert witness testimony in sexual assault cases', *International Journal of Evidence & Proof*, 9: 239–68.

Ellison, L. and Munro, V. (2009a) 'Reacting to rape: exploring mock jurors' assessments of complainant credibility', *British Journal of Criminology*, 49(2): 202–19.
—— (2009b) 'Of normal sex and real rape: exploring the use of socio-sexual scripts in (mock) jury deliberation', 18(3) *Social and Legal Studies* 1–22.
—— (2009c) 'Turning mirrors into windows?: Assessing the impact of (mock) juror education in rape trials', 49(3) *British Journal of Criminology* 363–83.
Finch, E. and Munro, V. (2008) 'Lifting the veil: the use of focus groups and trial simulations in legal research', *Journal of Law & Society*, 35: 30–51.
Fisher, B., Daigle, L., Cullen, F. and Turner, M. (2003) 'Reporting sexual victimization to the police and others: results from a national-level study of college women', *Criminal Justice & Behavior*, 30: 6–38.
Fischer, K. (1989) 'Defining the boundaries of admissible expert psychological testimony on Rape Trauma Syndrome', *University of Illinois Law Review*, 691–734.
Frazier, P. and Borgida, E. (1988) 'Juror common understanding and the admissibility of Rape Trauma Syndrome evidence in court', *Law and Human Behaviour*, 12: 101–22.
Freckelton, I. (1998) 'Sexual offence prosecutions: a barrister's perspective', in P. Easteal (ed.) *Balancing the Scales: rape, law reform and Australian culture*, Sydney: Federation Press, 151–5.
Friedland, S. (1989) 'On common sense and the evaluation of witness credibility', *Case Western Reserve Law Review*, 40: 165–225.
Home Office (2006) *Convicting Rapists and Protecting Victims – justice for victims of rape*, London: Home Office.
Jordan, J. (1998) *Reporting Rape: women's experiences with the police, doctors and support agencies*, Wellington: Institute of Criminology.
—— (2004) *The Word of a Woman? Police, rape and belief*, New York: Palgrave Macmillan.
Kauffman, G., Drevland, G., Wessel, E., Overskeid, G. and Magnussen, S. (2003) 'The importance of being earnest: displayed emotions and witness credibility', *Applied Cognitive Psychology*, 17: 21–34.
Konradi, A. (1999) ' "I don't have to be afraid of you": rape survivors' emotion management in court', *Symbolic Interaction*, 22: 45–77.
—— (2007) *Rape Survivors and the Prosecution of Rapists*, Connecticut: Praeger.
Koss, M., Dinero, T., Seibel, C. and Cox, S. (1988) 'Stranger and acquaintance rape: are there differences in the victim's experience?', *Psychology of Women Quarterly*, 12: 1–24.
Krulewitz, J. (1982) 'Reactions to rape victims: effects of rape circumstances, victim's emotional response, and sex of helper', *Journal of Counselling Psychology*, 29: 645–54.
Lees, S. (1996) *Carnal Knowledge: rape on trial*, London: Hamish Hamilton.
Littleton, H. and Radecki Breitkopf, C. (2006) 'Coping with the experience of rape', *Psychology of Women Quarterly*, 30: 106–16.
Massaro, T. (1985) 'Experts, psychology, credibility and rape: the Rape Trauma Syndrome issue and its implications for expert psychological testimony', *Minnesota Law Review*, 69: 395–470.
Petrak, J. and Hedge, B. (2002) *The Trauma of Sexual Assault: treatment, prevention and practice*, Chichester: Wiley.
Raitt, F. (2004) 'Expert evidence as context: historical patterns and contemporary attitudes in the prosecution of sexual offences', *Feminist Legal Studies*, 12: 233–44.

Sugar, N., Fine, D. and Eckert, T. (2004) 'Physical injury after sexual assault: findings of a large case series', *American Journal of Obstetrics and Gynaecology*, 190: 71–6.
Taylor, N. and Joudo, J. (2005) 'The impact of pre-recorded video and closed circuit television testimony by adult sexual assault complainants on jury decision-making: an experimental study', AIC Research & Public Policy Series (No. 68), Canberra: Australian Institute of Criminology.
Temkin, J. and Krahé, B. (2008) *Sexual Assault and the Justice Gap: a question of attitude*, Oxford: Hart.
Vidmar, N. and Schuller, R. (1989) 'Juries and expert evidence: social framework evidence', *Law and Contemporary Problems*, 52: 133–76.
Wessel, E., Drevland, G., Eilertsen, D. and Magnussen, S. (2006) 'Credibility of the emotional witness: a study of ratings by court judges', *Law and Human Behaviour*, 30: 221–30.
Wolchover, D. and Heaton-Armstrong, A. (2008) 'Debunking rape myths', *New Law Journal*, 158: 117–19.

Chapter 20

# The mythology of male rape
Social attitudes and law enforcement

*Philip N.S. Rumney and Natalia Hanley*

### INTRODUCTION: MALE RAPE AS A SOCIAL AND LEGAL ISSUE

In the last two decades, adult male rape and sexual assault have been the subject of a 'knowledge explosion' akin to the increase in research concerning female rape and child sexual abuse in the 1970s (Kelly 1988: 43). Scholarly responses have contributed greatly to our understanding of the prevalence, dynamics, nature and impact of adult male rape. This work has examined such issues as the problem of male sexual victimization within institutional settings (Banbury 2004; O'Donnell 2004), within the general population (Coxell et al. 1999; Sorenson et al. 1987), during wartime (Sivakumaran 2007), and within the gay community (Hickson et al. 1987; Kendall and Martino 2006). It has also explored the nature, dynamics and impact of male victimization (Light and Monk-Turner 2008; Walker et al. 2005a; Walker et al. 2005b; Allen 2002; Mezey and King 2000), including comparative analysis of male and female rape (Elliott et al. 2004). Male rape has a long recorded history (Jones 2000) and recent research provides detailed information on social and legal attitudes to this problem as far back as the seventeenth century (Sommer 2000: Ch. 4). Of particular relevance to this chapter, there has been a growth in research examining the treatment of male rape by the criminal law and criminal justice system, including the views and perceptions of criminal justice professionals (Saunders 2009; Abdullah-Kahn 2008) and victims (Jamel et al. 2008; Rumney 2008; Rumney 2001). Questions have also been raised concerning whether male victims suffer a form of secondary victimization within the criminal justice system, resulting from issues linked to sexuality and, in particular, homosexuality (White and Robinson Kurpius 2002; Anderson and Doherty 2008; Rumney 2009).

This chapter seeks to explore the extent to which social attitudes towards male rape are influenced by myths, misunderstandings and stereotypes. It draws on focus group research, conducted by the authors, which attempts to ascertain perceptions of male rape complainants and defendants by the use of fictional vignettes containing factual variables. This specific research builds on earlier focus group work (Anderson and Doherty 2008), by examining a series of factual variables that have not previously been considered in attitude research involving male rape. Given the amount of data generated by the focus group discussions, an exhaustive examination of these discussions is precluded. Consequently, this chapter will examine several specific issues. First, we examine the effect of complainant resistance and injury on participants' perceptions of his credibility. Secondly, we consider the use of sexuality and intoxication to judge complainant credibility, as well as the potential blameworthiness of the defendant in the vignette. Finally, building on work involving female rape complainants, this chapter explores possible linkages between the attitudes exhibited by the focus group participants and the wider criminal justice process.

## RESEARCH DESIGN

The primary aim of this research was to explore student attitudes towards adult victims and perpetrators of male rape through the use of vignettes featuring an alleged incident of male sexual assault (Davies et al. 2006; Anderson and Doherty 2008). Research studies which utilize hypothetical scenarios or vignettes have been accused of lacking ecological validity. In response, however, Davies et al. (2006) have argued that this technique has been useful in uncovering attitudes towards female victimization and, as such, can be effectively applied to the study of male victimization. Without trivializing the limitations of this methodology, we would similarly argue that the findings of this experimental study yield important insights.

Student participants in the present study were informed about the research through an electronic conferencing system attached to compulsory undergraduate Criminology modules, staff announcements in lectures and seminars, and email communications. There are a number of advantages to utilizing an opportunity sample derived from a student group (Jupp 1989; Davies et al. 2006; Bryman 2008). Most notably, for the purposes of this research, it ensures that participation in the research is voluntary and that participants are able to provide informed consent. Students decided which focus group session to attend. There was no attempt to seek to control, for example, the male/female mix of focus group participants. The self-selection approach resulted in four focus groups, which included male only (groups 1, N = 2; and 4, N = 3), female only (group 2, N = 7) and mixed group discussions (group 3, N = 6). Given that the study involved a small number of participants (18), a level of caution is clearly appropriate when considering the general application of the findings outlined below.

The focus group discussions were recorded and there were no researchers present. This was particularly important as it encouraged honest and open discussion of the vignette and minimized the impact of the student/academic relationship on participant responses. Each focus group lasted for 50 minutes. Focus group discussions were conducted at the university in order to provide a setting within which participants would feel comfortable and familiar (Hamby and Koss 2003). Owing to the sensitivities of the subject-matter, participants were fully informed of the nature, purpose and likely outputs from the research process. Participants completed a consent form and were advised that they could withdraw from the study at any time, without providing a reason. Details of support and advice services were also provided.

As participants were all undergraduate Criminology students, there is, of course, a danger that the views of students may not be representative of the general public. In addition, the majority of participants were aged between 19 and 23. This narrow age range may produce generationally and culturally specific understandings of sexual violence. However, much mock jury research has suggested that participants who are students and those drawn from the general public do not differ significantly or predictably in their decision-making (Temkin and Krahé 2008: 53–4). In addition, while it may be thought that the respondents in the present study would have some awareness of the issues and debates surrounding the academic study of sexual violence, which may have skewed their contributions, the content of the discussions suggest little prior knowledge about male or female sexual victimization.

Each focus group was provided with one of three fictional vignettes designed to encourage discussion of one of the following variables in the context of a male rape trial: complainant failing to resist during an alleged rape (groups 1 and 4), delayed reporting by the complainant to the police (group 2) and an involuntary physical response by the complainant during the alleged rape (group 3). The scenario featuring the first variable was run twice due to the small number of participants (2) in group 1 and it is this 'resistance' variable that will be the focus of this chapter. In summary, the standard information across all of the vignettes featured David and Ian. They met at a party and then went back to David's flat to watch a DVD and talk about football. Ian claims that, when he was getting ready to leave the flat, David restrained him, removed his trousers and raped him. By contrast, David claims that during the evening 'one thing led to another' and they had consensual sex. In line with provisions under the Sexual Offences Act 2003 in England and Wales, each group was directed to decide whether the complainant consented to intercourse and whether the defendant reasonably believed that there was consent. The aims of the research were to explore the effect of each variable, to investigate attitudes towards male sexual victimization and, finally, to analyse how group dynamics and interactions impact upon group discussions (Kitzinger 1994; Frith 2000; Hollander 2004; Finch and Munro 2008). It has been argued that the use of short, fictional scenarios may increase the likelihood of participants relying on rape myth stereotypes to 'fill in the gaps' in the vignette (Finch and Munro 2008: 35). Consequently, these findings should be viewed as exploratory at this stage.

## SOME THEMES IN FOCUS GROUP DISCUSSIONS

### Expectation of physical injury and resistance

There is a growing body of evidence across many jurisdictions which suggests that, to be seen as credible by others, rape complainants should resist their attackers and show evidence of injury (Estrich 1986; Human Rights Watch 1995: Ch. 7; Temkin and Krahé 2008). In their recent mock jury research on female rape, Ellison and Munro found that 'in trial scenarios in which the complainant displayed no signs of injury, jurors routinely emphasized the significance of this lack of bruising to their not guilty verdicts . . . Their commitment to the belief that a "normal" response to sexual attack would be to struggle physically was, in many cases, unshakeable' (2009a: 206; see also Ellison and Munro in this collection).

Within the current focus group research, groups 1 and 4 examined a vignette in which specific reference was made to the complainant, Ian, not physically resisting David. However, it is evident that there was little substantive difference between the discussions of any of the four groups concerning resistance or physical injury. The resistance/injury issue was one of the most commonly discussed aspects in all focus groups and there was a clearly pronounced belief amongst participants that male victims should resist and show signs of injury. For example, in group 3, the following comments were made: 'With what we have here, like being physically restrained and said he had his trousers pulled down, and I think Ian sort of would rather struggle, David would have known, if he was something and Ian didn't want him to'. Similarly, 'If David had pulled his trousers down, he would have had chance and get away . . . there doesn't seem to be any fight . . . even if David pulled his trousers down he's not fighting back'. Alongside the expectation of complainant resistance, there was an assumption that a male victim would be physically injured as a result of rape. This is illustrated in the following exchange between the two participants in group 1:

> A: . . . I think it would be quite interesting to know if there were any bruises to show restraint or something. If someone was about to get raped they're obviously not going to take it lightly, so they are going to fight back, and there would be some sort of marks whether it be scratches or bruises . . .
> B: There would have had to have been some sort of physical trauma to Ian's body, if it was a rape.
> A: Yes, exactly.
> B: Because from what I've read about anal intercourse, it does require some stimulation for it to . . . pass . . . But surely there would have been some sort of bleeding.

This exchange also raised another issue – the linkage of the complainant's credibility with his clothing. As one member of group 3 expressed it:

You would expect that there would have to be some sort of fight. It's not easy to pull someone's trousers down without them wanting to; especially if they had a belt, it would be a difficult thing to do to physically rape someone. There must have been some sort of fight or struggle for him.

This reasoning is akin to that adopted by an Italian court when it was suggested that it was unlikely that a woman could be raped if she was wearing a pair of jeans since 'it is a fact of common experience that it is almost impossible to remove jeans from a person, even in part, without their cooperation, given that this is a difficult operation for the wearer themselves' (Fenton 2000: 715; see also Fenton in this collection). It has long been argued that the female complainant's clothing will be relied upon to suggest that she provoked or contributed to the attack. While our findings suggest that the issue of clothing can also arise in the context of male rape, it must be left to future research to determine whether there are circumstances where men are also deemed to provoke sexual assault through the way they dress.

Arguably paradoxically, for some participants, the claim by Ian that he was restrained by David was actually taken as evidence supporting David's claim that sex was consensual. Such attitudes were illustrated in the following exchange amongst female participants:

A: The thing I can't get over is that he says they did talk about football and one thing led to another and it sounds like a perfectly reasonable thing [for David] to say.
B: Maybe that's why he said it though, because it was a defence.
A: If it was me and I had done this I would be thinking along these lines ... If it was me and I had done this I knew I had physically restrained him.
C: I would have said he said he wanted it rough; he made me hold his hands above his head.

Indeed, one of the above participants went on from here to suggest that the alleged use of restraint actually served to undermine Ian's assertion that the intercourse was non-consensual. In her mind, this claim raised a concern about dishonesty on his part, thereby reducing his perceived credibility: 'If he hadn't just said that I would probably have been more inclined to believe him but the fact he's exaggerating, he restrained me and ripped my trousers off.' Here, the participant 'read in' facts that were not present in the scenario: Ian, the complainant, did not allege that his clothing was 'ripped' off, only that he was 'restrained' and that his trousers were 'removed'. Amongst other things, these quotes illustrate the complexity of judgments regarding credibility. If Ian had indeed had his clothing 'ripped', that might, in fact, be seen to have corroborated his claim of non-consent. However, it is also suggested that any mere claim that it occurred may undermine his credibility because it is perceived to be an exaggeration. Of course, it is worth noting the limitations of the focus group method in this specific context and the dangers of assuming that such attitudes would operate in an actual male rape trial. For one thing, in an actual trial context the complainant's clothing would most likely be available to jurors to help clarify matters.

## Contextualizing the scenario: intoxication, sexuality and positioning

Several different explanatory frameworks were utilized by participants in the focus groups to contextualize the fictional scenario. Of particular interest here are frameworks relating to both intoxication and sexuality. Participants relied on 'positioning devices' – that is, they sought to understand and explain the scenario in terms of their own likely behaviour and experiences. In this regard, our findings support the suggestion from previous research that (mock) jurors make decisions based upon both their 'world knowledge' and subjective experiences (Pennington and Hastie 1986: 254). Throughout all four group discussions, references were commonly made to 'appropriate' behaviour, and to notions of risk and danger that were based on experience. Some participants also drew on knowledge gained from discussion with friends and films such as *American History X*, which included a scene involving a prison rape.

The fact that Ian and David met at a party meant that the issue of intoxication became integral to all the focus group discussions. Participants indicated that alcohol consumption might be a useful explanatory device for understanding the context of the scenario. Reflecting earlier mock jury research involving an intoxicated female complainant (Finch and Munro 2006), the issue of intoxication was interpreted in a variety of ways by participants. Some participants questioned whether a rape could have taken place if Ian had been intoxicated, on the basis that it would be 'pretty damn hard' for David to restrain or control a drunken victim. Meanwhile, others relied on the possibility of Ian's intoxication to explain and defend David's alleged restraint: 'If Ian was so drunk he couldn't stand, David may have thought he was holding him up, rather than physically restraining him.' At the same time, other participants insisted that intoxication on David's part would have increased the likelihood that he mistakenly believed that Ian was consenting to sex: 'From David's point of view, he's consented already by just coming back to his house. From his point of view, because he's drunk, well he's come back he's obviously willing ... I'm in basically.' Meanwhile, others emphasized that, even if David's judgment was impaired by intoxication, this did not provide a justification or mitigation for sexual assault:

> We all have responsible for our own actions, whether we're drunk or on drugs. Just because we're drunk doesn't mean, sometimes we do things we wouldn't do normally, but we're responsible for our actions.
>
> The chances are they were both equally drunk but they started sobering up and one started to sober up chances are the other one was getting

there as well. Because there's nothing here that says they continued drinking, besides the point you don't just rape someone because the person is over the limit. You change your mind sometimes, you go to some guy's house you've met, then you go over and decide half way through actually I don't want to continue and they have to stop and if they don't stop then that's rape.

As with intoxication, issues around sexuality were applied in complex ways in each focus group discussion. Participants explored both the complainant's and defendant's sexuality in order to contextualize the fictional scenarios, to explain delayed reporting and to decide whether the belief in consent was reasonable. Rape myths underpinned these discussions in all cases, particularly the belief that 'men who are sexually assaulted by men must be gay' (Chapleau et al. 2008: 603). A significant number of participants struggled, for example, to understand the complainant's decision to go to a man's house without considering the complainant's sexuality. This was apparent in the following exchanges from within two different focus group discussions:

> A: It wasn't about football, it was also going back to watch a movie and stuff.
> B: But why go if you weren't gay?
> C: ... it just doesn't make sense to me, like if you meet a guy at a party and afterwards he says do you want to come back to my flat and talk about football, it's just not something you do.
> D: Assuming of course that Ian says he isn't gay, he's not homosexual, but David it doesn't say anything about his sexuality. So maybe David thought Ian was gay as well and thought he's catching my hint come back to my place sort of thing.

Research examining attitudes to male rape has consistently found that gay male victims of rape are seen as more blameworthy than heterosexual victims (Wakelin and Long 2003; Davies and Rogers 2006). Recent focus group research by Anderson and Doherty found that participants 'project[ed] "subconscious" homosexual desires onto the alleged victim as a way of making sense of and dismissing the rape claim in the vignette' (Anderson and Doherty 2008; Doherty and Anderson 2004). In the current research, the credibility of the complainant's account was considered in relation to his purported sexuality, as well as the group's interpretation of his sexuality. When the complainant was perceived as heterosexual by the group, the rape allegation was more likely to be considered as credible:

> But see that's what I don't get, but if Ian definitely wasn't gay then they must have kissed if one thing did lead to another, and then if Ian says he wasn't gay then he would have got freaked out.

> So the story does sound a bit more feasible, that he was raped, because he is now insisting that he's not gay but then that's only us believing that he's not gay.

As with the focus group research by Anderson and Doherty, some participants imposed a gay identity upon Ian to explain his behaviour: 'If you weren't gay, you wouldn't go home with a man if you're drunk, unless it's something else like best friends.' Several participants also viewed the allegation of rape as false on the basis that Ian did consent to sex, but later regretted his actions, and one participant argued that a false allegation might be explained by the fact that Ian was a football supporter:

> There is a football culture, it's quite lads and quite masculine, I'm probably stereotyping but for someone, masculinity isn't normally associated with homosexuality, so as we were saying, that person just wanted to try it, or if he is gay and he doesn't want people to know, so he's just said he's been raped so really he did consent.

Operating within each of the discussions was a complex network of shared meanings and messages attributed by observers to our conduct towards one another. For example, some participants indicated that, by virtue of agreeing to go to the defendant's house, the complainant was, to some extent, responsible for any resultant sexual victimization:

> But that's sort of code isn't it, for going back to do other stuff [laughs]. If you met someone at a party, it's not like you have met someone you know then going to watch a film. If you've met someone at a party and you're going back at midnight to watch a film, if it was just a friendly thing and you've found someone to be your friend, maybe you would arrange to do it in a couple of days or next week, or something.

Positioning was also important here. Judgments around the 'messages' and meanings that could have reasonably been intended and interpreted by the defendant and complainant were considered alongside each participant's own likely behaviour in a similar situation. Where a group member indicated that they had made similar decisions to the complainant, the group as a whole were more likely to accept the credibility of the complainant's account and to conclude that agreeing to go to the defendant's house did not automatically imply sexual consent. On the other hand, some participants insisted that they would not do what the complainant in the scenario had done, and used this to attribute a level of contributory responsibility to him. For example, one participant described Ian's decision to go back to David's flat alone as 'very stupid or very innocent'.

These comments suggest that participants relied to varying degrees on sexual 'scripts' to interpret particular behaviour. Such scripts enable 'subject matter to be explained as incorporating a coherent sequence of events'

(Ellison and Munro 2009b). Through a series of inferences, expectations of normal behaviour and personal experience, many participants repeatedly questioned Ian's claim of non-consent. These discussions were influenced by a range of factors, including Ian going back to David's flat, his lack of resistance and injury, and inferring homosexuality on the part of Ian. In addition, in order to retain the coherence of the consent narrative, some participants suggested that the alleged use of restraint was evidence of exaggeration or fabrication, and/or argued that Ian might have made a false rape claim after the event to retain the image of his masculinity in the eyes of others. Amongst other things, what emerges strikingly out of these focus group discussions, then, is the extent to which reasoning that is normally seen as applying to female rape complainants (e.g. the idea that certain forms of behaviour imply consent) were explicitly also applied to Ian.

## SOME POSSIBLE IMPLICATIONS

The initial findings of this focus group research highlight attitudes which rely heavily on myths or misunderstandings regarding the nature of male rape and sexual assault. This research may serve to provide a 'bridge' between negative societal attitudes towards male rape and those exhibited within the criminal justice system. This research suggests that negative attitudes towards male rape in the legal process may partly derive from attitudes in wider society. As Jennifer Temkin and Barbara Krahé have argued in the context of female rape, there is a cyclical relationship in operation here: the treatment of cases by the criminal justice system is influenced by social definitions of 'real rape' and those '[r]ape stereotypes affect the judgments made by individuals dealing with rape cases . . . and thereby shape the understanding of rape as it is represented and dealt with in the criminal justice system' (Temkin and Krahé 2008: 209).

One of the most obvious linkages between the findings in this focus group research and the wider literature on legal responses to male rape concerns the expectation of resistance and injury. There is evidence from the historic, as well as contemporary legal literature, that the notion of male invulnerability to sexual harm has had a detrimental impact on perceptions of male rape complainant credibility. In his examination of legal and social attitudes to male rape in late Imperial China, Sommer found:

> the judiciary was highly skeptical that a man could be raped at all . . . Only a powerless male could be penetrated against his will – and the most unambiguous form of male powerlessness was youth . . . there existed a strong judicial bias against accepting an older male as a rape victim.
>
> (2000: 133–4)

In more recent times, the expectation of resistance also extends into the realm of prison rape. In the United States, an inmate named Roderick Johnson sued prison authorities for allegedly failing to protect him from repeated acts of rape. Prison officials disputed his claims of victimization on questionable grounds:

> In pretrial testimony, Jimmy Bowman, another defendant, explained that Mr Johnson's account was not credible because he had failed to resist the men he said raped him. 'Sometimes an inmate has to defend himself', Mr Bowman said. 'We don't expect him not to do anything.'
>
> (Liptak 2005)

In a recent survey examining the attitudes towards male rape that were held by Metropolitan Police officers in England, Abdullah-Kahn found officers who assumed that men would fight back when being raped. Indeed, the research concludes that, often, 'it is difficult for officers to see how an adult male can let himself get into a situation where he can get raped and be unable to physically protect himself' (Abdullah-Kahn 2008: 171). The problem with the expectation of resistance, of course, is that it is a myth which does not recognize the various ways in which male (and female) victims react to rape. Some men do verbally and physically resist their attackers. But there is also a consistent finding within the literature that 'men are either too afraid to resist or fight back, or [freeze] with fear' and that 'contrary to widely held beliefs that "real men fight back", men often do not or cannot fight back' (Abdullah-Kahn 2008: 208). Analysis of male rape trials also indicates that lack of resistance is sometimes used by defence lawyers to attack complainant credibility (Rumney 2001, 2008).

A further link between the focus group discussions and criminal justice responses to male rape can be found in the way in which participants were more likely to question the credibility of Ian if he were gay than if he were heterosexual. While this view does not necessarily rest on homophobic attitudes, and in the focus group discussions there was little evidence of explicit homophobia, it does reflect the fact that homosexuality and credibility concerns are linked in several ways (Rumney 2009). In research involving both police officers and male rape victims, Lees found that 'police officers are more likely to regard the testimony of homosexual victims as "unreliable" – either to assume that the sex was consensual or that the complaint was malicious' (Lees 1997: 94). Likewise, Abdullah-Kahn's recent research with the Metropolitan Police found that some officers made a range of negative assumptions regarding homosexual victims of male rape, including claims that gay male victims were more likely to make false rape allegations, and/or that they would be less traumatized by rape than heterosexual victims (Abdullah-Kahn 2008: Ch. 6).

## CONCLUSION

In this chapter, exploratory findings about the extent to which rape myths, stereotypes and misunderstandings might impact on societal attitudes towards male rape have been presented. In addition, the influence of the complainant's perceived sexuality and level of intoxication upon assessments of his credibility and culpability was also explored. Though an in-depth analysis of the effects of divergent gender compositions within the groups is outside of the scope of the present chapter, it is worth noting briefly here that there do not appear to have been significant differences in attitudes towards Ian or David based on participant gender.

Emerging findings indicate, in line with pre-existing research on both female and male rape, that participants considered the notion of resistance (as measured by physical injury) integral to their decision about the guilt or innocence of the defendant and the credibility of the complainant. Importantly, some participants also considered the complainant's clothing and concluded that clothing would present a physical barrier, which made claims to having been raped without incurring injury less credible. This finding has not emerged from any previous research investigating attitudes towards male rape, and merits further investigation.

There is also evidence that some participants 'added' information that was not present in the vignette to assist in the decision-making process. Participants also used positioning devices to understand and contextualize the vignettes in terms of their own likely behaviour in a similar situation. These discussions focused on the notion of 'reasonable risk' and the complainant's responsibility to consider his own safety. More broadly, some discussions centred on the culpability of the complainant and were victim-blaming in orientation. There was a linkage here with understandings of sexual scripts – in particular shared meanings and messages around sexual behaviour. A significant number of participants indicated that commonly held meanings and messages about the likelihood of a sexual encounter in the circumstances (i.e. agreeing to leave a party to go to a house with one other person) would have impacted upon the behaviour of both the complainant and the defendant. As a result, the complainant was often seen to be either providing unreliable information, or partly responsible for his own subsequent sexual victimization. These findings suggest that the majority of our participants held attitudes that can be located within a positivist victimological framework, in that they were supportive of a victim precipitation model of rape and advocated the idea of personal responsibility as a mechanism for preventing victimization (Wolhuter et al. 2009).

## Bibliography

Abdullah-Khan, N. (2008) *Male Rape: the emergence of a social and legal issue*, Houndmills: Palgrave Macmillan.

Allen, S. (2002) 'Male victims of rape: responses to a perceived threat to masculinity', in C. Hoyle and R. Young (eds) *New Visions of Crime Victims*, Oxford: Hart, 23–48.

Anderson, I. and Doherty, K. (2008) *Accounting for Rape: psychology, feminism and discourse analysis in the study of sexual violence*, London: Routledge.

Banbury, S. (2004) 'Coercive sexual behaviour in British prisons as reported by adult ex-prisoners', *Howard Journal of Criminal Justice*, 43: 113–30.

Bryman, A. (2008) *Social Research Methods*, 3rd edn, Oxford: Oxford University Press.

Chapleau, K.M., Oswald, D.L. and Russell, B.L. (2008) 'Male rape myths: the role of gender, violence and sexism', *Journal of Interpersonal Violence*, 23(5): 600–15.

Coxell, A., King, M., Mezey, G. and Gordon, D. (1999) 'Lifetime prevalence, characteristics and associated problems of non-consensual sex in men: cross sectional survey', *British Medical Journal*, 318: 846–50.

Davies, M. and Rogers, P. (2006) 'Perceptions of male victims in depicted sexual assaults: a review of the literature', *Aggression and Violent Behaviour*, 11: 367–77.

Davies, M., Pollard, P. and Archer, J. (2006) 'Effects of perpetrator gender and victim sexuality on blame toward male victims of sexual assault', *The Journal of Social Psychology*, 146(3): 275–91.

Doherty, K. and Anderson, I. (2004) 'Making sense of male rape: constructions of gender, sexuality and experience of rape victims', *Journal of Community and Applied Social Psychology*, 14: 85–103.

Elliott, D.M., Mok, D.S. and Briere, J. (2004) 'Adult sexual assault: prevalence, symptomatology, and sex differences in the general population', *Journal of Traumatic Stress*, 17: 203–11.

Ellison, L. and Munro, V.E. (2009a) 'Reacting to rape: exploring mock jurors' assessments of complainant credibility', *British Journal of Criminology*, 49: 202–19.

—— (2009b) 'Of "normal sex" and "real rape": exploring the use of socio-sexual scripts in (mock) jury deliberation', *Social and Legal Studies*, 18: 1–22.

Estrich, S. (1986) 'Rape', *Yale Law Journal*, 95(6): 1087–184.

Fenton, R.A. (2000) 'Separating law from facts: the difficulties faced by the Italian Corte di Cassazione in an appeal for illogicality of reasoning', *International & Comparative Law Quarterly*, 49: 709–19.

—— (2006) 'Breaking boundaries? Sexual consent in the jury room', *Legal Studies*, 26(3): 303–20.

Finch, E. and Munro, V.E. (2008) 'Lifting the veil: the use of focus groups and trial simulations in legal research', *Journal of Law and Society*, 35: 30–51.

Frith, H. (2000) 'Focusing on sex: using focus groups in sex research', *Sexualities*, 3(3): 275–97.

Hamby, S.L. and Koss, M.P. (2003) 'Shades of gray: a qualitative study of terms used in the measurement of sexual victimization', *Psychology of Women Quarterly*, 27: 243–55.

Hickson, F.I. et al. (1987) 'Gay men as victims of nonconsensual sex', *Archives of Sexual Behavior*, 23(3): 281–91.

Hollander, J.A. (2004) 'The social contexts of focus groups', *Journal of Contemporary Ethnography*, 33(5): 602–37.

Human Rights Watch (1995) *Violence Against Women in South Africa: state response to domestic violence and rape*, NW: Washington.

Jamel, J., Bull, R. and Sheridan, L. (2008) 'An investigation of the police service provided to male rape survivors', *International Journal of Police Science & Management*, 10: 486–508.

Jones, I.H. (2000) 'Cultural and historical aspects of male sexual assault', in G.C. Mezey and M.B. King, *Male Victims of Sexual Assault*, 2nd edn, Oxford: Oxford University Press, 113–24.
Jupp, V. (1989) *Methods of Criminological Research*, London: Unwin Hyman.
Kelly, L. (1988) *Surviving Sexual Violence*, Oxford: Oxford University Press.
Kendall, C. and Martino, W. (2006) *Gendered Outcasts and Sexual Outlaws: sexual oppression and gender hierarchies in queer men's lives*, Oxford: Harrington Park Press.
Kitzinger, J. (1994) 'The methodology of focus groups: the importance of interaction between research participants', *Sociology of Health and Illness*, 16(1): 103–21.
Lees, S. (1997) *Ruling Passions: sexual violence, reputation and the law*, Buckingham: Open University Press.
Light, D. and Monk-Turner, E. (2008) 'Circumstances surrounding male sexual assault and rape findings from the National Violence Against Women Survey', *Journal of Interpersonal Violence*. Online. Available at: <http://jiv.sagepub.com/cgi/rapidpdf/0886260508325488v1> (accessed 4 January 2009).
Liptak, A. (2005) 'Inmate was considered "property" of gang, witness tells jury in prison rape lawsuit', *New York Times*. Online. Available at: <http://www.nytimes.com/2005/09/25/national/25rape.html> (accessed 25 November 2008).
Mezey, G.C. and King, M.B. (2000) *Male Victims of Sexual Assault*, 2nd edn, Oxford: Oxford University Press.
O'Donnell, I. (2004) 'Prison rape in context', *British Journal of Criminology*, 44: 241–55.
Pennington, N. and Hastie, R. (1986) 'Evidence evaluation in complex decision making', *Journal of Personality and Social Psychology*, 51(2): 242–58.
Rumney, P. (2001) 'Male rape in the courtroom: issues and concerns', *Criminal Law Review*, 62: 205–13.
—— (2008) 'Gender neutrality, rape and trial talk', *International Journal for the Semiotics of Law*, 21: 139–55.
—— (2009) 'Gay victims of male rape: law enforcement, social attitudes and barriers to recognition', (2009) *International Journal of Human Rights*, 13: 233–50.
Saunders, C. (2009) *The University of Nottingham: School of Law Research profiles*. Online. Available at: <http://www.nottingham.ac.uk/law2/postgrad-research/Profiles/Saunders.php> (accessed on 30 January 2009).
Sivakumaran, S. (2007) 'Sexual violence against men in armed conflict', *European Journal of International Law*, 18: 253–76.
Sommer, M.H. (2000) *Law, Sex, and Society in Late Imperial China*, Stanford: Stanford University Press.
Sorenson, S.B., Stein, J.A., Siegel, J.M., Golding, J.M. and Burnam, M.A. (1987) 'The prevalence and adult sexual assault: the Los Angeles Epidemiological Catchment Area Project', *American Journal of Epidemiology*, 126: 1154–64.
Temkin, J. and Krahé, B. (2008) *Sexual Assault and the Justice Gap: a question of attitude*, Oxford: Hart.
Wakelin, A. and Long, K.M. (2003) 'Effects of victim gender and sexuality on attributions of blame to rape victims', *Sex Roles*, 49(9/10): 477–87.
Walker, J., Archer, J. and Davies, M. (2005a) 'Effects of male rape on psychological functioning', *British Journal of Clinical Psychology*, 44: 445–51.

—— (2005b) 'Effects of rape on men: a descriptive analysis', *Archives of Sexual Behavior*, 34: 69–80.
White, B.H. and Robinson Kurpius, S.E. (2002) 'Effects of victim sex and sexual orientation on perceptions of rape', *Sex Roles*, 46(5/6): 191–200.
Wolhuter, L., Olley, N. and Denham, D. (2009) *Victimology: victimisation and victims' rights*, London: Routledge-Cavendish.

Chapter 21

# Violence against women in South Asian communities in the UK

A culture of silence

Aisha Gill[1]

The central issue in this chapter is how, and to what extent, notions of culture dominate UK criminal justice approaches to dealing with violence against women (VAW), especially when its victims are from Black and Minority Ethnic (BME) – and particularly South Asian – communities. It is argued that the concept of intersectionality – which highlights the complex and interconnecting web of relationships that frame the context in which VAW arises – offers a possible remedy to the pitfalls inherent in current responses to VAW, including those that derive from a misunderstanding of how to embrace diverse cultural traditions in a multicultural society. This concept occupies the first part of this chapter, which then moves on to examine how other contextual difficulties, such as under-reporting of VAW (and especially crimes of sexual violence), complicate criminal justice system approaches to dealing with such crimes. VAW often derives at least in part from the social structures that support it. Therefore, the chapter examines one particular case – that of Zoora Shah, who was convicted of murdering her abusive partner – to illustrate how concepts of 'honour', shame and blame are used to mediate sexual violence and abuse. This case study demonstrates that official criminal justice responses often do not adequately address the complex interplay of social and psychological elements that support VAW. For instance, they do not address the fact that victims of VAW, especially South Asian ones, frequently find it difficult to discuss the crimes that have been committed against them, even as mitigation for offences that they may have committed towards their abuser(s). To move forwards, it is argued that the criminal justice system must engage with more complex discourses about agency, justice and culture in relation to VAW. The chapter then concludes with a discussion of how intersectionality – a victim-centred approach that seeks to more fully address the complexities of VAW – offers such a way forward. The chapter also highlights the need for the integration of victim-support services with services that attempt to prevent VAW; and it touches upon the importance of providing adequate funding for specialist services for BME communities in the UK.

## CONTEXT AND BACKGROUND

Women within BME communities are often represented as oppressed and lacking in agency, unlike putatively 'liberated' Western women, who are seen 'as educated, as modern, as having control over their own bodies and sexualities, and the freedom to make their own decisions' (Mohanty 1988: 65). This affects how women in BME communities are treated: discourses about rape and sexual violence in BME communities are generally attended by the application of specific cultural traits or religious attitudes (and the two are often viewed as interchangeable). Crucially, culture is not similarly invoked to explain the forms of violence that affect Western women from majority groups: a problem that transnational feminist scholars have highlighted in other contexts (Narayan 1997; Volpp 2000). This means that, broadly speaking, we can say that there is a tendency to treat VAW as a cultural problem when it affects BME women, whereas it is seen as a personal, individual crime when it affects Western women (Merry 2006).

This is the first thing that needs to be changed if the problem of VAW is to be properly addressed. Culture should be approached not as a monolithic entity that designates a specific and stable role for women, but with an awareness of the multiple – and often contradictory – strands that define it. If the criminal justice system is to address the problem of VAW, particularly in South Asian communities, then it must adapt, by allowing the voices of the women themselves to be heard and the complexities of their individual situations to be addressed. Crenshaw's (1992) theory of intersectionality is most valuable here because it permits an exploration of the interactions between the social and the personal that inform individual women's responses to violent abuse. The essence of intersectionality is that, in a society marked by multiple systems of domination (based on race, gender and class, among others), individuals' experiences are not shaped by single identities/locations (say, as a woman or a black person): instead, the experience of each individual is marked by multiple social influences and the complex web of structures surrounding the individual represent the myriad, but interconnecting, ways in which she is oppressed. Thus, crucially, intersectionality recognizes that women's experiences are often marked by multiple forms of oppression (Crenshaw 1992).

The simple fact of the matter is that not all women drawn into the criminal justice system as a result of violence they have experienced arrive there for the same reasons or receive the same treatment once there. An approach that moves away from a binary framework of 'woman' as compared to 'man' avoids the trap of essentializing women by viewing them as a unitary category and – consequently – of failing to recognize the important differences between them. For example, women can be situated in powerful/powerless ways in relation to other women and this can contribute to their ability to escape abusive situations. By rejecting binaries and meta-narratives, intersectionality foregrounds the multiple aspects of women's social (dis)location and identities, emphasizing the intersecting forms of oppression that shape their lives (Razack 1998).

It is only recently that work on VAW has begun to draw on intersectional conceptualizations (Batsleer et al. 2002; Horvath and Kelly 2007; Thiara and Gill 2009). An intersectional approach is necessary, not only for providing an understanding of the ways in which different social divisions impact on, and differentiate between, experiences of VAW among diverse groups of women, but also for challenging the problematic unidimensional articulation of cultures and communities in recent policy and legal developments (Thiara and Gill 2009). The ways in which women experience violence, the options open to them in dealing with that violence, and the extent to which they have access to services to help them, are all profoundly shaped by the intersection of gender with other dimensions, such as race, ethnicity, class, culture and nationality. Intersectionality, therefore, has much to offer in exploring women's diverse experiences of violence and their different needs in response to it. An intersection analysis can inform the development of both policies and services, which can thereby be targeted to meet the real needs of victims of VAW. However, it is not sufficient to use intersectionality to highlight the differences between individual women's experiences in relation to the major dimensions of power: there also needs to be an interrogation of the systems of power that (re)produce the many diverse types of subordination that women experience.

Professionals in the VAW field have increasingly used international laws and covenants to hold governments accountable, citing their obligation to protect women from violence (Sen et al. Kelly 2003). The circumstances in which VAW occurs in UK South Asian communities in particular mean that the conventional approach of the police and the judicial system, along with other key actors, remains inadequate. Governmental responses to VAW are failing women. Recent legislation in England and Wales (such as the Domestic Violence Crime and Victims Act 2004; Forced Marriage (Civil Protection) Act 2007) has been challenged on a number of grounds, not least because of its limitations in responding to the needs of BME/South Asian women. To address the issue of VAW directly and effectively, it will be necessary to reconceptualize both legal and social approaches, discarding faulty assumptions through listening closely to the voices of women who have been abused.

VAW has gradually received greater political attention in the UK in recent years. This has led to changes in the way that VAW is conceptualized. Until recently, 'domestic violence' has been used as a 'catch all' term, subsuming different forms of gendered violence, but many feminists are now arguing that the term 'violence against women' promotes a more integrated approach (Horvath and Kelly 2007). The concept of VAW looks beyond the physical and psychological harm that women suffer in order to examine the systems of inequality that support such violence: as such, VAW encompasses a plethora of discrete influences. Women's experiences of violence cannot be treated in a piecemeal way, as though each axis of injustice exists in isolation. On the contrary, VAW is the consequence of many colliding and interconnecting elements. It is part of a more widespread, systemic abuse of women, and can only be properly understood in this context (Horvath and Kelly 2007). It is not simply about rape or physical violence but can also involve abuses perpetrated by family members in order to assert and maintain power over women (for example, to regulate their behaviour and/or coerce them to comply with certain prescribed patriarchal norms and values).

In the context of South Asian communities, forced marriage and 'honour'-based violence, perpetrated in the name of 'culture', are also included under the umbrella of VAW. Moves to tackle VAW in these communities more effectively will require a greater understanding of what acceptable cultural 'traditions' can and should comprise, and especially how such traditions intersect with fundamental human rights. An approach must be forged within which it is possible to respect 'cultural differences' where appropriate, but without resorting to essentialist explanations thereof, which tend to ignore the complexities involved (Thiara and Gill 2009). The political dimension inherent in constructing notions of culture must also be recognized, so as to provide opportunities for scrutinizing and contesting cultural values, especially in terms of how they convey or deny power to members of the relevant group (Narayan 1997).

This is a complex undertaking. In South Asian communities, the silence that surrounds rape and sexual violence means that many crimes go unreported, or are reported long after the event, by which time victims have often suffered repeated abuse. Of particular concern is the belief held by many women from BME backgrounds that the authorities – and particularly the police – have entrenched racist attitudes and thus are likely to dismiss their experiences as simply forming part of, and emerging from, their cultural background (Southall Black Sisters 2007). This problem is further complicated by the fact that all areas of the criminal justice system are plagued by poor success rates in dealing with sex crimes. In recent years there have been efforts to improve the processing of sexual violence and rape cases in England and Wales (Munro and Kelly 2009). Legislation, in the form of the Sexual Offences Act 2003, has also been passed, along with a range of initiatives designed to improve arrest, prosecution and conviction rates. Nevertheless, the impact of this legislation, and its accompanying initiatives, has been limited (Munro and Kelly 2009); attrition rates continue to be high for sexual violence cases (Horvath and Brown 2009).

Statistics collected by the British Crime Survey show that between 47,000 and 61,000 incidents of rape are committed against women each year in England and Wales (Myhill and Allen 2002; Walby and Allen 2004). These statistics also reveal that many women fail to report the crimes committed against them to the police (EVAW 2009). Research suggests that there are four key reasons why South Asian women do not report sexual abuse. While these parallel the reasons provided by non-BME women to some extent, they also provide more particular insights. The first reason is that they feel 'betrayed' by the perpetrators of the crime, who are often well known to their victims as members of the same family or community (Gupta 2003; Siddique et al. 2007; Thiara 2003; Uberoi 1996). The second is that these women often fear that they will not be believed, especially since the criminal justice system struggles to prosecute in cases where the only evidence is the victim's testimony (Gill 2008; Patel 2008; Wilson 2006; Munro and Kelly 2009). The third is that some women believe that the assault is 'not violent enough' to constitute rape (Gangoli 2007; Haven 2008). Finally, professionals report that South Asian female victims experience heightened feelings of shame in relation to loss of 'honour'[2] when compared to their white counterparts for whom shame tends to take on a more personal character: the pressure of being responsible for their family's loss of 'honour', in addition to their own, often prevents South Asian women speaking out (Gangoli 2007; Gill 2009). Family and community responses play a crucial role in allowing women in South Asian communities to publicly discuss rape and sexual abuse. To date, however, the individual experiences of female victims remain largely undocumented (Ahmed et al. 2009). In order to understand the cultural milieu which generates, and too often sanctions, VAW, these women's voices need to be heard by other women, by community leaders, and by the various arms of the state and criminal justice system.

Violence against South Asian women thus needs to be understood in relation to the broader social context of their communities. South Asian women's experiences of violence and abuse cannot be reduced simply to issues of gender inequality or expressions of religion and culture. Instead, they must be examined in terms of the intersection of these and other axes of power. As Bograd states, 'intersections color the meaning and nature of domestic violence, how it is experienced by the self and responded to by others, how personal and social consequences are represented and how and whether escape and safety can be obtained' (in Sokoloff and Dupont 2005: 43). This also impacts on women's subjective construction of their experiences: for instance, whether they view themselves as victims or survivors of violence. Viewing women as victims of cultural practices shapes the service responses that they receive and decreases the likelihood of their pursuing criminal prosecutions. Because a woman's decision to remain silent or to speak out about abuse is shaped by a range of complex factors – personal, social, cultural and institutional – there is a clear need for the criminal justice system to take an intersectional approach.

In cases involving South Asian victims, reductive conceptions of culture are themselves partially responsible for the elision of women's voices. Simplistic notions of multiculturalism at best provide a partial solution, and at worst often serve to marginalize victims of VAW. Indeed, the UK state policy of multiculturalism ignores many of the warnings that have been flagged up by feminist writers about failures in current VAW-related practices and policies. The state has constructed minorities in homogenized ways, further marginalizing women's voices (Gill and Mitra-Kahn 2009; Patel 2008). This, in turn, has meant that responses to VAW have been further removed from real needs, especially the need to recognize and deal effectively with the complexities of individual situations. Too often, multiculturalism is applied in such a way that policies and practices fail to interrogate the norms and values of different cultures. There is an assumption that cultural diversity and sensitivity require these norms to pass uncontested, often even when they are arguably in tension with fundamental human rights (Patel 2008).[3] The case of Zoora Shah, discussed below, provides a vivid illustration of how the UK authorities can pay only nominal attention to the cultural context of the crimes at issue, and in so doing fail to respond effectively to the complexities of the situation.

## THE CASE OF ZOORA SHAH

Zoora Shah, a woman from rural Mirpur in Pakistan, came to Bradford (England) in the early 1970s after an arranged marriage. Her account of her suffering, though inevitably subjective, outlines a history of abuse that chimes with the experience of many other women. She reported in her statements to her lawyers that she was regularly beaten by her husband, and also forced to undergo several abortions to avoid giving birth to girls. She later lost a baby after receiving a severe beating, while another died only a few months after birth. After several pregnancies, she produced two daughters but only one son, so her husband threw her and the children out onto the streets. In 1980, Mohammed Azam, a prominent local Muslim, befriended her and helped her to get a mortgage on a property. However, Zoora claimed that he expected sexual favours in return, when and wherever it pleased him – such as in the cemetery where her two babies were buried, in the back of a car in the presence of a driver, or at home, while her family were in the next room: if she refused, he became violent. She turned to the (male) community elders, but they refused to help her. When Azam was sentenced to 10 years in jail for dealing heroin, Zoora described being plagued by men knocking on her door after their release from prison, demanding sex; Azam was 'pimping' her from prison. After Azam's release, he indicated that Zoora's daughter, Naseem (then aged 10), would be his new target. On a trip to Pakistan, Zoora obtained some arsenic, because she had been told that small doses would douse a fiery libido. However, she eventually gave Azam a larger, fatal dose.

Her testimony, though compelling, did not emerge in her trial for the murder of Mohammad Azam, and in December 1993, Zoora was sentenced to life imprisonment. Crucially, in her trial, Zoora did not mention the abuse she had suffered in mitigation for her actions, as she did not want to bring shame on her family. Her voice had been silenced by cultural forces that intersected and oppressed her. Only during her appeal against the conviction, which she lost, did she admit to poisoning Azam because of his sustained abuse. At her appeal, the judge called her credibility into question:

> We consider first the appellant's own evidence. Making every possible allowance for the difficulty of giving evidence through an interpreter to English judges whose experience of Asian culture is bound to be limited,

we have to say that we found the appellant to be a most unsatisfactory witness, and her evidence to be not capable of belief. For example, she said when giving evidence in chief that at the very beginning of their sexual relationship, before she went to number 251, Azam raped her. In cross-examination she said he treated her with respect 'when we first bought the house'.

(*R v Shah* [1998] EWCA 144: para. 8)

Although 'every possible allowance' was made for the cultural and language barriers she faced, the judge appears to have had little understanding as to why Zoora Shah found it so difficult to accuse her partner of abuse and why, under cross-examination, she claimed that he had treated her with respect. Her cultural background mandated that she preserve the family 'honour' at all costs, even though this prejudiced her own defence. The judge did not appear to fully appreciate the circumstances that made her, in 'Western eyes', a poor witness (for similar criticisms, see also Ellison and Munro, and Buss in this collection). The idea that 'every possible allowance' was made is at odds with the fact that a sensitive understanding of the impact of culture would have recognized that, in South Asian communities, powerful forces serve to render the possibility of women speaking in their own defence problematic: the assumption that a victim would be willing to do so draws on Western notions of how shame impacts on self-interest, and fails to recognize that in BME communities there are often other interests (such as those of the individual's family and community) at stake. What is crucial here is not the credibility of Zoora's testimony, but that the courts could not understand her silence; nor could they see that Zoora was influenced by a myriad of cultural forces that undermined her own testimony when, at last, it did emerge.

Zoora Shah was deemed untrustworthy by the court because of supposed inconsistencies in her testimony (Baker 2008; Carline 2005). However, survivors of sexual violence, and especially women who are bound by strong codes of 'honour' and shame, are not always able to provide the courts with the sorts of consistent, linear narrative that they demand (Gupta 2003). Consequently, courts of law often mistrust the natural voices of survivors and ignore the ways in which trauma may alter the nature and sequencing of a victim's testimony. Women who have survived sexual violence describe their abuse in terms far removed from the sterile language of the law (Smart 1989).

Throughout her trial and appeal, the defence portrayed Zoora in dismissive and essentialized terms as a 'stereotypical' Muslim, Asian woman: someone helpless, vulnerable, sexually accessible and insignificant. She was represented as passive but not – paradoxically – innocent. The Court of Appeal summarized her silence as follows: 'We appreciate that for someone from her background it may not have been easy to unburden herself' (*R v Shah* [1998]: 59). As this quotation demonstrates, Zoora's culture was deemed to define her and her actions. The judge at her appeal appears to have disregarded Zoora's interpretation of why shame and dishonour stopped her 'speaking up' at her original trial, suggesting that she had 'no "honour" left to salvage' because she had been involved in sexual relationships. Among other things, this comment ignored – and failed to problematize – the fact that it was her status as a divorced, isolated and poverty-stricken woman which made her vulnerable to sexual and financial exploitation by a series of predatory men (Carline 2005). Southall Black Sisters, who were involved in her appeal, argued that while the courts often accept cultural and religious factors into testimony when judging Asian men who kill female relatives for failing to comply with community norms (even when such men hold the balance of power in the family and community), they are reluctant to extend such leniency to women.

The application of an intersectional approach to VAW here would recognize how interweaving and mutually reinforcing systems of racial and gendered subordination work to influence South Asian women's encounters with the law. Structural intersectionality, the unique location of minority women at the place where race and gender meet, distinguishes their experience of rape, sexual violence and domestic violence from that of Caucasian women in ways that transcend monolithic definitions of 'culture'. However, the notion of structural intersectionality suggests that not all uses of culture are problematic, and that the legal system *should* take culture into consideration in individual cases. Volpp, for instance, suggests that courts should accept a broader view of cultural evidence that includes 'information on ... the dominant community, the inaccessibility of the local police department, economic constraints, racism and anti-immigrant violence, and the lack of accessible shelters for minority women' (1996: 1573). Schneider (2000) makes the case for linking the general with the specific in feminist law-making on violence, arguing that responses to VAW must take individual women's experiences into account, while simultaneously recognizing the ways in which VAW is connected to broad social patterns of gender subordination and inequality. This goal is difficult to achieve in practice, given the structure of the criminal justice system and the institutional tendency to implement uniform policies. Just as pro-arrest and pro-prosecution policies fail to deal with women's actual experiences, the criminal justice system as an institution fails to adequately address the gendered context in which the rape and sexual abuse of women occurs.

There is, thus, an urgent need for legal and criminal justice efforts to move beyond policy-making and instead look towards bringing about broader social change. Improving long-term specialist services for women – services designed to respond to the different types of VAW and the different contexts in which these occur – is part of the solution. However, there must also be a change in what Scheppele refers to as the 'habits of belief' (1992: 124) which persist across the criminal justice system and result in women being dealt with in ways that ignore contextual and cultural differences. Only after these habits of belief have changed will the discourse on VAW in BME communities – as well as the overarching quest for justice in all cases of VAW – contribute to the continued emancipation of women in the UK.

## AGENCY, JUSTICE AND CULTURE

Zoora Shah's case is representative of the ways in which South Asian women are defined by the legal system in a rigid, stratified manner, and shows how their agency is counteracted both by the authorities and their own cultural traditions. The legal subject must be reconceptualized to increase the power and agency of South Asian women. This reconceptualization must not reinforce culturally essentialist stereotypes: women must be viewed as individuals, not defined by their 'membership' of certain groups. Carline (2005) argues that Zoora Shah's failure to conform to existing essentialist gender and racial scripts led to the court labelling her as an 'unusual woman' and an unintelligible witness. When a cultural defence is introduced into a court case, pre-existing beliefs about culture, gendered violence and patriarchy can be either reified or dismantled (Volpp 1996; Phillips 2003). Defence solicitors often advance a cultural argument (Anitha and Gill 2009); however, while this tactic might secure the rights of some women in the short term, it risks defining them as victim-subjects. This is inherently problematic because 'culture' is never a neutral concept. Indeed, it may contribute to sustaining particular forms of VAW because it can be used to justify abuse. In certain situations, 'culture' is merely a construct – a formal, static system, defined by men – by which women can be judged. Although respect for diverse cultures is an essential part of an enlightened modern judicial system, this respect must not extend to allowing fundamental human rights to be violated. It is vital to recognize that such a faulty approach to multiculturalism may silence the voices of powerless members of different cultures, effectively preventing them from speaking for themselves and exposing the crimes committed against them. When South Asian cultural norms and values are not questioned, men are able to justify VAW by claiming, for example, that 'their' women's infidelity drove them to undertake retaliatory violence (Phillips 2003).

One of the most significant consequences of treating VAW as a cultural problem when it affects BME women but as a personal, individual crime when it affects Western women is that it encourages a conceptualization of cultural traditions as static and ahistorical. Thus, it effaces the ideologies and politics that underlie such practices. Not only does this elide the agency of women, but, by extricating gender from the social relations that produce particular constructions of femininities, the category of 'women' is homogenized. Thus, when South Asian women experience VAW, they become stereotyped as 'Third World women being victimized by Traditional Patriarchal Cultural Practices' (Narayan 1997: 57): that is, as victim-subjects. In women's rights movements, multiculturalism, community cohesion and 'culture' are viewed as sites of contestation, political struggle and domination – a fact often ignored within the broader public discourse. The notion of 'culture', either in its orientalist or occidentalist guise, supports various forms of oppression (Ertürk 2007), not least through the depiction of women from minority cultures as 'weak victims' who are left with little choice but to join forces with imperialist/hegemonic projects or comply with oppressive practices (Ertürk 2007: 3). Thus, a 'cultural focus' – as it has been operationalized in the UK context – risks essentializing women as 'victims', robbing them of agency and voice, and forcing them to conform to stereotypes that reinforce patriarchal dominance and female subordination.

To move beyond such stereotypes, the practices that underpin sexual violence – especially in BME communities – must no longer be represented as purely cultural. Instead, these practices must be examined in the light of the wider context of VAW. Essentialist, static, apolitical and ahistorical interpretations of cultural traditions are problematic because they contribute to reified conceptualizations that result in minority women being viewed as victims requiring the state's protection or as so unusual that their actions cannot be explained by their culture.

The risk in constructing women from BME communities as victim-subjects – cultural specimens rather than individuals – is that this denies them agency and invites protectionist responses from the state. This can be seen, for example, in recent changes in immigration law in the UK; one consequence of that change is that the age of marriage has been increased from 18 to 21 when one of the partners is from overseas. This is undoubtedly a decision intended to protect women, but it has the unfortunate consequence of placing them at greater risk of being taken from the UK and overseas to be married (Hester et al. 2008). The historic inability of the law to capture the multiple ways in which women exercise agency within (and despite) constraints, the preoccupation of the law with the victim-subject, the protectionist responses that often erode women's rights and the reinforcement of gendered stereotypes within legal discourses all encourage feminists to argue that the law remains an essential but insufficient route to gender justice (Kapur 2005). The way forward will involve conceptualizing the legal subject in ways that address individual experiences, but which are not constrained by essentialist assumptions about their attributes. Such an approach would recognize women's agency while recognizing that women often act within narrow cultural and/or structural constraints (Yuval-Davis 1997).

## CONCLUSION

Societies have a responsibility to address the needs of their most vulnerable members. In the UK, however, there is a general tendency to overlook the specific socio-economic and socio-cultural factors that affect BME women who are victims of VAW, placing them in multiple positions of powerlessness relative to men. Agencies and local authorities must acknowledge the complexity of minority women's experiences of, and responses to, gendered forms of violence and abuse. Poverty, health status (both mental health and physical well-being), race, class, language ability, sexual orientation, religious beliefs, disabilities and even place of residence (whether urban or rural), all have a profound effect on South Asian women's ability to access the services and resources they need (Crenshaw 1992). For example, BME victims of VAW may have been trafficked, or they may be asylum-seekers or refugees fleeing war and conflict with their children. These – and a range of other circumstances – contribute to an individual's unique, gender-based 'herstory'. Such complicating factors must be taken into account when designing preventative, protective and interventionist responses to VAW, and especially when responding to individual victims.

Too often the abuse suffered by women within BME communities is separated from the wider political and socio-economic environment within which it emerges, while culture and cultural tradition are simplistically viewed as sufficient explanation for these crimes, usually by construing these women as victim-subjects with little or no agency. A more victim-centred, nuanced approach to VAW must facilitate women's agency by treating them as active subjects rather than passive victims. Such an approach must include provisions to (1) establish victim safety, (2) offer women and their children the opportunity to access specialist support, including therapeutic assistance which recognizes the importance of allowing these women to express the impact of their experiences in their own words, without fear of censure, (3) create responses that recognize women's agency and their desire to have choices, (4) give women from BME communities the right to recourse to public funds when seeking asylum in cases of VAW and (5) provide outreach services to implement preventative measures.

Public support-providers working in the field of VAW are often unable to understand why they are ineffective in responding to the experiences of South Asian victims (Gill 2008). Since they are working in a sensitive area, these professionals must become more willing to explore their own beliefs, values and influences if they are to respond effectively. This is of crucial importance for ensuring that personal biases do not negatively influence their dealings with clients (Coy et al. 2009) and is a critical component of the intersectional, victim-centred approach proposed by Crenshaw. Of course, this is by no means a simple process: it demands an approach that proceeds outwards from the victim, connecting all the different agencies that aim to provide support and assistance. However, a more victim-centred approach may afford providers with the opportunity to learn more about why women under-report abuse and why they often flee their marital home without seeking support from the relevant authorities. Only with a greater understanding of such issues will it be possible to work to avoid the injustices that afflicted Zoora Shah and many others like her.

The critical issue remains the challenge of drawing together diverse legal approaches in order to better flag, detect and punish VAW. This means looking beyond criminal justice solutions in order to more fully engage with social justice approaches towards gender-based violence: evidence suggests that these offer the most promising avenues for effectively combating and preventing gendered violence in the long term (EVAW 2009). However, implementing such changes would require that all those working in public support systems understand the larger picture, in all its complexity. Criminal justice/health/

education/social care agencies must operate as a coherent whole if there is to be an integrated approach to addressing VAW, both in terms of supporting victims and attempting to prevent future crimes. More resources need to be directed towards supporting preventative measures and securing the financial status of specialist services, many of which are currently under threat in the UK from lack of funding. Insufficient funding leads, among other things, to competitive allocation, which – in turn – marginalizes some groups (often the most vulnerable) in favour of others (Imkaan 2008).

Change is possible. VAW in South Asian communities is not inevitable: it is a social problem that can be remedied. For VAW to be permanently eradicated there has to be both political will and socio-cultural motivation, coupled with investment in preventative work. Given the extent of gender-based violence, commitment to prevention and early intervention can no longer be postponed. A system of values based on a commitment to upholding women's human rights must underpin the provision of support to victims of VAW and also feature in long-term plans for eliminating all forms of VAW. Preventative measures must involve pragmatic sequencing of interventions aimed at challenging the normalized acceptance of VAW in certain communities. This ideal represents a truly intersectional approach: one which responds to the sophisticated interactions between women and their lived environment, and which turns its back on the monolithic view of culture once and for all.

## Notes

1   I wish to thank the editors, Vanessa Munro and Clare McGlynn, for their helpful comments and suggestions during the preparation of this chapter.
2   'Honour' (*izzat*) has multiple connotations and overlapping meanings relating to respect, esteem, dignity, reputation and virtue, which are equated with the regulation of women's sexuality and the avoidance of social deviation. Inherent in this code of 'honour' is the need to constantly strive to maintain 'honour' and avoid shame. However, even among communities which subscribe to this code, the specific acts that are deemed to increase or erode *izzat* are subject to constant contestation and change, and vary among particular groups of South Asian communities in both the diasporic context and in South Asia. Shame brings about feelings of humiliation and indignity that leaves individuals feeling exposed as defective in the eyes of others, even when they know that they were not responsible for what has happened to them. The shame experienced by women like Zoora is born from the stigma attached to being in a vulnerable position (Gill 2009); the wish to conceal this vulnerability is at the heart of many women's silence about the sexual violence they have experienced.
3   Many of the discussions on multiculturalism in the UK have focused on the following question: when, and under what circumstances, must the state 'intervene' in the norms of minority groups (see Parekh 2000; Phillips 2003)? More relevant to the case of VAW in BME communities in the UK are policy questions as to where and when the government may intervene based on these multicultural values. Most advocates of 'multiculturalist accommodation' agree that there are some cases where the state must intervene in group norms, and other cases where it should not intervene.

## Bibliography

Ahmed, B., Reavey, P. and Majumdar, A. (2009) 'Constructions of "culture" in accounts of South Asian women survivors of sexual violence', *Feminist Psychology*, 19(1): 7–28.

Anitha, S. and Gill, A. (2009) 'Coercion, consent and the forced marriage debate in the UK', *Feminist Legal Studies*, 17(2): 165–84.

Baker, H. (2008) 'Constructing women who experience male violence: criminal legal discourse and individual experiences', *Liverpool Law Review*, 29: 123–42.

Batsleer, J., Burman, E., Chantler, K. and McIntosh, H. (2002) *Domestic Violence and Minoritisation: supporting women to independence*, Manchester: Women's Studies Research Centre, Manchester Metropolitan University.

Carline, A. (2005) 'Zoora Shah: an unusual woman', *Social and Legal Studies*, 14(2): 217–40.

Coy, M., Kelly, L. and Foord, J. (2009) *Map of Gaps: the postcode lottery of violence against women support services*, London: End Violence Against Women Campaign.

Crenshaw, K. (1992) 'Mapping the margins: intersectionality, identity politics, and violence against women of color', *Stanford Law Review*, 43: 1241–2.

End Violence Against Women (EVAW) (2009) EVAW Campaign. Online. Available at: <www.endviolenceagainstwomen.org.uk> (accessed on 28 April 2009).

Ertürk, Y. (2007) *Elimination of All Forms of Violence Against Women: follow-up to the Secretary-general's in-depth study at national and international levels*, 1 March 2007. Online. Available at: <www.un.org/womenwatch/daw/csw/csw51/panelvaw/YE_CSW_Statement_07.pdf> (accessed 28 April 2009).

Gangoli, G. (2007) *Indian Feminisms: campaigns against violence and multiple patriarchies*, Aldershot: Ashgate.

Gill, A. (2008) 'Crimes of "honour" and violence against women in the UK', *International Journal of Comparative and Applied Criminal Justice*, 32(2): 243–63.

—— (2009) 'South Asian women's experiences of rape: analysis of the narrative of survival', in M. Horvath and J. Brown (eds) *Rape: challenging contemporary thinking*, Devon: Willan Publishing.

Gill, A. and Mitra-Kahn, T. (2009) 'Moving toward a "multiculturalism without culture": constructing a victim-friendly human rights approach to forced marriage in the UK', in R. Thiara and A. Gill, (eds) *Violence Against South Asian Women: issues for policy and practice*, London: Jessica Kingsley Publishers.

Gupta, R. (ed.) (2003) *From Homebreakers to Jailbreakers: Southall Black Sisters*, London: Zed Books.

Haven (2008) *Annual Report*, London: Haven.

Hester, M., Chantler, K. and Gangoli, G. (2008) *Forced marriage: the risk factors and the effect of raising the minimum age for a sponsor, and of leave to enter the UK as a spouse or fiancé (e)*. Bristol: University of Bristol.

Horvath, M. and Brown, J. (eds) (2009) *Rape: challenging contemporary thinking*, Devon, UK: Willan.

Horvath, M. and Kelly, L. (2007) *From the Outset: why violence should be a core cross-strand priority theme for the Commission for Equality and Human Rights*, London: End Violence Against Women Campaign.

Imkaan (2008) *Celebrating 'Herstory'*, London: Imkaan.

Kapur, R. (2005) *Erotic Justice: law and the new politics of postcolonialism*, New Delhi: Permanent Black.

Merry, S. (2006) *Human Rights and Gender Violence: Translating international law into local justice*, Chicago: University of Chicago Press.

Mohanty, C. (1988) 'Under western eyes: feminist scholarship and colonial discourses', *Feminist Review*, 30: 61–88.

Munro, V. and Kelly, L. (2009) 'A vicious cycle? Attrition and conviction patterns in contemporary rape cases in England and Wales', *Rape: challenging contemporary thinking*, Uffculme, Devon, UK: Willan.

Myhill, A. and Allen, J. (2002) *Rape and Sexual Assault of Women: the extent and nature of the problem – findings from the British Crime Survey*, London: Home Office.

Narayan, U. (1997) *Dislocating Cultures: identities, traditions, and third-world feminism*, New York: Routledge.

Parekh, B. (2000) *Rethinking Multiculturalism: Cultural Diversity and Political Theory*, Basingstoke: Macmillan Press/Palgrave.

Patel, P. (2008) 'Faith in the state? Asian women's struggles for human rights in the UK', *Feminist Legal Studies*, 16: 9–36.

Phillips, A. (2003) 'When culture means gender: issues of cultural defence in the English courts', *Modern Law Review*, 66(4): 510–31.

Razack, S. (1998) 'What is to be gained by looking white people in the eye? Race in sexual violence cases', in S. Razack (ed.) *Looking White People in the Eye: gender, race, and culture in courtrooms and classrooms*, Toronto: University of Toronto Press.

Scheppele, K. (1992) 'Just the facts, Ma'am: sexualized violence, evidentiary habits and the revision of truths', *New York Law School Law Review*, 37: 123–72.

Schneider, E. (2000) *Battered Women and Feminist Lawmaking*, New Haven, CT: Yale University Press.

Sen, P., Humphreys, C. and Kelly, L. (2003) *Violence Against Women in the UK: CEDAW thematic shadow report*, London.

Siddique, N., Ismail, S. and Allen, M. (2008) *Safe to Return: Pakistani women, Domestic Violence and Access to Refugee Protection – A report on a trans-national research project conducted in the UK and Pakistan*, Manchester, UK: South Manchester Law Centre.

Smart, C. (1989) *Feminism and the Power of the Law*, New York: Routledge.

Sokoloff, N.J. and Dupont, I. (2005) 'Domestic violence at the intersections of race, class and gender', *Violence Against Women* 11(1): 38–64.

Southall Black Sisters (SBS) (2007) *How Can I Support Her? Domestic Violence, Immigration and Women with No Recourse to Public Funds*, Resource Pack, London: SBS.

Thiara, R. (2003) 'South Asian women and collective action in Britain', in J. Andall (ed.) *Gender and Ethnicity in Contemporary Europe*, London: Berg.

Thiara, R. and Gill, A. (2009) *Gendered Violence in South Asian Communities in the UK: issues for policy and practice*, London: Jessica Kingsley Publishers.

Uberoi, P. (1996) *Social Reform, Sexuality, and the State*, New Delhi: Sage.

Volpp, L. (1996) 'Talking "culture": gender, race nation, and the politics of multiculturalism', *Columbia Law Review*, 96: 1573–617.

—— (2000) 'Blaming culture for bad behaviour', *Yale Journal of Law and Humanities*, 12: 8–116.

Walby, S. and Allen, J. (2004) *Domestic Violence, Sexual Assault and Stalking: findings from the British Crime Survey*, Home Office Research Study 279, London: Home Office.

Wilson, A. (2006) *Dreams, Questions, Struggles: South Asian women in Britain*, London: Pluto Press.

Yuval-Davis, N. (1997) *Gender and Nation*, London: Sage.

Chapter 22

# Sexual assault of women with mental disabilities
## A Canadian perspective

*Janine Benedet and Isabel Grant*

Women with mental disabilities confront sexual assault at an alarming rate. We have argued elsewhere that this reality should be reflected in our understanding of the concepts of consent and capacity in the criminal law of sexual assault (Benedet and Grant 2007a; Benedet and Grant 2007b). In this chapter, we examine recent developments in Canadian sexual assault law and consider whether they are adequate to recognize the experience of sexual assault for women with mental disabilities.

In using the term mental disability, we refer to any developmental disability, psychiatric condition or other chronic, non-episodic disability that affects cognition or decision-making. Of course, the range of conditions that might fall within this category is vast and its boundaries are not clearly fixed. Disability is both bio-medically and socially constructed in ways that shift with time and place. We are focusing on cases where the complainant is an adult woman with impairments in cognition, memory and/or intellectual development that affect her ability to understand and make decisions about her sexuality. Our cases include those with formal diagnoses, such as Down's syndrome or autism, as well as brain injuries and impairments for which there is no identified cause or label. This variation leads to different challenges for each woman, yet despite these differences we see several issues of common concern.

Women with mental disabilities are at a higher risk of physical and sexual violence than women generally. Indeed, studies suggest that women with mental disabilities are from two to 10 times more likely to be the victim of sexual assault than a woman without a disability (Roeher Institute 1995; Ticoll and Panitch 1993). In the specific context of Canada, one prevalence study suggests that 39 to 68 per cent of women with a mental disability will be sexually assaulted before they reach the age of 18 (Roeher Institute 1992). Sexual assaults against women with mental disabilities are also reported and prosecuted at a lower rate than sexual assaults generally (McCarthy 1999; Keilty and Connelly 2001). One study, for example, estimated that only one in 30 sexual assaults of a woman with a disability is reported, as compared to one in five for women who do not have a disability (Sobsey 1994).

There are many reasons for the high incidence of sexual assault against women with mental disabilities. Such women are more likely than other women to be dependent on others for their basic needs and their economic welfare. It may be more difficult for them to meet and to develop relationships with people who are not in a position of trust or authority over them. Women with disabilities face high levels of intervention and control in their lives, be it medical, social or parental. This may lead some women with mental disabilities to develop a high level of compliance toward people in a position of authority. They may not be aware that they can refuse to participate in sexual activity simply because they do not want to participate (McCarthy 1999).

There is also a high level of social segregation for women with mental disabilities both in institutions and in the community. Women with mental disabilities may be denied equal access to education, employment and housing. Poverty is widespread for women with mental disabilities, and poverty and social isolation are both risk factors for sexual assault (Petersilia 2001).

In most studies, caregivers, broadly defined to include doctors, teachers and other service providers, constitute a significant percentage of those who sexually assault women with mental disabilities (Sobsey 1994). Caregivers have ongoing access to women with mental disabilities and there is a relationship of dependency. In addition, a large number of offenders who are not personally in care-giving positions gain access to women through their caregivers (Sobsey and Doe 1991). Women with mental disabilities become targets for sexual assault, given the low rate of reporting and the tendency to disbelieve their claims.

Canada's criminal sexual assault laws have undergone several major revisions in the last three decades that have attempted to address some of the criticisms of traditional rape law by the women's movement. These changes are described in detail elsewhere in this collection (see Gotell). In this chapter, we describe the specific provisions that have been used to address disability in the context of sexual assault, concluding that they have been generally ineffective. Because most sexual assault cases involving women with mental disabilities are prosecuted using general sexual assault laws, we next consider how prosecutions using such laws have failed to offer substantive equality to these women. Instead, women with mental disabilities are often infantilized and disbelieved. Applying the current legal definition of 'non-consent' to women with mental disabilities can also be problematic. Judges, unsure of whether to prioritize protection from abuse or the promotion of sexual autonomy, in the end offer neither.

In our view, these conditions combine to require a reconsideration of basic principles of sexual assault law in a way that foregrounds the issues and concerns of women with mental disabilities. Specifically, we consider both the limitations of our understanding of consent for women with mental disabilities and whether *incapacity* to consent is a concept that should be used more frequently in prosecutions of sexual assaults against these complainants. However, because a focus on incapacity may deny a woman with a mental disability any opportunity to consent freely to sexual activity, we examine other options, such as the requirement that consent be 'voluntary' or a shift in focus to the exploitative conduct of the defendant. We evaluate the possibilities of these concepts against a framework that demands both respect for the entitlement of women with mental disabilities to develop a positive sexuality and their right to protection from men's exploitation and violence.

## CANADIAN LEGISLATIVE HISTORY

Canada has used a variety of legislative responses to address the sexual assault of women with mental disabilities (Benedet and Grant 2007a; Backhouse 2008). Canada's first Criminal Code of 1892 (SC 1892, c. 29) contained a provision making it an offence to have 'unlawful carnal knowledge' of any 'female idiot or imbecile, insane or deaf and dumb woman or girl, under circumstances which do not amount to rape but which prove that the offender knew, at the time of the offence, that the woman belonged to one of the groups listed'.[1] Later versions were expanded to include women who were 'feeble-minded', which the Code defined as 'a person in whose case there exists from birth or an early age, mental defectiveness not amounting to imbecility yet so pronounced that he or she requires care, supervision and control' (SC 1922, c. 16, section 10).

In the major 1982 redrafting of the sexual offences in the Criminal Code, the old offences of rape and indecent assault were replaced with the gender-neutral offence of sexual assault, which requires proof of the application of force (any physical contact) in circumstances of a sexual nature, without consent. The 'carnally knowing idiots' offence was repealed (SC 1982, c. 125). The only vestige of it is a reference in the Code's definition of consent, added in 1992, that 'no consent is obtained where the complainant submits or does not resist because of . . . the complainant's incapacity to consent' (RSC 1985, c. C-46, section 273.1(2)(b)).

In the 1980s and 1990s, disability rights groups campaigned for changes in the law which would recognize that persons with disabilities are especially vulnerable to sexual abuse from caregivers and other persons in authority. They lobbied for a specific criminal offence to address sexual assault of persons with disabilities, while also arguing that the law should not prevent women with disabilities from freely consenting to sexual activity, even in some circumstances with a caregiver (Department of Justice 2001).

In 1998, Parliament enacted the offence of sexual exploitation of a person with a disability in section 153.1 of the Code, which makes it an offence to have sexual contact with a person with a disability where there is a relationship of authority or dependency between the accused and the person with a disability, and where the complainant does not consent. The term 'disability' is not defined and consent has the same definitions as for other sexual assault offences. The maximum penalty for the offence is five years' imprisonment. This new offence was clearly modelled on the offence of sexual exploitation of a young person aged 14–17 by a person in authority, found in section 153(1) of the Code, but with one critical difference: it is not necessary for the Crown to prove non-consent in order to establish sexual exploitation of a young person, whereas the Crown must prove the absence of consent by the disabled person to convict under section 153.1.

The requirement of non-consent in section 153.1 means that the offence adds nothing to the existing sexual assault provisions. The crime of sexual assault already criminalizes sex without consent. Because sexual assault has a greater maximum penalty than the five-year maximum provided for in section 153.1, and is easier to prove, there is little incentive to lay charges under the new section.[2] It is therefore not surprising that in the 10 years since section 153.1 was enacted, it has rarely been used. Four of the seven cases we have found were guilty pleas; a fifth was a decision on a pre-trial procedural motion. In six of the seven cases, the accused was a caregiver or service provider to the complainant; in the seventh case he was the victim's brother (*R v Houle* [2002] JQ no. 9316 (CQ); *R v L (K)* [2004] JQ no. 6783); *R v Ashley-Pryce* [2004] 204 BCAC 186; *R v Sitch* [2005] OJ no. 5969 (CJ); *R v MacDonald* [2008] OJ no. 97 (SCJ); *R v Kiared* [2008] ABQB 767). In *R v Kiared*, the trial judge convicted the accused of the more serious offence of sexual assault causing bodily harm, but acquitted him of the charge under section 153.1 because the Crown had failed to prove that the accused, who had driven the victim's bus on a single occasion prior to the assault, occupied a position of trust or authority.

One of these cases resulted in an appeal to the Supreme Court of Canada, and demonstrates how issues of credibility take on particular significance in this context. In *R v Dinardo* (2008) 231 CCC (3d) 177, the complainant alleged that the accused taxi driver had touched her sexually after picking her up at 'a home for mentally challenged persons'. On cross-examination, the complainant testified that she did lie on occasion and that she sometimes made up stories. However, her assertions of sexual assault at the time of the event were consistent with her subsequent accounts. The trial judge disbelieved the accused and convicted him of sexual assault and sexual exploitation of a person with a disability. The Court of Appeal upheld the conviction but the Supreme Court of Canada ordered a new trial on the basis that the trial judge had not given adequate reasons for accepting the complainant's testimony despite its inconsistencies.

The Supreme Court essentially reversed the trial judge's finding on credibility in the guise of an inquiry into the adequacy of reasons for judgment. Even in the context of a provision specifically designed to protect complainants with mental disabilities, the Court was unable to understand that, even if the complainant occasionally made up stories, her repeated and consistent accounts of the sexual assault were not necessarily false. The Court did concede that most of her evidence about the allegations was consistent, but emphasized that she gave inconsistent evidence, particularly about whether and how often she made up stories. At one point during cross-examination she did state that the allegation was a 'story' but corrected herself on further questioning, making it clear that she stood behind her allegations. Cross-examination was clearly very difficult for this complainant who was easily led into giving the answer defence counsel wanted to hear. The Court never got to the question of consent because, it appears, it did not believe that a sexual touching even occurred.

This decision illustrates the tendency, even in Canada's highest court, to equate mental disability with an inability to give an accurate account of reality or to know what that reality is. The majority of the cases we reviewed involved women with developmental disabilities, not women who were psychotic or out of touch with reality. Yet the tendency to disbelieve women because of their disability is pervasive. Courts often disbelieve such complainants without any empirical support for the proposition that women with developmental disabilities are more likely to lie or be unable to convey the truth.

## NON-CONSENT IN CANADIAN CRIMINAL LAW

In most cases of sexual assault or exploitation of women with disabilities, sexual activity is acknowledged and proof of non-consent is the critical element. In a series of decisions culminating in 1999 in *R v Ewanchuk* [1999] 1 SCR 330, the Supreme Court has held that non-consent as an element of the *actus reus* must be seen from the perspective of the complainant. The issue is whether 'the complainant in her mind wanted the sexual touching to take place' (para. 27). If the trial judge believes that the complainant did not want the sexual activity to take place, then there is no consent. There is no such thing as implied consent, and silence or passivity cannot be substituted for consent. The accused's *perception* of whether the complainant was saying 'yes' is strictly a *mens rea* issue. Any assertion by the accused of honest belief in consent is subject to section 273.2 (b) of the Code, which requires an accused to take reasonable steps in the circumstances to inquire into whether consent was given.

*Ewanchuk* may be useful for some women with mental disabilities. For women who acquiesce in sexual activity although not wanting the sexual activity to take place (McCarthy 1999), *Ewanchuk* clarifies that acquiescence is not consent. However, in many cases involving women with mental disabilities, the *Ewanchuk* formulation is problematic because it focuses the consent inquiry on the complainant's thought processes, thus making her credibility a critical issue. The trier of fact must believe that the complainant did not want the sexual activity to take place. Credibility may be assessed in terms of her words and actions before and during the alleged assault as well as by her testimony at trial. This shift to a focus on credibility may disadvantage women with mental disabilities given that they are less likely to be believed both as complainants and as witnesses (Benedet and Grant 2007a). The recent decision in *Dinardo*, discussed above, shows how this tendency may exist even in Canada's highest court.

This is not the only problem with the *Ewanchuk* formulation. How does the test work, for example, for a woman who is unable to remember what was going on in her mind at the time of the assault (*R v Harper* [2002] YJ no. 38 (QL) (SC)), or the woman who has difficulty communicating those thoughts to a court (*R v Parrott* [2001] 1 SCR 178)? Similarly, what of the woman who never even thought about consent because she didn't know she had the right to say no to sexual activity, particularly with an authority figure? Or a woman who may acquiesce to sexual activity because she thinks it is the price of social inclusion? Clearly, *Ewanchuk* has its limits in addressing the nature of non-consent for some women with mental disabilities and it is these limits that lead us to look elsewhere for other legal doctrines that might better address the reality of sexual assault for women with mental disabilities.

## Voluntary consent

Section 273.1(1) of the Code defines consent as requiring 'the *voluntary* agreement of the complainant to engage in the sexual activity in question'. If a woman feels that she has no option but to consent, is that consent voluntary? In a leading case on voluntariness, *R v Stender* (2004) 188 CCC (3d) 514 (Ont. CA), aff'd [2005] 1 SCR 914, the accused and the complainant had been in a romantic relationship, which had ended prior to the sexual assault. The accused wanted to reconcile and threatened to disclose sexually explicit photos of the complainant if she did not have sex with him again; she complied. The accused was acquitted at trial because, although there was an abuse of power, the trial judge did not find that the coercion in question came within the scope of a criminal 'threat' that would vitiate consent.

The Ontario Court of Appeal overturned this finding on the basis that the apparent consent of the complainant was not voluntary. The complainant had repeatedly stated that she only went to the accused's apartment to delete the photos and that she had told him on both occasions that she did not want to have sex with him. Since she did not want the sexual touching to take place, no consent was present. The Supreme Court of Canada affirmed this decision. In order for consent to be voluntary it has to be the free choice of the complainant, and not the product of a 'deceived, unconscious or compelled will' (*St-Laurent v Québec* (1993) 90 CCC (3d) 291, leave to appeal to SCC refused, [1994] CSCR no. 55, quoted with approval in *Stender*, above).

One could extend this finding to a woman with a mental disability who believes she has no choice but to acquiesce to sexual activity. It remains difficult, however, to set clear boundaries around the concept of voluntariness. Decisions made to engage in sexual activity can be constrained by numerous factors. What about the woman who agrees to engage in sexual activity with her bus driver because she is afraid of losing access to adapted bus services (*R c. Gagnon* [2000] CanLII 14683 (CQ))? What if a woman is encouraged to engage in sexual activity in exchange for small gifts or tokens? It is not clear that such cases are qualitatively different from the woman who acquiesces in sexual activity to avoid the release of sexually explicit photos. Do any of the women in these instances really want the sexual activity to take place? The open-ended nature of voluntariness may render it no more helpful than the non-consent inquiry generally.

## Incapacity to consent

One option for avoiding the problems with the definition of voluntary consent is to make greater use of the doctrine of incapacity. In Canada, section 273.1(2)(b) of the Criminal Code states that no consent is obtained 'where the complainant is incapable of consenting to the activity'. This provision, added in the 1992 revisions, can be understood as codifying the common law, which always held that intercourse with an unconscious woman amounted to rape, and that resistance need not be proven where the women was incapable of resisting (*R v Ladue* [1965] 4 CCC 264 (YTCA)). However, it is also of potentially broader application and might be used to find a lack of consent where the complainant's decision-making ability is impaired by intoxication or mental disability.

Canadian courts have relied on the incapacity provision in both of these situations, but sporadically and without developing a clear standard for how to measure capacity to consent to sexual activity. In the cases involving mental disability that we have reviewed, the Crown typically concedes the complainant's capacity to consent, even where the 'mental age' of the complainant is fixed by experts at a point below the statutory age of consent which, until recently, was set at 14 years.[3] For example, in *R v Parsons* ((1999) 170 Nfld. & PEIR 319 (Nfld. SC)), the 26-year-old complainant was picked up by a stranger in a truck. The complainant was found to have the capacity to consent, notwithstanding evidence that she had a 'mental age' of seven years.[4]

We are critical of the practice of reducing women with mental disabilities to children through the application of crude measurements of intellectual ability, and our reference to the discrepancy between mental age and age of consent should not be understood as an endorsement of this practice. We simply find it surprising that where 'mental age' is measured, it is seldom related to the statutory age of consent so as to trigger a consideration of capacity.

The reluctance of the Crown to argue incapacity can be explained in a number of ways. First, as currently constructed, finding a complainant legally incapable of consent amounts to a statement that she cannot have any consensual sexual activity with another person. This approach is a significant limitation on women's sexual self-determination and thus ought to be applied sparingly. Indeed, Canadian cases that proceed on the basis of the complainant's incapacity to consent are typically ones in which the complainant has little or no understanding of sexual activity in even the most basic mechanical sense, let alone its consequences or social meaning. Thus in *R v Parrott* [2001] 1 SCR 178, the adult complainant had Down's syndrome with cognitive impairments that left her with mental abilities and communication facility similar to a pre-school child. The trial judge appears to have accepted her incapacity to consent. Other cases have found incapacity where the complainant has advanced Alzheimer's disease or no real awareness of the parts of her body or of the mechanics of sexual activity.[5] In most of these cases, the complainant's incapacity appears to be conceded by the defence, and the focus is on whether the sexual activity took place at all. Using incapacity only rarely may be a kind of recognition, however oblique, that women's sexual autonomy ought to be recognized.

Second, if the prosecution argues incapacity to consent, this may undermine the complainant's credibility generally. This can happen in two ways. First, a consideration of the complainant's capacity to understand sexual matters often opens the door to evidence about her sexual history, which can be extremely destructive of credibility. Where such evidence is introduced by the Crown to show the complainant's limited understanding of sexual matters, it is not even subject to the balancing process normally applied to defence applications to admit such evidence because section 276(2) of the Criminal Code, which creates a screening process for such evidence, refers only to evidence adduced by or on behalf of the accused. Some cases have used an inquiry into capacity as an opportunity to introduce evidence that the complainant is sexually promiscuous (Razack 1999). This kind of evidence fuels stereotypes of women with mental disabilities as over-sexed and sexually indiscriminate. More generally, a detailed inquiry into the complainant's cognitive limitations may cast a pall on her credibility by labelling her as child-like, unreliable and easily confused.

A focus on incapacity to consent does not avoid the possibility that the defendant will raise a mistaken belief defence with respect to consent and also a mistaken belief in capacity to consent (*R v RR* [2001] 159 CCC (3d) 11 (Ont. CA)). Such an argument has been successful in the intoxication context, where incapacity is raised more frequently (*R v Millar* [2008] CanLII 28225 (Ont. SC)).

Do the cases involving incapacity based on intoxication tell us anything by analogy about how to measure capacity to consent? Courts generally require a high degree of impairment by alcohol or drugs before a finding of incapacity is made. Incapacity has been defined as 'unable to understand the risks and consequences associated with the activity and the sexual nature of the act and [to] realize that [one] can decline to participate' (*R v Siddiqui* [2004] BCSC 1717: para. 55). Conversely, capacity has been defined as 'some awareness of what is happening and . . . a state of mind capable of processing the information and making a choice' (*R v Cedeno* (2005) 27 CR (6th) 251 (Ont. CJ)). The threshold for incapacity appears to be set at quite a high level; even passing in and out of consciousness is not necessarily sufficient for some judges. One challenge that flows from this high standard is that the only women who meet it are so intoxicated that they may have no memory of the events. This catch-22 is also present for women with mental disabilities in that those women incapable of consent may also be incapable of giving evidence in court.

Incapacity, under various definitions, is used much more frequently in American jurisdictions in cases involving sexual assault against complainants with mental disabilities. The American experience highlights another problem with over-reliance on capacity as a way of resolving these cases. Using incapacity as the litmus test may encourage courts to focus solely on the complainant and to ignore clear evidence of violence by the defendant. Once the court finds that the complainant is mentally capable of consent, the accused is acquitted, without further reference to the clear evidence of force that emerged from the testimony (Stefan 1993). While this result does not flow inevitably from an incapacity test, it is clearly influenced by the view that these are not real sexual assaults but are another form of technical 'statutory rape'. A similar pattern has been observed in American cases involving the age of consent (Oberman 1994; Oberman 2001).

For all these reasons, we are reluctant to encourage expanded use of 'incapacity' by prosecutors and judges, at least as that standard is currently applied. Adult women with mental disabilities ought to be presumed to have the right to form intimate sexual relationships, and ought to be supported, wherever possible, in developing such relationships in ways that do not leave them open to violence and abuse. The current judicial approach to incapacity tends to assume that the capacity to consent to sexual activity and the capacity *not* to consent to sexual activity are equivalent (*R v Jensen* (1996) 47 CR (4th) 363 (Ont. CA)). This leads courts to hold that it would be inconsistent to find both that the complainant was incapable of consent and that she did not consent. We are of the view that it is entirely possible that the complainant may have the capacity to withhold consent, in the sense of knowing that she does not want to be touched by the accused, even where she cannot be said to have the capacity to consent, in the sense of making a free and informed choice to engage in sexual activity. Thus, in the absence of any evidence that the complainant communicated a clear 'yes' to the accused, by her words or actions, it should be found that the complainant has the capacity to not consent and that she in fact did not consent.

The more difficult case is the one in which the complainant appears to go along willingly with the accused's requests, but there is real concern that the accused may be exploiting the complainant's disability. Such cases are hard to prosecute successfully. Under the current law, a finding of incapacity makes these women unable to have any legal sex, while a finding of capacity makes their disabilities disappear.

One solution to this problem is to reject an understanding of capacity as an all-or-nothing measure. Such an approach would be more consistent with the way that capacity is understood in other settings. Certainly, mental health professionals would not consider a client's ability to make financial decisions as an all-or-nothing assessment. The client might be considered capable of making decisions about how to spend a sum of discretionary income, but incapable of making investment decisions. The client might be capable of making certain kinds of financial decisions but only with some support. This situational approach to capacity recognizes that individuals ought to, in so far as possible, be given the opportunity to participate in self-care and decision-making about their own lives.

Applied to the context of sexual activity, we might consider, for example, that a woman with mental disabilities has the capacity to decide to engage in sexual activity with a friend of either sex, and the right to information and support that promotes her sexual health and sexual fulfilment, but that she does not have the capacity to decide to have unprotected sex with a man she does not know in exchange for token compensation. There are obvious problems with attempts to use such a situational capacity approach. The above example focuses not only on the kinds of decisions that a woman can make, but on the wisdom of those decisions. This is akin to saying that a person has the capacity to spend a sum of discretionary income if they spend it on an umbrella but not on lottery tickets. Our problem with either scenario is that it suggests that the woman does not have the capacity to make bad decisions, only good ones. Such a highly nuanced assessment of capacity may be workable in a care-giving capacity, but too vague as a threshold for criminal responsibility.

The real problem with capacity is that it places all the focus on the complainant and not on the accused and his predatory behaviour. What bothers us about so many of these cases is the clear and purposeful exploitation by the defendant of the complainant where he is so obviously taking advantage of a position of power based on both sex and ability.

## Exploitation

We remain troubled by the gap between what the courts recognize as sexual assault and the kind of abusive or exploitative sexual experiences reported by women with mental disabilities. Canadian criminal law fails to deal adequately with cases in which the woman's cognitive or intellectual challenges are exploited by a man who targets such a woman because of his belief that she is sexually deprived, compliant or eager to please. Such cases are similar to those where the complainant is intoxicated but not legally incapable of consent, and the accused targets the complainant because of that intoxication. Can these cases be recognized as abuse without disqualifying the complainant from all sexual activity on the ground that she is incapable of consent?

In several of the cases we found examples of what looked like consent, but which was only obtained as a result of the accused's exploitation of the complainant. The Criminal Code may partially deal with this situation in that section 273.1(3)(c) provides that no consent is obtained where the accused: 'induces the complainant to engage in the activity by abusing a position of trust, power or authority'. This section should capture some situations of exploitation, particularly where a caregiver, a teacher, a doctor or other person in a position of authority or trust is involved. However, there will be cases where exploitation is evident despite no formal relationship of trust, power or authority. In such cases, we would argue that it would be useful to add a similar clause that 'no consent is obtained where the accused induces the complainant to engage in the activity by exploiting her disability'.

The recent decision in *R v Prince* ((2008) 232 Man.R. (2d) 281 (QB)) demonstrates a number of the problems we have explored in this chapter. The complainant in *Prince* had a mental disability and was said to function at the age of a six- to eight-year-old in spite of the fact that she lived on her own. The accused lived in her building and had met the complainant in the hall on a couple of occasions. The accused walked into her apartment uninvited and began to kiss her and to feel her breasts. On the second occasion, he sat briefly with her on the couch and talked to her, then led her into the bedroom and had sexual intercourse with her. His main argument was that she did not say no and did not tell him to stop.

An expert witness testified that the complainant was likely to give the answers she thought the questioner wanted to hear. Despite this testimony, when there were inconsistencies in her testimony on cross-examination, the trial judge was unable to assess these inconsistencies in the context of a woman with a mental disability and instead declined to accept her evidence. While we agree with the trial judge's rejection of the Crown's argument that she was incapable of consenting to sexual activity in any circumstance, a more nuanced fact-specific approach might have inquired as to the relevance of her disability to her capacity to consent to sex with a near-stranger who entered her apartment uninvited.

Most importantly, we believe that the court's attention should have focused more on the accused's behaviour. The accused did not testify, but admitted to police that he was not interested in the complainant and that he felt badly afterwards because he had been 'just using her'. He indicated that she probably had said 'no' but he could not remember. He admitted to knowing that she had a mental disability and yet he took absolutely no steps to determine whether she was consenting. The trial judge found that there was nothing in the situation that should have alerted him to the need to make inquiries and, had the trial judge not found consent, he would have found that there was an honest but mistaken belief in capacity and consent. The trial judge characterized the accused as someone who 'regret[ted] his insensitive behaviour', not someone admitting to sexual assault.

This is precisely the type of case where we believe a provision dealing with the exploitative behaviour of the accused could be useful. Perhaps the complainant in *Prince* had difficulty asserting non-consent. However, *Ewanchuk* makes clear that compliance is not consent. Given his knowledge of her disability, Prince's failure to inquire into consent was exploitative and should have led to criminal liability. In *R v Kiared*, discussed above, the trial judge specifically noted that the accused's actions were exploitative of the complainant's disability and suggested that such a provision be added to section 153.1 to capture situations where there is no relationship of trust, authority or dependency.

## CONCLUSION

So long as Canadian criminal law measures proof of sexual assault according to a non-consent standard, it will be necessary to interpret that element of the offence in light of the realities of women with mental disabilities. If these women are even more likely to be sexually assaulted than other women, our understanding of non-consent, and of affirmative consent, needs to be developed in a way that treats these women as paradigmatic, rather than exceptional, victims. At a minimum, this means that behaviour that appears compliant should not be equated with consent, and the definition of voluntariness ought to be enriched by the recognition that capacity to consent exists along a spectrum and that the effect of external pressures on volition will vary accordingly. Finding that the complainant has the capacity to consent to sexual activity does not make her disability irrelevant. The law must also recognize that intellectual or cognitive disabilities do not make women more likely to lie about being sexually assaulted, even if they may have difficulty communicating their evidence in a way that meets the exacting standards of the criminal trial process.

A more robust understanding of non-consent by necessity shifts the inquiry to the defendant's state of mind and his awareness of that non-consent. Once again, disability is a relevant consideration here, even where the complainant does have the capacity to consent. Canadian law requires the accused to take reasonable steps to ascertain the presence of consent as part of the requirements for a mistake of fact claim. Where the complainant has a mental disability that is in any manner known to the accused, this ought to 'increase exponentially' the steps that are required as 'reasonable' in the circumstances (*R v RR* (2001) 159 CCC (3d) 11 (Ont.CA): para. 57, per Abella JA). No single provision will address the difficulties in prosecuting men who sexually assault women with mental disabilities. A complainant's disability must be understood as relevant to our understanding of consent and voluntariness. A more nuanced approach to capacity, recognizing that the threshold for capacity to say no to sexual activity may be lower than the threshold to say yes, and that capacity is not strictly an on/off switch, but exists in degrees, will help prevent women with disabilities being denied all sexual autonomy. Finally, a provision which focuses on the exploitative behaviour of the accused can assist in cases where it is difficult for a complainant to convey what was going on in her mind at the time of the sexual activity. Real reform, however, requires a more fundamental shift in attitudes. This means that women with mental disabilities are no longer to be seen as outside the circle of 'typical' complainants and that judges should not treat their evidence in court as inherently suspect.

## Notes

1 The provision first entered Canadian law in 1866: SC 1886 (49 Vic.), c. 52, section 1(2).
2 Both in the House of Commons and in Committee, MPs raised concerns that 'the current section 271, which refers to sexual assault for anyone, is much broader and calls for a stronger sentence of 10 years as opposed to 5'. MP Richard Marceau, Hansard, April 30, 1998 at 6383–6. See also *JURI* (12 March 1998) at 16:45–16:50 (Hon. Anne McLellan); Canada, *Senate Debates* (19 October 1997) at 269 (Hon. Noel Kinsella).
3 The age was raised to 16 in 2008: *Tackling Violent Crime Act, SC 2008*, c. 6, sections. 13, 54.

4 See also *R v Hundle*, (2002) 10 CR (6th) 37 (Alta. QB) [complainant's mental age substantially under 16]; *R v N.J.D.* [1990] 112 NBR (2d) 271 (CA) [complainant had mental age of 11-year-old child].
5 *R v McPherson*, [1999] BCJ no. 518 (SC); *R c. Duhamel*, 2002 CanLII 41275 (Que. CA).

## Bibliography

Backhouse, C. (2008) *Carnal Crimes*, Toronto: Osgoode Society.

Benedet, J. and Grant, I. (2007a) 'Hearing the sexual assault complaints of women with mental disabilities: consent, capacity and equality', *McGill Law Journal*, 52: 243–90.

—— (2007b) 'Hearing the sexual assault complaints of women with mental disabilities: procedural and evidentiary issues', *McGill Law Journal*, 52: 515–54.

Department of Justice Website, Index of Past Consultations. Online. Available at: <http://Canada.justice.gc.ca/en/cons/accea/I.Html> (accessed May 10 2001).

Keilty, J. and Connelly, G. (2001) 'Making a statement: an exploratory study of barriers facing women with an intellectual disability when making a statement about sexual assault to police', *Disability & Society*, 16: 273–91.

McCarthy, M. (1999) *Sexuality and Women with Learning Disabilities*, London: Jessica Kingsley.

Oberman, M. (1994) 'Turning girls into women: reevaluating modern statutory rape law', *Journal of Criminal Law & Criminology*, 85: 15–79.

—— (2001) 'Girls in the master's house: of protection, patriarchy and the potential for using the master's tools to reconfigure statutory rape law', *De Paul Law Review*, 50: 799–826.

Petersilia, J. (2001) 'Crime victims with developmental disabilities: a review essay', *Criminal Justice & Behaviour*, 28: 655–94.

Razack, S. (1999) *Looking White People in the Eye*, Toronto: University of Toronto Press.

Roeher Institute (1992) *No More Victims: a manual to guide counselors and social workers in addressing the sexual abuse of people with a mental handicap*, North York: Roeher Institute.

—— (1995) *Harm's Way: the many faces of violence and abuse against persons with disabilities*, North York: Roeher Institute.

Sobsey, D. (1994) *Violence and Abuse in the Lives of People With Disabilities: the end of silent acceptance?*, Baltimore: Paul H. Brookes.

Sobsey, D. and Doe, T. (1991) 'Patterns of sexual abuse and assault', *Sexuality and Disability*, 9(3): 243–59.

Stefan, S. (1993) 'Silencing the different voice: competence, feminist theory and law', *University of Miami Law Review*, 47: 763–816.

Ticoll, M. and Panitch, M. (1993) 'Opening the doors: addressing the sexual abuse of women with an intellectual disability', *Canadian Women's Studies*, 13: 84–7.

# Index

Abdullah-Kahn, N. 294, 303
Abrahams, N. 251–3, 259–60; and Jewkes, R. 251–3, 259–60
Adjamagbo-Johnson 127
Adjami, M.E. 124, 130
Adjetey, F. 123
Adler, Z. 140, 165, 268, 281
AFRC case, SCSL-04–160T, Trial Chamber, 20 June 2007: 57
Africa 122–33
African Charter on Human and Peoples' Rights 96, 122, 124, 127–8, 133; Article 18 124; Section 29 124
African Commission on Human and Peoples' Rights 100, 124, 127–9; Article 5 100
African Rights 1995 69
African Union 132
African Women's Protocol 122–33; Article 1 124–5; Article 2 125; Article 3 125; Article 4 126; Article 14 131; Article 16 128; Article 20 131; Article 25 128; Article 26 126; Article 27 126; Article 32 126
Ahmed, B. 312
*Akayesu* see *Prosecutor v Akayesu*
Albertyn, C. 251–6, 261; and Goldblatt, B. 255, 261
*Allan v HMA*, 2004 SCCR 278: 156
Allen, J. 142, 311; and Myhill, A. 142, 311; and Walby, S. 142, 311
Allen, S. 294
Alston, P. 109; and Steiner, H. 109
Alvarez, J. 61, 70
Amnesty International 83–4, 144, 147
Anderson, E. 32; and Pildes, R. 32
Anderson, I. 294–5, 300–1; and Doherty, K. 294–5, 300–1
Anderson, M. 164, 176, 227, 229

Andersson, U. 201, 204, 206
Anitha, S. 316; and Gill, A. 316
Archard, D. 27
Armed Forces Revolutionary Council 56
Artz, L. 253, 255, 258–61; and Combrinck, H. 253, 255, 258–61; and Smythe, D. 233
Ashworth, A. 20, 141, 143–4, 180, 268; and Temkin, J. 20, 141, 143–4, 180
Asia 12, 123
Asian Centre for Human Rights (ACHR) 100; Article 5 100
Askin, K. 49, 92
Asp, P. 200
Association of Chief Police Officers in Scotland 162
Association for Protection of Women's Rights (APWR) 96–9; Article 1 98; Article 11 97; Article 14 97
*AT v Hungary*, Comm. 2/2003: 103
*Attorney-General's Reference (no. 29 of 2008)* [2008] EWCA Crim 2026: 146
Australia 156, 159, 161, 237–49
Australian Bureau of Statistics, Personal Safety Survey 242
Australian Centre for the Study of Sexual Assault 243
Australian Institute of Criminology 243
Austria 95, 170, 269
*Aydin v Turkey*, ECtHR App. 25660/94 1997: 95, 100, 111, 113–14

Bačić, F. 174; and Pavlović, S. 174
Bacik, I. 26, 268–70
Baden, S. 251, 254
*Bagambiki* see *Prosecutor v Bagambiki et al.*
*Bagosora* see *Prosecutor v Bagosora*
Baird, V. 147

Baker, B. 23
Baker, H. 314
Baker, R. 33
Banbury, S. 294
Banda, F. 123, 125–7, 129, 132
*Barayagwiza et al.* see *Prosecutor v Barayagwiza et al.*
Bath, E. 104; and Byrnes, A. 104
Batsleer, J. 310
Beijing Platform for Action 98, 128
*Belgian Linguistics* (1979–80) 1 EHRR 252: 119
Belgium 269
Beloof, D. 270
*Bemba* see *Prosecutor v Bemba*
Ben-Ari, N. 83; and Harsch, E. 83
Benedet, J. 215–19, 228, 322, 324, 326; and Grant, I. 215, 218–19, 228, 322, 324, 326
Benn, M. 140; and Coote, A. and Gill, T. 140
Benninger-Budel, C. 93–4
Berglund, K. 204–5
Berlin 48
Bianchi, L. 76, 80
Binion, G. 94
*Black v Ruxton* (1998) SLT 1282: 274
Blackburn, S. 32
Blackstone, W. 226
Bluett-Boyd, N. 242
Boeschen, L. 281
Bono, P. 186; and Kemp, S. 186
Bonthuys, E. 252
Borgida, E. 281, 290; and Brekke, N. 290; and Frazier, P. 281
Bosnia-Herzegovina 50
Bower, L. 281; and Dalton, M. 281
Braithwaite, J. 82
Brekke, N. 290; and Borgida, E. 290
Brereton, D. 281
Brezsnyak, M. 37; and Whisman, M.A. 37
Brienen, M.E.I. 268–9; and Hoegen, E.H. 268–9
British Crime Survey 142, 311
Brodie, J. 211, 220
Bronitt, S. 281
Brouwer, A-M.L.M. 53
Brown, B. 140, 273
Brown, J. 20, 311; and Horvath, M. 311
Brown, W. 240
Brownmiller, S. 3, 48, 227
Brunet, A. 64
Bryden, D. 228; and Lengnick, S. 228

Bryman, A. 295
Buddie, A. 281; and Miller, A. 281
Bulgarian Criminal Code 113
Burchell, J. 255, 258–9
Bureau of Justice Statistics (US) 230–1
Burgess, A. 281; and Holmstom, L. 281
Burman, M. 165–6, 268, 273
Burt, C. 281; and Clay-Warner, J. 281
Burton, F. 147; and Scott-Ham, M. 147
Buss, D. 17, 55–6, 62, 70–1, 76, 78–9, 92, 314
Butegwa, F. 127
Byrnes, A. 103–4; and Bath, E. 104

Cadoppi, A. 188–91, 194
Calhoun, L. 284
Cambodia 59
Cameron, J. 270
Campbell, C. 85
Campbell, K. 62, 70–1
Campbell, R. 26; and Raja, S. 26
Canada 21, 161, 209–221, 270, 275, 277, 322–34
Canadian Charter of Rights 210, 270, 276
Canadian Criminal Code 209–14, 270, 324–31
Canadian Violence Against Women Survey 213
Carline, A. 314–16
Carlson, K. 84; and Mazurana, D. 84
*Carmichele v Minister of Safety and Security, Minister of Justice*, 2001 (4) SA 938 (CC): 256
Carswell, Lord 145
Cassese, A. 113–14
Cavallaro, R. 130
*Celebici* see *Prosecutor v Celebici*
Central African Republic 58
*Cesic* see *Prosecutor v Cesic*
Chalmers, J. 162, 164, 166
Chamallas, M. 115
Chambers, G. 272, 274; and Millar, A. 272, 274
Chapleau, K.M. 300
*Charles Sweenie* (1858) 3 Irv. 109: 155
*Charles Taylor* see *Prosecutor v Charles Taylor*
Charlesworth, H. 6, 48, 93, 109; and Chinkin, C. 48
Charter of the International Military Tribunal see International Military Tribunal
Charter of the International Military

Tribunal for the Far East *see* International Military Tribunal for the Far East
Chase, O. 270
China 49
Chinkin, C. 48, 93; and Charlesworth, H. 48
Chirwa, D.M. 124–5, 127
Civil Defence Forces case, SCSL-04-14-T, Trial Chamber, 2 August 2007: 56–7
Christie, M. 155; and Jones, T. 155
Christie, N. 8
Circeo Massacre 185
*CJLS v HM Advocate* [2009] HCJAC 57: 157
Clay-Warner, J. 281; and Burt, C. 281
*Clement Kayishema and Obed Ruzindana* see *Prosecutor v Clement Kayishema and Obed Ruzindana*
Coalition for Women's Human Rights in Conflict Situations 64
*Coker v Georgia*, 433 US 584 (1997): 225
Cold War 50
Cole, A. 17–18, 61, 63, 83
Combrinck, H. 132, 251–6, 258–61; and Artz, L. 253, 255, 258–61
Comfort Women Case, Judgment of April 27, 1998: 49
Committee on Economic, Social and Cultural Rights 96
Committee on the Elimination of Discrimination Against Women 96
Committee on the Elimination of Racial Discrimination 96
Committee on the Quality of Life and Status of Women (South Africa) 254
Commission for the Status of Women (South Africa) 254
Commission on Violence against Women (Italy) 197
*Commonwealth v Berkowitz*, 641 A.2d 1161 (Pa. 1994): 228
*Commonwealth v Lopez*, 745 NE 2d 961 (Mass. 2001): 230
Conaghan, J. 276
Connelly, G. 322; and Keilty, J. 322
Conot, R.E. 48
Constitution of the Republic of South Africa 108 of 1996: 254–5
Convention on the Elimination of All Forms of Discrimination Against Women (CEDAW) 93–4, 96, 104, 114, 118, 124–5, 127–8, 131, 133; Article 2 125; Article 6 93; Article 14 128; General Recommendation 1992 97
Convention on the Rights of the Child 104
Convention on the Rights of the Persons with Disabilities 2006 104
Coote, A. 140; and Benn, M. and Gill, T. 140
Copelon, R. 51, 54, 63, 92–3, 100
Cornell, D. 104
Council of Europe 109, 117, 120, 170, 269; Combating Violence against Women (2008) 120; The Position of the Victim in the Framework of Criminal Law and Procedure (1985) 269; Protection of Women against Violence (2002) 177
Cowan, S. 19, 22, 35, 126, 143, 156, 162
Coxell, A. 294
Coy, M. 143, 318
Crenshaw, K. 309, 317
Crew, A.B. 221
Crimes Act 1958 (Vic.) 240–1, 247; Section 37 240–1, 247
Crimes (Sexual Assault) Amendment Act 1981 (NSW) 239
Criminal Justice and Public Order Act 1994 (UK) 140
Criminal Justice Sexual Offences Taskforce 2006 (Canada) 213
Criminal Law (Consolidation) (Scotland) Act 1995 154, 156; Section 7 156
Criminal Law and Penal Methods Reform Committee 1976 (the Mitchell Committee) (Australia) 238–9
Crenshaw, K. 225
Croatia 10, 12, 50, 169–81
Croatian Code of Criminal Procedure 175–6, 179
Croatian Criminal Code 170–81; Article 188 175; Head XIII 171; Head XVI 171–2
Crowe, C. 225
*CT and KM v Sweden*, CAT Comm. 279/2005: 96
Cunliffe, E. 271
*Cyangugu* see *Prosecutor v Bagambiki et al.*
Cyprus 110
*Cyprus v Turkey* (1982) 4 EHHR 482: 110–11, 118

Dalton, M. 281; and Bowyer, L. 281

Darfur 85
Davies, M. 294, 300; and Rogers, P. 300
*DC and JC v UK* (2003) 36 EHRR 14: 115
de Londras, F. 61, 64
de Than, C. 276
Deisen, C. 198–9, 201–2, 205–6; and Deisen E. 199, 201, 205–6
Deisen, E. 199, 201, 205–6; and Deisen, C. 199, 201, 205–6
del Ponte, C. 64
*Delacic* see *Prosecutor v Delacic*
Dembour, M.B. 62, 70; and Haslem, E. 62, 70
Denmark 269–71
Desrosiers, J. 220
Dewar, D. 157
*Director of Public Prosecutions v Morgan* [1975] 2 WLR 913: 139–40, 144, 156
Doak, J. 26
Doe, T. 323; and Sobsey, D. 322–3
Doherty, K. 294–5, 300–1; and Anderson, I. 294–5, 300–1
Domestic Violence Act 2007 (Ghana) 133
Domestic Violence, Crime and Victims Act 2004 (UK) 310
Donini, M. 192
*Doorson v The Netherlands* [1996] ECHR 14: 276
Douzinas, C. 240
Draft Criminal Code for Scotland 154
Dripps, D. 19, 229
Dubois, T. 220
Duff, R.A. 31
Du Mont, J. 281; and Whyte, D. 281
Dupont, I. 312; and Sokoloff, N.J. 312
du Toit, L. 27
Dyer, C. 141, 147–8; and Morris, S. 147
Dylan, A. 218, 220

*E v UK* (2003) 36 EHRR 31: 112–14
Easton, S. 118
Ebeku, K.S.A. 123, 131
*Edwards v UK* [2002] 15 EHRR 417: 274–5
Edwards, A. 96–102, 109
Edwards, S. 140
Effange-Mbella, E. 80
*Egglestone v S* [2008] 4 All SA 207: 260
Ehrlick, S. 272, 281
Elliott, D.M. 294
Ellison, L. 25, 228, 231, 271, 281, 283, 286, 290, 297, 302, 314; and Munro, V. 25, 228, 231, 271, 283, 286, 290, 297, 302, 314
Elman, A. 197
England and Wales 19–20, 40–1, 139, 141–51, 156, 158–9, 161–2, 281, 310–11
Engle, K. 4, 71, 88, 92, 100; and Lottmann, A. 71
Enloe, C. 62, 72
*Ephrahim v Pastory* (2001) AHRLR 236 (TzHC 1990): 131
Equality and Human Rights Commission Scotland 161
Equality Network 160–1
Ertürk, Y. 102–3, 316–17
Estrich, S. 261, 268, 297
Ethiopia 122, 131
Europe 9–12, 109–10, 175, 199, 269–70
European Convention on Human Rights (ECHR) 109–20, 163, 273–6; Article 1 119; Article 3 100, 110–15, 118–19, 273–4, 276; Article 4 119; Article 5 119; Article 6 145, 173–4; Article 7 112; Article 8 112–13, 115, 273, 276; Article 13 276; Article 14 110, 117–19; Article 19 109; Article 33 109; Article 34 109; Protocol 12 110, 118–20
European Union (EU) 109, 170
Everhart, A.J. 186
Ewing, A.P. 99

Fairstein, L. 225
Falconer, Lord 145, 147
Farinelli, R. 185
Farley, M. 40
Fawcett Society 142
Fenton, R. 149–51, 185, 187, 193, 298; and Rumney, P. 149–51
Ferguson, P. 156, 162–3, 165–6; and Raitt, F. 156, 162–3, 165–6
Fiandaca, G. 186
Finch, E. 20, 144, 147, 149, 162, 164, 166, 283, 296, 299; and Munro, V. 20, 144, 147, 149, 162, 164, 166, 283, 296, 299
Finkelstein, C. 31
Fischer, K. 281
Fisher, B. 281
Fletcher, G. 27
Fletcher, L. 70; and Weinstein, H. 70
*Florida v Smith* (1992) (Kennedy-Smith case) 232
Forced Marriage (Civil Protection) Act 2007 (UK) 310

Foucault, M. 6
France 269
Francis, V.A. 253, 260
Franke, K. 70, 100
Fraser, F. 93
Frazier, P. 281; and Borgida, E. 281
Freckelton, I. 281
Friedland, S. 290
Friedman, E. 95
Frith, H. 296
*Furundijza* see *Prosecutor v Furundijza*

Gangoli, G. 312
Garačić, A. 175
Gardner, J. 21, 31, 34; and Shute, S. 21, 160
Garkawe, S. 272
*Garvock v HMA*, 1991 SCCR 593: 160
Gender at the International Criminal Tribunal for the Former Yugoslavia 76
Geneva Conventions 52–7; Article 2 52; Common Article 3 52–7
Genocide Convention 54
Germany 12, 170, 269
Gibb, F. 147–8
Gill, A. 310–12, 316, 317, 319; and Anitha, S. 316; and Thiara, R. 310–11
Giobbe, E. 40
*Goekce (deceased) v Austria*, Comm. 5/2005: 103
Goffman, E. 77, 80
Goldblatt, B. 255, 261; and Albertyn, C. 255, 261
Goldfarb, S.F. 97
Goodman, J.E. 225
Gormley, L. 96, 102
Gotell, L. 161, 169, 180, 211–18, 243, 275, 323
Government Equalities Office (UK) 142–3
Grant, I. 215, 218–9, 228, 322, 324; Benedet, J. 215, 218–19, 228, 322, 324
Graycar, R. 21, 239; and Morgan, J. 21, 239
Green, L. 38
Greenspan, E. 268, 271
Gregory, J. 141; and Lees, S. 141
Gross, H. 37
Gupta, R. 311, 314

Haddad, R.I. 233–4
*Hadijatou Mani Koraou v Niger*, Judgment no. ECW/CCJ/JUD/06/08 of 27 October 2008: 129

Haffajee, R.L. 61
Hale, Baroness 145
Hale, Sir Matthew 1, 19, 226
Halfwordson, A. 203
Hallet, Lady Justice 146
Halley, J. 4–6, 79
Hamby, S.L. 296; and Koss, M.P. 296
Hanciles, E. 132
Hancock, B. 271; and Jackson, J. 271
Harsch, E. 83; and Ben-Ari, N. 83
Haslem, E. 62, 70; and Dembour, M.B. 62, 70
Hastie, R. 298; and Pennington, N. 298
Hattem, T. 220
Hayner, P. 83
Heaton-Armstrong, A. 282; and Wolchover, D. 282
Hedge, B. 281; and Petrak, J. 281
Heenan, M. 241; and Murray, S. 241
Hengehold, L. 240
Herring, J. 30, 32, 35–38; and Madden Dempsey, M. 30, 32, 35–6, 38
Hester, M. 317
Hickson, F.I. 294
Hoegen, E.H. 268–9; and Brienen, M.E.I. 268–9
Hoff-Summers, C. 11
Hollander, J.A. 296
Holmes, Justice 6
Holmstom, L. 281; and Burgess, A. 281
Hope, Lord 145
Horney, J. 273; and Sphon, C. 273
Horvath, M. 310–11; and Brown, J. 311; and Kelly, L. 310–11
Human Rights Act 1998 (UK) 141, 145
Human Rights Commission 96, 102
Human Rights Committee 118–19
Human Rights Watch 70, 82, 297
Hume, Baron 154–5
Hungary 103
Hurd, H. 34

Iceland 270–1
ICC Rules of Procedure and Evidence 58, 277; Rule 16 277; Rule 88 58
ICC Statute 52, 53, 58, 92, 277; Article 7 92; Article 8 92 ; Article 68 58
ICTR Statute 53; Article 3 53; Article 4 53
ICTR Rules of Procedure and Evidence 53
ICTR Sexual Violence Committee 80
ICTY Statute 50–2; Article 3 52; Article 5 50–1

ICTY Rules of Procedure and Evidence 50; Rule 96 50; Rule 34 50
*Illhan v Turkey* (2002) 34 EHRR 36: 114
*In re MTS*, 609 A.2d 1266 (NJ 1992): 229
Inter-American Convention on the Prevention and Punishment and Eradication of Violence Against Women (IA-VAW) 96, 99; Article 1 99; Article 2 97, 99
International Center for Research on Women 86
International Center for Transitional Justice 84
International Crime Victim Survey (ICVS, Croatia) 171, 180
International Criminal Court (ICC) xiii, 9, 47, 57–9, 177–8; Elements of Crime (2002) 177–8
International Convention on the Elimination of All Forms of Racial Discrimination 104
International Convention on the Protection of the Rights of All Migrant Workers and Members of Their Families 1990 104
International Covenant on Civil and Political Rights (ICCPR) 93, 100, 104, 118–19, 120, 125; Article 3 118, 120; Article 7 93, 100, 118; Article 8 118; Article 119; Article 26 120
International Covenant on Economic, Social and Cultural Rights 104, 125–6
International Criminal Tribunal for the former Yugoslavia (ICTY) 7, 9, 17–18, 47, 50–9, 61, 73, 83, 88, 114, 116, 170, 177–8
International Criminal Tribunal for Rwanda (ICTR) xiii, 2, 6, 9, 17, 21, 47, 53–9, 61–73, 76–83, 100, 116; Office of the Prosecutor 61, 63–6, 71; Witness and Victim Support Section 71
International Law Commission 58, 102
International Military Tribunal 49; Charter of, 49; Official Documents 1945–46
International Military Tribunal for the Far East Indictment 49; Charter of, 49
*Ireland v UK* (1978) 2 EHRR 25: 110–11
Italy 183–194
Italian Statistics Office 184, 194

Jackson, J. 271; and Hancock, B. 271
Jamel, J. 294
*Jamieson v HMA* 1994 SLT 573: 156
Japan 49
*Jane Doe v Metropolian Toronto Police* (1998) 39 OR (3d) 487: 220–1
Jeeves, P. 146
Jefferson, L.S.R. 83
Jeske, D. 36
Jewkes, R. 251–3, 259–60; and Abrahams, N. 251–3, 259–60
Jiwani, Y. 218; and Young, M.L. 218
Johansson, L. 203; and Wersäll, F. 203
Johnson, H. 213–4; and Sacco, V. 213
Jones, T. 155; and Christie, M. 155
Jordan, J. 281
Joudo, J. 281; and Taylor, N. 281
Jung, H. 270
Jupp, V. 295
Justice Committee Official Report (Scotland) 157, 160–5

Kaldal, A. 196, 204, 206; and Sutorius, H. 196, 204, 206
Kanusher, C. 227
Kapur, R. 317
Karmen, A. 272–3
Karuganjo Segawa, R. 124–5
*Katanga and Ndjulu-chou* see *Prosecutor v Katanga and Ndjulu-chou*
Kauffman, G. 284
Kaufman, N.H. 97; and Lindquist, S.A. 97
Kazibwe, S. 123
Keenan, A. 82; and Nesiah, V. 82
Keilty, J. 322; and Connelly, G. 322
Kelly, L. 20, 115, 140–3, 147, 158, 199, 254, 258, 267, 274, 294, 310–12; and Horvath, M. 310–11; and Lovett, J. 142, 199; and Munro, V. 20, 311–12; and Regan, L. 26, 109, 141–2, 158, 267
Kelsall, M.S. 70, 83; and Stepakoff, S. 70, 83
Kemp, S. 186; and Bono, P. 186
Kendall, C. 294; and Martino, W. 294
Kennedy, D. 86–8
Kesić, V. 170
Kitzinger, J. 296
Klein, R. 227, 233
Klug, F. 276
Konradi, A. 283
*Kordic and Cerkez* see *Prosecutor v Kordic and Cerkez*
Koskenniemi, M. 61
Kosovo 56
Koss, M. 286

Krahé, B. 20, 142, 144, 166, 281, 290, 296–7, 302; and Temkin, J. 20, 142, 144, 166, 281, 290, 296–7, 302
Krulewitz, J. 284
*Kunarac et al.* see *Prosecutor v Kunarac et al.*
*Kupreskic et al.* see *Prosecutor v Kupreskic et al.*
*Kvocka et al.* see *Prosecutor v Kvocka et al.*

Lacey, N. 150, 165
LaFree, G. 233
Latin America 12
Lattimer, M. 61; and Sands, P. 61
Leebaw, B.A. 61
Lees, S. 140–1, 281, 303; and Gregory, J. 141
Leijonhufvud, M. 201, 203, 205–6
Lengnick, S. 228; and Bryden, D. 228
Lesbian, Gay, Bisexual and Transgender (LGBT) Domestic Abuse 161, 163
Liberia 95
Light, D. 294; and Monk-Turner, E. 294
Limann, L.H. 125
Lindquist, S.A. 97; and Kaufman, N.H. 97
Liptak, A. 303
Lither, O. 133
Littleton, H. 283; and Radecki Breitkopf, C. 283
Llewellyn, K. 6
Lombardi, J. 233
London Agreement, 8 August 1945: 49
Londono, P. 114, 177, 273–4, 276
Long, K.M. 300; and Wakelin, A. 300
*Lord Advocate's Reference (no. 1 of 2001)* 2002 SLT 466: 155–6
Łoś, M. 161, 210
Lottmann, A. 71; and Engle, K 71
Lovett, J. 142, 199; and Kelly, L. 142, 199
*Lubanga* see *Prosecutor v Lubanga*
Lundgren, E. 198

McCarthy, M. 322–3, 326
McColgan, A. 119
McDonald, S. 270, 275; and Wobick, A. 270, 275
McEwan, J. 270
McGlynn, C. 19, 101, 113–14, 156, 161
McGregor, J. 181
McIntyre, S. 210–13
MacKinnon, C. 2–4, 7, 18–21, 24–6, 33–4, 36, 92–4, 100, 113, 115–16, 119, 127, 144, 160, 240, 259

Macedonia 50
McSherry, B. 156
Madagascar 130
Madden Dempsey, M. 30, 32, 35–6, 38, 40; and Herring, J. 30, 32, 35–6, 38
Mahoney, K. 93
Mamdani, M. 82
Manna, A. 183
Maogoto, J.N. 61
Marcus, S. 221
Mardorossian, C. 5
*Maria Da Penha Maia Fernandes v Brazil*, I-ACtHR case no. 12–051 2001: 103
*Marr v HMA*, 1996 SCCR 696: 155
Marshall, G. 271
Martino, W. 294; and Kendall, C. 294
*Maslova v Russia* (2009) 48 EHRR 37: 111, 113, 115
Massaro, T. 281
Mathews, S. 123
Matoesian, G. 272
Mazurana, D. 84; and Carlson, K. 84
*MC v Bulgaria*, ECtHR App. 39272/98 2003: 96, 100, 102, 113, 115–18, 177, 198, 205, 276
*Meek v HMA*, 1983 SLT 280: 156
*Mejia v Peru*, I-A Comm. HR 5/96 case 10.970 1996 95: 100
Mendeloff, D. 70
Merry, S.E. 94, 309
Mertus, J. 62, 70
Merzagora Betsos, I. 183–5, 194; and Ponti, G. 183, 185
Meyers, D. 27
Mezey, G.C. 294; and King, M.B. 294
*Miguel Castro-Castro Prison v Peru*, I-ACtHR 2006: 96, 100
Millar, A. 272, 274; and Chambers, G. 272, 274
Miller, A. 281; and Buddie, A. 281
Miller, Z. 82, 85
Mills, S.W. 161, 255
Milosevic, S. 50
Minow, M. 61, 70
*Miranda v Arizona*, 384 US 436 (1966) (Miranda Rules): 224
Mohanty, C. 309
Mohr, R. 161, 166, 275; and Roberts, J. 161, 166
Monk-Turner, E. 294; and Light, D. 294
Montreal Massacre 210–11
Morgan, J. 21, 239; and Graycar, R. 21, 239

Morris, S. 147; and Dyer, C. 147
Mosteller, R.P. 234, 268
*Muhimana* see *Prosecutor v Muhimana*
Munro, V. 7, 20, 22, 25, 34, 55, 115, 117, 144, 147, 149, 156, 162, 164, 166, 169, 176, 180, 228, 231, 258, 271, 283, 286, 290, 296–7, 299, 302, 311–12, 314; and Ellison, L. 25, 228, 231, 271, 283, 286, 290, 297, 302, 314; and Finch, E. 20, 144, 147, 149, 162, 164, 166, 283, 296, 299; and Kelly, L. 20, 311–12
*Munyakazi* see *Prosecutor v Munyakazi*
Murray, R. 127–8, 132
Murray, S. 241; and Heenan, M. 241
*Musema* see *Prosecutor v Musema*
*Muvunyi* see *Prosecutor v Muvyani*
Myhill, A. 142, 311; and Allen, J. 142, 311

Naffine, N. 20
Narayan, U. 309, 311, 316
National Centre for Knowledge about Men's Violence against Women (NCK) (Sweden) 199, 206–7
National Commission for Social Action, Sierra Leone 88
National Network Against Violence Against Women (South Africa) 254
National Working Group on Sexual Offences (South Africa) 254
Native Women's Association of Canada (2009) 218
Naylor, N. 251, 255–8, 260
Nesiah, V. 82, 84; and Keenan, A. 82
New Tactics in Human Rights 86
New Zealand 156
Ni Aolain, F. 71; and Rooney, R. 71
Niemi- Kiesiläinen, J. 204
*Nikolic* see *Prosecutor v Nikolic*
Nikolic-Ristanovic, V. 70
Norway 270–1
Nourse, V. 150
Novoselec, P. 174
Nowak, M. 103
Nowrojee, B. 55, 61–2, 64, 76, 78, 80–1, 83, 88
Nsibirwa, M. 124
Nuremberg 9, 47–52, 58; *see also* International Military Tribunal

Oberman, M. 330
Obote-Odora, A. 80–2
Ocran, C. 132
Odinkalu, C.A. 99
O'Donnell, I. 294
Office for Criminal Justice Reform (England and Wales) 281, 290
Okuizumi, K. 51; and Sellers, P.V. 51
*Olden v Kentucky*, 488 US 227 (1988); 227
Olowu, D. 124, 127
Olsen, F.E. 94
O'Neill, S. 146
Onoria, H. 124
Oppong, F.R. 130
*Opuz v Turkey*, 33201/02, 9 June 2009: 109, 118–19
Orentlicher, D. 61
*Owens v HMA*, 1946 JC 119: 156

Padovani, T. 185, 187, 189
Paglia, C. 11
Palumbieri, S.R. 188, 191
Panitch, M. 322; and Ticoll, M. 322
Patel, P. 312–3
*Paton v HMA*, 2002 SCCR 57: 166
Pavarini, C. 187
Pavlović, S. 174; and Bačić,F. 174
Pearce, H. 100
Pennington, N. 298; and Hastie, R. 298
*People v Bryant* (2003) (Kobe Bryant case) 233–5
Petersilia, J. 323
Peterson, I. 18; and Schomburg, W. 18
Petrak, J. 281; and Hedge, B. 281
Philips, B. 86
Phillips, A. 316, 319
Philpart, M. 122–3
Physicians for Human Rights 85
Picotti, L. 193
Pietila, H. 48; and Vickers, J. 48
Pildes, R. 32; Anderson, E. 32
Pillay, Navanethem 2, 54, 63, 67
Pillsbury, S.H. 228
Pineau, L. 213
Pizzi, W. 267–8, 270
Policing and Crime Bill (UK) 41; Section 13 41
Ponti, G. 183, 185; Merzagora Betsos, I. 183, 185
Pottier, J. 68
*Prosecutor v Akayesu*, ICTR-96-4-T, Judgment 2 September 1998 xiii-xvi, 2, 4, 6, 17–19, 21, 23, 54–5, 63, 72, 76–80, 92, 116
*Prosecutor v Bagambiki et al.*, ICTR-99-46-T, Trial Chamber, 25 February 2004: 64–5

*Prosecutor v Bagosora*, ICTR-96–7, Trial Chamber, 18 December 2008: 55, 69
*Prosecutor v Bemba*, ICC-01/05–01/08: 58
*Prosecutor v Charles Taylor*, SCSL-03–01-PT: 57
*Prosecutor v Celebici*, ICTY-96–23 & 23/1, Trial Chamber, 16 November 1998: 51–2
*Prosecutor v Cesic*, IT-95–10/1-S, Trial Chamber, 11 March 2004: 53
*Prosecutor v Clement Kayishema and Obed Ruzindana*, ICTR-95–1-T, Trial Chamber, 21 May 1999: 69
*Prosecutor v Delacic*, ICTY-96–21: 114
*Prosecutor v Furundijza*, ICTY-95–17/1, Trial Chamber, 10 December 1998: 51–2, 92, 116
*Prosecutor v Gacumbitsi*, ICTR-2001–64-A, Judgment 7 July 2006: 18, 55
*Prosecutor v Jean-Bosco Barayagwiza, Hassan Ngeze and Ferdinand Nahimana*, ICTR-99–52-T, Trial Chamber, 3 December 2003 69
*Prosecutor v Katanga and Ndjulu-chou*, ICC-01/04–01/07: 58
*Prosecutor v Kordic and Cerkez*, IT-95–14/2, Trial Judgment, 26 February 2001: 52
*Prosecutor v Kunarac, Kovac and Vukovic*, IT-96–23-T & IT-96–23/1-T, Judgment 22 February 2001: 17–18, 51–2, 55, 57, 92, 116–17, 177–8
*Prosecutor v Kupreskic et al.*, IT-95–16, Trial Judgment, 14 January 2000: 52
*Prosecutor v Kvocka et al.*, IT-98–30/1, Trial Chamber, 2 November 2001: 52
*Prosecutor v Lubanga*, ICC-01/04–01/06: 58
*Prosecutor v Muhimana*, ICTR-95–1B-T, Judgment 28 April 2005: 18, 55, 65, 69–70
*Prosecutor v Munyakazi*, ICTR-97–36-R 11 bis, Appeals Chamber, 8 October 2008: 68
*Prosecutor v Musema*, ICTR-96–13-A, Trial Chamber, 27 January 2000: 67–9
*Prosecutor v Muvyani*, ICTR-2000–55A-T, Trial Chamber, 12 September 2006: 65–6, 69
*Prosecutor v Nikolic*, IT-94–2, Trial Judgment, 18 December 2003: 53
*Prosecutor v Semanza*, ICTR-97–20, Trial Chamber, 15 May 2003: 55
*Prosecutor v Tadic*, ICTY-94–1-T, Trial Chamber, 7 May 1997: 51, 54
*Prosecutor v Todorovic*, IT-95–9/1, Trial Judgment, 31 July 2001: 52
*Prosecutor v Vasiljevic*, IT-98–32-A, Appeals Chamber, 25 February 2004: 57
Protocol on the Prevention and Suppression of Sexual Violence against Women and Children (Great Lakes Protocol) 129, 132; Article 6 129

Quinlivian, K. 109

*R v A (no. 2)* [2001] UKHL 25: 141
*R v Ashlee* [2006] AJ no. 1040: 216
*R v Ashley-Price* [2004] 204 BCAC 186: 325
*R v AJS* (2005) 192 Man. R. (2d) 4 (Man. CA): 217
*R v Billam* [1986] 1 All ER 986: 140
*R v Black; R v Gowan* [2006] EWCA Crim 2306: 146
*R v Bree* [2007] EWCA Crim 256: 148–5
*R v Cedeno* (2005) 27 CR (6th) 251 (Ont. CJ): 329
*R v Cornejo* (2003) 68 OR (3d)(Ont. CA): 216
*R v Corran* [2005] EWCA Crim 192: 145–6
*R v Daviault* [2004] 3 SCR 63: 212
*R v Dinardo* (2008) 231 CCC (3d) 177: 325–6
*R v Doody* [2008] EWCA Crim 2394: 282
*R v Dougal* (2005): 147–9
*R c. Duhamel*, 2002 CanLII 41275 (QUE. CA): 333
*R v Ewanchuk* [1999] 1 SCR 330: 215, 217, 219, 326–7, 332
*R v G* [2006] EWCA Crim 821: 146
*R v G* [2008] UKHL 37: 145
*R c. Gagnon* [2000] CanLII 14683 (CQ): 327
*R v Garvey; Attorney General's Reference (no. 104 of 2004)* 2004 EWCA Crim 2672: 159
*R v H* [2007] EWCA Crim 2056: 149–50
*R v Harper* [2002] YJ no. 38 (QL)(SC): 326–7
*R v Houle* [2002] JQ. No. 9316 (CQ): 325
*R v Hundle* (2002) 10 CR (6th) 37 (Alta. QB): 334
*R v JR* (2006) 40 CR (6th) 97 (Ont. SCJ): 216

*R v Jenson* (1996) 47 CR (4th) 363 (Ont. CA): 330
*R v Jheeta* [2007] All ER (D) 164: 162
*R v Kaired* [2008] ABQB 767: 325, 332
*R v L (K)* [2004] JQ. No. 6783: 325
*R v Ladue* [1965] 4 CCC 264 (YTCA): 328
*R v MacDonald* [2008] OJ no. 97 (SCJ): 325
*R v McKearney* (2004 JC 87): 166
*R v McPherson* [1999] BCJ no. 518 (SC): 333
*R v Malcolm* (2000): 216
*R v Malone* [1998] 2 CAR 447: 148
*R v Martin* [2004] EWCA Crim 946: 141
*R v Millar* [2008] CanLII 28225 (Ont. SC): 328
*R v Mills* [1999] 3 SCR 688: 275
*R v Mukadi* [2003] EWCA Crim 3765: 141
*R v O'Connor* [1995] 4 SCR 411: 212, 276
*R v Parrott* [2001] 1 SCR 178: 327–8
*R v Parsons* (1999) 170 Nfld.&PEIR 319: 328
*R v Prince* (2008) 232 Man.R (2d) 281 (QB): 331–2
*R v R* [1992] 1 AC 599: 112, 140
*R v RR* [2001] 159 CCC (3d) 11 (Ont. CA): 329, 333
*R v Sadaatmandi* (2008): 217
*R v Seaboyer* [1991] 2 SCR 577: 211
*R v Shah* [1998] EWCA 144: 313–318
*R v Shearing* [2002] 3 SCR 33: 274–5
*R v Siddiqui* [2004] BCSC 1717: 329
*R v Sitch* [2005] OJ no. 5969: 325
*R v Stender* [2005] 1 SCR 914: 215, 327
*R v Tang* [2008] HCA 39: 237
*R v White* [2004] EWCA Crim 946: 141
*R v Williams* (1923) 1 KB 340: 156
Radačić, I. 170, 177
Radecki Breitkopf, C. 283; and Littleton, H. 283
Radin, M.J. 41
Raitt, F. 156, 162–3, 165–6, 269, 281; and Ferguson, P. 156, 162–3, 165–6
Raja, S. 26; and Campbell, R. 26
Rape Crisis Scotland 159, 163, 165–6, 177
Rasool, S. 251, 253
Raz, J. 27, 35–6, 38–9
Razack, S. 218, 309, 329
Regan, L. 26, 109, 141–2, 158, 267; and Kelly, L. 26, 109, 141–2, 158, 267
Revolutionary United Front 56

Roberts, G. 147–8
Roberts, J. 161, 166, 275; and Mohr, R. 161, 166
Rocco Code 1930, Italy 183, 185
Roeher Institute 1995 322
Roeling, B.V.A 49; and Ruter, C.F. 49
Rogers, P. 300; and Davies, M. 300
Roiphe, K. 11
Romany, C. 94
Rome Statute of the International Criminal Court *see* ICC Statute
Rome Statute of the International Criminal Court Rules of Procedure and Evidence *see* ICC Rules of Procedure and Evidence
Rooney, E. 71; and Ni Aolain, F. 71
Ross, F.C. 70–1
Ross, Lord Justice-Clerk 155
Roth, K. 82
RUF Forces case, SCSL-04–15-T, Trial Chamber, 20 June 2007: 57
Rumney, P. 19, 140, 142, 149–51, 166, 294, 303; and Fenton, R. 149–51
Ruparelia, R. 215, 218
Rush, P. 161, 242, 245, 249; and Young, A. 242, 245, 249
Russell, D. 114
Ruter, C.F. 49; and Roeling, B.V.A 49
Rwanda xiii, 3, 53, 61–2, 64, 68, 76, 78, 80, 92, 100

*S v S*, 1971 (2) SA 591 (A): 258
*S v Swiggelaar*, 1950 1 PH H61 (A): 259
*S v Volschenk*, 1968 2 PH H283 (D): 259
*S v Zuma* (2006) 3 All SA 8: 254–5
Sacco, V. 213; and Johnson, H. 213
*Salman v Turkey* (2002) 34 EHRR 147: 114
Sands, P. 61; and Lattimer, M. 61
Saunders, C. 294
Scales, A.C. 93
Scheppele, K. 315
Schneider, E. 315
Schomberg, W. 18; and Peterson, I. 18
Schulhofer, S. 228
Schuller, R. 290; and Vidmar, N. 290
Scotland 19, 154–167, 267–77
Scotland Act 1998 271; Section 4 271
Scott-Ham, M. 147; and Burton, F. 147
Scottish Crown Office and Procurator Fiscal Service 157
Scottish Law Commission 154–5, 157–9, 161–2, 165–6
Scottish Women's Aid 159–60, 162

Sebold, A. 268
Sellers, P.V. 51; and Okuizumi, K. 51
*Semanza* see *Prosecutor v Semanza*
Sen, P. 310
Serbia 50
Sex Offences Act 2001 (Republic of Ireland) 270; Section 34 270
Sexual Offences Act 2003 (England and Wales) 40, 141, 143–7, 150, 156, 164, 281, 296, 311; Section 1 40, 143; Section 5 144; Section 74 147
Sexual Offences Act 2007 (South Africa) 254–7; Section 1 257; Section 3 257
Sexual Offences Act (Criminal Law (Sexual Offences and Related Matters)) Amendment Act 32 of 2007 251
Sexual Offences (Amendment) Act 1976 (England and Wales) 140
Sexual Offences (Procedure and Evidence)(Scotland) Act 2002 273; Section 8 273
Sexual Offences (Scotland) Act 2009 10, 154, 157–65; Section 1 157, 164; Section 2 159; Section 12 161–2; Section 13 161–3; Section 14 163–4; Section 16 164–5
Shute, S. 21, 31, 160; and Gardner, J. 21, 160
Siddique, N. 311
Sierra Leone 56, 82–4, 88, 132
Sivakumaran, S. 70, 101, 294
Slovenia 50
Smart, C. 6, 71, 214, 216, 314
Smythe, D. 252–4, 260; and Artz, L. 253; and Waterhouse, S. 252–4, 260
Snider, L. 214
Snyman, C.R. 258
Sobsey, D. 322–3; and Doe, T. 323
Socialist Federative Republic of Yugoslavia (SFRY) 169–70
Sokoloff, N.J. 312; and Dupont, I. 312
Solemn Declaration on Gender Equality (2004) 132
Sommer, M.H. 294, 302
Sorenson, S.B. 291
South Africa 11, 122, 161, 251–61, 308–319
Southern African Economic Development Community; Declaration on Gender and Development 130; Protocol on Gender and Development 129–31; Articles 20–25 130

*Southern Pacific Company v Jenson*, 244 US 205: 6
Southall Black Sisters 311, 315
Spain 95
Special Court for Sierra Leone (SCSL) 9, 47, 51, 53, 56–9, 83
SCSL Statute 83
Spencer, J. 144
Sphon, C. 273; and Horney, J. 273
*Stallard v HMA*, 1989 SLT 469: 154
State Responsibility for Internationally Wrongful Acts (2001) 102; Article 2 102; Article 4 102; Article 5 102; Article 7 102; Article 9 102
*State v Finnerty* (2006) (Duke Lacrosse case) 233–5
Status of Women, Canada 219
Steele, J. 146
Stefan, S. 330
Stefiszyn, K. 132
Steiner, H. 109; and Alston, P. 109
Stepakoff, S. 70, 83; and Kelsall, M.S. 70, 83
Stewart, L. 164
*St-Laurent v Québec* (1993) 90 CCC (3d) 291: 327
Strandbakken, A. 271
Sugar, N. 281
Sutorius, H. 196, 204, 206; and Kaldal, A. 196, 204, 206
*SW v UK* (1996) 21 EHRR 363: 112, 115
Sweden 41, 196–206, 270–1
Swedish Penal Code 196

Tackling Violent Crime Act, SC 2008 (Canada) 333
*Tadic* see *Prosecutor v Tadic*
Tadros, V. 21, 31, 34, 115, 162–3
Tamale, S. 123
Taslitz, A. 228
Taylor, N. 281; and Joudo, J. 281
Temkin, J. 20–1, 139–44, 166, 180, 267, 271, 275, 281–2, 290, 296–7, 302; and Ashworth, A. 20, 141, 143–4, 180; and Kelly, L. and Griffiths, S. 141; and Krahé, B. 20, 142, 144, 166, 281–2, 290, 296–7, 302
Thailand 86
Thiara, R. 310–11; and Gill, A. 310–11
Ticoll, M. 322; and Panitch, M. 322
*Todorovic* see *Prosecutor v Todorovic*
Tokyo Indictment 50
Tokyo Trials 49
Tomkins, S. 76

Torrey, M. 178
Travis, A. 142
Truth and Reconciliation Commission 56, 83–4, 88
Tshwaranang Legal Advocacy Centre 255
Tunisia 95
Turkey 110, 118
Turković, K. 172–3, 175

Uberoi, P. 311
United Kingdom (UK) 112, 139, 157, 267–77, 282, 308–319
United Nations (UN) xiii, 56, 92, 170
UNAIDS 123–4
UN Charter 50, 53, 56; Chapter VII 50, 56; Chapter XII 53
UN Commission for Human Rights xiii
UN Convention Against Torture (UNCAT) 93, 100, 104, 113; Article 1 100, 113; Article 16 100
UN Declaration on the Elimination of Violence Against Women (DEVAW) 95–8, 103, 110, 125; Article 1 98; Article 2 96–8
UN Development Fund for Women 95
UN Development Programme 132, 171; Human Development Index 132
UN General Assembly 95–6, 98
UN Office for the Coordination of Humanitarian Affairs 82
UN Secretary-General 92, 96, 122
UN Security Council 50; Resolution 827 50; Resolution 789 50
UN Special Rapporteur on Human Rights 50
UN Special Rapporteur on Violence Against Women 95–6, 102, 126
UN The World's Women 92
United States of America 11, 19, 32, 95, 224–36, 270, 281, 329
*Unity Dow v Attorney-General, Botswana* (2001) AHRLA 99 (BwCA 1992): 131

*Van Mechelen v The Netherlands* [1997] ECHR 22: 276
Van Schaack, B.: 61, 63–4
Vandervort, L. 178–9
*Vasiljevic* see *Prosecutor v Vasiljevic*
*Velásquez Rodriguez v Honduras*, I-ACtHR Ser. C no. 4, judgment 29 July 1988: 102
Veneziani, P. 192
Vetten, L. 251–4, 260

Vickers, J. 48; and Pietila, H. 48
Victim Support Scotland 159–60, 164
Victorian Law Reform Commission Final Report on Sexual Offences (2004) 165
Vidmar, N. 290; and Schuller, R. 290
Viljoen, F. 123–4, 127–8
Virgilio, M. 193–4
Viseur-Sellers, P. 76
Volpp, L. 315–16
von Hirsch, A. 31

Wakelin, A. 300; and Long, K.M. 300
Walby, S. 142, 311; and Allen, J. 142, 311
Walker, J. 294
Warren, G. 272
Waterhouse, S. 252–4, 260; and Smythe, D. 252–4, 260
Weinstein, H. 70; and Fletcher, L. 70
Welch, C. 127
Wendt Höjer, M. 197
Wersäll, F. 203; and Johansson, L. 203
Wertheimer, A. 22, 34, 226
Wessel, E. 283
West, R. 181
Westen, P. 226
Whisman, M.A. 37; and Brezsnyak, M. 37
White, B.H. 294; and Robinson Kurpius, S.E. 294
Whyte, D. 281; and Du Mont, J. 281
Williams, J. 86
Williams, R. 142
Williams, Z. 149
Wilson, A. 312
Wilson, L. 268–9
Wobick, A. 270, 275; and McDonald, S. 270, 275
Wolchover, D. 282; and Heaton-Armstrong, A. 282
Wolhuter, L. 304
Woods, G. 240
World War II 47–50, 59, 88, 109
Wright, J. 258

*X and Y v Netherlands* (1986) 8 EHRR 235: 112, 114

*Yildirim (deceased) v Austria*, Comm. No. 6/2005: 103
Young, A. 240, 242, 245, 249, 268, 276; and Rush, P. 242, 245, 249

Young, M.L. 218; and Jiwani, Y. 218
Youth Justice and Criminal Evidence Act 1999 (UK) 141
Yugoslavia (former) 3, 50, 92, 170

Yuval-Davis, N. 317

Zilli, L. 111
Zirima, P. 130

# eBooks – at www.eBookstore.tandf.co.uk

## A library at your fingertips!

eBooks are electronic versions of printed books. You can store them on your PC/laptop or browse them online.

They have advantages for anyone needing rapid access to a wide variety of published, copyright information.

eBooks can help your research by enabling you to bookmark chapters, annotate text and use instant searches to find specific words or phrases. Several eBook files would fit on even a small laptop or PDA.

**NEW:** Save money by eSubscribing: cheap, online access to any eBook for as long as you need it.

### Annual subscription packages

We now offer special low-cost bulk subscriptions to packages of eBooks in certain subject areas. These are available to libraries or to individuals.

For more information please contact webmaster.ebooks@tandf.co.uk

We're continually developing the eBook concept, so keep up to date by visiting the website.

### www.eBookstore.tandf.co.uk